No Angel

NO ANGEL

The Secret Life of Bernie Ecclestone

TOM BOWER

faber and faber

First published in 2011
by Faber and Faber Limited
Bloomsbury House
74–77 Great Russell Street
London WC1B 3DA

Typeset by Palindrome
Printed in the UK by CPI Mackays, Chatham

The right of Tom Bower to be identified as author of this work
has been asserted in accordance with Section 77 of the Copyright,
Designs and Patents Act 1988

A CIP record for this book
is available from the British Library

ISBN 978–0–571–26929–7

4 6 8 10 9 7 5

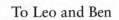

To Leo and Ben

Contents

Acknowledgements

The originator of this book wants to remain anonymous. A major personality in Formula One, he persistently urged me over some years to expose Bernie Ecclestone's dishonesty. Sharp, ruthless and evasive have been familiar descriptions of Ecclestone's career, often blemished by scandal and accusations of bribery and chicanery. But what is the truth? In our first meeting in Knightsbridge in late 2009, arranged by John Bloom, I replied to Ecclestone's offer of cooperation with the assurance that I would publish any evidence I found of wrongdoing and criticism. Ecclestone smiled. 'Tom, I'm no angel,' he countered. Over the months of research and writing, I enjoyed unprecedented access to Ecclestone, most of Formula One's leading personalities, his personal friends and Ecclestone himself. Many asked Ecclestone, 'What should I say?' He replied, 'The truth. Don't worry about me.' The result is an extraordinary insight into Britain's most successful tycoon.

To achieve that portrait, I relied on many people. The majority asked for their contributions to remain anonymous. Of the others, I would like to thank the following.

Pino Allievei, John Blake, Herbie Blasch, John Bloom, Michel Boeri, Flavio Briatore, Aleardo Buzzi, Alistair Caldwell, John Coomb, Don Cox, Ron Dennis, Patrick Duffeler, Ed Gorman, Gerhard Gribkowsky, Katja Heim, Alan Henry, Damon Hill, John Hogan, John Howett, Johnny Humphries, Alexandra Irrgang, Anne Lodge, Eddie Jordan, Stefano Lai, Scott Lanphere,

ACKNOWLEDGEMENTS

Niki Lauda, Terry Lovell, Jon McEvoy, Patrick McNally, Luca Montezemolo, Max Mosley, Gordon Murray, John O'Connor, Adam Parr, Marco Piccinini, Nelson Piquet Senior, Brian Powers, Stuart Pringle, Tony Purnell, Bernard Rey, Peter Rix, Tamas Rohonyi, Tom Rubython, Robin Saunders, Joe Saward, Tony Scott Andrews, Monty Shadow, Ron Shaw, Brian Shepherd, Jackie Stewart, Rachel Sylvester, Walter Thoma, Alice Thomson, Tuana Tan, Tom Walkinshaw, David Ward, Peter Warr, Richard Williams, Frank Williams, Richard Woods, Allan Woolard and John Young.

Bernie Ecclestone's staff have been particularly helpful, including Lucy Hibberd, Enrica Marenghi, Pasquale Lattuneddu, Ross Mercer, Mike Lawson and especially Sacha Woodward-Hill.

As always, I am grateful for undiminished support from David Hooper, who undertook the legal reading, and to Jonathan Lloyd of Curtis Brown for endearing loyalty. At Faber and Faber I owe a special debt to Julian Loose, who bravely embraced the idea when others in London proved to be notably weak, and sincere thanks to Kate Murray-Browne and to Paula Turner for her thoughtful editing.

I owe a special thanks to David Cornwell whose insight into the human condition is invaluable; and to Veronica, my wife, who keeps the flame alight.

Finally, thanks to Bernie Ecclestone himself. Until we met he seemed to have adopted the attitude, 'I've got to cope with my life, I don't want to know about my life.' But as the months together passed he occasionally said, 'I'm looking forward to reading the book. I want to know what I've done in my life.' He took a gamble. For my part, the ride was thrilling. It is tantalising to speculate on his opinion – whether he decides in the end that he scooped a jackpot, came out evens or lost to the bank.

Illustrations

1 Ecclestone and Frederick Compton. Private collection.

2 Frederick Compton's forecourt. Private collection.

3 Ecclestone winning at Crystal Palace, 1950. Private collection.

4 Car dealers of Warren Street, 1949. Photo by Charles Hewitt/Picture Post/Getty Images.

5 Ecclestone with his first wife, Ivy, Jack Brabham and friends. Private collection.

6 Bertha Ecclestone and her grand-daughter Debbie. Private collection.

7 Sidney Ecclestone. Private collection.

8 Ecclestone and Tuana Tan. Private collection.

9 Tuana Tan and friends. Private collection.

10 The Brabham-Alfa Romeo team, Nürburgring, 1976. © Grand Prix Photo

11 Ecclestone and Patrick Duffeler. Private collection.

12 Ecclestone with Niki Lauda, Österreichring, 1978. © Sutton Images

13 Ecclestone with Nelson Piquet, Dijon-Prenois, 1979. © Grand Prix Photo

14 Ecclestone with Max Mosley and Jean-Marie Balestre, Hockenheim, 1981. © Grand Prix Photo

15 Enzo Ferrari, Maranello, 1981 © Grand Prix Photo

16 Ecclestone with Michael Schumacher and Damon Hill. © Grand Prix Photo

Acronyms

ACEA Association des Constructeurs Européens d'Automobiles
BRDC British Racing Drivers Club
EBU, European Broadcasting Union
FIA Fédération Internationale de l'Automobile Motor racing's
supreme authority with the Fédération Internationale du Sport
Automobile (FISA), a subordinate organisation, responsible for
the organisation of the Formula One. FISA was abolished in
1993. In this book, the organisation is uniformly called FIA.
FOPA Formula One Promotions Administration was a
company owned by Ecclestone. In 1977 the company was
called Motor racing Developments (International) Ltd and it
was renamed FOPA in 1989.
F1CA restyled FOCA in 1974) Formula One Constructors'
Association the club organised in 1963 by Colin Chapman so
that British teams could jointly transport their cars to the races.
FOH Formula One Holdings
FOA Formula One Administration Ltd
FOM Formula One Management, formerly Petara
FOTA Formula One Team Association
GPWC Grand Prix World Championship
GPMA Grand Prix Manufacturers Association
WCR World Championship Racing, a breakaway group
excluding FOCA

Monaco, Sunday 16 May 2010

'Bernie! Bernie! Darling!' A tall, beautiful black girl is smothering the diminutive man with kisses. Trapped against the wall of a rickety metal cage, the seventy-nine-year-old smiles up to the exuberant model, 'Hi, Naomi.' Silently watching from the corner of the descending makeshift lift is a lined face hidden behind sunglasses and a baseball hat. Seconds later, the doors clang open. Thirty screaming cameramen greet Mick Jagger, Naomi Campbell and Bernie Ecclestone as they walk into the Monaco sunlight. 'Where can we watch the race, Bernie?' shouts Jagger. 'My motorhome,' replies the impish man pushing burly cameramen from his path. A twenty-four-stone bodyguard stands helpless on the side. Pursued by the cameras, the group heads towards the security gates guarding the 'motorhome' – a grey, black-windowed, air-conditioned, sound-insulated, leather-upholstered coach equipped with concealed cameras to cover every angle – parked at the entrance of the Paddock, the exclusive harbour area squeezed between a hill and the sea reserved for Formula One's players. Looking twenty years younger than his age thanks to the teenage cut of his hair, Ecclestone is enjoying the unpredictability. 'Water?' Ecclestone offers his guests, as they sit back to watch the beginning of the sixty-eighth Monaco Grand Prix.

Forty minutes earlier, Bernie Ecclestone had fought his way out of the same lift facing a bigger scrum. 'This way, Jennifer!' the paparazzi screamed. 'Jennifer, we love you!' roared the crowd from the hill and stands overlooking the race circuit. Jennifer Lopez had unexpectedly dropped in to see Bernie. 'Jennifer wants to see the cars,' explained Sir Philip Green, the retailer, and Lopez's host on *Lionheart*, his 206-foot yacht moored nearby. In three days Green would be in London to open a store in Knightsbridge and any publicity attendant on the Hollywood star and Formula One was valuable. 'Okay, I'll help,' said Ecclestone, abandoning the lobster lunch he had personally bought that morning in a Monaco supermarket. Side by side, preceded by a wall of backwards-lurching photographers, Ecclestone, Lopez and Green had headed towards the pits, the twelve garages where mechanics were preparing the cars for that afternoon's Grand Prix.

'They're so small,' cooed Lopez, gazing at the bare axles of Robert Kubica's Renault. 'Where are the wheels?'

'They've been sold,' quipped Ecclestone.

'I couldn't get into that car,' J-Lo laughed. 'The driving seat is so small.' 'We'd squeeze you in,' laughed Green, 'and then sew your clothes on.' 'Thanks for the publicity, Bernie,' Renault's chief said.

Ecclestone and Lopez moved on to the adjacent Ferrari pit. Pictures of J-Lo alongside the red car were the publicist's dream. It justified spending $400 million on Ferraris for nineteen races in just one year.

Twenty minutes before the race, the mood was tense. Visitors were usually unwelcome but the rule was broken for the man who had made everyone rich. 'Hi, Bernie,' greeted the white-haired man among the crowd outside the Ferrari stop. 'Good to see you, Michael,' replied Ecclestone. 'How's your daughter, Bernie?' 'Great,' replied Ecclestone, being pushed on.

'Michael Douglas is a good man,' said Ecclestone seconds later, regretting that he had not spent more time with the actor who had flown over from the Cannes film festival.

Lopez was heading back to the harbour as Ecclestone began

wandering through the grid, the line-up of twenty-two cars getting ready to start. To loud cheers of 'Bernie' from the stands, the true star of this show took the stretched-out hands and returned smiles greeting his wandering gaze.

'You look relaxed,' Ecclestone said, greeting Nico Rosberg, who was standing by his Mercedes.

'Inside I'm a shaking mess,' replied the German driver.

Prince Albert, the reigning monarch of Monaco, swept past. Ecclestone had shunned his party at the palace the previous night. At the end of the grid, Ecclestone walked past two Virgin cars.

'A nickel-and-dime operation,' commented Ecclestone about Richard Branson's attempt to speed into the Formula One spotlight. 'He's paying economy and should be in first class. I told him, "You're trying to get a Rolls-Royce job with a Cortina." He won't last.' Formula One only suits the seriously rich.

'That's Lakshmi Mittal,' he murmured, spotting the Indian steel magnate worth over £20 billion speaking to Vijay Mallya, the owner of the Kingfisher beer company, standing by two Force India cars. Two days earlier Ecclestone had visited Mallya's huge yacht, moored alongside Philip Green's. Plans to stage Formula One races in India in 2011 relied on Ecclestone's negotiations with the Indian government. The huge diamond studs screwed into Mallya's ear lobes glittered while they briefly resumed discussions about his plans to become the subcontinent's Grand Prix maestro.

'Bernie! Bernie!', roared hundreds of British spectators from stands bedecked with the Union Jack. They pointed their cameras at the icon as he walked down the sunlit track, but he barely acknowledged their presence. 'They cheer today but they'll boo tomorrow,' observed the anti-hero.

Beyond the stands, on terraces and balconies, thousands of flamboyant party-goers clasping champagne glasses were focusing their binoculars on the white-shirted figure striding along the middle of the road. In their gleaming Rolls-Royces, Bentleys and Ferraris, the mega-rich club has returned every year since 1929 to Formula One's Mecca – a bolt-hole confirming Somerset Maugham's truism that Monaco was a 'sunny place for shady people'. Ecclestone was a hero for the members of that club.

Over the previous thirty-six years Ecclestone had transformed Formula One from a mere enthusiasts' sport into one of the world's most-watched entertainments. The catcalls – and there have been plenty over the years – had come from the original team owners whom Ecclestone had enriched to buy yachts, private planes and countless homes. Gratitude for the source of their fortunes was begrudging. Only insiders knew that since the previous year's Monaco Grand Prix, the scars of Formula One's most recent internecine war were still raw. The puppet-master lived in a self-constructed golden cage surrounded by misfits. Parading with the stars, the billionaire knew, confirmed his indispensability. In the recession Monaco's opportunities were gold dust.

That morning a procession had entered 'The Kremlin', Ecclestone's motorhome, to broker deals. Each was greeted by him with a few words in his south London accent asserting his negotiating position, often terminated by, 'Just do it. We'll sort it out later.' Outside, Flavio Briatore, the discredited Italian businessman, had arranged something different. To restore his reputation in Formula One, Briatore posed for photographs with Ecclestone. As forty cameras whirred, the two spotted Michael Schumacher giving interviews. The German, like the Italian, was trying to make a comeback. Cynics would call them 'poseurs with their playthings'. No one even noticed Richard Branson as he walked past towards his dark motorhome in the distance.

Minutes before the race started, Ecclestone, Mick Jagger and Naomi Campbell were seated on deep leather upholstery insulated from the ear-shattering blast of twenty-two high-tuned engines built to speed at 200 miles an hour. The narrow street circuit is the ultimate challenge for drivers' skills. Within the first minutes of the race weaving around Europe's most expensive real estate, a Williams car crashed into a metal barrier. A wheel and wing splattered across the bend.

'A goner,' said Mick Jagger, asking a friend to take a photograph of himself watching television with Ecclestone. A few minutes later smoke poured from Jenson Button's McLaren engine. The previous year's world champion had been defeated by a careless mechanic.

'A lot's happening in the first five minutes,' muttered Jagger.

'There's a lot of nerves and it's not easy here,' agreed Ecclestone. Two stars, both raised in Dartford, south London, shared a gritty mateyness.

'It's a sensational challenge,' Mark Webber, the Australian driver, said about Monaco just before the race. 'The track is a law unto itself because at Monaco there's no difference between a small mistake and a big mistake. The result is the same – a trashed car.'

Scary rides linked Jagger and Ecclestone. 'Doing any tours?' the sports czar asked the rock king over his shoulder. 'Nah,' replied the emaciated sixty-five-year-old glancing across at L'Wren Scott, his six-foot-tall girlfriend. 'If you're here on Wednesday, Bernie,' continued Jagger, 'come to Cannes and see our new film. There's a party.' Ecclestone barely nodded. He avoids parties.

'Darling, I'll call you when I wake up,' Naomi Campbell was drawling down the phone. Seated at the other end of the motorhome, the model was rejecting work. 'And then I'll decide if I can see you. I don't want to let you down.'

After ending the call, she turned to a friend. 'I'm hungry. I want lunch.' Jagger's group was waiting for a launch to take them to *Lionheart*.

'The boat's here,' said the voice of an unusually fat gofer, known for attaching himself to celebrities. *Lionheart* was moored just fifty yards away. Campbell pushed through the coach to say farewell. 'You'll be just six boats down from *Force Blue*,' said Ecclestone, laughing. 'I know,' she smiled. 'I won't be going there.' The insiders' joke was that *Force Blue* was owned by Flavio Briatore. Seven years earlier, Flavio Briatore and Campbell had been dating. At the time, he was a Formula One celebrity. Since then, he had become notorious in the sport.

'Flavio's past has never been a problem for me,' Ecclestone would tell those questioning his friendship. Some guessed that his loyalty towards the Italian exhibitionist had been sealed after Ecclestone uncharacteristically exposed a vulnerability.

Ecclestone was staying on Briatore's gleaming gin-palace for the weekend. Danielle Steele, the writer, and other multi-millionaires chartered the craft from Briatore for €250,000 a week, with food, fuel and tips extra. Flying together four days earlier from Biggin Hill, the airport in south London that Ecclestone personally owns, to Nice on Ecclestone's Falcon 7X, one of the world's fastest private jets, the two had discussed restoring Briatore's tumultuous career in Formula One. Briatore's star had soared as the principal of the Renault team only to crash in 2009 amid scandalous accusations. His prosecutor and judge was Max Mosley, also tainted by scandal. The backstabbing and recrimination between Mosley, Briatore and Ecclestone over the previous two years matched the finest Shakespearean drama. 'Max is jealous of me,' Briatore complained to Ecclestone during the flight. 'I even agreed to employ Alexander,' added Briatore, referring to Mosley's son, who had died in 2009 of a suspected drug overdose. Both agreed that Mosley enjoyed exercising power but disagreed about the man himself. Ecclestone and Mosley's relationship in Formula One started in the late 1960s and despite disagreements was glued by their extraordinary success. Flavio Briatore's arrival was more recent. His wealth owed much to Ecclestone, yet in 2009 he was universally accused of seeking to oust his mentor as Formula One's supremo. Their reconciliation baffled everyone. 'People say I shouldn't be associated with Flavio and people who cheat,' admitted Ecclestone. 'I couldn't care. I know what I know. Everyone cheats in Formula One and he shouldn't have got caught. He's suffered more than he should have done.'

Life on Ecclestone's $78 million jet reflected the owner's abstemiousness. Briatore was offered water or coffee. At lunchtime there was no food. Looking through a locker Ecclestone discovered a tube of Smarties. He shared them with his two passengers. Then, after rummaging some more, he found a packet of Hula Hoops. Briatore, tanned and paunchy, the owner of Cipriani restaurant in London, and with homes in London, New York and Sardinia, declined the crisps. Before the plane landed in Nice, Briatore had consented to invite Mosley to a dinner party on *Force Blue*. On the eve of the Grand Prix the two would be reconciled. While Briatore was briefly absent from his seat, Ecclestone compared the Italian with Ron Dennis, his life-long nemesis and the architect of McLaren's success. 'When Flavio stuck a knife in my back, he charmed me and said, "It's good for you to let out some blood." But when Ron puts the knife in, he wants you to know that he's in charge and he's killed you.' Ecclestone had survived many ambitious assassins but was equally wary of the self-righteous: 'You don't want to believe people who tell you they're honest.'

From the plane Ecclestone and Briatore were driven to Nice's helicopter terminal. Ecclestone paid the fares from a wad of folded €500 notes. Fortunately for the ticket-seller, Ecclestone refuses change. After a six-minute flight, the two men stepped from the plane into a waiting launch and a welcome by *Force Blue*'s seventeen-man crew.

Three days later, on the eve of the race, Flavio Briatore and Elisabetta Gregoraci, his thirty-year-old wife and former Wonderbra model, were generous hosts to seventy guests for dinner. Several were familiar to gossip columnists. Boris Becker, Tamara Beckwith, Nick Candy and Goga Ashkenazi regularly feature in glossy magazines. Briatore was pleased that Robert Kubica, Renault's driver, arrived for a drink dressed in corporate gear. Formula One had made Briatore rich and he wanted to re-enter the show. Mosley had cried off.

'Flavio has given an unhelpful interview about me to an Italian newspaper,' he explained from his Monaco apartment.

'He's told a journalist that he has forgiven me.' Briatore was unapologetic about his venom. Mosley, he believed, had ruined his reputation and his fortune. Instead, Mosley attended a dinner party for eighty guests hosted by Jean Todt, his successor as president of FIA (Fédération Internationale de l'Automobile, based in Paris), on the *Maltese Falcon*, the world's biggest private sailing yacht, moored nearby. Among Todt's guests were Michael Schumacher and other Formula One stars. At midnight Briatore led a handpicked elite to his 'Billionaire' club in Monte Carlo. Tables cost up to €10,000 for an evening and the club was nearly full, an achievement during the recession. One week later *Force Blue* was seized by the local police while sailing through Italian waters. Briatore was accused of failing to pay £4.5 million in taxes. Mosley did not express his sorrow. Ecclestone was pragmatic. Bruised egos were common in his business. Throughout his stay in Monaco, he mediated conflicts, resolved problems and, in between, had negotiated the supply of tyres for the following season.

Races can be won or lost on the quality of the tyres. Over the previous twelve years, Bridgestone, the Japanese tyre manufacturer, had supplied Formula One teams with up to 30,000 tyres every year – worth about $40 million – at no cost. In return, the regular advertising on television in over a hundred countries during races had transformed Bridgestone into a global success. In 2009, sated by the marketing triumph, Bridgestone decided to terminate the contract. Three suppliers – Michelin, Pirelli and Avon – offered to supply the teams but for a price. A few weeks earlier, Jean Todt had promised Michelin, a French corporation, that the teams would each pay $3 million for a season's supply of tyres. Ecclestone suspected that Todt may have been partial towards Michelin, not least because his son was hoping to establish a new racing team. Ecclestone was cool towards Todt and had opposed his election. During his stay in Monaco he negotiated that Avon would offer their tyres for $1.5 million and simultaneously encouraged Pirelli to make a winning offer. 'The teams will decide, not Todt,' Ecclestone told the managers of the Formula One teams. 'Leave it to me,' he said in his familiar south London tone. This was one battle he was going to win. 'I'm not going to lose to Todt,' he pledged.

Since 1974 Ecclestone had brokered Formula One's business. Dealing was in his genes and few could rival his skill. Negotiating a bargain for 200 sets of tyres for each team was, for him, a piffling chore but the successful execution was his oxygen. Before leaving Monaco, Michelin's negotiator agreed with Ecclestone to reduce the price by 50 per cent. During a visit to Ecclestone's motorhome Norbert Haug, the head of the Mercedes team, approved the arrangement. But Ecclestone wanted more. Every minor success, multiplied across the sport's annual $1 billion budget, reconfirmed his dominance. Daily, one man balanced the demands of twelve teams, nineteen race circuits, countless sponsors, eighteen governments, over a hundred broadcasters and the sport's regulators to produce seamless entertainment. But Ecclestone rarely stayed at any race to watch the end of it.

Halfway through Ecclestone left his motorhome, bid farewell to those crowding into his private canteen, including Niki Lauda, and headed towards the heliport. Unwilling to be caught in traffic, Ecclestone never stayed at any race to watch the chequered flag come down. Seated twenty minutes later in his Falcon, he leaned back into the deeply upholstered leather armchair and read the *Observer* newspaper's preview of the Monaco race. Under the headline 'The streets where heroes are made – disaster is only ever a moment away' was a grainy black-and-white photograph of Monaco's 1957 race. Featured in the lead of eight cars was Juan Manuel Fangio, the legendary Argentinian driver. 'I've got those two Ferraris, that Maserati and the Lancia,' said Ecclestone pointing with pride at the photograph of the speeding old cars racing around houses demolished many years ago. Ecclestone spoke with nostalgia about the 'old days' and his collection of eighty vintage Formula One cars arranged like museum exhibits in a hangar at Biggin Hill.

As the Falcon descended over the Thames estuary heading towards his personal runway, he looked down at Dartford. 'Never been back since I left,' he said. 'Not interested.' After a brief pause he pressed closer to the window. 'I owned that house, and that one . . .' His voice trailed off. Few eyewitnesses at the start of his personal race to the top are still alive but the survivors whisper about the casualties during his triumphant progress. 'I'm no angel,' he admits. Time has softened the rough edges but the steel core remains.

Driving himself home to Knightsbridge from Biggin Hill airport, Ecclestone was thinking of the next race in Istanbul. His motorhome, he realised, was about to be shipped from Monaco across the Mediterranean. 'That's a waste,' he softly remarked. At the back of his four-wheel drive, Pasquale Lattuneddu, his Sardinian fixer recruited by Slavica, his former wife, understood the message. Within seconds, he was speaking to Karl-Heinz Zimmerman, the Austrian 'host' of Ecclestone's motorhome. 'The bus is booked to be shipped from Italy to Istanbul,' said Zimmerman. 'Mr E. wants that cancelled,' said Lattuneddu. Careful with money, Bernie Ecclestone's frugal manner matched his origins.

2

Gambling

Celebrations were unfamiliar for Bernard Ecclestone's parents. At Christmas they never exchanged presents or enjoyed the traditional lunch, and Bertha Ecclestone never arranged a birthday party for her son. That changed on his eighth birthday after they moved to south-east London. On 28 October 1938 Aunt May, his mother's sister, baked a cake, prepared sandwiches and invited neighbours. Bewildered, Bernard fled the house and wandered around Dartford until nightfall.

'They were worried about me,' he realised when he eventually returned. Over the following seventy-two years, as he gambled, bargained and battled to accumulate his fortune, at least $4 billion in cash, Bernard Charles Ecclestone avoided celebration of his life and success.

At regular Saturday coffee mornings at Fortnum & Mason in Piccadilly, his oldest Dartford friends – a bookmaker, a tailor, a horse trainer and a property developer – all in their late seventies, speculated on whether their host was ever truly happy. Despite the private jets, the luxury yacht, the mansions in Chelsea and others scattered across Europe, and all his billions, the gang searched for signs of emotion behind the mischievous banter and the urchin face concealed by tinted glasses and a grey fringe. In unison they agreed he never forgot his roots but never mentioned happiness.

Hardship was ingrained in the circumstances of his birth in St Peter in Suffolk on 28 October 1930. Sidney Ecclestone, a small, quiet twenty-seven-year-old fisherman, was scraping a living on the *Elnet*, a rickety trawler sailing from Lowestoft to catch herring and mackerel in the North Sea. Bertha, his twenty-three-year-old wife, dominated the household. Sharing the chores with Rose Westley, her mother, who lived nearby, the housewife demanded that Sidney hand over his earnings on pay day. Strict discipline about money, cleanliness and morality pervaded Hawk House, their thick-walled home without an inside lavatory or water from a tap. Isolation was a natural way of life for those living in the hamlets around South Elmham linked only by narrow tracks across the Suffolk wheat fields. Until Bernard's birth the only noteworthy event in the Ecclestones' life was the *Elnet* being tossed on to a beach during a storm in 1928. Ever since, Sidney had sought to escape the harsh seafarer's life.

At the turn of the century Sidney Ecclestone's family had moved from Kent to work in the nascent printing industry in Norwich but Sidney lacked the self-confidence to keep a skilled job. Famous for always polishing his shoes, Sidney even gave up fishing to work as a farm hand soon after Bertha became concerned about her son's health. Around Bernard's second birthday, she became convinced that her son's eyesight was defective. With the baby strapped to her back, she cycled twenty miles to the hospital in Norwich. The diagnosis was brutal. Her son was nearly blind in his right eye and the defect could not be remedied.

Three years later he arrived on a horse-drawn milk wagon at the infant school in Wissett, a nearby village. In the afternoons, under the disciplinary eyes of his mother and grandmother who taught him 'right from wrong', he obediently did domestic chores, even collecting horse manure for his mother's garden. 'Never waste,' he was told by Sidney, 'but always buy the best you can afford.' That was about the only homily his father uttered. On reflection Ecclestone realises now that throughout his childhood there was sparse home life. His parents rarely spoke except when his mother became angry and they never went on holiday, not even to the nearby beaches. Ecclestone only saw the sea twice, thanks to a visit arranged by a kind neighbour.

By the mid-1930s Bertha and her family realised there was no future in St Peter for their son. Pumping water in the back yard, poor education and health facilities and no job prospects made life too difficult. In 1935 Bertha's sister May moved to Dartford in Kent with her husband, a fishmonger, followed by their mother. In 1938 Bertha, pregnant with her second child, decided to join the exodus. Renting a bungalow in Priory Close, Sidney found a job as a crane driver at a local engineering factory while Bernard joined the West Hill infant school, a half-mile walk from his home. That year, Bertha's second child, a daughter called Marion, was born. She would barely feature in her brother's life. One year later, the Second World War began and the Ecclestones had good reason to consider the folly of exchanging their sanctuary in Suffolk for living under the flight path of German bombers heading along the Thames estuary towards London. 'They'll bomb us tonight,' Sidney announced on 3 September 1939. Bernie watched his parents tape up the windows to protect themselves from flying glass and fix the blackout curtains. An air-raid siren sounded that night, a false alarm.

Regardless of the danger, Bertha refused to evacuate Bernard with the majority of London's children to the countryside. Deciding that her family would be adequately protected by a flimsy Anderson shelter erected in the garden, she made a critical decision that would forge her son's character and career. By example and love rather than lectures she allowed her son to foster his own life. Little was ever spoken between the son and his parents. The family lacked overt emotional bonds. Feelings were never expressed or analysed. Bertha was merely demanding and supportive, making her son self-critical and ambitious. Most importantly, Bertha never expressed doubts about any decision. The most obvious was her choice to stay in Dartford.

In May 1940, as the British army was being evacuated from Dunkirk, the Luftwaffe bombers began raids on the munitions factories located near Ecclestone's home before heading on towards the London docks on the River Thames, visible in an uninterrupted view across the fields from the bottom of their garden. Daily, German bombers passed over the Ecclestones' neighbourhood, dubbed by the locals as 'Bomb Alley'. Every night during the Blitz Ecclestone could see from the shelter the London skyline covered by shooting flames. During the daytime he watched the dogfights of Spitfires, scrambled from nearby Biggin Hill airfield, attacking the Luftwaffe. During the Battle of Britain, Ecclestone played with friends in the bomb sites, especially the burnt-out local labour exchange, collecting live and spent ammunition, catapulting shrapnel at each other and examining the detritus of blasted offices and homes.

The war disrupted all schoolchildrens' education. Most English teachers had been called up for military service and were replaced by refugees. At West Hill the thirty children in Ecclestone's class were taught by Poles and Belgians. Among the rigorous disciplinarians was an outstanding maths teacher, a crucial factor in the fate of the unusually small but self-confident boy in the playground. In the era of poverty, rationing and shortages, it became normal for schoolboys to swap their possessions. 'Swapping' assumed a particular attraction for Ecclestone. Initially he swapped the milk and biscuits provided by the school. Next he began swapping his toys. Trading up, obtaining a better toy, became instinctive. To the surprise of Don Cox, a friend, Ecclestone even swapped his birthday presents. 'Doesn't your mum mind?' asked Cox. 'Nah,' replied Ecclestone.

At home, Bertha had allowed 'Bungay', as she called her son, to commandeer a wooden shed adjoining the bomb shelter at the bottom of the garden. Despite the musty atmosphere, Ecclestone spent hours pulling apart motors, engines and old bicycles. Taught by Sidney, a perpetual tinkerer with machines, he cleaned ball bearings, chains and wheels and, after reassembling his artefacts, looked for another machine to renovate. 'Do the best you can with what you've got,' Bertha told her son.

Moving up to the Dartford West Central secondary school in 1941, when Ecclestone was eleven, provoked a change in life. Confronted by the limited finances at home and a desire to be independent, he completed two newspaper rounds early every morning before school. He could always be heard approaching the houses. On Sidney's instructions his shoes were studded with Blakeys to last longer. At the end of the rounds he set off for school, passing a baker at the railway station. Using the income from the newspaper round, he bought biscuits and buns to sell in the playground during the break for 25 per cent profit. 'Titch', as Ecclestone was ungenerously called, realised that his physical and financial survival depended upon ingenuity. Bullied in the playground – 'I got knocked over quite a few times,' he admitted – he befriended and paid taller muscular boys to protect his business and money. 'Short people have to fight a lot,' he murmured. 'Small people have to fight to survive. I learnt to fight the battles I had a good chance of winning. Or I'd run.' His ambition was to purchase a bicycle.

'I didn't want to bother my family to buy me something,' he explained. 'I wanted to earn my own money. I knew they didn't have it anyway. When I wanted things, I hustled and hustled until I got them. I was an independent bastard.'

The following summer, to supplement his income during the holidays, he picked vegetables on a Kent farm. In 1942 he finally bought the bike. After school he raced with his friend Don Cox around Herne Hill and at weekends cycled to Brighton and back on the same day, a round trip of about seventy miles. Returning to Ecclestone's home for tea Cox was always struck by Bertha's habit of 'table thumping', complaining about the government. 'Your mum's very political,' commented Cox who, after his father was killed on a minesweeper in 1943, drew closer to Ecclestone. 'You've always got your dad here,' said Cox, grateful that Ecclestone shared his sadness. Sidney had escaped war duty. 'He doesn't want to go to fight,' Ecclestone explained. Instead of joining the army, Sidney became an air-raid warden. His son joined the Sea Scouts but soon quit. 'Too much discipline,' he complained. 'I don't like camping and sleeping out. I can't see the point.' In compensation Aunt May offered her nephew and Cox 'a treat in London'. Arriving at Hamley's, the toy shop in Regent Street, she told the two, 'Have anything you like.' Poignantly, Ecclestone chose a red racing car. The tin Dinky toy was never offered for a swop in the schoolyard.

During that summer the school friends cycled to the sea wall, famous as an eighteenth-century smuggler's hideaway, near an army practice range for mortars. They built a raft from drift wood and empty oil drums. Inevitably, 'Titch' fell into the water and was pulled out by Cox.

Over the following months Ecclestone and Cox cycled around Bexleyheath, stopping regularly outside the camps for American GIs preparing for the invasion of Europe. In conversations through the fences, the boys agreed to deliver messages to the soldiers' local girlfriends in exchange for chewing gum. Ecclestone quickly chewed his gum and demanded that Cox hand over his own. Accustomed to trading comics and marbles with Ecclestone, Cox resisted, recalling his suspicious mother's advice: 'Don't do too much bargaining with Bernard. He gets the better of every deal.'

In the summer of 1944 Ecclestone was earning money digging potatoes. Suddenly, he heard the engine of a V1 rocket flying to London cut out. Looking up, he saw the rocket lurching towards the field. Running madly, he threw himself into the mud just before an explosion. He returned to find the potatoes lying neatly on the earth. His narrow escape was soon followed by another on a Saturday morning. Cox rushed into his garden to watch a V1 rocket pass low across his house. Seconds later the engine cut out and it fell vertically towards Ecclestone's bungalow. After the explosion Cox ran towards Priory Close. The rocket, he discovered, had hit a neighbouring friend's house. The boy, sleeping in the loft, was scrambling out of the rubble. His mother was dead. Cox did not hear the Ecclestones express any relief.

When the end of the war came, the Ecclestones had survived unscathed. No member of their family had been killed or even injured and in the house, Ecclestone knew, 'We had a cupboard that was full of boxes of Black Magic chocolates and sugar and all other things you could not get.' Ecclestone's parents had been trading in the black market. On VE day their street was decorated with balloons and Union Jacks for a jubilant celebration. But the Ecclestones did not party. Instead, after careful saving, the family moved to a bigger house nearby in Marcet Road. Aged fifteen, Ecclestone took his matriculation exams and failed in all subjects except maths. He would dismiss his school years as irrelevant and never kept any school reports. Nevertheless, he was admitted in 1946 to the Woolwich Polytechnic to study physics and chemistry. Uninterested in the course, he spent Sunday mornings at Petticoat Lane market buying fountain pens to sell to other students and searching for a more interesting occupation.

Cyril Clisby, a fellow student, was racing motorbikes at Brands Hatch in south London and suggested that Ecclestone join him on Saturday morning. Ecclestone was already enthralled by bikes. Throughout the war he had travelled in the sidecar of his father's motorbike. Bikes were in the family's genes. Although without a driving licence and hampered by near blindness in one eye, he joined locals in impromptu competitions, scrambling on a Velocette bike fuelled with alcohol to overcome petrol rationing, up hills and through woods across Kent's countryside, and then to more organised competitions at Brands Hatch.

Fiercely competitive, the by-product of being small and a target for mockery, he raced to win. 'Show me a good loser,' he would later say, 'and I'll show you a loser.' Winning at any price became a virtue, probably the principal source of his happiness. Every weekend Sidney drove his son, the bike and equipment in a newly acquired van to Brands Hatch to compete. After the races the Ecclestones did not socialise in the local pub. They simply returned home, and in the kitchen Ecclestone and his mother cleaned the mud off the bike until it sparkled.

On Good Friday 1946, not wearing a crash helmet, he crashed and went to hospital at Fawkham with concussion. Lying in the accident ward he experienced an epiphany. Studying, he concluded, was a waste of time and, at sixteen, past the legal school-leaving age, he decided to leave the Poly. Reluctantly, Sidney agreed on condition that he worked in the laboratory of a friendly neighbour, Mr Richardson, a Gas Board chemist. Paid £5 per week to check the purity of the gas, Ecclestone possessed no qualifications that promised a successful career. Uneducated and unsophisticated, his best attributes were his wits and a passion to become rich. The Gas Board was merely a convenient venue for his first office. He spent most of his time searching through the classified advertisements of local newspapers for sales of motorbikes and parts. Throughout the day he used the Gas Board's telephone to arrange visits to sellers and prospective buyers. If he was away from the telephone, Richardson took the messages. After work Ecclestone scuttled around south-east London, riding the bikes from sellers to buyers, temporarily storing any unsold bikes in the garden shed. Without help from anyone, his trade was self-financing.

In 1947 Ecclestone opened his front door to Jack Surtees, the pre-war British motorbike champion, responding to an advertisement for a 250cc Excelsior Manxman. The famous rider, a dealer in cars and bikes at his shop in Forest Hill, was surprised to discover Ecclestone repairing the spotless Manxman in the kitchen. Standing next to Surtees was John, his twelve-year-old son. Having agreed the price with the seventeen-year-old and paid in cash, Jack Surtees loaded the Excelsior into his van.

By now Ecclestone's expertise was established. Earning more money from his sideline than his Gas Board wages, he approached Les Crocker, the owner of Harcourt Motor Cycles in a shopping centre in Bexleyheath, near Dartford, for a job. To his father's bewilderment, his son gave up the security of the Gas Board and began a daily routine with Crocker. After searching through classified advertisements in the newspapers, the two men drove across London in an estate car, returning to the showroom with five bikes for renovation and resale. Crocker was impressed by Ecclestone's manners and methods but noticed his habit of frequently washing his hands, straightening his tie and then making sure that no speck of dust could be found on the bikes before positioning them in an impeccably straight line. He was so fastidious that even the labels on each bike were placed precisely in the same position.

Jack Surtees was among the first to witness how Ecclestone had brought refinement to Crocker's presentation of his goods. 'That Ecclestone gets everyone bamboozled,' he told his son on his return home one evening. 'He's buying whole showrooms. The sellers think they're getting good prices but only later do they realise his trick. By offering a price for the whole lot they don't see they're getting much less than they think.' Ecclestone was developing a party-piece of casually arriving in a showroom and nonchalantly offering a price. Not realising that he had spied on the shop in advance to calculate a price, the shopkeeper was won over by the impression of exaggerated values.

After one year Ecclestone decided that Crocker's business was too limited. Across the road was Compton & Fuller, a large garage selling second-hand cars. Ecclestone asked Fred Compton to lease the forecourt to sell second-hand motorbikes. 'No,' replied Compton, unwilling to have motorbikes contaminating his showroom and doubtful of Ecclestone's credibility. Ecclestone was eighteen years old. His call-up papers had arrived for national service. 'I had a decent sense of business and I didn't see the point,' Ecclestone would say. With bad eyesight, his potential in the military was limited but his exclusion was sealed when he complained of 'bad stomach pains'. Soon after the medical examination, he told his mother, 'They've decided they don't want me.' He walked back across the road to Fred Compton and persisted. The offer from the well-dressed teenager wearing a suit and tie became irresistible. Not only would Ecclestone pay rent, but Compton would receive a percentage of the profits.

Ecclestone was given the forecourt and a dilapidated office. 'I'm going over to Fred,' Ecclestone told Crocker. There was no bitterness. 'He probably thinks I'll buy him out one day,' thought Ecclestone as he established his first business. By the end of the year Compton was pleasantly surprised. The profits from Ecclestone's motorbikes were sustaining the sluggish car business. Without any argument, Compton agreed that Ecclestone should move from the forecourt into the showroom. Days later Ecclestone's area was immaculate and regularly filled with new bikes bought in bulk from other dealers. 'His brain was like a calculator,' Compton noted, equally impressed by Ecclestone's innovation of telling customers, 'No need for a test drive. The bikes are covered by my personal guarantee.' There was a natural progression into Compton's car trade.

Brands Hatch had become south London's meeting place for those interested in cars and motorbikes – traders and racers. Among his new friends was Ron Shaw, a motorbike dealer who would become a business partner, and Jimmy Oliver, a Peckham car dealer. 'I understand you're in the car business,' the youth dressed in brand new leathers for racing said to Oliver. 'I've got a customer who wants an American car. Have you got anything?' 'Come to my showroom,' replied Oliver. On the customary sale-or-return basis, without payment or anything written, Oliver watched Ecclestone drive a Hudson Straight Eight out of the showroom and return with cash.

In the post-war era, the centre for trading used cars in London was the network of side streets to the west of the Tottenham Court road. Parking their cars along the kerbs, the city's sharpest dealers or 'spivs' stood on the bleak pavements of Warren Street even in the fog and snow with an air of conspiracy, their pockets stuffed with car logbooks and banknotes, expecting a touch of dishonesty to transform their lives. Shuffling between those characters mixing rackets and honest enterprise was a real-time education, transforming street fighters into elite traders.

In an era of petrol rationing and smuggling of alcohol into the country, the honours were earned by those scooping profits in spite of drab socialist authoritarianism.

Introduced by Derek Wheeler, a veteran trader, Ecclestone ambled along the street, avoiding hardened criminals and stolen cars, exuding deadpan ambivalence when buying or selling in a market notorious for bluff and brutalisation. Distinguishing between the good and the bad in a world where lies flourished, Ecclestone learned the crucial difference between price and value. His fundamental rule was to decide a value before starting negotiations and let the profit follow automatically. After listening to seasoned traders, he perfected a cunning style of 'take it or leave it' to put the other side at a disadvantage. A cardinal rule was to ignore the question, 'What will you give?', and put the burden on the other trader to name a price. The skill was timing, never flinching and 'letting the other side blink first'. The image was of a man whose heart had turned into dust, for whom nostalgia was a burden. Temperamentally ice cold, his success depended on stifling his opponents' will-power. No profit, no fun became his credo. Dubbed by rivals as 'The Whippet' for being fast, he enjoyed haggling and dangling the bait while sidestepping the latent aggression. Showing the slightest interest guaranteed less profit. Indifference was the shield to daily duplicity. In that murky world, trust was paramount. Cheques were written but never presented to a bank. Settlement was eventually in cash. Pockets stuffed with banknotes became a regular feature of Ecclestone's life. 'Folding doesn't tell stories' was the Street's mantra. 'Keep up with me, Fred,' he shouted at Compton, the man with the money. Among the low-life Ecclestone encountered along the bomb-damaged streets was Stanley Setty, a trader of stolen cars whose corpse was dropped by his murderer in 1949 from a plane into the English Channel. Then there was Victor White and Harry O'Connor, two much older dealers from Blackpool who, while not particularly gifted, were reliable and introduced Ecclestone to a riskier, more profitable trade.

All-night car auctions were regularly held at the Midland Hotel in Manchester for horse traders who had graduated to become car dealers. 'To beat them,' O'Connor warned Ecclestone, 'you'd have to wake up early in the morning.' None of the occasional bidders attracted to the sales was aware that the auctions were rigged by twelve dealers. Ecclestone was introduced into the ring by O'Connor, who whispered to the others that his young friend from London was 'a nutter who inherited a fortune after his father's death and would be easy pickings'. Cars were not traded singly but in packages of three or four. Those outside the ring did not realise that the trade was contaminated by a ruse of including into the package non-existent cars which needed to be 'bought back' at the end of the session for less than the original selling price. To profit from that audacious game required a glacial expression, nerves of steel and a love of gambling. 'You're a car short,' one canny dealer mumbled to Ecclestone at the end of a ferocious session. Ecclestone hated being caught out: it would expose any weakness. Survival meant showing no sympathy, especially for himself.

Alternating between Bexleyheath, Warren Street and Manchester, Ecclestone graduated within months into a master dealer. Smartly dressed and sharp, he won respect as a trader who cared about his increasing wealth and his image as a hawk who could make trouble. 'He's the man at the top of the motor trade,' a Warren Street dealer told Jimmy Oliver. Ecclestone had crafted his skills. He walked away from every deal satisfied about winning but never chortling.

'I don't like others to think I'm sharp,' he explained, 'then they're more careful, and that's a disadvantage. I want to buy from someone who thinks he's smart and sell to someone who is not that smart. Most of all, I'm happy if the other side is happy – then it's a good deal for both sides, but so long as it suits me I never care what others think.' Few claimed to have scored against Ecclestone. The trader, whose favourite relaxation was watching black-and-white Hollywood westerns with sheriffs chasing outlaws, adopted the maxim, 'Until someone is quicker on the draw, then I'm alive.' Hailed as 'ballsy' for 'giving all', he mixed with men who had either avoided military service or were too young to fight in the war. Together they shrugged off bleak post-war austerity by embracing daredevil recklessness.

Risking his life in competitive racing became Ecclestone's search for the thrill of real danger. The high point was racing a Manx Norton on Brands Hatch's new tarmac in 1950 against John Surtees, then fifteen years old and at the beginning of his career. In 1956 he would win the first of seven world motorcycle championships and become the Formula One world champion in 1964. Soon after Surtees defeated him in that race, Ecclestone decided to 'upgrade'.

The partnership with Compton had become one-sided. While Ecclestone transformed the business, Compton was playing golf. 'That's good for the partnership,' said Ecclestone. 'Means there's no arguments.' Ecclestone's ambitions were profitable for Compton but the twenty-one-year-old demanded recognition. In late 1951 Ecclestone bought Derek Fuller's share and, as a partner, modernised the showroom, renamed Compton & Ecclestone. At the same time, he bought derelict industrial premises in Greenwich, his first property deal, and joined the Ideal Endeavour Freemason's lodge in Kent. His final 'upgrade' was to stop racing motorbikes and switch to racing motor cars.

Italian, German and French manufacturers had revived the construction of sleek Formula One cars. In Britain, motor-car enthusiasts had converted the concrete runway at Silverstone, a wartime RAF base, into a racing track. In May 1950 they invited European car manufacturers to compete in Britain's first Grand Prix, watched by King George VI and the Queen, and 100,000 spectators. Alfa Romeo won. Passionate to join the crowd, Ecclestone persuaded Compton that his participation in Formula Three racing should be borne by their business as an advertising cost and headed to the Coopers' factory in Surbiton, the Mecca for aspiring drivers. Watched by enthusiasts, Charles and John Cooper were fitting 500 cc motorbike engines on to metal chassis and beating post-war shortages by manufacturing vital parts. Ecclestone ordered the Coopers to install a Norton motorbike engine and cover it with a blue body. In 1951, dressed in a new leather suit, with his gel-slicked hair swept back from his thin face, Ecclestone arrived at Silverstone driving an American Ford and towing the car. Compton followed in a van bearing the company's name painted on the side. 'Going into racing', Compton acknowledged, 'was a way of getting our name known. It worked. Everyone in the south of England knew us. Everything about Bernard had to be that way – organised and professional.' Mixing with Stirling Moss, Mike Hawthorn, the legendary Juan Fangio and other swashbucklers who had already completed the first world championship, Ecclestone's persistent daring won several heats but he failed to beat Stirling Moss. There was also a cost.

On 8 April 1951 Ecclestone won the Junior Brands Hatch Championship in a Cooper MK5/JAP driving at 62.03 miles an hour. Later that year he won his heat in the Brands Open Challenge Final. In the final Ecclestone was battling against three others as another car spun out in front of him: Ecclestone steered sharp right and, according to a local newspaper, 'his Cooper climbed up the safety banking, jumping on to a spectator's parked Riley car, unfortunately breaking a spectator's leg as a result'. Others were also injured but, as the newspapers recorded, 'The race continued uninterrupted. St John's gallant ambulance men and the mechanics cleared up.'

Ecclestone felt rich. Five years after leaving school, he was driving an expensive Austin Healey sports car around Bexleyheath and his pockets were stuffed with banknotes. Well dressed and good company among like-minded dealers, he was known as 'the bravest man in the car business'. He now wanted his independence.

Moving out of home was only possible by marriage. Through a racing friend and neighbour, he had met Ivy Bamford, a pleasant brunette, two years older than himself, employed at the local telephone exchange. Every day Ivy, the daughter of a carpenter and only faintly interested in motor racing, connected callers by pushing the plugs at the end of telephone lines into sockets. Although the two had little in common, Ecclestone was a virgin and liked the idea of moving into his own home. Marrying Ivy, he also hoped, would stop their arguments. Ivy had every reason to grab the material advantages Ecclestone offered. He had bought Fred Compton's 1930s four-bedroomed semi-detached family house in Pickford Close, Bexleyheath, for £1,000.

The ceremony was planned for 5 September 1952 at the Dartford Registry Office. But a few days earlier, Ecclestone was plagued by uncertainty. 'Let's forget about this and do it another day,' he suggested. Ivy was insistent. Disregarding his fluster, she arrived for the marriage with her mother and an aunt. All three, Ecclestone thought, were crying. 'Sure you want to go through with this?' he asked. 'You don't have to.' Ecclestone was waiting with Fred Compton and his wife Jean, who had agreed to be the witnesses. Although he would later say that his parents were not present – 'I didn't tell them,' he said – they were at the ceremony and noticed his irritation that the registrar was a woman. Once the formalities were over, Ecclestone turned to leave. Halfway out of the room, the registrar asked, 'Haven't you forgotten something Mr Ecclestone?' 'What?' he replied. 'Your bride.' There was no photographer to record the moment, nor drinks or a meal after the ceremony. Even marriage celebrations were alien to the Ecclestones.

Ivy Ecclestone was unaware that his regular bouts at Brands Hatch were increasingly dangerous. Handicapped by poor eyesight and lacking the skills of Stirling Moss, he could not manoeuvre safely at high speeds around the crudely constructed bends. Eventually the inevitable happened. In 1953 he collided with Bill Whitehouse, a friend, and drove through a fence into the spectators. Whitehouse was the first to arrive, to find him dazed in the smashed car and drooped over the steering wheel.

'Are you all right, Bernard?' shouted Whitehouse. Ecclestone mumbled. 'Good,' said Whitehouse. 'Now stay still because you've killed someone in the crowd and they'll kill you.' Ecclestone froze. Gradually Ecclestone realised that he was the victim of a prank like the many he himself had played. But after his arrival in a hospital ward, while gazing at the ceiling he considered his options. He was enjoying life, was earning serious money and realised that over the previous years he had 'woken up four or five times in hospital but was lucky never to break anything nor even draw blood'. Harry Epps, a Ford dealer, had recently crashed and lost part of an arm. Deaths were quite common. 'I realised that I didn't want to risk lying in bed for the rest of my life looking up at the ceiling because I had a broken back, so I decided to concentrate on my business.'

On his return to dealing, there was one score to be settled. The opportunity arose when, after speeding too fast around Bexleyheath in a silver Mercedes sports car, he crashed into a bus. Walking away with a wounded arm, he distanced himself from any responsibility. 'That car', he told the onlookers, 'belongs to Bill Whitehouse. He's run away.' News about his accident quickly reached Whitehouse who owned an identical car. Rushing to his garage, he pulled open the doors. Everything fell into place.

Risk fed his hunger for serious wealth. He loved gambling. During evening visits to friends' homes, he regularly played roulette, gin rummy and Monopoly for money. There was a bigger challenge. From older Warren Street dealers he heard about Crockfords, one of London's few casinos. Membership in that era was not required. Having reserved a table for a gala show and wearing black tie, with Ivy in an expensive cocktail dress, Ecclestone arrived in Mayfair from Bexleyheath. Both were overwhelmed by the opulence. The dazzling show and dinner were a revelation to those still accustomed to food rationing and bomb sites. 'Real glamour,' Ecclestone told his wife. The principal attraction was the baize-covered tables. Clusters of men were playing chemin de fer, blackjack and roulette. Until then Ecclestone's serious bets were on horses and greyhounds with Tony Morris, his friend and bookmaker. Crockfords was in a different class, not only for its style but also the scale of betting. Gambling became Ecclestone's passion, not because he was compulsive or addicted but because chance, risk and weighing the odds matched his philosophy of life. Individuals, he believed, could not be protected from making mistakes or the consequences of their errors and should look after themselves. The underdog was discarded with an unnerving lack of sympathy. 'I'm a gambler,' he said, 'and gamblers do it to prove they're right.' Gambling had much in common with dealing.

'With cars', he explained, 'I could add up in my head the value of all the cars in a showroom without writing it down. It was not back-of-the envelope stuff. At Crockfords, I weighed up the probabilities. I had no system. I'd love to be the banker when somebody believes he has a system. I realised that the best chance was by looking for players who were unlucky. I like playing against unlucky people.' As he brushed with that society, Ecclestone's taste for money as a passport out of his childhood poverty grew. While the guest of Jimmy Oliver for lunch at the Poole Yacht Club in Dorset in 1954, Ecclestone spotted Sir Bernard and Lady Docker, famous high-living millionaires. 'I suppose if you've only got a hundred thousand you'd be regarded as a pauper here?' he asked with slight envy.

That year he gave his semi-detached house to his parents and bought a detached home nearby in Danson Road. After builders had gutted and renovated the building to his meticulous design, he searched for his next home. Dealing in houses was akin to dealing in cars. He had no need for permanence. The following September, Deborah Anne, his daughter, was born. Regularly the ecstatic father returned home with clothes and toys – giving presents instead of emotion – but the sense of a contented family life was missing. Rows erupted if he discovered breakages, dirt or any disorder. His meticulousness at work extended to his home. Ivy disliked his long working hours; he disliked her lack of interest in his business. He was irritated by her demand that he stop working and even celebrate Christmas. Nevertheless, his parents were invited on Christmas Day for turkey and presents, and he was pleased that Debbie stayed overnight regularly with his parents while he, brushing aside Ivy's complaints, took off for the cinemas and Crockfords in London. His wife was the unwitting passenger in his dash to become a millionaire.

Fred Compton was the first obstacle – and the first casualty. Arguments became frequent. 'I couldn't live with Ecclestone and his methods of business,' admitted Compton. 'I wasn't doing any business at all in the end. It wasn't his fault, but I had become a useless object.' Ecclestone wanted to be rid of his partner. His approach was intentionally casual. 'Either I'll buy you out or you can buy me out,' said Ecclestone. 'You decide.' Although Compton was, like Ecclestone, a used-car dealer, he was caught short when his partner suggested, 'Just write your price down.' Compton, Ecclestone shrewdly guessed, would assume his inability to pay a high price. Just as Ecclestone planned, Compton's price was lower than he wanted but, he assumed, beyond Ecclestone's means. Instead, Ecclestone instantly accepted and shepherded his surprised partner to conclude the purchase at the solicitor next door. 'It's the price of freedom,' said Ecclestone after bidding Compton farewell.

As the sole owner of the business Ecclestone traded more aggressively. He bought the Barnhurst garage in Bexleyheath from Ron Frost and signed for an option on the premises of the Strood Motor Company in Kent which was later resold for a profit. Even Compton was impressed: 'It was a major property on a plum location but it took a lot of nerve to pull it off.' He made an offer with Ron Shaw to buy Brands Hatch for £46,000 but at the last moment they were double-crossed. In 1956 he sold his house, a car in the garage and some adjacent property for development to move into Barn Cottage, a five-bedroomed house in Parkwood Road, Bexley. As with the previous houses, the family lived among builders during the house's reconstruction. He had not bought the latest house because it was 'nicer' but because 'it was cheap and a good deal'. The sharply dressed car dealer walking around Bexleyheath with his British bulldog was always happy to deal: 'Buying and selling is a state of mind. People usually buy what they don't need; and you need to convince people you are a real buyer. I don't like the Arab way of dealing – asking for 100 and expecting to get 60. You can't insult people. Everything has a value, but no one really knows the value of anything. Everything has a different price for different people. I assess the price and then ask for it. When buying, I always wait for the owner to state the price. I say, "It's your property not mine." If you offer blind you'll offer too much.'

Among the fraternity of rival dealers in Bexleyheath socialising in the local pubs and at Brands Hatch was Lewis 'Pop' Evans and his son Stuart Lewis-Evans, the same age and height as Ecclestone. In the early 1950s, he had raced Cooper cars against Ecclestone and won. By 1957 Stuart had graduated to drive a Connaught Formula One car at Monaco against the legendary Fangio. Excited by his friend's success, Ecclestone offered to manage the commercial side of his driving career. After Lewis-Evans beat Stirling Moss that year at Goodwood, Ecclestone negotiated with Tony Vandervell for Lewis-Evans to switch from the unreliable Connaughts to join Moss at the Vanwall team. Ecclestone, Vandervell also agreed, could negotiate Lewis-Evans's appearance fees with each of the circuits where he raced.

The racing business enjoyed by rich enthusiasts, businessmen and some minor aristocrats was financially primitive. Each driver and team negotiated separately with individual circuit owners for the appearance fee and the prize money. To attract spectators, the circuit owners or promoters paid more for Ferrari's and Fangio's appearance than to the unknown drivers and their lack-lustre cars. Rightly, the promoters calculated that the less qualified owners and drivers cared less about money than enjoying a non-stop party embracing thrill and risk. In that hectic world cars regularly crashed and burst into flames; and every week motor sport magazines featured obituary notices alongside frenzied descriptions of gladiatorial contests. Passionate about racing, Ecclestone seized the opportunity to join the party when the Connaught team went bankrupt in 1958.

Abroad when the receiver announced the auction to sell three Connaught cars and spares, Ecclestone ordered an employee at his showroom in Bexleyheath to buy everything. 'What price?' he was asked. 'I don't care,' Ecclestone replied, 'just go and buy.' Merely owning the obsolete cars would be his passport into the elite club. Nostalgia played no part in his venture. A profit, he hoped, would follow victory for the two Connaughts entered to race in the New Zealand Grand Prix. Stuart Lewis-Evans and Roy Salvadori were persuaded to fly around the world and ordered to sell the cars after the race. After a miserable performance in the Grand Prix, however, there were few buyers. Salvadori telephoned Ecclestone with the news that the best offer for the Connaughts was a stamp album. Ecclestone lambasted the driver and the deal was off. The cars were shipped back to Europe in time for Ecclestone to enter the Monaco Grand Prix. Arriving in the town, Ecclestone was intoxicated by the atmosphere. Unlike other circuits, the race through the principality's streets, under the prince's palace and along the quay for millionaire's yachts was unforgettable. Unimpressed by the driver he had hired, he pushed the hapless man aside to drive the car himself. Competing against thirty entries, he failed to qualify but enjoyed the glory in what was officially described as 'not a serious attempt'. Worse, he lost in the casino.

Defeat rarely dampened Ecclestone's spirit. Any anger or desperation was concealed by the comfort that his business was growing. Travelling across the country, his challengers were outwitted. Rivals hailed the younger man as 'pretty fantastic, a genius in finance and organisation, and a miracle'. His poker face concealed his mastery of mathematics. Typically he would buy the best cars with high mileage from sellers blind to potential profits. Inevitably the trade was lubricated by tricks. 'Clocking' or falsifying mileage meters was common. In the pre-electronic era, a car's mileage was recorded by numbers engraved on small mechanical wheels. To increase a car's value, dealers turned the wheels backwards to reduce a car's apparent mileage. In south London John Young, the owner of a large franchise of Mercedes and Jaguars, was especially wary of 'Bernard' who, he noticed, had 'a knack of knocking back the mileage'. Usually the customer was fooled but a complaint sparked an official investigation. Ecclestone told the inspector in a jocular quip, 'All my cars are "clocked".' Then, in a serious tone, he added, 'If you prosecute me, you'll put a lot of people out of work.' Tricking authority with fast talk, a smile and a good story was an escape from 'a tight corner'. Ecclestone eventually avoided conviction by persuading the court that the car's milometer had been doctored while on loan to another dealer.

His sales operation in Bexleyheath grew inexorably. In 1956 he bought Hills Garage, a rival selling Mercedes, and two years later he merged his business with James Spencer Ltd, the biggest dealer in the area with the franchise to sell new Morris, Austin, MG and Wolseley cars. Ecclestone now owned a money machine. The demand for new cars, especially from the suburban middle classes, was insatiable. Since the war, they had stashed huge sums of cash to avoid punitive income tax and were hungry to spend their savings. But dealers faced an obstacle: the limited number of new cars available from the manufacturers. To beat the shortage and rival dealers, 'back-handers' were given to the manufacturer's sales managers. Ecclestone was proud to be ahead of the game. For those unable to buy new cars, he offered top-quality second-hand cars renovated by six mechanics employed behind the showroom. To expand the business, he designed a massive conversion of the James Spencer garage into an ultra-modern showroom.

In the midst of that reconstruction, he flew in October 1958 with Stuart Lewis-Evans to Casablanca to compete in the

Moroccan Grand Prix. His friend was battling in a Vanwall against Stirling Moss and Mike Hawthorn, both British stars. Standing in the pits beside the dusty circuit with a stopwatch in each hand, Ecclestone monitored his friend's progress until, in the second half of the race, a huge flash of flame and smoke erupted on the far side. Running across the track, Ecclestone discovered that Lewis-Evans's car engine had seized up and, after losing control, he had crashed through the barriers. The driver was taken to the local hospital suffering seventy-degree burns. Sitting beside his friend, wrapped with a blanket while he waited endlessly for a doctor, Ecclestone was racked by anguish. To spare Stuart further pain and possible death from the primitive medicine, Tony Vandervell chartered a plane and they returned to England. Six days after the crash, Ecclestone was sitting with his friend while he died. Lewis-Evans's obituarists, brushing aside the risks as 'the throttle works both ways', praised 'the little man with a big heart' joining the long list of Formula One's fatalities. A few days later Ecclestone had his twenty-eighth birthday. Watching a close friend die so painfully had been excruciating. His appetite for the sport was spent. The Connaught cars were sold and he turned his back on all Formula racing. He would focus exclusively on selling cars, dealing in property – and becoming richer.

The James Spencer showroom on Bexleyheath Broadway had been transformed into a futuristic emporium. Fastidious about design, Ecclestone had devoted an inordinate amount of time to every detail, aiming for perfection. The sheet-glass exterior and the gleaming white interior was an unprecedented spectacle for car showrooms in the post-austerity era. Obsessively Ecclestone ordered that the shining cars were lined up exactly straight on white tiles, illuminated by beams of light and surrounded by thick carpets. Sliding doors in the rear led into a showroom for specialist second-hand cars – Rolls-Royces, Maseratis and Jaguars. Access was possible only by Ecclestone's personal invitation. 'I don't like the customers coming in here,' he told a salesman. 'They're bloody pests. They make the place dirty.' Comfortable sofas were placed in recesses near an unusual spiral staircase leading to Ecclestone's glass-walled office. On his desk were three telephones – yellow, cream and red. Constantly adjusting the cords and straightening papers, he would walk across to Ann Jones, his secretary, and, like a mother hen, remove flecks of dust from her desk and square her papers. 'Everyone's tucked under the Governor's wing,' thought Jones until the uneasy peace cracked. 'I'm a secretary, not a cleaner,' she spluttered after Ecclestone complained that her desk was untidy. Ecclestone was deaf to complaints. He was a one-man band, micro-managing his business and demanding unquestioned loyalty. Allegiances were tested with explosive curses against suppliers failing to fulfil their promises or by cutting telephone connections. Frustrated by the primitive telephone system and racked by stress, Ecclestone flung telephones at a wall or on to the floor, expecting secretaries in a nearby office to dodge the flying plastic and ignore his outbursts. Telephone engineers were frequently summoned to replace the smashed instruments while Ann Jones faithfully cleared up the mess for a man she admired. Then, watching another tearful secretary flee his lacerating curses, she patiently called an employment agency for a replacement.

Amid the constant drama, the most fearful was the showroom manager, Sidney Ecclestone. The first to arrive every morning, Sidney was alerted to his son's appearance by a succession of warning telephone calls, 'He's here.' At night Sidney locked up and was the last to leave. During the day he served customers, acutely vulnerable to Bernard's reprimand. 'You shouldn't have let that customer go. You should have got that deal.' To find calm, Sidney would go out on to the forecourt and wipe a leather over the cars. Some visitors, including Ron Shaw, who were counted among Ecclestone's close circle, thought that their friend appeared to outsiders to be ill at ease with his father. After all, Sidney and his son seemed to have little in common.

In Ecclestone's opinion that judgement would be mistaken. 'I didn't terrorise my father,' he explained. 'I just had an opinion.' Eventually, they forged a convenient system. Sidney would greet customers and signal to his son the possibility of a sale, and Ecclestone would descend the spiral staircase. With awe Sidney watched his son persuade a walk-in customer enquiring about a Morris to buy a more expensive MG. In an undemonstrative way, the father was proud of his son's achievements, grateful to have a respectable job and, in that uniquely English manner, showed no obvious affection. Whenever Ann Jones was provoked to storm out of the building, Sidney was dispatched to her house with a gift – flowers, chocolates and even an embroidered handkerchief from Ecclestone's mother – beseeching her to return. The cycle was repeated and loyalties were continually tested. Spotting a bunch of flowers for Jones with a card signed, 'from a secret admirer', Ecclestone disparaged the gift as 'probably from a competitor trying to find out our secrets'.

Mastering the tight control of his staff, costs and the presentation of the cars was the bedrock of Ecclestone's business style. In 1960, at the beginning of the Swinging Sixties, all the elements came together. The all-white James Spencer showroom was cool, the cars were sparkling – especially the new MG sports series – and in the suburbs husbands started buying second cars for their wives and children. To finance the boom the Conservative government introduced 'hire purchase', allowing Ecclestone to lend customers the purchase money. To earn profits as the borrower in March 1961 he established Arvin Securities, taking a hefty profit from the interest payments. Unlike in other areas in Britain, the middle-class inhabitants of Kent rarely defaulted on their monthly repayments. The few who fell into arrears were visited by Ron Smith, his bulky debt collector, driving a green TR3, who as a last resort reclaimed the cars. 'We had very little trouble,' Ecclestone volunteered.

Beyond the glitz, a hint of Warren Street's atmosphere was still present. Customers occasionally noticed that well-built men were hanging around the premises, not least Jack 'Spot' Cromer, a familiar East End criminal. Dealing with criminals was not unusual for Ecclestone. When a well-known gangster appeared in his showroom to sell a car, Ecclestone handed the man a cheque for the agreed price. Later that day Ann Jones discovered a hire-purchase loan was charged against the car. 'Stop the cheque,' ordered Ecclestone. A few days later the criminal reappeared. 'You shouldn't have stopped the cheque,' he growled, pulling out a gun. 'If you don't pay up I'll shoot you.' 'If you shoot me I can't pay you,' snapped back Ecclestone. Both broke out laughing. 'I'll tell you what I'll do,' said Ecclestone. 'I'll pay off the finance and give you the rest in cash.' 'Right,' replied the gangster still holding the revolver as Ecclestone peeled off the banknotes. To Ecclestone's amusement, a few weeks later the gangster returned to buy one of the newly launched Austin A40s. 'As good as gold,' laughed Ecclestone, waving goodbye. Shortly after driving the bright red car out of the showroom, the gangster stopped at traffic lights. As the lights changed to green, he found the new gears difficult to shift and was honked at by the car behind. He got out of his car, opened the boot and snatched the metal lever used to change tyres; he walked to the noisy offender, pulled the driver on to the street and split the man's head open with a single blow. Arrested, he was taken to Bexley police station. Pulling the gun from his pocket, he told the police officer, 'I don't like being arrested,' and walked out. He was subsequently prosecuted for murder.

Ecclestone's reputation for dealing with criminals became common gossip among south London's car dealers. At their regular lunch at the George pub, Bill Whitehouse and his employees at the Westmount garage regarded Ecclestone with measured respect. Peter Rix, one of those employees, asked Ecclestone over a pint, 'Have you got a good second-hand MG?' 'Yes,' replied Ecclestone. 'A bright red one.' 'Has it got a heater?' asked Rix about the optional extra. 'Yes,' replied Ecclestone. The car was bought and delivered, and Rix discovered there was no heater. He telephoned Ecclestone and complained. 'Are you calling me a liar?' Ecclestone murmured. 'You want to be careful, boy. I've had fingers cut off.' Rix apologised. 'I got the message,' he would later say. 'You didn't cross Bernard. He didn't care about tucking me up.'

Ecclestone's fearlessness attracted many admirers. Speeding around Bexleyheath and London in the new Mini rather than status symbol cars, his love of racing had been revived. Recklessly, he competed in an American car at stock car tracks in West Ham and Essex, becoming notorious as 'Mind the Paint Ecclestone' for avoiding crashing into his rivals. 'I hate my car being damaged,' he grumbled. After completing a pilot's course at Biggin Hill, he frequently swooped across Kent in his own four-seater Beagle. 'I can't see,' he admitted after failing the test for a licence. Unwilling to be beaten, he applied for a licence in America but, after contemplating the transatlantic trips, the plan was abandoned. As consolation he bought twelve Beagle aircraft from an insolvent company at Biggin Hill which were promptly resold.

Compared with profits at this level, those in the motorbike trade palled. In 1959 he sold Harcourt Motor Cycles to Robert Rowe, a successful racing competitor. During their negotiations, Rowe persuaded Ecclestone to organise his sponsorship and start-up money. As Rowe's agent, Ecclestone supplied a 500 cc Norton for the Isle of Man TT race, obtained sponsorship money from Shell and even loaned Rowe the leather overalls. Rowe had some success, although Ecclestone missed his victory at Brands Hatch when he left early to avoid the rain ruining his clothes and Italian shoes.

The same year Ecclestone sold Compton & Ecclestone to Les Crocker, his original employer. Within months Crocker was failing. Ecclestone agreed to pay off Crocker's £25,000 overdraft in return for a debenture giving Ecclestone the first claim on all the company's assets. Three months later a receiver was appointed. By June 1961 Ecclestone discovered his mistake. The company owed £9,700 to the Inland Revenue and the debt would, according to the law, be paid before Ecclestone could recover his own £25,000. He reversed his strategy. After arranging with Crocker to become the legal owner of all the properties and any cash, he dismissed the receiver and sold the showroom on to his old friends, Victor White and Harry O'Connor. The two were equally unsuccessful and now not only Ecclestone but other creditors were owed money. Ecclestone swiftly pocketed over £6,000 by selling the buildings and stock before BSA Motorcycles, a major supplier, petitioned to have Compton & Ecclestone wound up. At the bankruptcy hearing in Carey Street, Ecclestone learned another lesson. To the receiver's irritation, Victor White, wearing a vicuña suit, arrived late for the afternoon hearing. His excuse was honest. 'I had some money on the two o'clock,' said White blowing the smoke of a large cigar, 'and I've got to leave soon because I'm catching a plane to get to St Moritz.' Left to negotiate with a new receiver, Ecclestone was asked to pay £9,700 owed to the Inland Revenue. 'Would you like to make an offer?' asked the receiver. 'Yes, one third of what I owe,' replied Ecclestone. 'You don't understand, Mr Ecclestone. You've got to pay the whole lot plus a fine. It's tax plus.' Ecclestone offered less than previously. 'You play poker, don't you?' the receiver asked. Ecclestone nodded. 'Well,' replied the receiver, 'I don't want to play with you.' Ecclestone was satisfied. The receiver, he thought, had been outsmarted and the debt would be forgotten. 'Most successful businessmen', he reassured himself, 'have luck and take opportunities.'

One sign of emboldened self-confidence was his change of tailor. Previously Reg Cox, his school friend's brother, had cut his suits. He switched to Edward Saxton in Savile Row, and ordered tailored shirts by Frank Foster. Perfectly dressed, most Saturdays he took Ivy for dinner at a Park Lane hotel and then headed for Crockfords to play chemmy not only against rival car dealers but also against Otto Preminger, Cubby Broccoli, Lord Beaverbrook and once Lord Lucan. By then he had become famous at Crockfords – for spotting two flies climbing up the wall and taking a bet which would reach the ceiling first. If, just before dawn on a Sunday, he was down £10,000, he would take over the bank, risking to double his losses or swing the other way to double his stakes and walk out with a profit. 'If you're the richest man at the table,' he would say, 'you can't lose; and if you can't afford to lose, it's not gambling.'

Among those attracted to the amusing, sharp-talking gambler at Crockfords was Eve Taylor, a show business agent and pop star manager. Taylor's clients, the trailblazers of the Swinging Sixties, were advised to rely on Bernard, her new friend, for an honest deal in cars. James Spencer in Bexleyheath became the destination for Lulu, Sandie Shaw, John Barry, the composer, and Twiggy who arrived with Justin de Villeneuve, her boyfriend, and a large Afghan dog. Twiggy departed in a light green Lamborghini. None of Taylor's clients was more important than Adam Faith, enriched by his 1959 hit song, 'What do you want, if you don't want money?' The pop idol drove out of Ecclestone's showroom in a pale blue Rolls-Royce.

Selling those cars was Ecclestone's introduction to the new aristocracy: they often met in San Lorenzo, a new Italian restaurant in Knightsbridge. Mara and Lorenzo, the generous owners, welcomed Ecclestone along with Princess Margaret, Tony Snowdon and a galaxy of world-famous film stars, musicians and writers. Ecclestone changed his appearance. Instead of wearing his hair Brylcreemed back, he let his locks fall over his ears and brow like the Beatles, the emerging pop group who also appeared at the restaurant. At weekends he adopted a new clothes style: a white shirt, dark trousers and moccasin shoes. Unlike other car salesmen known as the 'laughing boys', Ecclestone's quick, dry humour and straight-laced jokes appealed to San Lorenzo's habitués.

Social success encouraged his gambling, and he headed – but now without his wife Ivy – for a second regular session at Crockfords on Thursdays until nearly dawn. Gambling had become a passion, although he would never risk his business or his home. Punctually at nine o'clock on a Friday morning, as he arrived at work, he could not disguise his fortunes from Ann Jones. If his face was taut, by midday Jones knew she would be told by the club the amount required to settle his losses. While she wrote out cheques for amounts sufficient to buy a large house, she could hear Ecclestone in the showroom below arguing with a customer about the last £5 of a deal which would usually end with Ecclestone's challenge, 'Right, I'll toss you for it.' As he climbed the spiral staircase to order Jones to settle the paperwork, he whispered, 'It's not the money but the deal.' Then, to prevent another argument, he would buy Ivy a mink, jewellery or a new wig. Overall, Ecclestone covered his losses at Crockfords by a succession of property deals of derelict land in Greenwich and the purchase of Jennings, a bankrupt store on Bexleyheath High Street. Breaking it down into small units, he resold the site for a hefty profit. The business technique never changed. Hours after buying the Strood Motor Company, the biggest distributor of Leyland cars in Kent, he inspected his new acquisition. No one was working. 'Fire them,' he ordered, pointing at the staff playing darts. Cutting costs and improving the building, he traded out within one year.

Flush with money, he travelled with Adam Faith to Monte Carlo. 'I met this geezer who sold me a Roller,' Faith told John Bloom, famous for selling the first cheap washing machines to England's middle classes. 'Can I bring him down?' In 1962 Bloom was enjoying his new millions on his yacht, *Arienne 3*. Ecclestone arrived without Ivy and enjoyed the weekend with Max Bygraves, the entertainer, playing chemin de fer at the casino. He lost. With men Ecclestone's banter cemented strong relationships, forging new business opportunities. On his return to England, he began negotiations to buy Faith a cabin cruiser but decided the price was too high. No deal was done.

There were no sharp frontiers between business and friendship. Walking into the Alfa Romeo showroom in Surrey owned by

Roy Salvadori, the former racing driver, Ecclestone asked whether all the cars were for sale. 'Yes,' replied Salvadori. 'I'll give you £52,000 for the lot.' Salvadori was surprised and became unsettled as Ecclestone pushed hard for an answer. 'Will a cheque do?' asked Ecclestone. Salvadori was on the verge of agreeing when he remembered Ecclestone's business methods. Clearly, he had assessed the value before entering and conjured up a sum which seemed enormous but allowed himself a sizeable profit. Salvadori declined the offer. After Ecclestone left, he painstakingly calculated his cars' value. Ecclestone's profits would have been enormous.

In 1965, driving home at night 'with someone I shouldn't have been with', recalled Ecclestone – an 'Indian girlfriend' according to a friend – Ecclestone spotted flames bursting out of the James Spencer showroom. The building and the cars inside were destroyed. 'The fire brigade was already there and they had called the fire assessor,' Ecclestone remembers. What followed entered folklore. Ecclestone's rivals would later paint a scenario of the ruins cleared by eight o'clock in the morning with Ecclestone operating his telephones from a Portacabin delivered at the forecourt before dawn to sell a new range of cars which had been stored outside the building overnight. In their scenario, Ecclestone's insurance policy paid for the reconstruction of a dowdy pre-war building as a modern, gleaming, white emporium. The cynics forgot that the building had been modernised five years earlier. In reality Ann Jones and other eyewitnesses saw Ecclestone 'choking up' as he scrambled over the smoking debris and climbed the metal stairs to his office to spot three pools of plastic – yellow, cream, red – the remnants of his telephones. His insurance broker revealed that the cover was inadequate to replace the used cars in the rear, gutted by the flames sparked by an electrical fault. 'Insurance is a big con,' Ecclestone told Ann Jones, who rescued the undamaged logbooks from the safe. For the first four days Ecclestone and his staff moved into an empty house adjoining the showroom, using orange boxes as tables and chairs. Then a Portacabin was delivered, the area was cleared and business restarted. But the reconstruction, with identical design and materials, took several months. The latest Trimline telephones replaced his previous ones. 'If you throw these new ones around, Mr Ecclestone,' warned the engineer, 'they can't be replaced. There's a shortage.'

That Christmas Ecclestone was particularly antagonistic towards the idea of festive celebrations. Irritated that his staff had organised a meal at the local pub, he remained in the showroom waiting for their return. 'You're no good for work,' he told Jones as she wobbled up the spiral staircase. He would have preferred to open the showroom on Christmas Day. There was little joy at Melcot Road, his latest rebuilt house with his 'suburban' housewife. He had outgrown Ivy. Unable to keep up with his lifestyle and with no shared interests, she spent her time shopping and complaining about his perfectionism at home – some would say his obsession – and his need to control women. She was, he suspected, having a relationship with a local electrician.

'This Chinese girl keeps giving me the eye,' Ecclestone mentioned to Ann Jones on a Friday morning in 1967. At a Crockfords dinner for regular gamblers the previous night, he had met Tuana Tan, a pleasant Singaporean, and her American husband. Born on 7 December 1941, the day the Japanese bombed Pearl Harbor, the attractive woman had grown up in a wealthy family which funded her father's professional gambling. While Tuana's husband stood by the crap table, she and Ecclestone played chemin de fer. Tuana, he discovered, arrived in London in 1961 to study art and was dissatisfied with her one-year marriage. To some, Tuana was quiet. Others remarked on her obedience.

Tuana Tan suited Ecclestone. Intelligent, caring and undemanding, she was refined compared with Ivy and was uncomplaining about his prime interest – business and accumulating money. Nor was she troubled by his unemotional relationships and perfectionism. For a year they met secretly in

London until one evening Ecclestone returned home to be told by Ivy that Tuana's husband had telephoned. Ivy and the American agreed that neither knew the whereabouts of their spouses. 'Bernie's having an affair with Tuana,' the husband revealed. Ecclestone was not upset by Ivy's demand for a divorce. The only issue was the fate of their twelve-year-old daughter Debbie and, in return for adequate alimony, the arrangements were speedily agreed. Carrying a single suitcase, he departed.

His new life with Tuana caused few waves. Attentive and subservient in the Oriental manner, the demure woman happily acquiesced to Ecclestone as the master and cared for him and their new home in Chislehurst. Once again, he gutted and rebuilt a house, and added a waterfall in the garden. Without a fuss she cooked his meals, laid out his clothes and even squeezed the toothpaste on to the brush in the morning. 'I'm like a mouse,' she cheerfully admitted. 'I make everything perfect for him.' The only imperfection was her messages. The telephone rang ceaselessly and rather than admit not understanding the caller, she wrote gibberish. 'Featherhead,' Ecclestone cursed when he returned. For a man who adored the unpredictability of work, his routine at home never changed. After entering their home, he first cleaned his shoes, then straightened the curtains, next, he moved any ornaments which were not properly squared, and finally he sat down, content that every part of his world was perfect. Whatever the stress, he never discussed any problems. There was little demonstrative love other than presents – and embarrassment if the gifts were reciprocated. He would be the strong one but sentiments were concealed except towards Debbie, who became a frequent visitor and forged a close relationship with Tuana.

His lifestyle had become enjoyable. He would take a car from the showroom, often a Rolls-Royce, and, barely able to peer above the steering wheel, race up to Crockfords with Tuana, cutting up any competing car in frequent outbursts of road rage. Or, after an evening at the greyhound races or watching ice hockey, they might head for Beaverwood on the A20, an expensive nightclub with dinner and dancing. On the first floor, Johnny Humphries, a bookmaker whose business partner Tony Morris was Ecclestone's closest friend, had opened a casino. In contrast to Ivy, the gang liked Tuana and noticed how Ecclestone had relaxed. His relationships with men were intense, none more so than with Jochen Rindt, a German racing driver, and a frequent visitor to his new home.

3

Embryo

In 1965 Ecclestone abandoned his self-imposed ban on any involvement with motor racing. Casting aside the gloom since Stuart Lewis-Evans's death, he travelled with Roy Salvadori and John Cooper to enjoy the Mexican Grand Prix and the capital's nightlife. Just before the race, Cooper became frustrated. His Cooper-Climax was unreliable and Jochen Rindt, the German contracted to drive the car, was openly angry. Ecclestone volunteered to scour Mexico City to find a spare radiator but the car failed halfway through the race. John Surtees won in another Cooper. The following year Ecclestone followed Rindt around the European circuits and shared his continuing disappointment. Despite Ecclestone's and Salvadori's attempts to improve the Cooper's performance, Rindt repeatedly retired during races. 'You drive the cars hard,' Ecclestone lamented, 'and the Cooper can't take it.' United by misfortune, during endless low-stake games of gin rummy and backgammon, Ecclestone and Rindt had become close friends. Ecclestone's pragmatism soothed Rindt's misery and, while gambling in the days before Rindt's unsuccessful race at the Kyalami track in Johannesburg, they agreed that Ecclestone should become his business adviser. Ecclestone's first suggestion was that Rindt should switch to Brabham, a team created by two Australians, Jack Brabham, a former champion driver, and Ron Tauranac, a designer. Among the few following Rindt from Cooper to Brabham was Ron Dennis, a junior grease mechanic.

Ecclestone and Rindt had become inseparable. Frequently, the taciturn chain-smoker entered Ecclestone and Tuana's home and waited in the kitchen for 'Bernie', as he renamed his friend, to return and start another marathon session of gin rummy. Dressed in flared trousers bought in Carnaby Street, a floral shirt and hand-made shoes, Rindt spoke staccato English punctuated by expletives. Born in Germany in 1942 he had moved to Austria after his parents were killed during an Allied bombing raid. The orphan regarded Ecclestone as his elder brother, whose loyalty and guidance solidified their relationship. Rindt had even insisted that Ecclestone and Tuana join him on his honeymoon with his wife Nina in Mexico in 1968. The two men played gin rummy on the beach from noon till dusk. The bond forged a unity on the race track against Jackie Stewart. Rindt was low in the pecking order for the world championship, and the Scotsman, who would come second that year, had snubbed Ecclestone. Tuana noticed the slight: 'Bernard will never forget. He has a super-elephant's memory.'

To help Rindt win, Herbie Blash, the Brabham engineer, resorted to 'every trick in the book' by adjusting the car's weight and imperceptibly twisting the wings to improve the aerodynamics. The secret adjustments were not enough. Potential victories were ruined by faltering engines. Brabham's glory had passed. Ranked fourth in the champion's league and ambitious to win one world championship before retiring to partner Ecclestone in various business ventures, Rindt was offered the chance in 1969 to drive Colin Chapman's winning Lotus cars alongside Graham Hill, the reigning world champion.

Colin Chapman was a visionary. Every car manufactured in the world owed something to his innovations in design, materials and suspension. But Chapman's engineering was fraught with risk. Reducing weight and crafting aerodynamics to increase speed had intensified the Lotus's fragility. Fear of unexpected hazards had deterred Jackie Stewart from accepting Chapman's offer that same year of higher pay to switch from Ken Tyrrell's cars and take the place of Jim Clark, a shy Scottish farmer and world champion killed months earlier in a Lotus. Rindt was willing to take the risk. Ecclestone negotiated Rindt's contract with the warning, 'Chapman's cars are not as safe as Jack's but you'll get a better chance to win the championship.'

To increase speeds Chapman was experimenting with high wings, to force the car down on to the ground for the tyres to maximise the engine's power. His drivers paid the price. In 1969 both Rindt and Graham Hill crashed at the Spanish Grand Prix, the season's second race. Rindt emerged from the crash suffering a hairline fracture of his skull. Both drivers blamed Chapman's experiments. To shield Chapman from Rindt's abrasive English, Ecclestone mediated from the Spanish hospital. With ill temper Chapman recoiled and the new wings were abandoned for the season's remaining nine races. During the course of their heated arguments, Ecclestone noted Chapman's priorities. His ruthlessness, covered by infectious enthusiasm, won universal respect although his priority was Lotus's profits rather than the drivers' euphoria. Unashamedly Chapman raced for business with pleasure as a bonus. Ecclestone probed Chapman's commercial model. He discovered that while Chapman's income from the circuit owners in prize money and appearances was substantial, his income from the corporations providing free fuel, tyres and brakes who advertised in the media about their association with Lotus's success was potentially enormous. The most intriguing revenue was £100,000 paid to cover his cars' bodywork with the words 'Imperial Tobacco', who replaced Esso as a sponsor. This was the start of a long relationship between tobacco and Formula One.

No other team owner was as focused as Chapman on money. Eking out the financial support they received from the circuits and suppliers, his rivals' lives were consumed by the excitement of travel, high living and the thrill of competition. Flying with Rindt around Europe, Ecclestone became intoxicated once again by the atmosphere. Among the living legends, including

Jackie Stewart, Graham Hill and Piers Courage, a handsome and charming Englishman, Ecclestone shared the fun of that unconventional gang's daring and skill alongside their beautiful wives – Helen Stewart, Sally Courage and Nina Rindt. Enjoying a glamorous lifestyle, none expected special protection but they were unwilling to squander their lives for show business.

As a former racer, Ecclestone understood Jochen Rindt's skill, hurtling at excessive speed just off the ground, around sharp bends, either wheel-to-wheel or separated by a fraction of a second from a rival car. Dripping sweat, pummelled by constant vibrations, deafened by the engine and occasionally suffering burning sensations from the juddering metal, the driver was constantly calculating between daring and disaster when to make the break. Their spirit and decisions determined their rank as the best and the fastest. Throughout, Rindt was dependent on Chapman's genius to balance the components' weight and tensions, carrying a powerful engine on the lightest body. The margin of error was the difference between tragedy and the magic of the chequered flag followed by the spotlight on the podium.

In the four months after his crash in Spain, Rindt repeatedly won the valuable pole position in the qualifying sessions only to watch Jackie Stewart snatch victory in the actual race. At Monza, near Milan, in September Stewart won by a split second, pushing down the throttle for a last minute surge after a crafty deception. Four weeks later the tables were turned. At a thrilling race at Watkins Glen in America, Rindt forcefully beat the British drivers and won his first Grand Prix. The only omen that day was Graham Hill's crash, breaking both his legs. With Hill out of the picture Rindt was tipped as the potential champion for 1970. Ecclestone knew this was the moment to negotiate Rindt's new contract with Chapman.

During the inactive months in winter Ecclestone and Rindt planned their future businesses. Based in Switzerland, Rindt spotted the value of selling branded sports clothing. Together, they agreed, they would create Jochen Rindt Racing, a Formula

Two team, promoting a range of goods. Luc Jean Argand, a Swiss lawyer employed by Rindt, was told to complete the legal formalities. During those weeks they were enthused by the sheer pleasure of working together and the relationship between them deepened. Ecclestone enjoyed Rindt's 'sense of humour and his feeling for fun made him a wonderful mate'. Rindt was equally attracted to the Englishman's unselfish encouragement, which fed his passion to become world champion.

From the outset, the 1970 season was marked by accidents and funerals. Among the famous, Bruce McLaren was killed first while testing a new car in England, followed by Piers Courage, crashing during the Dutch Grand Prix and trapped within a fireball. 'It was total despair,' Frank Williams admitted about the loss of his friend and the possibility of bankruptcy.

Rindt arrived in Monza with Ecclestone in September. By then, after a disappointing start of the season, Rindt had won spectacularly at Monaco and had accumulated five victories out of nine races. He was on course for the world championship. Both felt excited by the circuit, which was not far from the Ferrari factory. The Italians are passionate followers of Grand Prix racing and the raucous crowds fed Rindt's hunger for victory. After driving hard during the practice sessions, Rindt had told Ecclestone just before he drove to the starting grid, 'I'll win the world championship and retire.' Ecclestone said nothing as his friend boldly pushed his Lotus, equipped with an unusual combination of tyres and a new braking system, at a record 205 miles an hour around the circuit. Unseen by Ecclestone, on the far side Rindt entered a curve and lost control. Hitting a metal barrier, he slipped down into the fuselage. Crushed metal severed his foot and the harness cut his throat. Within seconds, as blood gushed from an open vein, he was unconscious. Back in the pits, Ecclestone was still unaware of his friend's fate. Without television coverage, the spectators only became aware of a problem when noise levels fell and the cars failed to appear.

Then began the nerve-racking anticipation of being told what the cause was and who was the casualty. 'Jochen's gone off the track,' he was told.

Jackie Stewart was among the first to arrive at the scene. To his dismay, Rindt's corpse already lay in the back of a Volkswagen ambulance. A few yards away, Nina Rindt was sitting limply on the grass. 'I've seen things no man should ever see,' Stewart said afterwards. 'It was all so pathetic.' Following behind, Ecclestone burst through the police cordon and ran along the track amid the chaos of officials, photographers and spectators. By the time he arrived, the ambulance was heading towards the hospital. In Italy, to avoid races being cancelled, no one was allowed to 'die' at the track. 'Is he OK?' Ecclestone asked. In motor sport no one ever asks 'Is he alive?' The expressions on everyone's faces gave him the answer. Picking up Rindt's helmet, Ecclestone watched the wrecked car dragged past the pits, its front ripped away. Someone, he knew, would be tasked to separate the remains of Rindt's body from the metal to perform the mechanical autopsy and identify any technical problems. At the media building, there was still no formal announcement, but an official, seeing Ecclestone, drew his hand across his throat, '*E morte* [He's dead].' Impassive and drained of emotion, Ecclestone drove with Nina to the hospital. Chapman, in shock, was waiting. They were met by Peter Warr, the Lotus manager, walking down the corridor from the theatre to confirm the news. The paramedics at the track had aggravated Rindt's fate, he said, by 'banging on his heart, and that's where the aorta was ruptured!' Ecclestone went into the room to see his friend for the last time. 'Courageous. He was one of the boys,' was his glowing testament. To avoid the police investigation and automatic arrest, Chapman flew out of Italy immediately. Ecclestone remained to clear up. Accidents, he knew, were part of the spectacle drawing crowds to the races. Death attracted the mawkish and even they, by the following day, had forgotten Rindt's fate. Joyous Italians filled the stands to watch Ferrari win the race, the ideal outcome for

Monza's spectators. Amid the roars, Rindt would win the world championship posthumously. The final ritual was to send Herbie Blash to collect Rindt's personal belongings from the hotel and deliver them to his widow in Switzerland.

Ecclestone returned to England in a trance. Ever since Lewis-Evans's painful death, he had avoided close attachments to men, aware that only one in three Formula One drivers would survive a severe crash. His attachment to Rindt had broken the rule and he was suffering. First he went to a memorial service for Piers Courage and then flew to Graz in Austria for Rindt's funeral. He emerged, stricken by misery, from an unusually sombre event lacking any celebration of a life. On his return home, he felt unwell. Bedridden, he was shaking and feverish. Uncertain of the diagnosis, the doctor eventually concluded that his patient was suffering from anxiety caused by his friend's death.

'When Jochen was killed,' Ecclestone told Tuana, 'it was a terrible time for me. I have been close to a lot of men who have been killed but Jochen's death was such a shock that I can't describe it.' In those extreme circumstances, the gambler revealed unexpected emotions. Racked by grief and, some suspected, guilt, he teetered on the verge of completely abandoning racing. In the end, the attractions outweighed the torments but the profound effect of Rindt's death was to make him avoid close friendships with drivers in the future.

Aged forty, Ecclestone had reached a crossroads. Tuana complained that she was tired of living with builders and decorators. Every time he had ripped apart and completed a home, another car dealer would arrive, offer a good price, and they would move again. Ecclestone seemed unwilling to 'nest'. His office was his home. Some commented that his restlessness was 'sad', others that he was 'dysfunctional'. Possibly the absence of any children at home made him regard houses as investments. Although he would never recognise the gap in his life, a son might have closed the circle. His fevered pace was the substitute for a natural companion, a son to help him to tinker with machines or to introduce to racing – just what he had enjoyed with Sidney. Even his move with Tuana into a seven-bedroomed house in Farnborough Park, Kent, was only a scaling-up of his lifestyle rather than a curb on his frenzy. Partly financed with a £95,000 loan from a Guernsey corporation to Pentbridge Properties Ltd, his own company, the renovation confirmed his wealth but not the desire to create a family. Guided by instinct rather than painful introspection, he failed to articulate the absence of a son in his life. Surrounded by twenty-six acres of woodland, the principal attraction was a large lake filled with perch and golden orfe. Friends and his father, now seventy years old, were invited to fish with rods kept in a lakeside house on condition that anything caught was returned to the water. In an adjoining house was a full-sized snooker table and kennels for two bulldogs, one called Oddjob. Every week Ron Cunningham called to clean his shoes and iron his shirts, suits and even his jeans. His plan to develop the woodland would be rejected by the council. Other property ventures were more successful.

To expand his car business, Ecclestone had bought three and a half acres in Frith, Kent. He built three single storey buildings for commercial rent and cleared the ground to establish Mid-Week Car Auctions, a rival to British Car Auctions, the country's principal auctioneers, owned by David Wickens. After lunching with Wickens, Ecclestone decided to attract traders by providing better facilities, especially an elegant restaurant equipped with crafted furniture and carpets. Few dealers arrived on the first day to bid for the fleets of cars Ecclestone had bought at Wickens's auction to kick-start his new business. Unable to lure Jack Mosley, Wickens's auctioneer, to his company, he became dissatisfied with the dull substitute and grabbed the microphone and gavel. Nothing saved the first week from disaster. The debacle was compounded by the collapse of a concrete ornament on to the restaurant's roof. By the second month, sales still languished and the grubby dealers had damaged his restaurant. The land was worth more than the business and the effort was not commensurate with the profits. Ecclestone plotted to abandon his venture. He challenged Wickens that unless he bought his rival, British Car Auctions would be permanently damaged. 'He had them over a barrel,' was one opinion, suggesting that Wickens was forced to buy out a dangerous competitor in order to close it down. Wickens would deny that suggestion, but he did buy the business – just at the moment when Ecclestone was discovering the profits to be earned from trading small planes.

There was a healthy trade in two-seater planes, often bought and resold for cash, but those involved were surprised to be confronted by ethics familiar in Warren Street. Chris Marshall, a Southampton dealer, had advertised a two-seater Tripacer Piper in *Flight* magazine for £3,750. Ecclestone called and offered £3,500 if Marshall flew the plane to Biggin Hill. Ecclestone was not actually at the airport, but Marshall was persuaded to drive to Ecclestone's showroom in Bexleyheath. While Ecclestone unsuccessfully sought to persuade Marshall to take some cars in part exchange, an associate at the airfield was demonstrating the plane to a potential buyer. A telephone call from Biggin Hill confirmed that the deal was finalised, so Ecclestone agreed to buy the plane from Marshall. But, angry that Marshall had refused to buy any cars, he threw down the draft for the money, while refusing to arrange for a taxi to take Marshall to the station. 'Why?' asked Marshall. 'Because you've been bloody awkward,' replied Ecclestone. His brusqueness, experienced by many individuals, did not come to public attention until December 1971.

It was in that month, ten years after he had assumed that his refusal to pay Compton & Ecclestone's tax arrears would be forgotten, that the Inland Revenue's pursuit of £9,700 plus costs and interest arrived in the High Court. Ecclestone's refusal to pay was punished by a judgment familiar to many brash, aspiring tycoons. Mr Justice Goff described Ecclestone's 'machinery' towards the receiver as 'altogether extraordinary . . .

The documents themselves and the admission made out of court cry out for an explanation . . . and [Mr Ecclestone] does not condescend to give one.' The judge ruled that Ecclestone had broken company law. Ecclestone was displeased. Convinced that the judgment would never be publicised, he would insist thirty years later that he had acted on the advice of lawyers and his accountant and had been unfairly rewarded with a hefty bill.

Apologies and explanations did not feature in Ecclestone's lexicon. In the dealers' world, fines were paid and shysters hoodwinked in revenge. No bad deed passed unpunished. One dealer who had tricked Ecclestone was pleasantly surprised to be offered 'a Mercedes 230SL hard top', a convertible sports car with a detachable hard roof, for an advantageous price. After paying in cash, the dealer was told by Ecclestone: 'The hard top's in the street outside.' The dealer found the hard roof sitting on the tarmac – but no car. John Young, a rival dealer in south London, never sought to outwit Ecclestone. Over a weekly lunch, Young told Ecclestone that he had bought a silver Bentley from the tearful widow of Pedro Rodriguez, a Mexican driver who had been killed on 11 July 1971 racing a Ferrari in Germany. 'You know, Bernie, I believe that I lent that same car to you some time ago and you sold it?' 'Yes,' replied Ecclestone. 'It's only', continued Young, 'that when you took it away there were 23,000 miles on the clock, and now there are 14,000. You're a bastard.' Unfazed, Ecclestone replied, 'I thought you'd forgotten about that. Well, don't worry. See how you get on and if you lose call me.' 'Someone's going to bump Bernie off one day,' Young told John Coomb, another South London car dealer. 'Bernie', replied Coomb, 'was offered by me a new Jaguar which had been driven just 800 miles.' 'Nah, thanks,' replied Ecclestone. 'Why?' asked Coomb, surprised. 'No clocking,' Ecclestone explained, meaning he wouldn't touch a car lacking the potential to be clocked. This brazenness reflected Ecclestone's weariness with the car business. He wanted a new challenge and a new life. Despite the trauma of Rindt's death, his passion for motor racing was ineradicable.

His wealth was sufficient to finance a bid to win the world championship. His vehicle, he decided, would be Brabham, the team that Rindt had abandoned.

Jack Brabham had won the South African Grand Prix, the season's first race, in March 1970 but knew that his performance could not be sustained. After successive embarrassments, Ecclestone had discussed Brabham's fate with Ron Tauranac, the car's designer, during the Monaco Grand Prix. Tauranac's designs had enabled Jack Brabham to win the world championship three times since 1961 but after their third victory in 1966 the cycle of failure for previously victorious teams was apparently irreversible. At the end of 1970, accepting his decline, Jack Brabham returned to Australia and Tauranac struggled as the sole owner of Motor Racing Developments, the holding company. Ron Dennis, his chief mechanic, had departed to set up his own racing team; Goodyear, the lead sponsor, had abandoned Brabham in favour of McLaren; and Graham Hill was negotiating to return as the lead driver, even though Chapman had declared the former champion was unfit after breaking both his legs. Tauranac, an excellent engineer but a prickly individual, needed a commercial partner and Ecclestone offered himself.

Negotiations between Ecclestone and Tauranac began in autumn 1970. Ecclestone proposed a partnership, which Tauranac rejected, preferring a sale so he could buy back into it if Ecclestone was successful. They had not been able to come to terms by the time of Rindt's death. In 1971 Ecclestone offered to buy Brabham outright and employ Tauranac as the joint managing director. The price, they agreed, would be the value of the assets. Diligently, Tauranac completed his calculations and told Ecclestone that the assets were worth £130,000. Naively assuming that his valuation would be accepted, Tauranac began spending the money. Waiting until the last moment, Ecclestone met Tauranac at the solicitors to sign the agreements and told the Australian: 'I don't agree with your price. I think it's all worth £100,000.' Disconcertingly Ecclestone announced the steep difference without emotion or apology. 'But we had a verbal agreement to sell for the asset value,' spluttered Tauranac, mentioning that he was selling two cars and five engines. 'Well, whatever it means is whatever it means,' replied Ecclestone, implying a flaw in Tauranac's supposedly independent valuation. 'If you don't think my valuation is true, then do another one properly.' Ecclestone's style was deadly. Knowing that Tauranac was committed, Ecclestone minimised the deal's importance. 'You can pull out if you like,' said Ecclestone. 'I do need to think about this again,' replied Tauranac, 'because I'm not sure whether I want to sell.' 'It's up to you entirely,' breezed Ecclestone. After a few moments, Tauranac accepted the cut. 'Nobody told him to go ahead,' Ecclestone later insisted. 'Nobody told him to do anything.' Tauranac later admitted to inexperience but acknowledged, 'people in business, that's the way they work. It was down to me.' Ecclestone was not a charity. 'Bernie bought Brabham for the fare home,' laughed Ecclestone's friends when they heard the story at their regular Saturday morning coffee in the Queen's Café off Bond Street. Ecclestone became a member of the Formula One fraternity for a pittance. 'Buying Brabham', he would later say, 'was like having all my birthdays at the same time . . . I couldn't get the feeling for racing out of my blood. I just loved it.'

The first casualty was Tauranac. Ecclestone could not tolerate any relationship other than master and servant. In Ecclestone's world he decided his own fate, untroubled by others. His earlier suggestion that Tauranac act as a joint managing director was ignored. 'I don't run a business on other people's opinions,' Ecclestone said. 'I get rid of people who offer opinions.' On his first day as owner Ecclestone walked into the workshop in Weybridge in Surrey, gazed at the grubby tin sheds, the reek of inefficiency and was offended by the amateur slapdash attitudes. He needed wholesale change. 'Everyone is dispensable,' Ecclestone declared, 'but *I* don't dispense with them.' Brian

Shepherd, his auditor, was told to marginalise Tauranac. 'You can't do without me,' Tauranac protested. 'We'll have to try,' winked Ecclestone. 'Others at Brabham want him out,' declared Ecclestone unapologetically, forcing Tauranac's departure in 1972. 'He was too set in his ideas.'

Gordon Murray, a tall South African junior designer, was deemed to be the only employee worth keeping. Ecclestone could smell his workaholic ambition, hungry for invention and cost-conscious improvisation. The rest of the design team was fired. 'I want a whole new car. One that's going to win in '73,' he told Murray. 'It's up to you.' Ideal employees, for Ecclestone, were eager and talented. Colin Seeley, a thirty-five-year-old former British motorbike champion, fitted that mould. Seeley had met Ecclestone at the end of 1970 while buying a Ford Capri at the James Spencer showroom. Despite supplying bikes to world champion riders, Seeley's racing bike factory was being harmed by Japanese imports. He was grateful that Ecclestone tried to negotiate a sponsorship deal for Seeley's bikes with John Player & Co., the cigarette manufacturer. Although his attempt failed, Ecclestone recognised an honest, hard-working engineer who could replace Tauranac. He proposed that Brabham and Seeley's bikes should merge, with Colin Seeley as the joint managing director of Motor Racing Developments and Ecclestone investing sufficient cash to save Seeley's business. Agreement was swift and the partners arrived together at the Brabham facility. Standing on a box Ecclestone introduced Seeley and invited the inarticulate engineer to speak. Seeley spluttered a few words and the meeting dispersed. Unused to publicity, Ecclestone shortly after told an inquiring journalist that he intended a 'major assault' on both Formula One and motorbike racing 'to compete with the best in the world championship by producing the best cars and bikes and attracting lucrative sponsorship'.

Ecclestone's real character, formerly seen only by his father, Ann Jones and a handful of mechanics at James Spencer, surfaced. The same mentality that had driven him to take apart and reassemble bicycles in his parents' garden shed and later scrupulously design the Spencer showroom created havoc in Brabham's three buildings. 'I've got a neat and tidy mind,' he said. 'I like things in nice boxes so I know where everyone is and who's in charge of each box.' Free movement and open-plan production amounted, in his opinion, to chaos. His remedy was instant. Doors were filled in, fences installed and breeze-block walls built across the production floor to compel orderly movement between the buildings. Grime, grease, posters and junk were eradicated and replaced by white paint and white tiles. Even Brabham cars were resprayed white rather than racing green. Toolboxes were repainted dark blue and were, he ordered, to be placed on identical spots on work benches. 'Anyone got a problem with that?' he asked sharply. Intolerant of anything except hard work and perfection, his purpose was obtaining value for his money. Even if he *was* rich, he would not tolerate disobedience or waste in a loss-making business. Excuses were unacceptable. War was in the genes of a man who embraced confrontation.

His employees, he hoped, would be uncertain about his mood. He would plan his arrival at the building in a way calculated to cause trepidation. Frightening his employees with outbursts was a weapon of choice. Mud splashes on his car or open office doors provoked his anger. Telephones ringing during meetings could rouse him to throw the devices across a room. Spotting a cleaner using a pay phone, he ripped the instrument off the wall. Even a telephone ringing in an adjacent office incited a dash through doors to yank the wires from the socket. His irritation spread to the workshop. When Ecclestone spotted a mechanic damaging a bench, Gordon Murray watched him kick the headlamp of the mechanic's car. When he became displeased with the quality of the bodywork for the Brabham, Murray saw his employer stamp over the metal until it was broken. Remarkably there was never a protest or even a murmur after an outburst. A spell was cast over his intrigued employees. No one dared to protest about his night-time telephone calls querying small details. The uncertainty stimulated not anger but awe. 'Right, let's go for lunch,' he would announce at the end of a tirade. On his return from a convivial beer and sandwich, his anger was easily retriggered. 'Shut up or piss off,' he told Keith Greene, a team manager who complained about the overwhelming pressure to prepare the cars for a race. Even Greene's request for an additional £10 a week in compensation for long working hours was parried. 'I'll think about it,' Ecclestone said repeatedly, until Greene resigned.

Few were allowed to feel indispensable, and that included Seeley. Working an eighteen-hour day, Seeley continued to manage the production of his bikes at his own factory in Belvedere in north-east London, then drive across the River Thames to meet Ecclestone at Bexleyheath and finally head west to the Brabham works, completing over a hundred miles on narrow roads. In contrast, just once a week Ecclestone chose a Rolls-Royce or a sports car from his showroom to visit the Brabham works. Within months he had become disenchanted by his agreement with Seeley. Although Barry Sheene, the world motorbike champion, was winning races on Seeley's bikes in the British and European championships, Ecclestone's £4,252 investment was proving insufficient. The debts were also mounting at Brabham. The annual £80,000 costs, he knew, were barely covered by the earnings from the sport and would exhaust his own income. For his own survival, Formula One needed to be transformed from a rich man's pastime into a profitable business.

Owning Brabham automatically made Ecclestone a member of the Formula One Constructors' Association (F1CA), the club organised in 1963 by Colin Chapman so that British teams could jointly transport their cars to the races. Ecclestone's arrival at his first meeting in 1971 at the Excelsior Hotel at Heathrow was surrounded by mystery. The owners and representatives of the nine other teams were puzzled about Ecclestone's ability to finance Brabham. The uncertainty was compounded by Ecclestone's discretion about his wealth and a certain obsequiousness evinced by his willingness to pour the tea. For his part Ecclestone was curious. Gazing around the barren conference room, he identified a group of oddballs united by racing but divided about everything else. Listening to their conversation revealed their stubbornness to consider anything other than their own opinions. Concessions were rare among a group enjoying success. British ingenuity had exposed the traditional 1950s victors – Ferrari, Maserati, Alfa Romeo and Mercedes-Benz. Driving a Vanwall at the British Grand Prix in 1957, Stirling Moss had cracked the European manufacturers' domination. Over the following years, the revolutionary designs of Charles Cooper, Jack Brabham and Colin Chapman repeatedly challenged the Europeans not only with better cars but also more skilful drivers. After 1958 Lotus had a winning spree of seven world championships. In anger Enzo Ferrari, Formula One's grand master, had scoffed about the English 'garagistes', meaning Chapman, Frank Williams and Ken Tyrrell. Unlike the European teams' relationship with production-line manufacturers – Ferrari was owned by Fiat – the British were self-financing former mechanics or motor enthusiasts. That fed their creative strength but perpetuated financial weakness. With hindsight, Ecclestone recognised his luck. Timing, as all successful businessmen confess, is everything. He had arrived just as the British teams had become vulnerable.

Excited by competition on the circuits, the growing numbers of spectators had increased the race organisers' profits. Yet nearly all the British teams were on the brink of bankruptcy. Each team negotiated directly with the eleven circuits – eight in Europe and the rest in South Africa and America – for their fee but the haphazard balance between income and costs was crippling. In the scramble for money – the total prize money never exceeded $10,000 – Enzo Ferrari, the star attraction, extracted the largest appearance payment in cash before each race, while the other teams, earning just a few hundred pounds for appearing, suffered as payments were either delayed or occasionally forgotten. Ecclestone offered to help Andrew

Ferguson, Chapman's appointee, to administer F1CA from a cottage on his estate outside Norwich.

On his first visit he grasped the problem. While planning their trip to Montreal, Ecclestone suggested, 'Tell the organisers that they should also provide twenty-five hire cars for the teams, at their expense.' 'Oh, we can't do that,' replied Ferguson. 'We've never done that before.' Such incompetence, Ecclestone knew, was incurable. 'This is driving me crazy,' he thought and suggested at the next F1CA meeting how the teams could earn more. Instead of separate negotiations with eleven race organisers, he said, an F1CA representative should negotiate the fees on their combined behalf and, at the same time, organise cheaper transport for the cars and teams. His audience agreed. 'Well, why doesn't one of us do it?' asked Ecclestone. The faces staring back were blank. None of his competitors were interested. 'Well, I'll do it,' said Ecclestone giving the impression of a sacrifice. 'But I want a fee.' Colin Chapman expected Ecclestone to charge 10 per cent, so was pleasantly surprised when Ecclestone mentioned 2 per cent. There was unanimous agreement to the cheap deal, although Peter Warr, keeping the minutes, recalled writing 4 per cent and Brian Shepherd, who would audit Ecclestone's accounts, read the commission as 7 per cent. Just how, in the those early days, F1CA's accounts were presented would get lost in the mists of time but one crucial fact was never forgotten: Ecclestone had offered to do all the work and the others unanimously consented to pay a commission.

Among those around the table at the Excelsior was Max Mosley, the thirty-one-year-old owner of the March racing team, a new manufacturer of Formula One cars. Created with two friends in Bicester for £10,000, they had in 1969, their first year, sold ten cars, including two models to Ken Tyrrell, a well-established racer. To the annoyance of the established teams, March cars during that year were the fastest around the tracks. Mosley himself had been racing cars since 1964. Although he had first noticed Ecclestone at circuits alongside Rindt in 1968, Ecclestone only acknowledged Mosley properly at his first FICA meeting. There was an immediate bonding. Like Ecclestone, Mosley could not believe the mutual distrust among the teams and their poor behaviour. By contrast, Ecclestone stood out for Mosley, 'as someone I recognised who understood life'. There was, Mosley would say, 'an immediate natural alliance with compensating talents'. Ecclestone, although he only had a sketchy awareness of Mosley's background, was pleased to have found an apparent ally to serve his interests. One bond between the two was an attraction to conflict. In order to advance, each impatiently grasped every opportunity to fight.

Mosley's mother, Diana Mitford, was the beautiful, intelligent wife of Oswald Mosley, an adventurous Conservative and then Labour MP who had finally switched in 1932 to the far right to promote a more radical solution for the Depression. In 1933 Mosley allied himself with Nazism, and when he married Mitford, recently divorced from Bryan Guinness, at Josef Goebbels's home in Berlin in 1936, Adolf Hitler was a witness. Mosley transformed himself rapidly into a violent pro-Nazi agitator. Long before the outbreak of the war, he had attracted venomous denunciation. Just ten weeks after Max was born in 1940, his mother joined her husband in jail in London as a dangerous Nazi sympathiser, leaving Max to live with a nanny near the prison. After the war, the Mosleys left England, educating their son in Ireland, France and Germany. Multilingual and sophisticated, Max returned to England in 1958 to study physics and law at Oxford and was elected secretary of the Union. While at university he went with Jean, his future wife whom he had met aged seventeen at a London party and married three years later, to Silverstone and became a committed enthusiast of motor racing, a passion which continued as he struggled as a young barrister. By the time he met Ecclestone, Max Mosley knew that, despite success, March's survival would be precarious without better organisation and secure finances.

During trips across Europe, both realised that the Formula One's regulatory agency, FIA, based in Paris, was prejudiced against the British teams. With FIA's approval Formula One was tilted in favour of the foreign teams, especially Ferrari, while the British were regarded as mere ballast to fill the circuit. Less obvious but more important, an FIA balance sheet obtained by Ecclestone revealed the enormous profits earned by the race organisers. The teams were paid about $10,000 per race but the circuits could afford over $100,000. Astutely, they protected their interests by extracting pledges from each team not to reveal the terms of their individual contracts. Effectively, Ecclestone discovered, the British teams were financing their own races. Under Ecclestone's plan, speed was essential during the remainder of 1971 to change fundamentally the F1CA teams' relationship with the eleven circuits. Demands were dispatched, replies received and the negotiations began with an entrenched enemy. During their plotting, Ecclestone once arrived late at Mosley's home on the Gloucester Road.

'What's wrong?' asked Mosley, perplexed because Ecclestone was usually punctual.

'Some old dear came through the windscreen,' replied Ecclestone dryly, referring to what had been a serious incident. Their differences and complementary talents became obvious.

'Your problem is,' Ecclestone told Mosley, 'you always want things absolutely clear and sometimes it's better if things are not clear.' Ecclestone's sharpness was exploiting weaknesses, both among his rival team managers and the circuit owners. Second-hand-car dealers, Mosley realised, operated in a special world: 'Even the honest ones still took out the radio.' In the compartmentalisation of tasks, Mosley decided that 'Bernie can handle the lies'.

While they were flying together around Europe in a B.125 twin-engined Beagle Bulldog, part of a batch Ecclestone had bought from a receiver, Ecclestone used the opportunity to sell one to Mosley for £10,000. 'It's a lovely plane,' Mosley later told Ecclestone 'but it can't fly and I can't afford the repairs to make it airworthy.' Ecclestone, unrepentant and phlegmatic as ever, pointed out, 'At least it hasn't cost you much to run.' By the autumn of 1971 Ecclestone had negotiated improved terms with the circuits and the freight contractors. The next step was to negotiate with governments.

In late 1971 a team of Argentinian officers flew to London to meet Ecclestone and Mosley at the Excelsior. Argentina was ruled by a military junta and, to enhance their international credibility, the generals wanted the Formula One race to be held, as usual, the following January. To Ecclestone's surprise, the officers insisted that their meeting should be recorded. His love of pranks proved irresistible at this moment. While feigning disinterest as Mosley spoke, Ecclestone slipped some paper into the large tape recorder causing the blank tape to spill silently on to the floor. The prank did not undermine the agreement to stage the race. The deal was done. Flying with eleven teams including two of his own cars and three of Mosley's March models to Buenos Aires, Ecclestone arrived with a purpose: for Brabham to win the race and prove his organisational abilities.

'Don't worry about the money,' he told the team owners who feared that currency restrictions would prevent the transfer of Argentinian pesos to Europe. 'I've arranged it all,' he explained, promising that funds would be provided in London in exchange for blocked funds in Argentina. The settlement fuelled the amusing fairy tale among the community that Ecclestone controlled 200 bank accounts across the world and knew exactly how much each contained.

In the pits he proved fearless. Told there was friction between his two drivers, Graham Hill and Carlos Reutemann, about the selection of engines, he summoned the two world champions. 'Right, I'm not having any more arguments. What we are going to do now is decide the engines for the year. OK?' Ecclestone flipped a coin and ordered the drivers to call. 'Right, I don't want to hear any more about engines.' Neither driver won any glory in the race.

By the time the Grand Prix circus reached Kyalami, near Johannesburg, for the South African Grand Prix in March 1972, Ecclestone had mastered the logistics and had an appetite to fashion a good deal. The financial risk, he knew, was considerable but his attempt to convince the other teams to invest jointly with him in a company to promote their interests provoked a uniform reply: 'No, you do it.' Having negotiated good rates with Cazaly Mills, a freight company he would later buy with Ron Shaw, he summoned the teams to meet at the Ranch Hotel outside Johannesburg to present his plan. 'I'm guaranteeing you a better deal with the race organisers,' he said, proffering to cach of the team owners an envelope outlining his offer to save costs on transportation of their cars across the world and a guaranteed income from each Grand Prix. In return the teams would contractually assign to him the right to negotiate on their behalf. The teams' agreement would, said Ecclestone, trigger an increase of his commission to 4 per cent of the prize money. None of those around the table doubted Ecclestone's sincerity. During their conversations, the car dealer had persuaded his rivals that his word was his bond and an agreement would be sealed by his handshake. No one demurred. Unanimously the team owners expressed their acceptance of his offer. None would question whether Ecclestone was pocketing additional commission on the transport costs or whether he expected an additional payment for himself from each circuit. Shedding the burden of negotiating fifteen separate race fees in the 1973 season and the transportation of the cars and people around the world at cheaper rates was a double relief. They could focus on racing, winning and enjoying themselves.

'There wasn't a strategy,' Ecclestone would later admit, 'because I didn't know what would happen. I was just taking a huge risk.'

To improve his operation, he replaced Andrew Ferguson with Peter Macintosh, a former RAF serviceman who spoke unconvincingly about his membership of the elite Red Arrows flying team, and appointed Ann Jones, his secretary, to collect and pay out the money to the teams. The teams' signatures on a sparse agreement to assign the administration to Ecclestone offered the newcomer a remarkable coup. Ecclestone could transform F1CA from an agency into a business. Remarkably there were no competitors.

Four weeks later Ecclestone proposed that the teams race in Rio de Janeiro. He had negotiated a contract with the circuit and sponsorship with Rede Globo, the Brazilian television network. Since the event had not been approved by FIA as part of Formula One, the F1CA teams agreed to participate on condition that Ecclestone guaranteed payment. While the teams waited at Heathrow's cargo zone with their cars, Mosley was in Rio de Janeiro to secure payment from the television company. His report to Ecclestone was discouraging. The money, said Mosley, would only be paid from the turnstile cash after the race. There was a chance of a double-cross. 'Right, we're off,' announced Ecclestone. 'Don't worry about the money. I'll sort you all out.' The gambler took the risk. The teams with their cars and equipment boarded the chartered aircraft grateful that Ecclestone had arranged everything. Colin Chapman, Ken Tyrrell and Frank Williams were bonding with Ecclestone as if Formula One were a family business.

Crossing the Atlantic, Williams interrupted Ecclestone and Teddy Mayer, the McLaren chief, playing non-stop backgammon, to request a loan. The former mechanic and grocery salesman, who had begun racing in an Austin A35 and ran his business from a telephone box near his garage, had first met Ecclestone at San Lorenzo restaurant. He had arrived with Piers Courage, with whom he shared a home, while Ecclestone was accompanied by Jochen Rindt. Unable to afford their lifestyle, Williams 'hung around the fringes', notorious for his financial struggles. In Brazil he was looking forward to cash in a brown envelope but in the meantime he needed finance. Throwing the dice, Ecclestone agreed to a loan secured against an engine. Williams's verbal agreement sufficed. Ecclestone was proving himself invaluable. The race itself satisfied the teams and the Brazilians. Ecclestone collected the television money in cash and the team managers stuffed it into briefcases.

The only dissatisfied group was the Grand Prix denizens at their citadels in Paris and Monaco. Ecclestone's negotiation with the circuits was intentionally taking control of Formula One from the race organisers. His agenda was to transform the sport within a few months. Michel Boeri, the organiser of the Monaco Grand Prix, was particularly upset. With FIA's support, Boeri plotted the counter-attack. To prove that the circuits rather than the teams would control the sport, Boeri announced that the number of cars allowed to race in Monaco would be reduced to sixteen. Mosley arranged a meeting with Boeri in Madrid to negotiate a truce, and departed with an agreement that twenty-six cars could compete. Soon after the English teams arrived in Monaco, Boeri changed his mind. The race, he said, would be limited to twenty-two cars. After consulting the teams, Mosley told Boeri that the race would be boycotted unless their agreement was honoured. In retaliation the Monaco police impounded the F1CA cars by locking the garage doors with padlocks. There was deadlock. None of the teams would agree to race until twenty-six permits were issued, and by then spectators were arriving. Agitated, Boeri offered oral assurances but Ecclestone refused. Without twenty-six signed documents, he said, there would be no race. Boeri capitulated. Clutching his document, Ecclestone went into the garage, sat in the cockpit of his Brabham and released the brake. His feet could not touch the pedals as the car was rolled on to the grid. Beyond his control, a wheel rolled over a policeman's foot. He smiled at the irate officer.

Success was emboldening. Ecclestone had set out to prove that he was not only efficient but committed to serve the teams' interests. Chapman, Williams and Mayer recognised an unusual animal. At their meetings, Ecclestone was scribbling every request in unintelligible handwriting on yellow stickers and promising to provide solutions. With their support, Ecclestone began demanding increased fees from the race organisers. European tracks had begun to pay about £15,000 to the smaller teams. Ecclestone set his rate at $150,000 for each race and more for races outside Europe to cover expenses. F1CA, he said, would distribute the money. The circuit owners pleaded that the fixed income from entrance tickets prevented higher payments. To discover his opponents' strategies, he would encourage a break midway during negotiations with the circuit owners at Heathrow for each side to consider their positions. 'We'll wait for you in here,' said Ecclestone, suggesting that the others leave the room. Once they were outside, he dived into the waste-paper basket to retrieve the messages they had passed to one another during the discussion. The image confounded any attempt to classify Ecclestone. In conversation, he promoted his reputation as a straightforward businessman but as Mosley noted wryly, 'If you blew your nose during a flight, Bernie's elbow would be on the arm-rest after you put your handkerchief away.'

With mixed success, at the beginning of the 1973 season all fifteen race circuits had signed agreements with F1CA. Three non-European circuits – Argentina, South Africa and Brazil each agreed to pay $110,000. In Europe the circuits had raised their offers to $56,000. Not all were profitable. Racing at Watkins Glen outside New York would be a loss, but Ecclestone did not tell the teams. They would not, he knew, have cared. 'They don't want to take the risk,' he told Mosley. Since the teams trusted his organisation, and he was responsible for the distribution of money, he proposed the winner-takes-all prize. He devised a complicated formula based on rankings not only in the actual race but also the practice trials, the place on the grid, the results in previous seasons and whether a car finished the race. Agreeing the system was fraught. F1CA meetings had become serious. To establish his credibility with the circuits and sponsors, Ecclestone wanted to solve the race organisers' constant fear of teams failing to appear at the last minute and causing the spectators disappointment. To avoid that grief, Ecclestone planned to guarantee with his own money that all eighteen F1CA cars would race at every event. Implementing that contractual pledge, he realised, would trump FIA's powerlessness to compel appearances. At an F1CA meeting during 1973 he described his plan, with the financial penalties for any team breaking their contract. Anticipating a protest, he then began telling jokes and speaking about something completely different, only returning to the topic to squash a protest. Once he was satisfied that the teams were confused and in disagreement, he began elaborating on his plan. 'How much will we get?' asked the team managers, keen to pin down Ecclestone's financial interest. But total candour was alien to Ecclestone. To divert attention, he again dived off into another topic and then looked to Frank Williams for support.

Williams was a reliable ally because he was a used-car dealer living beyond his means, to the extent that the previous year, even as he drove to Heathrow to race at Watkins Glen, he had stopped at his bank to seek a loan to pay his mechanics. He would frequently borrow £5,000 from Ecclestone and return it on the agreed date but on a recent occasion he had asked straightaway, 'Can I now borrow £8,000?' To Ecclestone's amusement, Williams would next be seen buying expensive cashmere pullovers. But in 1973 Ecclestone drew the line. Williams had failed to repay a loan collateralised against an engine. 'Bernie's Boys' – two Eastenders known around Warren Street – were dispatched to recover the engine. Ecclestone offered his friends loyal support but his generosity did not extend to acting against his own interests. So Williams repaid the loan and the cycle started again. Naturally, in return Ecclestone expected Williams's support if required at F1CA meetings, and he needed Williams's voice to finalise the guarantees to the circuits. Every decision required unanimous consent.

Ecclestone's principal critic was Ken Tyrrell, a tall, suspicious timber merchant who, on a previous occasion, had jumped on to the conference table to intimidate Ecclestone. 'I'll throw you out of the window if you don't fuck off,' smirked Ecclestone to the bigger man. Inevitably, Tyrrell opposed the proposed guarantees and Ecclestone relied on Williams to distract his audience. Eventually, exhausted by the arguments, the teams approved the plan in return for Ecclestone's guarantee of their income. With relief, everyone fled from the hotel. Over the following hours, the team managers individually grasped that Ecclestone had won again but on balance they favoured Ecclestone mastering the negotiations and taking the financial risk. There was no reason to oppose raising his commission to 8 per cent.

Success also bred enemies. Henri Treu, an authoritarian Dutch executive at FIA, encouraged by French and German members, began a counter-attack. He sought allies at the Royal Automobile Club (RAC), a receptive audience. The English blazers-and-sherry brigade, the flag carriers of conservatism, agreed that Ecclestone's authority should be diluted. 'The RAC is a gentleman's club without gentlemen,' responded Ecclestone, ignoring their protests. Next, Treu offered money to teams to break away from Ecclestone. He was rebuffed by all except Graham Hill. Disliking Ecclestone, Hill had left Brabham and, sponsored by a tobacco company, raced under his name without F1CA.

Since Hill's departure, Ecclestone had reorganised the Brabham team. Learning from Colin Chapman about balancing the mix of engines, chassis, tyres and race strategy, he encouraged Gordon Murray in 1973 to redesign the car while he contemplated Brabham's precarious finances. The British economy was in trouble and, after the Arab invasion of Israel and a cut in the supply of oil to the West, Britain was ravaged by widespread strikes, failing banks, inflation and a burst of the property bubble. Ecclestone was not seriously exposed to debts – he rarely borrowed money – but he detested any losses.

Seeley was the first casualty. Ecclestone had limited patience for losers. Like so many engineers, Seeley lacked any proper sense of business. His company, Ecclestone knew, would have folded without his money and any more would be wasted. 'I'm just paying out for your pleasure,' Ecclestone told him. 'Just pouring money into your sinking ship and I'm picking up the bill for your mistakes.' Seeley's company, he decided, would be declared bankrupt. Seeley's unhappiness was irrelevant. He could buy his machinery back at the receiver's auction. Ecclestone was impervious to the sight of Seeley's misery.

'It was nothing to do with me that Seeley's company folded,' he said. 'It was already in trouble before. That's why he came to us. He didn't come to me because he had a thriving business.' Seeley was allowed to continue working at Brabham but Ecclestone showed no affection when, arriving one morning, he saw Seeley covered in oil after working throughout the night to prepare two engines for a race in Belgium.

'Get yourself cleaned up,' Ecclestone instinctively commented. Formula One, he knew, exploited enthusiasts prepared to work around the clock for a pittance. But even that could be excessive. 'Seeley upset other people at Brabham' was Ecclestone's reason for refusing to allow the mechanic to borrow a truck to rescue a marooned racing friend.

'That's the last straw,' Seeley decided about Ecclestone's refusal. 'He was a good mate and needed a bit of help. That really upset me.' Seeley resigned but became embroiled in a protracted dispute with Ecclestone over a National Insurance payment of £1,200. In pursuit of his money, Seeley realised that he did not have a copy of his signed contract with Ecclestone – a feature that would recur in Ecclestone's professional relationships with some employees. Ecclestone abided by his agreements – whether by handshake or contract – but understanding the precise terms of the agreement was critical, as was possession of a written contract, occasionally overlooked by the eager employee as Ecclestone stuffed the paper into his ubiquitous briefcase. In Seeley's case, their agreement was 'lost' until a copy was mistakenly sent to Seeley's solicitor. Seeley settled the dispute for £600 from Ecclestone's company.

Seeley was a casualty at a critical moment in Ecclestone's life. Formula One, which had started as a hobby financed by his car dealerships, had become the focus of his life. The lifestyle was marvellous, managing F1CA was profitable, and Chapman had shown how, with sponsorship and victories, Formula One could be financially enriching. By contrast, the motor trade had become difficult. Car sales were dwindling and his prolonged absences from James Spencer had reduced the profitable finance business to what Brian Shepherd, his auditor, called 'piffling'. The introduction of VAT in 1973 complicated trading for cash. The motor trade, Ecclestone concluded, had changed. 'I'm retiring,' he joked. 'I don't want to be a tax collector for the government. I'm going to travel around the world with Brabham cars.' James Spencer was sold and he moved his office to Creek Road in Greenwich, near the *Cutty Sark*.

In rooms above the Alfa Romeo engine shop used by Brabham, he employed only Ann Jones. His income dropped sharply, dependent on rent from a few properties and the remnants of his car finance. Nevertheless, the Lloyds bank manager from Bexleyheath still called to meet his best client, although he rarely borrowed any money. 'What was his name?' Ecclestone asked Jones after the manager left. On Wednesdays he visited Weybridge. Gordon Murray had promised to design a rival to beat Lotus. Around the white-bodied car, Murray's engineers, dressed in new uniforms with their tools perfectly organised, appeared disciplined. Outside stood Ecclestone's pride: Formula One's first road transporter with the Brabham name painted on the metallic outside and a new kitchen installed inside for his use at Grand Prix meetings. He had taken a risk but saw the reward. The whole Formula One business was wide open to be signed up. Ecclestone could not believe his luck.

'There's all to play for,' Ecclestone wistfully told Mosley. Ecclestone, Mosley realised, was gambling on building an empire.

At their original meeting in 1971, Ecclestone had reassured the teams about equality and how nothing could be changed without unanimous agreement. Two years later, Ecclestone was taking over.

'I gave up worrying,' Mosley admitted, 'and I didn't try to stop it.' The original purpose of their own partnership had also shifted. Mosley was to be the intermediary when the RAC's chairman relented and suggested that the club repair its relationship with the former car dealer.

4

Squeeze

To his friends in the motor trade Ecclestone had changed. Convinced he was on the brink of a fortune, his easy-going charm disappeared. 'Don't go there,' he snapped aggressively when Ron Shaw, an old friend, jokingly suggested during the regular Saturday coffee that he too might like a slice of the Formula One pie. His co-ownership of Cazaly Mills with Shaw had ended abruptly but that did not interrupt his banter with Tony Morris, his bookie friend, Harold Duffman, a currency dealer, Brian Gilbert, who had just bought some of Robert Maxwell's companies after the tycoon's collapse, and Frank Foster, his tailor. Max Mosley was invited to join them on one occasion. Before he arrived, the waitress was told that their visitor had just been released from prison and that she should serve a very full English breakfast. 'He's a proud man and will refuse it,' said Ecclestone, 'but insist that he takes it.' Inevitably Mosley did refuse the fat-laden meal. 'No, I don't want it,' said Mosley. 'You've got to have it,' she replied. 'It's disgusting,' protested Mosley, unaware that his hosts were enjoying his discomfort at their joke. Soon after, they moved their meeting place from the Queen's Café to Richoux in Bond Street. Going upmarket matched Ecclestone's ambitions.

Britain's Formula One teams were not financed, like Ferrari and Mercedes, by assembly-line manufacturers with ample funds. Even the increased income from the races was insufficient to support the costs. To bridge the gap, the British teams needed corporations paying to use their cars as advertisements. Ever since Colin Chapman covered his Lotus with the colours of Gold Leaf cigarettes in 1968, other tobacco corporations had negotiated to have their brands placed on rival cars and the drivers' overalls. British American Tobacco had signed a two-year agreement for £50,000 a year with British Racing Motors (BRM), the winning car for Graham Hill, to promote Yardley soaps and scents, its subsidiary. The cars were painted pink. In 1971 the stakes rose. To launch Marlboro cigarettes across Europe, Philip Morris outbid BAT's contract with BRM and paid £100,000 a year, nearly sufficient to finance a year's racing. The Marlboro BRM car was introduced at a flashy presentation in a gigantic cigarette packet. At every race meeting, beautiful girls dressed in the Marlboro logo handed out cigarettes and entertained Philip Morris's guests. But Louis Stanley, BRM's extrovert and spendthrift chief, was losing his genius to deliver a winning car and driver. The fading glory harmed Marlboro's image and in 1972 Philip Morris ended its sponsorship. The corporation's search for a new team electrified Formula One. Their only condition was that the chosen team employ Emerson Fittipaldi, an Brazilian driver. The emerging favourites were McLaren, run by Teddy Mayer, a likeable and trustworthy expert, and Ecclestone's Brabham, whose ratings were improving. McLaren's chance, Ecclestone knew, was hampered by their cast-iron sponsorship contract with Yardley. Brabham had no unbreakable links. Indeed, when compared to Chapman's new contract with John Player, Brabham's small-scale sponsorship with an oil supplier, a watch manufacturer and a brewery irked Ecclestone. The major obstacle to attracting Philip Morris, he knew, was Patrick Duffeler, the intelligent thirty-two-year-old Philip Morris executive responsible for sport sponsorship. The American multilinguist preferred McLaren but agreed to meet Ecclestone at a villa in Switzerland where he and Fittipaldi were resting.

The meeting ended badly. Duffeler, a passionate supporter of Formula One, did not warm to Ecclestone or appreciate his ambitions within Formula One. In his version of what occurred during Ecclestone's visit, there was an exchange of opinions and the two men walked on to a balcony. 'Bernie', said Duffeler later, 'asked me if he could take care of me, that is, with a financial gift.' Some might interpret Duffeler's version to suggest that Ecclestone was offering personal help in return for giving Brabham the sponsorship.

Thirty-seven years later Duffeler refuted the idea that the 'help' was a bribe. 'It was nothing more than an offer of help,' he said. In 2004 Ecclestone was challenged about Duffeler's version of their meeting. Ecclestone could not remember offering a 'gift' or even speaking on the balcony. 'You know,' Ecclestone told Terry Lovell, 'if you put me against a wall and put a machine gun to my head, and you said, "Are you absolutely 100 per cent sure you never said that?" I would have to be honest with you and say, "I couldn't" because I don't remember that much. But I may have said, "Let's take care of you for the efforts you made." It's the sort of thing that happens all the time in these situations. Normally, people say first "I want a percentage." Y'know, they're part of the business arrangements. People actually come up and ask for "commissions". Unfortunately, that's the way the world goes round.' Six years later, in 2010, while repeating that he could not recall the conversation, Ecclestone quipped, 'I probably didn't offer him enough.' To refresh his memory, Ecclestone spoke to John Hogan, Duffeler's deputy at the time. Hogan reported that Philip Morris considered Duffeler to be 'a fantasist'. The misunderstanding about 'help' between Formula One's prominent sponsor and the British teams' organiser assumed particular importance in Ecclestone's battle to grasp control of the sport over the next seven years.

Following their inconclusive conversation, Duffeler drove Ecclestone to Geneva airport. Although they parted coolly, Ecclestone telephoned Duffeler over the following days to discover his fate. Unknown to him, Teddy Mayer had escaped from BAT's contractual veto and was finalising a new contract with Philip Morris to begin what was to become a twenty-two-year relationship. When Duffeler broke the news personally to Ecclestone in London, he recalls their meeting ended acrimoniously. 'I didn't warm to Duffeler,' admitted Ecclestone. 'He fancied himself as a hero.' Duffeler's expectation that Ecclestone might disappear as an irrelevant parvenu was undermined at the 1974 Grand Prix in Argentina.

Ecclestone arrived in Buenos Aires in early January 1974. Gordon Murray, he believed, had produced a winning car. Carlos Reutemann, his star driver, was hungry for fame, especially in front of a home crowd. The atmosphere among the Formula One family hanging around the hotel pool was sparky. Watching a German driver swimming two lengths underwater, Ecclestone belittled the achievement. Challenged that he could not do the same, he replied, 'Are you saying that I can't swim two lengths underwater?' 'Yes,' replied the chorus around the pool. 'Right, what's the bet?' asked Ecclestone. '$100,' shouted the choir. 'Let's get the bet exactly,' repeated Ecclestone. 'You're saying that I can't swim two lengths underwater?' Heads nodded. 'Right,' said Ecclestone to Herbie Blash. 'Go and get me a snorkel.' All the losers concluded that Ecclestone used the same tactics to negotiate Formula One agreements. Honed as a car dealer, Ecclestone's contracts depended not only on the agreed terms, but equally on what was omitted – in this case, a snorkel.

After coming seventh in Argentina and again in Brazil, Ecclestone and Carlos Reutemann arrived in South Africa. Kyalami was always fun. The Ranch Hotel was as usual full of attractive air hostesses and tens of thousands of spectators were arriving in anticipation of an electric race. To everyone's amazement, Reutemann won. The owner showed no surprise, however, and refused to celebrate his first Grand Prix victory. Nor would Ecclestone celebrate the next victories in Austria and the United States. Consistently, he left the circuits before Reutemann passed the chequered flags. 'I don't like to be at the end of anything,' he told his driver. Sentiment could be misinterpreted as weakness. Happiness was limited to watching a crazy gamble materialise and sweeping up the stakes. He was a one-man operation and employees were not friends. Brabham's fortunes had revived but Ecclestone still fumed. 'The cars weren't clean,' he cursed Blash. Murray was also scorned for a misdemeanour. The only happiness was a telephone call and an invitation from Count Vittorio Rossi to visit Monaco. 'Can you imagine a used car salesman having dinner with a count?' he asked Blash after he returned with Martini's offer of sponsorship in 1975. Red stripes would be painted over the white cars.

Victory on the track released Ecclestone's natural method of generating money, a style familiar to those who had traded on Warren Street. The first to experience his manners were the organisers of the Grand Prix in Canada, where Formula One was the country's most popular sport. In Canada and the United States, Ecclestone increased his demand to $350,000 from each circuit. The Canadians refused to pay extra for the 1975 season and Ecclestone issued an ultimatum: the race would be abandoned unless they paid by the deadline. When the deadline passed, Ecclestone announced that the Canadian Grand Prix was cancelled. The Canadians quickly offered to pay the extra amount but, to their surprise, were rebuffed. 'When I say I'll do something, I do it,' he said quietly. That was not a threat, but merely an explanation of his inflexible terms of business. The teams who questioned Ecclestone's tactics were reassured by Mosley. Having learned the lesson, the Canadian organisers produced the extra cash and Ecclestone agreed to return to Montreal in 1976.

The next to experience Ecclestone's tactics were FIA's officials in Paris. Ecclestone's income from FOCA (renamed from F1CA) had become substantial but he was pressing for more money. He wanted $270,000 from each European circuit to stage a Formula One race and for the organisers to pay for the teams' costs. Their inevitable resistance was as putty in Ecclestone's greater scheme.

Televising races, he knew, was Formula One's most lucrative prospect but satellite television was still in its infancy. With no chance of live broadcasts, television stations recorded bursts of the race on film, and these were then physically transported back to the studios where, after processing and editing, clips were transmitted on news programmes. But even that limited exposure had been halted in Britain. The BBC refused to broadcast Formula One after John Surtees's car carried a prominent advertisement for Durex. Changing the BBC's attitude seemed impossible unless there was public demand and competition for the broadcasting rights. An unexpected encounter in Rio with Mark McCormack, the American sports agent, and his description of selling the broadcasting rights of tennis, triggered Ecclestone's imagination – and not only for broadcasting but also for providing hospitality to corporate sponsors. McCormack, the founder of IMG, was also the agent for leading sportsmen including Jackie Stewart and Graham Hill. His vision was to share Formula One's management with Ecclestone. 'McCormack's falling over his own ego,' observed John Hogan, 'and it's too complicated.' Ecclestone declined McCormack's proposition but used his ideas.

Without any notice, he inserted clauses into the contracts with the circuits assigning the television rights of Formula One races to FOCA. Since television was peripheral, the new clause was uncontested by the circuits. Their preoccupation was to resist Ecclestone's demands for more money for the teams. In reply, he raised the fee to $300,000 per race for all the teams. Frustrated by their own divisions – Ecclestone insisted on meeting them individually rather than as a group – and furious about Ecclestone's ability to present a united front, the circuits' organisers appealed to FIA in Paris to bring Ecclestone into line. FIA responded with an ultimatum. Unless Ecclestone withdrew his demands for more money, FIA would exclude British teams from competing in the 1976 season. The declaration of war was unexpected but certainly appealed to Ecclestone.

A meeting was arranged at the Excelsior at Heathrow with Pierre Ugueux, a retired Belgian civil servant delegated by FIA to assert the regulator's authority. Just after everyone had assembled in a conference room, a fire alarm sounded. Fearing an IRA bomb, some fled towards the foyer. With characteristic sangfroid Ecclestone ordered, 'Follow me,' and headed towards the rear. 'Let the others go that way. A bomb's more likely to be in the front.'

A new meeting was arranged in Brussels in November 1975. On entering the room with Mosley, Ecclestone spotted some paintings hanging crooked. After impassively making the adjustment, he stared blankly at Ugueux. The representative of an arcane bureaucracy of motor enthusiasts, brandishing the big stick, was proclaiming that the 1976 championships could not proceed until FIA had approved the terms between FOCA and the circuits. In Ecclestone's world, rules and laws existed only to be circumvented. 'We've put money into this,' said Ecclestone. The contracts, he continued, were between himself and the circuits. 'Where's your cash?' he challenged Ugueux. 'We won't race and then you'll have no Formula One.' To Mosley's enjoyment, Ugueux gaped. Whatever FIA's threats, the races would be ruined if the British withdrew. 'So let's be serious,' continued Ecclestone. Next to Ugueux sat Jean-Marie Balestre, a wealthy and quarrelsome French publisher who had served and been photographed as a uniformed member of the French SS during the Second World War. The motor enthusiast enjoyed dressing immaculately and wielding power. Ecclestone spotted his weaknesses. Intemperate, vain and considerably less intelligent than he imagined, he flat-footedly walked into many traps. 'We want the money, not you,' shouted Balestre impatiently and broke a pencil. Ecclestone's riposte to the blusterer was theatrical. Serenely, he rose, walked purposely towards the door and turned off the lights: 'See, I'm not even afraid of the dark.' The two officials were silenced by a man offering no comfort. Mosley recognised in Ecclestone's stone-cold eyes an

unemotional, nerveless force obliterating the opposition. Ugueux
agreed that the organisers should pay $270,000 a race. To prove
his prowess, Ecclestone could not resist demanding an additional
$5,000. Mosley was impressed. '*Bon*,' announced Ugueux with a
smile to conceal defeat. Luck, Ecclestone knew, always has to be
earned. The races for 1976 were approved.

The next to learn was Carlos Reutemann. Brabham had initially
scored well in the 1975 season, taking high places in Argentina,
Brazil and Germany, but then luck faded. Niki Lauda stormed
to victory in an unbeatable Ferrari, followed by Fittipaldi in a
McLaren. Reutemann was a distant third. In the penultimate
race at Monza in September, Lauda's chance to win the world
championship was endangered. An FIA official took a sample
of the fuel from his car, which had come third. 'Is the fuel OK?'
Lauda asked Luca Montezemolo, the Ferrari team principal.
'Yes,' replied Montezemolo. 'Are you sure?' 'Well, we're trying
something,' admitted Montezemolo. Lauda ran to Ecclestone:
'They're checking my fuel. Can you help?' Ecclestone found the
FIA steward. 'Let me look at that sample,' he ordered, grabbing
the test-tube. 'It doesn't look like fuel to me,' he scoffed as he
poured it out. 'It's piss.' Lauda went on to win the championship.
  Ecclestone hoped for better fortunes in 1976. He switched
engines from Cosworth to Alfa Romeo, provided free by
the manufacturer. From the outset in Brazil the engine failed.
Reutemann repeatedly retired from races. Disappointed, he
demanded more money but Ecclestone refused. 'There's always
someone else,' he reasoned, echoing Enzo Ferrari's refusal to
feel indebted to any driver because the cars, he believed, won
the races. He did not blame the driver if the car didn't win.
Reutemann decided to leave. In exchange for paying a fee to
Ecclestone for breaking the contract, Reutemann signed for
Ferrari. 'I even helped him get more money from Ferrari,' said
Ecclestone, trusting that the replacement driver Carlos Pace, a
thirty-two-year-old Brazilian, would succeed. Financially he was

unconcerned. Martini's sponsorship and the free engines had eased Brabham's costs.

With a gambler's luck, the attraction of Formula One grew in Europe during 1976. Not only was the racing unusually exciting, but the wild sex life of James Hunt, a handsome fair-haired champion driver for McLaren, constantly featured in the headlines. During the year, Hunt had lost his wife Suzy to Richard Burton, the actor, and in retaliation had intensified his chase for girls and partying. Newspapers eagerly followed his prowess during the season, reporting the envy of rivals. To stymie his success, they had on one occasion anticipated his return to his hotel room, inevitably with a girl, by filling every space up to the ceiling with television sets all tuned and blaring.

On the track Hunt's challenge to Niki Lauda for the championship was initially unsuccessful. His McLaren repeatedly faltered and Lauda won his fifth race of the season at Brands Hatch in July. 'A shrewd bugger,' was Ecclestone's comment on the Austrian, now in his prime and who either charged from the starting point to the front or 'waited to pick up the pieces after the front runners crashed'. 'Magic,' was Ecclestone's view about Hunt's unpredictable racing, as his varying performance against Lauda swayed with his mood.

The theatre rose to compelling heights at Long Beach in California. Ecclestone had urged 'The Brethren' to try the old track south of Los Angeles. 'Too far,' they complained and criticised the town, saying it was dilapidated. Only after Ecclestone offered to take the financial risk, paying the teams regardless of the outcome, did they reluctantly fly west. Clint Eastwood and a clutch of Hollywood stars were persuaded to come for the day, guaranteeing media interest. At the end of the race, Ann Jones gathered the cash taken from the turnstiles and, after counting out each team's share, discovered there was nothing left for Ecclestone. In compensation there had been explosive drama on the track, epitomised by the sight of Hunt, forced out by an accident, standing on the edge of the pit, shaking his fist in fury at his rival as Lauda finished second. Their hectic competition appeared to end on 1 August 1976 at the Nürburgring, a perilous track in the Eifel mountains. Lauda crashed and after being pulled to safety from his burning Ferrari was expected to die from severe burns. Instead, with his head heavily bandaged and his face disfigured, he returned just six weeks later to defend his title at Monza. To the adulation of Italian fans, despite his open wounds, he came fourth. The ferocious duel between the sex-mad blond and the bandaged hero descended on America and Canada. Both races were won by Hunt. By the final race of the season in Japan in October, only one point separated the two drivers and they were barely speaking to each other after a spectacular argument about Lauda's accident. The world championship depended on whether Hunt or Lauda won the race beneath Mount Fuji. Interest in the swashbucklers' fate spread across the globe. Ecclestone spotted the chance of finally ensnaring the television companies but first he had to squash an irritant.

Patrick Duffeler had been keen in 1975 to mount a Grand Prix around Tokyo and, encouraged by FIA, had gathered allies among the Japanese government, the media and other international sponsors eager to join Philip Morris's campaign to spread the Marlboro brand across Japan. Ecclestone had been equivocal. Other countries, including Saudi Arabia and the Philippines, were possible new venues for Formula One but some of the teams were reluctant to race more than sixteen times a year. They even ridiculed the idea of staging a Grand Prix in Japan as an unaffordable expense. Nevertheless, Ecclestone had persuaded the teams during 1975 to fly directly from New York to Japan. Duffeler proudly announced the breakthrough. At that moment, Ecclestone struck. In Ecclestone's world, until a contract was enshrined in concrete, nothing was sacrosanct if there was a chance to squeeze additional money. Casting aside his Brabham hat and adopting his position as FOCA's negotiator, he spotted a chance to take some revenge on Duffeler. The ambitious promoter, Ecclestone knew, believed that the circuits rather than the teams should run Formula One.

Approaching the Japanese organisers at the French Grand Prix in July 1976, three months before the race, Ecclestone revealed that he could not recommend approval of the Grand Prix without more money to cover the teams' costs to Japan. Infuriated by Ecclestone's trade union tactics, Duffeler urged the Japanese not to capitulate. 'Don't yield,' he yelled, convinced that he had closed every loophole to prevent Ecclestone's ruses. Duffeler loved motor sport but realised that Formula One existed in 'a vacuum of mismanagement'. FIA was a joke, staffed by men who loved running around in blazers but who were weak and unintelligent. Henri Treu, in particular, was blatantly aggressive and had made a mess of their tactics towards Ecclestone. In spite of those bunglers, Duffeler longed to defeat Ecclestone.

'Come on Patrick,' said Mosley gently, 'Why fight us? Come over and work with us.' Observing Ecclestone outsmarting everyone, Duffeler refused 'I don't approve of Bernie's approach to business,' he replied. 'Bernie's God is money. He just wants to weaken institutions.' Mosley demurred. 'A lot of people', continued Duffeler, 'are afraid of Bernie: team mechanics, drivers and managers. He's abrasive. He knows what he wants and won't tolerate opposition.' Mosley shrugged: 'We'll have to agree to disagree.' Duffeler, everyone knew, was being encouraged by Huschke von Hanstein, a former director of Porsche, to oppose Ecclestone. Von Hanstein's passionate hatred of Ecclestone as 'a little, ill-bred man' was fed by his wartime membership of the Nazi party. His loathing of the British as 'idiots' was wrong-footed by Ecclestone's ruse. Despite Duffeler's careful planning, anticipating every possibility, Ecclestone – sharp, edgy and purposeful – had found a loophole in the contract. The Japanese agreed to pay more. 'FIA is a monster of inefficiency,' moaned Duffeler, 'my plan was doomed not to work.' A few weeks later Duffeler met Ecclestone in France. Still wounded he asked, 'Bernie, why did you do that?' 'Because I can,' answered Ecclestone without adding a single word.

Before the teams arrived in Japan, the public's interest in the rivalry between Lauda and Hunt had been stimulated by the frequent transmission of a fan's 8-mm film of Lauda's crash, followed by stories about Hunt's tangled love life. The newspapers' fascination and the expectation of huge numbers of spectators were persuading broadcasters to abandon their reticence about showing advertisements festooned over the cars and to overcome the obstacles of transmitting pictures back to Europe. The opportunity, Ecclestone realised, was enormous, except for one hurdle: he had no legal authority to sell the television rights to the broadcasters. Nevertheless, knowing that Colin Chapman and Enzo Ferrari were uninterested and the other team owners were too disparate to interfere, he opened negotiations as FOCA's representative with the European Broadcasting Union (EBU), a non-profit agency representing all the state-owned European networks. The EBU, he soon realised, was a cumbersome bureaucracy. Instead, he encouraged the BBC to film the race and air-freight the celluloid to London. The drama guaranteed huge interest although the cheers turned to jeers when Lauda, fearing a crash in torrential rain and creeping darkness, retired from the race and immediately headed for the airport. To his surprise, the rain suddenly stopped and Frank Williams ordered his driver to allow Hunt to pass, so that a Briton could win the world championship.

On his return to Europe Duffeler persuaded Ugueux that Ecclestone threatened FIA's control of Formula One. Ecclestone's pressure on the organisers to pay more or suffer the 'unfortunate' withdrawal of the teams from races because of 'unsatisfactory safety arrangements' was undermining FIA, said Duffeler. 'Ecclestone believes', he continued, 'in the theory of maximum pressure and he's clever at it.' But he added, 'Although I like Bernie, I don't like how he's decided to dominate world motor sport.'

Duffeler proposed that FIA unite the circuits against Ecclestone and FOCA. This was the kind of conflict Ecclestone adored. Duffeler, he believed, would be outwitted because of his own good relations with each circuit owner.

The American was unwilling to surrender. To reassert FIA's authority, Ugueux was cast aside and Duffeler was appointed to confront Ecclestone. At their meeting Ecclestone refused to stop negotiating with the circuits. To make it clear that he was not listening, he got up, straightened the paintings in the room again, and announced that he would organise a Grand Prix in Holland without FIA's authority. In response Duffeler announced the creation of World Championship Racing (WCR), a breakaway group excluding FOCA. Eight circuits sided with Duffeler's WCR and eight sided with Ecclestone. The battle lines were drawn.

Successfully outmanoeuvring Duffeler depended on maintaining the unity of the teams. At their regular meeting at Heathrow, Ecclestone listened silently to his congregation. The mutual suspicions of the temperamental egoists around the table allowed him to play each off against the other, while they in turn relied upon Ecclestone to solve their problems: to obtain a visa for a South African driver banned under the anti apartheid sanctions, produce a spare part or persuade a sponsor not to withdraw. His reliability had secured their support as their unity was tested in November 1976. But Duffeler too had scored a trick. The Argentinians had sided with his WCR for the Grand Prix in January 1977. The race, Duffeler warned Ecclestone, would be cancelled if the teams did not comply with his terms. Moreover, he had the support of Michel Boeri and others in FIA. Ecclestone's temperature rose. He had resurrected the Argentinian Grand Prix and now the organiser had switched sides. To stymie Duffeler, Ecclestone cancelled the race.

Duffeler launched a media campaign to raise the stakes, comparing Ecclestone's 'unscrupulous' tactics to the Mafia's. The sports pages of British and European newspapers reported a ferocious battle. 'I know that in the past the constructors' association has been likened to the Mafia,' replied Ecclestone, 'and people have even called me the Godfather, but that's not true. I wish I was a Godfather. They have millions of pounds, don't they? And travel about in jets instead of railway trains like me. Believe me, if I was a Godfather I would not be getting involved in wrangles over racing cars roaring round a circuit.' Duffeler, Ecclestone decided, had miscalculated.

'What, my friend, does unscrupulous mean? I don't understand the word. This fight is about money.' He was, he pleaded in the media, merely the servant of the teams. He had not profited from the sport he loved, rather he had invested his personal money and was not even claiming expenses. Ecclestone delighted in tongue-in-cheek salesmanship. He may be small, he admitted, but he loved a battle. 'I'm not a little girl,' he said, 'and I believe in fighting for what is right.' In a style familiar to astute politicians, he characterised himself as a misunderstood victim of bullies. Although Brabham was a business and his FOCA activities were earning him a fortune, he unashamedly told an interviewer, 'I have taken nothing out of motor racing.' He also injected a sinister tone into the argument. Those scheming behind his back, he warned, would become 'history' and anyone attempting to get the better of him was 'dead'. No one could ever recover from worsting him. 'I could take you to the cemetery where I buried people,' he would later tell enquirers. Brinkmanship and talking tough, he hoped, would obliterate Duffeler and his plans for World Championship Racing.

Like every good poker player, Ecclestone knew when to fold. By early January he realised that the Argentinians' loyalty to Duffeler was solid, and that he had to be pragmatic. The British teams wanted to race, so he arranged for their cars and equipment to be loaded on to a chartered 747 to fly to Buenos Aires. 'I've beaten Ecclestone,' chortled Duffeler. Ecclestone could contain his anger. There was no shame in waiting for the next hand and there was always time for pranks. To irritate Ferrari, he arranged with the circuit organiser to announce that the duration of the race would be reduced because Brabham's Alfa Romeo engine was consuming excessive oil. Ecclestone watched with Colin Chapman and other English managers as Marco Piccinini, the leader of the Ferrari team, was handed the statement. The Italian's face contorted and, outraged, he rushed to the stewards complaining of favourable prejudice towards Ecclestone. The stewards smiled, shrugged their shoulders and turned away. Returning to the pits, Piccinini saw Ecclestone and the English teams laughing. Ecclestone also laughed at the end of the race. Carlos Pace came second in a Brabham, two seconds ahead of Carlos Reutemann in a Ferrari.

Two weeks later Ecclestone meekly led the teams to the Brazilian Grand Prix, again on Duffeler's terms. As they lay by the hotel pool in Rio, Ecclestone turned to Mosley. 'What's this hotel worth?' he asked. Mosley was nonplussed. To while away his time, Ecclestone had calculated the value based on the number of rooms, the rate they were paying and the running costs. Then he speculated about the commercial possibilities. The combination of Ecclestone's love of deals and Mosley's precise legal analysis was forging a solid alliance. From England, Debbie, his daughter, telephoned with the news of her marriage. 'It will be a quiet wedding, Dad,' she explained. 'Well, you'd better wear your slippers,' replied Ecclestone, declining the invitation to join Ivy and his parents and five others. He had a good excuse to avoid a type of celebration he particularly hated. The race had ended badly. Pace failed to finish after an accident and Reutemann won. Seven weeks later, after another bad result in South Africa, Pace was killed in an aircraft accident. Ecclestone was devastated and left without a winning driver. He offered James Hunt $1 million to race for Brabham for one season but was rejected.

Duffeler's repeated successes threatened Ecclestone's financial prospects. There was no alternative but to defeat the American in Europe. Ecclestone's message to the European circuits was raw-knuckled: if they refused to stage races on FOCA's terms,

Formula One would move to another track or even to another country. Duffeler, Ecclestone continued, could not guarantee the arrival of any Formula One team. Only Ecclestone could do that. Appeals to Duffeler, Ecclestone added, would be pointless. Duffeler could not coordinate races in seventeen different countries and languages. Finally, Ecclestone played his ace. FIA and Duffeler assumed there would be eighteen races in 1978. Sadly, Ecclestone countered, the teams would tolerate only twelve. His warning he knew would strike fear among those circuits siding with Duffeler who risked exclusion from the next season, especially the least profitable tracks. The Swedes were the first to crack. Others followed.

Duffeler was nonplussed. Worse, he was irritated by criticisms from Pierre Ugueux who was insisting on taking back control of the negotiations. Before relinquishing control to the 'supercilious and self-righteous' Ugueux, Duffeler arranged a final meeting with Ecclestone. He emerged, he would admit, 'out-psyched. I realised that Bernie was going to win. He did divide and conquer well. I had my fill of it.' Negotiations resumed between Ecclestone and Ugueux. Ecclestone calculated that while he refused to participate in the WCR races, Ugueux could not afford to disrupt the existing fixtures in Europe. Victory, both knew, depended on securing Enzo Ferrari's support. Ugueux expected Ferrari to tilt towards FIA. After all, FOCA opposed the manufacturers.

Enzo Ferrari enjoyed his authority. No Grand Prix could be staged without the glamorous Italian team, the oldest in the sport. Although the English had successfully challenged Ferrari on the track, the seventy-nine-year-old based in Maranello outside Modena bided his time, knowing that eventually Ecclestone would need to pay homage to solve the dispute with FIA. The Italian prided himself that motor racing negotiation was in his blood. Even before Ecclestone was born, he had transported his cars to the Italian frontier and refused to cross into France to compete in Monaco until he had extracted a good appearance fee from the organisers – and had received payment in cash. Ecclestone's request to meet the master was not unexpected, nor was Ferrari's assumption that any meeting would be in his office. Just as the Pope expected people to come to the Vatican, so Ferrari expected Ecclestone to travel to Modena.

Over the previous three years, Ecclestone and all the British teams had occasionally flown to Bologna for a day-trip to meet Ferrari. Little business was discussed during the excellent lunch he provided. In 1976 they had all laughed when Ferrari ordered a huge Parmesan cheese, blessed as an aphrodisiac, to be placed on Ecclestone's plate with Ferrari's audible whisper, 'This will get the little man going.' To show respect, all conversations were addressed through Ferrari, a tedious process undermining any spontaneity. The upside was Ferrari's invitation to his inebriated guests – Ecclestone, Mosley, Chapman, Tyrrell, Mayer and Williams – to visit the test track and drive Ferrari cars, a special treat for the former drivers. During snatched conversations, Ecclestone realised that Ferrari respected cars and engines more than the drivers who were expected to prove their courage and skill. At least they were assured of decent mourning if they died. In particular, Ferrari admired Chapman. The founder of Lotus was not only a brilliant engineer but also brave. Shortly before arriving in Italy, Ecclestone had arranged to fly with Chapman in a Cherokee from Biggin Hill to Gatwick. After Chapman took off, there was a hard knock underneath the fuselage. Glancing back Ecclestone saw loose telephone wires swinging wildly. Even worse, the door was open. 'We'll close it when we land,' laughed Chapman. They both remembered only too well the previous year's visit to Maranello and their hazardous journey through freezing fog back to Bologna airport where Ecclestone's Citation aircraft was parked.

Ecclestone's pilot was shaking his head as they approached. 'No take-offs possible,' he announced. 'The airport's closed and I've found hotel rooms for everyone.' Keen to return to London, Ecclestone told Chapman, 'Take the pilot to his plane on the runway and show him how to take off.' Chapman returned also shaking his head. 'The "Follow Me" car can't find the plane in this fog,' explained Chapman. 'Well,' said Ecclestone, 'let's all sit in the plane, turn on an engine and keep warm.' Through swirling fog, the group eventually found the plane and Ecclestone persuaded the control tower to turn on the runway lights. 'Turn on the other engine,' ordered Ecclestone, adding, 'Just to keep warm.' 'Look,' said Mosley, 'we can now see two runway lights.' 'No, three,' countered Ecclestone. 'Take off quickly,' he ordered. Under pressure from his passengers, the pilot raced the plane down runway. Two minutes into the flight, the plane burst through the fog into bright sunlight. Ecclestone had proven himself unbeatable.

The following year, on 16 February 1977, Ecclestone flew alone with Mosley to meet Ferrari in Maranello. Theirs was a journey with a serious purpose. Although Ferrari did not speak English and Ecclestone spoke no Italian, communication was a limited problem. Ferrari, like Ecclestone, understood business in any language and there was an interpreter. As they studied each other through their tinted glasses, the two men sensed a common appreciation of the power of performance. Both were former used-car dealers, street fighters joined by their love of racing and gambling. Both shunned ostentatious habits. Ferrari drove to his office in an old Renault, a gesture appreciated by the English visitor who was starting to grow fond of his mentor. Still struggling to bear the grief of his young son's death in 1956, Ferrari did nothing to disabuse Ecclestone's belief that he could be the 'old man's' protégé'. In their bouts of mutual admiration, Ecclestone especially praised Ferrari's salesmanship. Before they sat down, he watched his host play with a customer thinking about buying a Ferrari. 'I'm afraid there's a two-year waiting list,' said Ferrari, watching the customer's anguished face. In the garage, Ferrari knew, were stacks of unsold cars but over the next minutes, in front of Ecclestone, Ferrari's face twisted in contortions as he summoned his staff to perform the ritual of the pained ally seeking to please one customer while wrecking the hopes of another whose order would 'sadly be delayed'. After squeezing the drama to discover a scarce car, the grateful customer paid the full price. Ferrari's charisma, undisguised by the translator, barely concealed his brutal egocentricity. 'You speak too much about money,' Ferrari scolded Ecclestone during lunch. Banging on the table he pronounced, 'On top of the table is the sport, and underneath is the business.' Like a pupil, Ecclestone nodded.

Adulation of Ferrari was Ecclestone's trump card to win the Italian's support against Ugueux. Naturally, he expected Luca Montezemolo, Ferrari's young assistant, to tilt one way and another to extract the best deal in transportation costs and prize money. 'Montezuma', as he was dubbed as a figure of fun, was replaced by Marco Piccinini, the young son of a Monte Carlo banker whose clients included Enzo Ferrari. 'Why did Enzo promote Marco?' Ecclestone asked Montezemolo. 'Because he speaks three languages and he's cheap,' replied the protégé of Gianni Agnelli, Fiat's chairman and Ferrari's owner.

Ferrari would expect special treatment to ally himself against FIA and their shared hypersensitivity about wealth prompted Ferrari to repeat his advice to speak less about money. 'After all,' Ferrari told Ecclestone, 'if you are going to run a brothel, you wouldn't put up a big sign saying "Brothel". You would put up a sign saying "Hotel" and run a brothel in the basement.' Ecclestone nodded in agreement. Ferrari, he acknowledged, prided himself on being the cat, while Ecclestone, Ugueux and the rest were the mice. 'I knew it would be a game,' Ecclestone later told John Hogan, 'and he was very good. He's got a mind like a steel clamp. You can't get anything past him.' Ferrari was equally suspicious. 'Don't get too close to FOCA and Ecclestone,' he told Piccinini. 'But we'll support them.'

The combination of FOCA and Ferrari persuaded the circuits to side with Ecclestone. There would after all be seventeen races in 1977. Ugueux was defeated. Mosley stood back impressed. Ecclestone, he realised, would say anything expedient and, if caught out, would think fast to escape. Ecclestone's own description was more lyrical. 'In fighting my battles,' he explained, 'I prefer close, silent wrestling rather than noisy open warfare.' His war with FIA, he knew, would continue.

Ferrari's support had been important but Ecclestone's warm relationship with Enzo was secondary to his business interests, especially the need to cure Brabham's regular defeats on the track. Everything had gone wrong. His best drivers were lost and the Alfa Romeo engine was unreliable. His commitment, however, was undiminished. Brabham's workshop had been moved from the ramshackle buildings in Weybridge to a hangar – four times bigger – on an industrial estate in Chessington. To stack the odds more in his favour, Ecclestone had approached Niki Lauda. The Austrian, he knew, was dissatisfied. Ever since Lauda's accident, Enzo Ferrari had doubted his ability to overcome his injuries and had relegated the 1975 world champion to number two in the team. The driver suspected that Ferrari, convinced he was 'bust', wanted to 'grind me down mentally and turn me out to pasture' because 'they didn't know what to make of a defending champion with a disfigured face.' To compound the insult, Ferrari refused to discuss Lauda's fee, although he was on the verge of winning the 1977 world championship. Hearing about his unhappiness, Ecclestone deliberately bumped into the champion in the Paddock at Monza. 'Do you want to change?' he asked. Lauda nodded. 'Let's meet in the park,' suggested Ecclestone. Terms were agreed and sealed with a handshake. 'I was happy that my departure would be like a slap in the face for Enzo Ferrari,' wrote Lauda. 'I pretty much had my fill of Ferrari – Il Commendatore and all his entourage.' Enzo Ferrari would not speak to Lauda for the next two years.

Lauda was more than a brave driver. He was also a shrewd businessman, enjoying the tough negotiations against Ecclestone. Among his attractions was to bring to Brabham sponsorship from Parmalat, the Italian manufacturer of dairy products. In return for Brabham's £10 million annual costs, Ecclestone agreed to repaint the cars in Parmalat's colours, red, white and blue, and promote Parmalat in the UK – although the company in the end abandoned the idea. Lauda emerged from all the negotiations bewildered by Ecclestone's technique of using 'any excuse, any half-truth to give a new twist to the conversation. He'll argue that black is white and two plus two equals five – or vice versa – whatever comes into his head . . . He twists and turns to such a degree that there is no thread running through his conversation that you can grasp. However, immediately you have reached an agreement with him, you can be sure that the deal is cast iron.'

Lauda arrived at Brabham just as Ecclestone and Gordon Murray were acclimatising themselves in the new workshop. Ecclestone had naturally made some improvements. The lavatory windows had been blocked by bricks, walls had been erected and, to save electricity, timing switches had been installed to cut off the lights after two minutes in the lavatory. He was furious when he discovered that his electricians had effortlessly overridden his device. He also locked the blinds on the windows in Murray's design office to fix the amount of sunlight to suit himself. Murray was not consulted. Beyond his soulless office – with just a large desk, a paper shredder and a secretary – he had also changed the view. Irritated by a lamp post on the street, he asked the council to move it. Undeterred by a refusal, he paid workmen to dig up the road and move the concrete pillar beyond his eyeline. The tension he caused was matched by his frugality. Standing with his executives by the bar at the Star pub at lunchtime, his pocket stuffed with a roll of banknotes, just like the Warren Street days, he pulled out a coin and challenged 'heads or tails', before ordering either a sandwich and a pint of beer or a British fry-up with brown sauce. The tense atmosphere of the workshop evaporated. Bernie provided a safety net to catch anyone who tripped up. Punctually, at ten to two, everyone headed back to the workshop.

Murray was perfecting a new plan. The technical competition between the teams had been elevated beyond engines, tyres and fuel systems. The focus was now on the shape of the cars. Following Chapman's experiments, speeds were being increased by constant changes to the aerodynamics which forced a car's weight down on to the ground. Cheating was elevated to a new level.

In the early days, aware that weight was critical to a car's speed, cars had been weighed before the race by the scrutineers. The cheating occurred between the weighing and the race. Over lunch at the Star, Ecclestone enjoyed retelling the story of Frank Williams's chief engineer rushing to his employer at Monaco in 1975 with the news, 'I've just seen Ecclestone loading extra lead into his Brabham.' 'I know,' replied Williams, 'but keep quiet about it because I lent it to him.' Since then, the designers' skills were focused on using aerodynamics to increase the downward pressure. In 1977 the regulations stipulated that cars could not be equipped with movable aerodynamic devices. To overcome that rule, Colin Chapman had installed skirts along the Lotus's body which forced air under the car, increasing the pressure and, accordingly, the car's speed. His innovation caused uproar and protests. 'Rules', said Chapman, 'are for the interpretation of wise men and the obedience of fools.' Murray came up with a response that was executed in great secrecy. Some might call it cheating, others would say he was just bending the rules. To the scrutineers it appeared that the Brabham was equipped with a second fan to cool the engine but in reality the new fan pushed air down on to the ground, propelling the car faster.

The debut for the ruse was the Swedish Grand Prix at Anderstop. Jean-Marie Balestre, newly elected as FIA's president, knew that any meeting he had with Ecclestone was certain to be difficult. The Englishman epitomised everything the Europeans hated and in his manifesto Balestre had pledged to recover control of Formula One from FOCA. Ecclestone's response was to provide a special welcome in Sweden for the immaculately dressed president. Knowing that Balestre assumed he would be staying in the presidential suite of the town's best hotel for the weekend, Ecclestone reserved all the rooms and arranged that

Balestre would sleep on a couch in the living room of a private house in the suburbs. He delighted in imagining Balestre's limousine driving from the airport, past the hotel towards the outskirts. The scene was set for confrontation between pomposity and profit.

On the track Lauda was unaware of Murray's ruse. Indignantly he heard Ecclestone order the fuel tanks to be full for the qualifying sessions. 'I want to win pole,' Lauda protested. 'The car will be too heavy.' 'Shut up and do as I say,' snapped Ecclestone, conscious that he needed his rivals to remain unaware of the plot. Lauda qualified a poor tenth. Just before the actual race the following day, Ecclestone ordered 'Push the accelerator down when you see the others in trouble. You'll be OK.' Realising that something special had been added to the car, Lauda obeyed. When his rivals suddenly started skidding on puddles of oil, he throttled the engine and won the race. 'The challenge', he later wrote, 'was not to let my lead appear too great.' Ecclestone's rivals were not deceived. 'Bernard's pulled a fast one,' Colin Chapman told Peter Warr. Chapman had good reason to be suspicious. Until then, Lotus had won four races and Ferrari had won two. Brabham had consistently failed. Led by Chapman, everyone protested. The moment of reckoning was temporarily delayed as Herbie Blash deceived the FIA inspectors by blocking the fan's air-intake with his foot. 'The car's legal,' the inspectors told Chapman. 'Bernard, I love your car but if that's legal I will have a car within four races with four fans.' 'OK, I pushed the envelope,' admitted Ecclestone, but refused to back down. 'But, Bernard,' said Chapman, 'how can you represent Brabham against all of us and at the same time represent all the FOCA teams? That's a conflict of interest.' 'Don't give in,' Murray urged Ecclestone. 'I've spent months working on this.' Ecclestone was prepared to fight until he realised he was putting something more important at risk. 'OK, I'll withdraw it,' he conceded, to Murray's disappointment.

To scoop Formula One's financial potential, Ecclestone was

lobbying Colin Chapman and Teddy Mayer to formalise his management of FOCA. He should, he explained, be officially recognised as FOCA's president and chief executive. His argument was strengthened by Balestre's tempestuous protests about his poor accommodation and the Brabham fan. Repelled by Balestre's outburst, Chapman and the others agreed that Ecclestone needed some status to negotiate with Balestre and the circuit owners but hesitated about any legal commitment. Their informal agreement to recognise Ecclestone's authority was enough. To his advantage, they did not quite understand what was happening. Only Mosley properly grasped Ecclestone's opportunistic take-over plan. After selling the March racing team, Mosley volunteered to help as FOCA's legal adviser. Diplomatic and intelligent, Mosley could be relied upon during their nightly conversations for sound advice. The first test arose later that year in South Africa.

For the white establishment, battered by the international anti-apartheid campaign, Formula One racing at Kyalami confirmed the country's international sporting status. To continue staging Formula One, Ecclestone told Louis Luyt, the organiser, would cost more in 1978. No less than £350,000. Reluctantly, Luyt paid up. Ecclestone was not antagonistic to South Africa's whites nor had he expressed any opinion about the racist regime. He was simply unsentimental about its vulnerability. His preoccupation was money.

On the track Ecclestone's fortunes declined. 'It's not working,' Lauda complained to Ecclestone and Murray. Since his victory in Sweden in June, Lotus had consistently won. Finally, at Monza in September, Lauda burst into the lead only to watch Ronnie Peterson crash his Lotus. As Hunt pulled Peterson from the burning car, Ecclestone hurried towards the flames with Giuseppe Marrone, Monza's chief of police. To his surprise, the police had formed an armed cordon around the site. A policeman turned his gun on the Englishman to prevent his access. Monza's chief of police pulled his revolver on his subordinate and the two men were allowed to pass. Peterson died in hospital during the night. 'We won't race here again unless you improve the medical facilities,' warned Ecclestone. Formula One was being blighted by too many deaths. The only consolation was Lauda being declared the winner.

Partly in revenge for his frustration, Lauda wanted more money for the 1979 season. '$2 million,' he announced, more than any other driver. 'Are you mad?' Ecclestone replied, predictably. During their negotiations, Lauda heard Ecclestone rant and rave one day and on the next be conciliatory. Over four months Lauda refused to budge: 'All I did was repeat my price.' Having endured a bad season, he was losing interest in racing. 'Beating down the financial wizard is a damn sight more fun than driving,' he thought. Ecclestone's lack of respect for drivers, Lauda anticipated, would provoke retaliation. His method was crude. To cut Lauda off, Ecclestone telephoned his rivals. 'That Lauda is off his 'ead. He wants $2 million but don't pay more than $500k.' By the time Lauda rang Frank Williams and Teddy Mayer, their replies were identical, 'There's no way I can even speak to you.' Crossing Ecclestone, they knew, would be in his own words 'at your peril'. Lauda was furious. 'Ecclestone is ahead of me,' he cursed. Worse, Ecclestone was freezing Lauda out just to enjoy the pleasure of defeating the driver.

Lauda held one ace. Brabham depended on Parmalat's sponsorship. Unsuspecting, Ecclestone travelled with Lauda to the corporation's headquarters in Parma, Italy. Lauda had primed the chief executive about his problem. After agreeing the sponsorship's renewal, the Italian asked Ecclestone, 'Who's driving?' 'Niki,' replied Ecclestone. 'No, I'm not,' interrupted Lauda. 'We haven't got a contract.' Ecclestone was outwitted. With barely a pause, Ecclestone replied, 'I've agreed to pay Niki $2 million.' 'You fucker,' Ecclestone cursed Lauda as they left the office. '*C'est la vie*, Bernie,' smiled the Austrian.

Gordon Murray also wanted to cash in. Ford, he told Ecclestone, had made a huge offer for him to transfer. Ecclestone perked up. However reluctant, he would need to match a rival to keep Murray. Instead of agreeing a big pay hike, Ecclestone dangled the prospect of selling Brabham and splitting the profits. Reassured by Ecclestone, Murray declined Ford's offer and waited for the sale. In Buenos Aires, at the beginning of the 1979 season, Ecclestone knew there was no chance of Brabham beating Ford, Ferrari or Williams. Lauda and Murray's disappointment would grow. To keep the group together, he contemplated daredevil stunts in helicopters and planes, flooding hotel rooms with fire extinguishers and taking the wheels off a rival's car. His revelry by the pool was interrupted by Mario Andretti, the American driver who won the 1978 world championship for Lotus. 'I'll give you $1,000 if you push Bernie into the pool,' Colin Chapman told Andretti. Fearful of the consequences, Andretti approached Ecclestone by the pool edge and revealed the plot. 'Pay me half and you can,' replied Ecclestone. That was the only moment of humour in Buenos Aires. Lauda retired from the race. Brabham appeared paralysed – just as Ecclestone's own life was changing dramatically.

Ecclestone and Tuana had moved from Kent to London, although they kept the acres of parkland adjacent to the Farnborough house. Their new home was a penthouse flat on the Albert Embankment with panoramic views across the River Thames to Westminster. The flat, with its twenty-five-foot-high windows, had for a short time been the home of Frank Sinatra while he worked in London. Ecclestone redesigned and rebuilt the apartment, painting the living area chocolate brown and filling it with miniature Japanese sculptures, paintings including a fake Modigliani and bric-a-brac he had bought during his regular Sunday visits to auctions. A crane hoisted a green carpet for the main bedroom through the panoramic windows. By the end of the week, the dark shade displeased Ecclestone. Two men were summoned and, after opening the windows, he ordered them to throw the carpet out. 'Make sure no one is in the street,' urged Tuana, who was convinced that they had finally stopped moving. To his old friends, Ecclestone's new sophisticated tastes had smoothed some edges of a brash car salesman. Others found his home chilling, more like a set displayed at the Ideal Home Exhibition. His height, his furtive restlessness and secretive manner all aroused suspicion among those who were struggling to stereotype him. The lack of information about his life and past inspired lurid rumours. The unseen reality was occasionally banal.

Ecclestone's dislike of celebrations and Christmas in particular had not changed. The plan for Christmas 1979 was that the day would be spent sharing a turkey with Oddjob, the bulldog. Lunch was, however, delayed by Ecclestone's sulking. Usually Tuana tolerated his moods but on this occasion she abandoned the kitchen, left the turkey to burn in the oven, the pans boiling on the hob, and walked out. Alone and bewildered by her first rebellion, Ecclestone panicked and agreed never to shout again. This was a rare victory for Tuana, only shared by Oddjob, whose occasional illness dented his master's steely exterior.

In business, however, he offered no self-restraint. Brabham's faltering performance on the track and the potential income from televised races had aggravated his clash with the French FIA president, Jean-Marie Balestre. Ecclestone was about to embark on the next stage of his extraordinary journey.

Ecclestone annoyed Balestre. As Formula One's finances improved from the increase of tobacco company sponsorship, the corporations' hospitality tents followed. Spread across the Paddock and close to the pits, they encouraged a carnival atmosphere that Ecclestone disliked. The fans and the 'pit popsics' trampling around the cars upset his love of cleanliness, especially at Silverstone where rain had wrecked the race in 1978 and the teams lost valuable equipment. Calling it 'disastrous and expensive', Ecclestone had damned the British organisers and warned that Formula One's future in Britain was in doubt. The organisers, he said, needed to replace tents with purpose-built garages with fixed water and electricity supplies, and better emergency medical facilities. Casualness annoyed Ecclestone. His solution was electronic ticketing and an attempt to charge journalists £5,000 for an annual pass. He enjoyed spurning anxious demands for access to the pits and Paddock. Those complaining, especially about sterility and a loss of atmosphere, were ignored. Balestre was planning to crush the usurper's independence at the outset of the 1979 season in Argentina.

To reassert his authority over Formula One, FOCA and Ecclestone, Balestre imposed a £3,000 fine on McLaren's John Watson for an allegedly dangerous movement during the early stages of the Argentinian race. Balestre had not consulted anyone or given the driver a chance to defend himself. While the teams travelled to the next race in São Paulo, Ecclestone and Mosley plotted a showdown. To galvanise them, Ecclestone also decided to inject the race with a new excitement. Frank Williams suggested that they invite Ronnie Biggs, the notorious criminal, to visit the circuit. In 1963 Biggs had participated in the famous Great Train Robbery and, after escaping from prison, had flown to Australia and then fled to Brazil in 1969. Herbie Blash was dispatched to Biggs's home with the invitation. He reported that Biggs knew Frank Williams but had never heard of Ecclestone and was not interested in Formula One. He refused the offer. Nevertheless an envelope with two tickets was left for the fugitive at the Intercontinental Hotel's reception.

Seeing Biggs's name written in large letters, many of the Formula One personnel believed there must be a connection between the fugitive and Ecclestone. This undoubtedly added to the party spirit as they headed towards the pool on the eve of the race. Ecclestone had gathered twenty stunning local girls. Each was told to walk along the 'catwalk' in a skimpy bikini with a team's colours. Ecclestone appointed himself the chairman of the panel to judge the 'Miss Grand Prix' competition. 'Votes,' called Ecclestone, collecting the slips. After a studied glance, the papers were stuffed in his pocket.

'Miss Brabham is the clear winner,' he announced without a hint of embarrassment.

The following morning, just before the Brazilian Grand Prix started, Mosley invited Balestre to meet him and Ecclestone in a basement room at the Interlagos stadium. In fluent French, Mosley told Balestre that the teams would withdraw from the race unless John Watson was allowed to compete without paying the fine. Balestre protested his outrage. In a moment of exquisite theatre, with their opponent confused, the showdown came to a climax as Mosley added that the Brazilian organisers agreed with the boycott. Helpless, Balestre surrendered. At the end of the race, won by Jacques Laffite in a Ligier with a Ford engine, the teams waited at the Intercontinental to be paid. Eventually two trucks arrived with sixty binliners containing banknotes. 'We can't count all this stuff,' said Blash. 'Let's measure it. One foot is about £500.' 'Bernard has brought a sense of self-respect to Formula One,' Frank Williams told his rivals as they sat by the pool surrounded by Brazilian girls. 'He's moved fast and the race money is going up.'

Williams and his fellow mechanics did not fully understand the power struggle Ecclestone was waging. In individual negotiations beyond their view, he was extracting higher fees from every circuit. In response to any organiser's procrastination, he mentioned the possibility of transferring the race to another country. To avoid that disappointment, the Argentinians had reluctantly increased their fee but Ecclestone had cancelled the Swedish Grand Prix. Balestre was uncertain about his enemy's tactics. Perspiring under a tree at Kyalami – the race following Brazil's – Balestre sat down beside Ecclestone to discuss an accommodation. Despite his humiliation in Brazil, he sought to retrieve FIA's control but found Ecclestone stonily deaf to any compromise. Unable to conceal his contempt for the businessman's grubby sentiments, Balestre exploded, accusing his neighbour of exaggerating his own and the English teams' importance. 'You're just little men playing with toys,' said Balestre, 'making cars in garages. Who do you think you are? You don't own motor sport. Your group are just a bunch of nobodies living off the back of the sport.' Balestre's tirade exposed his weakness, rousing Ecclestone's taste for conflict, the natural ingredient for earning money, but the final goal still remained unclear. Ecclestone was not a far-sighted strategist motivated by precise visions of an empire but a tactician protecting a healthy income by arranging the races for like-minded Britons. They, like him, resented a pompous Frenchman's dictate. Provoking the Frenchman's anger confirmed his success but the final outcome still remained uncertain.

For others, Ecclestone's combativeness was too personal. Lauda was drained by their arguments. 'I feel completely empty,' he told his friends. 'After a big fight with Bernie, I've got no positive emotions.' Sitting wearily in his Brabham on the grid in Montreal towards the end of the season, with the engine turning, he sensed an unfamiliar tickle in his back. In the previous twelve races, his car, cursed by a woefully inadequate engine, had crossed the line only twice. Soaked by the 'misty and shitty' Canadian weather, he was sunk in gloom. 'The bubble's burst,' Lauda realised. Halfway through the practice session, he returned to the pits and found Ecclestone in his motorhome. 'I've had enough,' Lauda told his employer. 'I can't drive any more.' 'You must be barking mad,' said Ecclestone. 'You've just signed a $2 million contract.' 'I don't want to drive in circles any more,' said Lauda. 'I want to do different things in my life.' 'Think again,' urged Ecclestone with an expressionless face. 'I want you to take the right decision.' 'I've decided,' said Lauda. 'OK. Just leave your helmet and overalls.' 'Why?' asked Lauda. 'Because whoever I hire won't have any.' Dashing into the Paddock, Ecclestone found Ricardo Zunino, an Argentinian, wandering aimlessly. 'You're hired,' said Ecclestone to the inevitable loser. By nightfall, Lauda had flown out of Montreal to Long Beach to buy a DC10 aircraft for his new airline.

Looking around for a replacement driver, Ecclestone offered $2.5 million to Jackie Stewart to drive for one season. Stewart had retired six years earlier and refused. Eventually, Ecclestone chose Nelson Piquet, a twenty-six-year-old Brazilian whom he had met in 1977 at Monza. The Brazilian had entered his motorhome clutching a contract he was about to sign for a Formula Three race. 'Would you check this for me?' he asked. 'If you're any good, you'll be sorry,' advised Ecclestone after reading the agreement. 'If you sign this, you're going to be trapped for three years.' In unusually clear handwriting, Ecclestone wrote an escape clause. Months later, that gesture allowed Ecclestone to lure Piquet to sign a Brabham contract to drive in the last race of the 1978 season. 'Write on the contract, "I have read and understand the English," ' Ecclestone ordered Piquet, dropping the only copy afterwards into his briefcase. 'By the way,' he added as an afterthought, 'I'm paying you $50,000.'

Few in Ecclestone's world were indispensable and no one was paid a penny more than necessary. Lauda could be replaced but Gordon Murray was special. To cure Brabham's problems he needed help and, as usual, the best solution was to poach a rival's designer with some new ideas. Alastair Caldwell, a New Zealand draughtsman, was hired after twelve successful seasons at McLaren. From the outset, Caldwell realised that he and Ecclestone were 'circling each other and knew it would not last'. The atmosphere at Brabham's headquarters in Chessington, Caldwell discovered, was unusually frugal. To save money, Ecclestone had banned tea-making equipment because when mechanics drank tea they were not working. He continued to be fanatical about turning off lights. When Caldwell installed fluorescent lights because the draughtsmen were finding difficulty seeing their drawings, Ecclestone switched them off. Caldwell turned them on. Ecclestone erupted. Aggravation was consistent with keeping control. He was quite happy for Caldwell to witness his anger on another occasion when, on returning to his Albert Embankment flat, he noticed a Jaguar pulling into his reserved parking place. Hearing the driver quip, 'I'll be back . . .' and disappear, Ecclestone drove his Mercedes directly into the Jaguar. Stepping out of the car, Ecclestone went up to his flat to collect a bag and returned. Without a word, he walked past the incredulous owner of the Jaguar staring at his severely damaged car and drove off. Years later Ecclestone would deny the incident had occurred but did not object to the allegation being publicised.

Ecclestone's anger reflected his frustration with Caldwell. At the Canadian Grand Prix in 1980 Caldwell had opposed Ecclestone's orders to change a worn engine on the qualifying car before the race. After Piquet crashed his race car during the Grand Prix, he was forced to use the inferior engine and lost. Next, they clashed at the Brazilian Grand Prix. Ecclestone wanted to use wet tyres but Caldwell insisted on dry tyres. Piquet was leading until the rain started and then lost the race. Brabham's fortunes were not improving. Ecclestone blamed Caldwell's lack of commitment: they would part on bad terms in 1981 after more arguments, not least about Caldwell's bonus. 'He's a sad, little, unfulfilled twerp,' cursed Caldwell, 'whose real name is Ecclestein and whose father was probably a multimillion-pound trawler owner and he's robbed billions off the Grand Prix teams.' To Caldwell and other critics, Ecclestone appeared to flourish on sharp practice. His critics highlighted his sale to the teams of Avon tyres, manufactured in England, for cash. Jean-François Mosnier, a Frenchman, transported the tyres across Europe to the race circuits, took the cash and deposited the takings in various bank accounts. Gossip circulated that Ecclestone was running an untaxed sideline. After Mosnier's death from cancer, Ecclestone seemed reluctant to explain the operation. 'Jean ran the business for me,' said Ecclestone. 'He did whatever had to be done. If there was money coming in or money going out, he did everything.' One explanation about cash-for-tyres was that Ecclestone didn't trust the teams to pay if he gave them credit. But occasionally Ecclestone preferred not to clarify misunderstandings. Instinctively private, he preferred to confuse enquirers by conjuring a mystique among the Formula One fraternity. This only served to reinforce his influence. Uncertainty was a barrier to jealous rivals who wanted to find out how much he earned from FOCA. As his wealth grew, he actually encouraged ludicrous tales to divert attention from the truth.

A few rival car dealers could not understand how one of their kind had become so wealthy. A story began circulating that Roy 'The Weasel' James, a former Formula Three driver who drove a getaway car from the Great Train Robbery, was linked to Ecclestone. When combined with anecdotes about the envelope with tickets awaiting Ronnie Biggs at the hotel's reception in Brazil, a wild rumour spread that Ecclestone's wealth may have been related to the robbery itself, possibly as the mastermind. Since even the police could not believe that the crime had been organised by the gang they had so easily arrested, Ecclestone was mentioned as a possible 'Mr Big'.

Roy James's connection to Ecclestone began in 1970. Writing from Parkhurst prison on 6 September to Graham Hill, James introduced himself as a former racing driver and asked whether, on his release, he could return to the sport. Three years later, freed from prison, James contacted Hill, who passed the request on to Ecclestone, his employer at the time. Intrigued, Ecclestone asked a Brabham manager to allow James a test drive. The report confirmed Ecclestone's misgivings. James was too old, but in compensation, Ecclestone met James, whom he discovered was a silversmith, and commissioned a silver trophy for Formula One. The significance of that brief acquaintanceship snowballed into assertions that Ecclestone's wealth clearly dated back to the robbery. The first journalist reporting the link received a legal threat. Ecclestone's draconian reaction encouraged suspicions of a link. Mischievously, Ecclestone began to enjoy the notoriety. By crafting a response – 'Why would I want to rob a train with only £1 million on it? That's not even enough to pay one driver. I suppose it does not do any harm people thinking things like that' – he did not appear to resent his reputation as a sinister hard man. He quite liked a friend telling a newspaper, 'Don't tell stories that upset Bernie as you might find yourself as one of the uprights in the new M4 extension.' The image suited his purpose at the next Spanish Grand Prix, one year after his argument with Balestre in South Africa. As the same friend said, 'Bernie had every trick in the book. He's done it all by outwitting everyone else.'

5

Hard Man

War was declared by Bernie Ecclestone against Jean-Marie Balestre on 1 June 1980 at the Jarama race circuit in Spain. Armed police, dispatched to the race course at Ecclestone's request and with the approval of King Juan Carlos, confronted FIA's president at gunpoint to assert control of the circuit.

Ecclestone's enjoyment of the conflict was second only to Max Mosley's. Balestre's taste for travelling at FIA's expense in a Rolls-Royce, staying in the presidential suite of the best hotels and receiving unlimited tickets and hospitality for his friends increased their anger. Both men might have tolerated Balestre's personal indulgences if he were not manipulating the FIA's technical rules to favour foreign manufacturers against British teams. His overt prejudice particularly annoyed Mosley. Three months earlier in Kyalami, Mosley had arranged for a local official to push Balestre physically from the winner's podium. 'What was he doing there?' Mosley asked waspishly, waving aside Balestre's impulsive retaliation, that he would ban the competition in South Africa the following year. 'Don't worry,' Mosley reassured the local organiser. 'We'll have won by then.' Three months later Mosley was vindicated as he witnessed Balestre's humiliation when he faced the armed Spanish police. His and Ecclestone's battle was not about the sport's heart and soul but, under the fig-leaf of disputing FIA's technical regulations, about power and money.

Formula One is not only a competition between drivers but

also among engineers. Pitting Ferrari against the British teams to improve performances had challenged the ingenuity of the best designers. Technical developments were Enzo Ferrari's daily oxygen and until 1981 the British teams' lighter cars combined with aerodynamic skirts gave them an advantage. To restore his fortunes, Enzo Ferrari had developed a turbo-charged engine to beat the traditional Cosworth engines used by the British. 'Ferrari's always got the advantage of better engines and more money,' lamented Ecclestone, who had fatefully switched from Cosworth to Alfa Romeo to compete with Ferrari's twelve-cylinder engines. 'That didn't work,' Ecclestone admitted mournfully, acknowledging that the British teams lacked the finance to develop turbo engines. To tilt the balance firmly in favour of the European manufacturers, Balestre had issued a regulation banning skirts and requiring all Formula One cars after 1981 to be heavier – a necessity if they were to carry the turbo engines. To Ecclestone, Balestre's motives were transparent. The expensive innovation had been introduced at Enzo Ferrari's request and copied by Renault, France's biggest car maker, knowing that FOCA members would suffer. As usual, deploying crude politics and emotional manipulation, Enzo Ferrari had mesmerised Balestre and allowed him to punch above his weight.

There was little reason for Ferrari to love Ecclestone. Lauda's switch to Brabham and Ecclestone's organisation of the British teams had left Ferrari isolated against McLaren and Williams, both blessed with body designs superior to Ferrari's. Although he would tell Marco Piccinini, his team manager, to say that the battle was about the turbo engine and not about Ecclestone's bid to control Formula One, Ferrari masterfully exploited his natural Latin bond with Balestre during their excited discussions about girls, food and politics to encourage opposition to Ecclestone. To Ferrari's satisfaction, Balestre had manipulated the votes at FIA meetings to pass binding technical changes on the English, deliberately ignoring adverse votes. Yet simultaneously, in his emotional moments, Ferrari mentioned how meeting Ecclestone was 'my destiny', beguiling Ecclestone to recount, 'Enzo is always on my side against Balestre. He feels there's a bit of me in him which Balestre doesn't have.' One 'bit' was Ecclestone's ambition to dominate the sport, the very commercialisation which Balestre so opposed. Amid those conflicting relationships at the heart of Formula One, everyone's vanity could be tolerated until Ecclestone scented a threat to his commercial ambitions. Like every true street-fighter, Ecclestone acknowledged Balestre's justified protection of FIA's legitimate interests but, in the cause of his own fortunes, he would do his utmost to defeat him comprehensively.

Since their argument under the trees in Kyalami, Balestre had not only ignored Ecclestone's repeated advice to retreat but, in the week before the race at Jarama, he sought to recover control of Formula One by fining the drivers of British teams for minor transgressions of FIA's rules. With gusto Ecclestone ordained that the fines would not be paid. In reply Balestre threatened to ban the drivers from all Formula One races and, to sustain his edict, secured the support of twelve national associations hosting Formula One races. The first ban would be effective immediately at Jarama. Ecclestone retaliated by threatening a boycott of all Balestre's races. In Ecclestone's scheme, a showdown meant a shoot-out.

On the night before the Jarama race, Mosley contacted Balestre and suggested that they meet in his office at the circuit at seven o'clock the following morning. Mosley's self-deprecating mild manner reassured the Frenchman that the English would be surrendering. Simultaneously Ecclestone was personally arranging with King Juan Carlos, with whom he had developed a personal friendship at Formula One circuits, that the race would not be run unless the FOCA teams participated. With that assurance Mosley and Ecclestone met Balestre. With Mosley acting as interpreter, the conversation quickly degenerated into an argument until Ecclestone produced his ace: FOCA and not FIA owned the exclusive legal rights to race at Jarama and at most of the other national circuits used by Formula One. Balestre and FIA, said Ecclestone, would be unable to stage Formula One races at any of those world-famous stadiums. Stubbornly, the Frenchman refused to acknowledge Ecclestone's trump card. 'He's quite mad,' Mosley whispered to Ecclestone. 'Shall I fuck him now?' 'Knock his table over,' Ecclestone replied. The lawyer dutifully obliged and in the mayhem of Balestre's papers cascading to the floor, Ecclestone seized his precious list of the twelve supporting countries. 'I can't find my papers,' screeched Balestre, searching frantically, unsuspecting that his list was in Ecclestone's pocket. 'The race is cancelled,' shouted Balestre. 'We'll see,' whispered Ecclestone, expecting chaos to extend across the circuit.

On Ecclestone's orders FIA officials were removed at gunpoint by the local police, followed by Balestre. Running along the grid, Ecclestone ordered the drivers, fearful or confused, to race. Twelve teams entertained the crowds but three teams – Ferrari, Renault and Alfa Romeo – refused to participate. The result was irrelevant after Balestre declared the race would not count towards the world championships. Balestre's sanction, Ecclestone exhorted, was worth suffering. His euphoria was short-lived. In the days after the race, some sponsors threatened to withdraw, complaining about lawlessness, the absence of Ferrari and low television audiences. The fractious mood encouraged Balestre's conviction that he would defeat Ecclestone. For Ecclestone retreat was inconceivable. Winning depended upon maintaining the momentum and time was short. Under pressure from dissatisfied sponsors, divisions among the teams and the risk of twelve circuits supporting Balestre, Ecclestone needed a swift victory.

Following the debacle Balestre had flown on a private plane from Spain to Athens. The Frenchman was claiming the support of the world federation and manufacturers. 'He's got all the cards,' admitted Mosley. 'All the strength.' Ecclestone refused to consider defeat, although he did laughingly remind Mosley about the offer three months earlier at the Rio circuit from a bunch of local hoods to send a team to Europe to murder Balestre with the assurance, 'They'll be back before anyone knows.' 'No thanks,' both instantly replied. 'You're either a gangster or you're not,' Ecclestone had later told Mosley.

In pursuit of their quarry, the two men found that no commercial flights to Athens were available. Scouring Madrid airport, they hitched a lift on a private plane to reach Athens by nightfall. Checking in to the same hotel as Balestre, they had no master plan other than to discover a weakness in Balestre's armoury. 'He's never going to tell you his hand,' Ecclestone told Mosley. 'You have to grab it.' A discreet payment to the hotel's telex operator secured a copy of every message Balestre was sending and receiving. The telexes showed that in organising his campaign, Balestre was seeking an alliance with Colin Chapman. The two, Balestre suggested, should meet at Le Mans to discuss Chapman replacing Ecclestone as FOCA's president. If Chapman agreed, wrote Balestre, he would arrange for FIA to approve skirts on the cars. By sundown, Ecclestone's apprehension was confirmed. In a telex Chapman accepted the offer and, to seal the deal, agreed to fly immediately with Balestre to meet Enzo Ferrari. The following day, Ecclestone and Mosley watched Balestre leave the hotel to fly to Le Mans. Ecclestone feared the worst. Chapman, unlike the other team owners, suspected Ecclestone's motives and had good commercial reasons to side with Balestre. Stranded in Athens, Ecclestone began telephoning the race circuit to speak to Chapman. His rival, Ecclestone knew, was telling the other British team owners, 'Bernie can't win.' Some agreed with Chapman, saying in the wake of the Jarama race, 'Balestre's got control of the sport.' To survive, Ecclestone realised that he needed to persuade Chapman to side with him against Balestre. Much to his relief, Chapman came to the telephone at Le Mans just before he boarded his plane. In that critical moment, Ecclestone guessed that the odds were even. 'He's conning you,' said Ecclestone. 'He'll never allow skirts.' Then he began praising Lotus's technical genius and massaging Chapman's vanity. 'It's stupid to go. We're all together on this. If we don't stick together, we'll blow up.' By the end of the conversation, Chapman acknowledged that Ecclestone had improved the business and, despite his self-aggrandisement, could be trusted. 'Don't worry about Enzo,' Ecclestone told Chapman. 'He'll sit back and refuse to take a position until he has to.' The flight to Italy was cancelled.

Capitalising on that small victory, Ecclestone contrived a confrontation and announced that the FOCA teams refused to race at the French Grand Prix in June. Balestre, he knew, would be severely embarrassed in his own country. The FIA president was vexed by the discovery of a wartime photograph of himself wearing SS uniform, posing under a banner of Adolf Hitler. To suppress the obvious conclusion, Balestre was suing newspapers for libel. He claimed that he had been an undercover member of the resistance but unfortunately all the French co-conspirators who could verify his brave record were dead. At that moment, Balestre did not need more problems in France, so Ecclestone was not surprised that he offered a truce to reinstate the skirts and negotiate a peace treaty. Trustfully, Ecclestone accepted the olive branch and followed Balestre's gilded procession around the Paul Ricard circuit near Marseille. Soon after the race, Balestre reintroduced the ban on skirts and resumed his war with FOCA.

Over dinner at his home in Saint Cloud with the managers of Renault and other manufacturers, Balestre explained how, together with the race organisers, he would retrieve Formula One from Ecclestone. If the manufacturers' support for himself remained solid, he promised, Ecclestone would be defeated. Foolishly Balestre did not subscribe to Ecclestone's philosophy: act first, threaten after. Soon after the dinner, he disclosed his plan to *L'Equipe*, the French daily sports newspaper. His boast was picked up by Ecclestone, smarting from Balestre's double-cross. 'They shouldn't start these things,' he said about Balestre's latest declaration of war. 'They should pick on someone their own size.'

Summoning an emergency meeting of the teams in October 1980, Ecclestone was vengeful. FOCA, he explained, represented the seven leading independent teams employing the best drivers. His contracts with the organisers, he continued, would prevent Balestre's group racing on those circuits. He proposed that FOCA break away from FIA and establish the World Federation of Motor Sport to compete in the World Professional Drivers' Championship. Ecclestone was advocating a draconian step – the destruction of Formula One – and he could not imagine the outcome.

'These people don't know what they are in for,' Balestre scathingly retorted. Ecclestone soon realised the strength of Balestre's scorn. In December 1980 the balance was tilting towards FIA. Balestre's tenacity had won the support of the Italian and French manufacturers, the members of FIA's affiliated motor sport clubs and some circuit owners who feared Balestre's threats if they failed to break their relationship with Ecclestone. The FOCA teams were also nervous. Their sponsors were reassessing contracts and their banks were hesitant to grant loans in case the races were cancelled. The war's outcome, Ecclestone knew, depended on Enzo Ferrari. On 16 January 1981 Ecclestone and Mosley flew to Maranello. To their dismay, Ferrari expressed his doubts about the breakaway's plan and refused to participate in any FOCA race. Anticipating Balestre's glee, Ecclestone urged the British teams not to be deflected. The risk of financial ruin for Ecclestone drew a line in the sand. Attack rather than discussion was his response. Lawyers were hired to seek injunctions across the world to prevent FIA sabotaging FOCA's contracts with the organisers. But Ecclestone's certainty of legal success would evaporate if insolvency crippled the teams. Without admitting any anxiety, he corralled the FOCA teams to head for South Africa to race in February 1981. Each received his personal guarantee that he would pay all the costs and bear any losses.

Balestre's instant reaction was predictable. The race, he declared, would not count towards the world championship.

Ecclestone was not deterred. Keen to host any sporting event that would undermine the global boycott against apartheid, the organisers at Kyalami had agreed to cover the costs. Mosley, providing legal expertise to clarify and obfuscate as required, drafted Ecclestone's defiant reply to Balestre: 'Who the hell is FIA? They are a bunch of nobodies. They appointed themselves and think they own racing, when all they really are is a bunch of clubs around the world and self-important people living off the back of the sport.' Two outcasts from British society, spurning links to the 'establishment' clubs, the RAC and the British Racing Drivers Club, were leading a group of unconventional risk-takers on the basis of Ecclestone's pledge, 'If someone wants to cross me, they do that at their peril. I will defend myself.'

The Ranch Hotel was a perfect venue for sealing the teams' solidarity. The mood encouraged Ecclestone and Mosley to irritate Balestre. Posing as a South African telephone operator, Ecclestone called Balestre in France and announced, 'Call from Mr Nelson Mandela.' Balestre, assuming that the leader was telephoning from his prison, and unable to distinguish the accents of English speakers, was unaware that 'Mandela' was Mosley. 'I'm told that you are visiting South Africa for the Grand Prix,' said 'Mandela'. 'I am delighted. I would be proud if you agree to visit me.' Balestre's strangled excuses about the impossibility of a visit was only cut short by the 'prison operator' announcing, 'Time's up.'

Thereafter, the mood in Kyalami soured. Washed out by rain, few spectators and a meagre field, the race on 7 February 1981 was a flop, but the tightly focused television pictures obscured the depth of the disaster. Ecclestone admitted to Mosley that he could not afford to stage another 'pirate' race. Support from the sponsors and circuits was fading fast. Goodyear's refusal to provide tyres for the race had been minimised by using Ecclestone's own warehouse of Avon tyres, but compensating other withdrawals would be impossible. The gambler's trick was to pretend the contrary. Cards face down on the table and with a fixed stare, Ecclestone announced that the breakaway was a roaring success and the FOCA teams were heading for the next circuit. To those in Europe relying on the television pictures, Ecclestone's Grand Prix did appear to be a triumph. Balestre blinked first. The disaster was transformed into a winning opportunity. 'Great,' said Mosley relieved. 'All he had to do was wait.'

The peacemaker was Enzo Ferrari. Kyalami, he admitted, removed his doubts about Ecclestone's determination and further conflict risked financial ruin for everyone. He asked Aleardo Buzzi, the European president of Philip Morris, to broker the peace. Hearing the news, Ecclestone finally understood Ferrari's strengths and weaknesses. Using his own legend he manipulated emotions to cloak his bids for power but, while he loved the sport, he lacked Ecclestone's energy, intrigue and attention to detail to exert his authority beyond a simple veto. Isolated in Maranello and relying on the television pictures from Kyalami, he decided to abandon Balestre and trust Buzzi to save the sport. The mandate, confirming the tobacco industry's influence in Formula One, naturally delighted Buzzi. Summoning only Teddy Mayer and Marco Piccinini to the Palace Hotel in Lausanne, Buzzi discussed Ferrari's peace formula. Ecclestone had good reason to fear the old adage, 'If you're not at the table you become part of the menu.' To compensate for his absence, he brought pressure on Mayer to argue the case in favour of the British teams which in turn persuaded Buzzi to oppose Balestre about the advantageous outcome. Once Ferrari and McLaren had agreed, Ecclestone was told the solution and invited to gather with all the teams in Modena to confirm the agreement. Balestre's supporters swiftly dispersed. Renault, Ferrari and Alfa Romeo agreed to attend the next race at Long Beach in March on Ecclestone's terms.

Ecclestone's victory was unconditional: Balestre accepted that FIA could not authorise a Grand Prix except on the terms Ecclestone negotiated with the circuits, for which he would receive 8 per cent of the gross income. In return, the teams indisputably recognised FIA's authority to make, change and enforce technical rules. Unnoticed in the drafted settlement, Ecclestone had included a clause assigning all of Formula One's television rights and income for four years to FOCA. Oblivious to the implications, Balestre approved this critical concession.

Mosley and Ecclestone met Balestre in Paris to sign the peace agreement formally. Over breakfast at the Hôtel de Crillon on the Place de la Concorde, the three men initialled the paragraphs. On completion, Balestre made one request. The agreement conceived in Maranello, discussed in Lausanne and concluded in Modena should be called the Concorde agreement. Ecclestone did not object to the vanity but he did refuse Balestre's request to lift the worldwide injunctions against FIA's interference with FOCA's contracts with the organisers. 'Sign and announce the contract and we'll get them lifted,' Ecclestone told Balestre. He would not risk another double-cross. Balestre was not offended. 'Let's keep the argument going for a few more weeks,' he said, smiling at Ecclestone. The president, Ecclestone knew, loved posturing in the spotlight. By delaying an announcement, the tension would increase before he would summon journalists to his headquarters in the neighbouring building and declare 'victory'. Ecclestone nodded. Balestre's harmless posturing suited a man who profited by inhabiting the shadows. His prize was incalculable. Nothing could in the future be decided without his approval. Formally, the war ended on 11 March 1981. The foundation stone of Bernie Ecclestone's fortune was legitimised that day in Paris.

Balestre's defeat liberated the teams to cast aside their unnatural cooperation and resume their inter-team hostilities. McLaren was in turmoil. Teddy Mayer had been usurped by John Hogan, the deputy marketing head of Philip Morris. 'Teddy doesn't know what's going on,' said Ecclestone after hearing that Philip Morris had decided to finance a take-over by Ron Dennis, formerly a junior mechanic at Brabham. Although Dennis was criticised as a chippy man who 'can't get out of bed without being awkward', he had pioneered the use of carbon fibre as a stronger and lighter alternative to aluminium for the cars' bodies. And he was hungry for success. At his first FOCA meeting at Heathrow, Dennis got a glimpse of the man who did not, he believed, play like himself by the Queensberry rules. At the end of the negotiations, after the circuit owners had left, Ecclestone as usual dived for the waste-paper bin. 'You've got to see what they were saying to each other,' chortled Ecclestone, straightening out crumpled pieces of paper. 'No wonder', thought Dennis, 'that Bernie has a huge shredder in his office.' Dennis thanked Philip Morris for his promotion.

To forge a good relationship with Dennis, Ecclestone and Tuana invited the victor and his wife to Crockfords for dinner. By the end of the meal, Ecclestone's dislike of Dennis was irreversible. 'No rapport and no mutual liking,' Tuana said as they bid farewell to their guest and walked towards the gambling tables. Two weeks earlier, the couple had won handsomely at chemmy against Prince Fahd, the eldest son of Saudi Arabia's ruler sitting at the table with a beautiful girlfriend. The following week, Ecclestone had lost £100,000 at punto banco. 'You play and I'll watch,' he had ordered Tuana. Over the next hour, Tuana had recovered the £100,000. After Dennis's departure, they hoped to win another £100,000. 'It's the Big One,' Tuana laughed. Instead, Ecclestone lost £100,000. 'Right, home,' he ordered. 'Bad omen about your relationship with Ron,' said Tuana. As usual, Ecclestone slept soundly that night. Tuana recognised he was a good loser, determined not to show any weakness. He was not wealthy enough to suffer serious losses regularly but accepted that, as in business and love, he must accept the consequence of his mistakes. The following morning, she knew, he would set off to earn money and recoup the thrashing.

No one could enjoy beating Ecclestone for long, as the seller of fake Brabham merchandise outside the Spa circuit had recently realised. The previous year, Ecclestone had backed his car into the stall and driven off. But on the second occasion, his retaliation had been more sophisticated. 'This is wonderful,' he had told the unsuspecting seller. 'I'll just get my money and buy the lot.' He returned in a van with two men. 'Load the lot. I'm buying it all,' he said. 'How much is that in dollars?' 'I want Belgian francs,' replied the stall's owner. 'I've only got dollars. Let's work out the conversion rate.' Finding a newspaper and agreeing the rate took more than an hour. 'You know,' said Ecclestone as the Belgian awaited payment, 'I don't want to pay. Drive,' he ordered his employees. Summoning the police, the seller discovered Ecclestone's influence. 'There's nothing we can do,' he was told.

On the track Brabham's principal foe remained Chapman's Lotus. For some months, Murray had been perfecting a ruse to increase the car's speed. The challenge was to circumvent the rule stipulating a six-centimetre gap between the car and the ground. Murray's innovation – beyond the sight of FIA's scrutineers and his rivals – was a system of fluids which, once the car was moving, lowered the car's body down to within a centimetre of the track to increase the downward pressure which would automatically increase the speed. Flashing past the scrutineers, the minor adjustment would be invisible but, if suspicions were aroused, the FIA scrutineer would find on the car's return to the pits that the stationary car was six centimetres off the ground. To Ecclestone's surprise, Chapman had arrived at the Long Beach Grand Prix in March 1981 with his own circumvention of the same rule, except that it was blatantly obvious. The new Lotus was built on two chassis with a telescopic suspension which rose and fell with speed. His revolutionary design, argued Chapman, adhered to the rule which stipulated that anything which influenced the car's aerodynamic performance had to be immobile. Not only was Ecclestone irritated that Chapman's technical genius had outmatched Murray's but he knew that no team could hope to beat Lotus. The only recourse was to organise a universal protest, urging Balestre to outlaw the Lotus. Chapman's rage was matched by Ecclestone's placid response that the rules must be obeyed. Balestre's eagerness to oblige – ordering the Lotus's withdrawal – surprised some but not Ecclestone. Ever since the Crillon breakfast, he had fashioned an understanding with Balestre that, in return for permitting Balestre's luxury lifestyle, the FIA president would be more benign towards his new friend's tactics.

In the race Nelson Piquet's Brabham, helped by the secret advantage, finished third. One month later, with his rivals still bewildered as to how Murray had transformed the car, Piquet won the Argentinian Grand Prix. Midway through the season Murray's secret was exposed, but too late to prevent Brabham leading the field. Consistent with their new relationship, Ecclestone persuaded Balestre not to ban the Brabham but to allow other teams to copy Murray's design. By then Chapman had initiated a succession of costly appeals for an unwinnable cause. FIA's rules, as everyone understood, were biased to protect prejudices. As Ecclestone enjoyed recalling, when Ken Tyrrell had been spotted pouring gunshot into his fuel tank to add weight and was threatened by loss of points at an FIA trial, he had also insisted on appealing. But he then decided to accept Ecclestone's advice: 'You've been fucked. Take your punishment.' Chapman, however, objected to the charade of FIA's 'justice' and, preoccupied by his protest, failed to prevent Ecclestone's tightening grip over Formula One.

Walking through the pits carrying a black briefcase (whispered to contain cash), Ecclestone's restless, I-am-never-satisfied appearance stoked rumours about never forgetting a slight, prompting his disparaging quip, 'He's afraid to step out of line.' Wearing expensive Italian shoes and tailored clothes, his carefully combed hair fell over tinted glasses emphasising deep lines embedded on either side of his face. To one observer quoted in a magazine profile, 'He has the spruce, spry look of an archetypal used-car salesman as he gingerly prods a Formula

One world championship Brabham car, then wipes his hand with the exaggerated care of a fastidious pastry cook.' Another newspaper judged that the grim atmosphere in the pits reflected widespread fear of the fifty-one-year-old multimillionaire. The image matched his decision to stage the season's final race at Caesar's Palace in Las Vegas on 17 October 1981.

Nelson Piquet was on the verge of becoming Formula One's world champion. The owner of Caesar's Palace promised that the circuit would start and finish at Steve Wynn's Bellagio hotel and wind its way around the famous Strip. The deal had been negotiated with Billy Weinberger, the son of the Caesar's Palace founder. After welcoming Ecclestone to the hotel, Weinberger escorted his guest to meet his board of directors in a dark room deep underground – built to withstand eavesdropping, bombs and bullets. 'I want you guys to know', announced Weinberger with Ecclestone at his side, 'that we've got Bernie here to have a race here which will be good for the city. And do you guys have any questions?' One mundane question was asked and Weinberger concluded, 'Right, that's done then.'

Ecclestone was paid handsomely to bring the race to Vegas and attract huge crowds to stay and gamble. But by the day of the race, Ecclestone feared the worst. The circuit was limited to Caesar's Palace's car park surrounded by the hot Nevada desert, few spectator tickets had been sold and the American television networks had expressed no interest. Ecclestone's compensation was a thrilling race. Exhausted and almost comatose at the end, Piquet beat Carlos Reutemann and won his first world championship. Ecclestone had good reason to be proud of his driver and Brabham's designer. But instead of celebrating, he disappeared before the end of the race. 'All he did was do the job he was paid for,' said Ecclestone. Riding up in a lift together to their hotel rooms, Ecclestone sighed to Piquet, 'Your win has made our lives much easier,' and disappeared. Piquet was not disturbed. Ecclestone, he knew, disliked high-profile employees. Nor was he sorry that there was no celebration with Ecclestone.

He would party with his own crowd. That evening, Ecclestone headed with Mosley for a big card game against a group of Chinese. 'Let's go halves,' Ecclestone suggested to Mosley. 'I can't afford it,' replied Mosley. Over the next three hours, looking increasingly angry, Ecclestone lost $100,000.

Piquet's victory encouraged Ecclestone to crush those opposing his authority. 'We have got to get our act together otherwise we won't be around in two years time,' he warned those whose anonymous bickering and jealousies encouraged dark predictions in newspapers. He blamed the drivers for being particularly prone to self-destruction: 'They think they're angels,' complained Ecclestone, 'but they're generally overpaid, live as tax exiles, think only about short-term interests and, within one season, will smash four cars, blow up fifty engines and then break their contracts and walk out. I don't socialise with them any more.' His proposed solution was to limit the drivers' freedom to auction their services between rival teams. Instead, like football players, the drivers' contracts would hinder transfers by imposing onerous fees on those switching teams. With little argument, the team managers and Balestre approved Ecclestone's scheme. The new terms of employment were published just before the South African Grand Prix in January 1982, the first race of the season.

The drivers were furious. The day before the first practice session, Ecclestone heard that Niki Lauda, lured back to racing by Ron Dennis, was urging a strike. Ecclestone, Lauda told everyone, was behaving like a Mafia Don, spreading the message that anyone who got the better of him was 'dead' while schemers were destined to become 'history'. 'But don't be deterred,' Lauda urged. Piquet was among those who opposed Lauda's proposed strike until he met Ecclestone at the Ranch Hotel. Tension had developed between the two because Ecclestone objected to Piquet's eighteen-month romance with Ann Jones, Ecclestone's secretary. 'If you're not in my car at 8 a.m. tomorrow,' Ecclestone told Piquet, 'you'll never drive for me again.' 'I can't stand how you want to control everything,' Piquet retorted and joined the strike.

At seven o'clock the following morning, Lauda was waiting for the drivers to arrive at the Kyalami race track. Before they could enter, he shepherded them on to a hired coach. Once all were on board, Lauda ordered the driver, 'Take us to a hotel as far away as possible.' Didier Pironi, a Ferrari driver, remained behind to negotiate with Ecclestone. Lauda did not underestimate Ecclestone's determination. Recently, while flying together in a helicopter towards Silverstone, they had hit impenetrable fog. 'We'll have to return,' said Lauda. 'We can't land in this.' The pilot agreed, 'We'll go back.' 'It'll be OK,' ordered Ecclestone. 'Just land.' Lauda's face whitened as Ecclestone's grit pushed the pilot towards the ground. Piquet had mentioned the same fear. In Belgium he had refused to sit in the front seat of a saloon car while Ecclestone drove. 'He's so dangerous,' Piquet complained. Lauda agreed but recently he had witnessed the breaking-point of Ecclestone's vulnerability after he was hit by a passing car in Bexleyheath. The hard man had cracked. His nerves were clearly jittered as he recovered on the pavement. In the South African battle, Lauda expected ferocious passion but not lingering resentment by whoever was defeated.

For the first hours in the Sunnyside Park Hotel's banqueting suite, the drivers were entertained by Elio de Angelis, a Lotus driver, playing the piano. But gradually they became restless. 'Do something, Nelson,' Lauda asked Piquet, to prevent a drift back to Kyalami. Dropping his pants, the Brazilian shouted, 'Bernie can lick my arse and I'm still not going back.' Angelis struck up a dramatic tune. The rebellious mood was restored. Ecclestone's counter-coup relied on the police's agreement to break the strike. Spotting the officers arrive at the hotel, Lauda ordered the piano to be pushed against the ballroom door. The stand-off lasted throughout Friday night.

In Kyalami Ecclestone vented his anger against the 'bloody fools' who could easily be replaced by drivers on the rungs below. 'And then,' he raged against the strikers, 'those buggers, those prima donnas who go on strike will have plenty of time to sit on their private jets, count the zeroes and add up the figures on those great fat contracts – those who can read that is – and realise how bloody lucky they are.'

The following morning, Ecclestone capitulated. The licence scheme was abandoned. The coach brought the tired drivers back to the track. Piquet's first sight was Ecclestone standing agitated on the curb. Ecclestone darted towards his driver, grabbed his shirt and screamed, 'Go to a doctor and he'll tell you you're not fit to drive.' The driver was equally determined to defend his championship. For ninety minutes, the two argued. 'Listen, sunshine,' said Ecclestone having recovered his self-control, 'Sit out the practice. I'm not putting up with this. You're not driving.' Piquet's response was truculent: 'If you don't let me drive in the qualifying session which starts in fifteen minutes, you'll have broken my contract and I'm off.' Silenced for a brief moment, Ecclestone surrendered. 'Right, get in,' he said.

The season started badly and deteriorated. To gain aerodynamic advantages the teams were cheating with fuels, weight, suspension and the wings. In retaliation against a ban on Piquet and other drivers by the FIA's stewards, Ecclestone organised a FOCA boycott of the race in Imola in March. Only Tyrrell ignored their conspiracy, straining the relationship between himself and Ecclestone. Two weeks later Gilles Villeneuve, a popular Canadian driver, was killed racing in Belgium. Then, after another fatal crash on the track, Piquet won in Canada, only to lose his lead in Germany after another driver caused a crash and was rewarded by a punch in the face from Piquet. Ecclestone appeared to be immune to the carnage. 'When a driver dies,' he explained later, 'he goes out doing what he wants to do. I don't find that depressing at all.' Others were affected by the misery and deaths, especially Colin Chapman. 'Formula One', said Chapman in a coded complaint about Ecclestone, 'has degenerated into power struggles and political manoeuvrings between manipulators attempting to make more money out of the sport than they put in.' The future, he warned, was blighted by a 'quagmire of plagiarism, chicanery and petty rule interpretations'. Outbursts, in Ecclestone's reckoning, revealed weakness. Chapman, he knew, was losing his grip over Lotus and the company was heading towards insolvency. Ecclestone lent Lotus £100,000 but it was too late. On 16 December 1982 Chapman died of a heart attack, aged fifty-four, probably provoked by his partnership with John DeLorean, a dishonest American businessman who had defrauded the British government with his futuristic sports car factory in Belfast. Ecclestone went to the funeral, amused by the congregation's speculation that Chapman had staged his own death to hide abroad and avoid inevitable imprisonment. The unpredictability of Chapman's demise was just one among hundreds of incidents during the year which made Ecclestone's life in Formula One quite extraordinary. Another incident was a chance encounter at Monza in September.

During his frequent journeys to the circuits, Ecclestone rarely travelled with Tuana but rather with Sandra, the Brazilian daughter of a banker whom he had met on Concorde. Finding successive new women was easy for those associated with Formula One, and the owner of the sport was attractive to the 'pit popsies', especially in South America. His passive relationship with Tuana suited his lifestyle until he spotted a twenty-three-year-old, six-foot-tall Croatian model standing in the pit with Nelson Piquet. Employed by Fila fashions, one of the race's sponsors, Slavica Malic had been invited to the Monza track by Monty Shadow, a Croatian photographer, well known for introducing models to drivers and team principals. 'Get out of here,' Ecclestone ordered the model. 'I'm staying here,' she replied brusquely. 'It's my duty.' 'I don't care. No girls in the pits. Out!' insisted Ecclestone. Reluctantly Slavica moved to a nearby wall. Even the sight of an attractive woman standing on a wall offended Ecclestone's eye for tidiness. 'Off,' he ordered. 'If you come any nearer, I'll kick you,' she retorted. Attracted by the feisty woman, Ecclestone introduced himself and offered her a Coke in his motorhome. Understanding no English, she agreed but insisted on bringing a Dutch model to translate. At the end of a stilted conversation, Ecclestone asked for a telephone number. Reluctantly, Slavica wrote down some random figures. After she disappeared, Ecclestone discovered the number was wrong but, with the help of the local police, had the right number at the end of the day. By then Malic had returned to Shadow's home, a converted monastery outside Milan. 'I met this guy who was trying to break my balls,' said Slavica, 'and he said he's in charge of Formula One. Do you think it's true?' The telephone call to arrange lunch the following day confirmed Ecclestone's attraction to the opinionated street survivor. Tuana was a loyal friend who submitted to Ecclestone's domination but Slavica was the opposite – fiery, fun and a challenge. The twenty-eight-year age-gap and the twelve-inch height difference was not a barrier to a relationship. 'Come to Las Vegas next week,' he suggested. With Shadow's frantic help, Slavica obtained a visa and arrived for the season's last race. Making her way beside Ecclestone to a vast suite at Caesar's Palace, she felt conscious of 'dirty looks' thrown in her direction for being with a man half her size and old enough to be her father. There was added reason for her to be wary. A recent newspaper profile described Ecclestone as 'a mysterious figure . . . at the centre of so much intrigue' and 'the subject of lurid speculation'. The 'mystery' was compounded by Ecclestone's unwillingness to provide accurate biographical details to newspapers. A recent profile in *The Times* wrongly asserted that he had been awarded a BSc in chemical engineering, his car dealing was described as a 'hobby', there was confusion about his racing career and even his age was depicted as 'unknown'. Maintaining misunderstandings, Ecclestone believed, enhanced his control.

During dinner with Jackie Stewart, John Frankenheimer and Ecclestone, the Croatian was silently assimilated into

Ecclestone's kingdom. At the end of the race the following day – the conclusion of a disastrous season for Piquet and Brabham – Ecclestone and Malic returned to Europe and supposedly to their separate lives – in London and Milan. Thanks to Shadow, she was given a contract by Armani, and thanks to Ecclestone she was to be introduced to unlimited luxury. He landed in a helicopter in the garden of Shadow's home to start a turbulent relationship that would last twenty-five years. Her innate anger was one of her attractions.

At the beginning of the 1983 season in Brazil, Ecclestone met Malic in São Paulo. Determined to win the world championship again, Murray had calculated a new ruse to undermine FIA's regulations. To accommodate Ferrari's heavier car using a turbo engine, FIA stipulated that a car's weight could not be less than 580 kilogrammes. To make the Brabham lighter than permitted under the regulations and therefore faster, Murray modified the car's weight by fitting additional water tanks 'to cool the brakes'. The tanks were full when the car was weighed by FIA's stewards before the race and emptied as the race progressed. At the end, and before the car was reweighed by the stewards, the water tanks would be filled up again. The subterfuge worked perfectly in the first race. Piquet won. Naturally, Ecclestone did not see the victory, nor did he celebrate with Piquet that night. 'Bernie and Slavica', Piquet told his girlfriend, 'are fighting like hell.' He added, 'Bernie takes no shit from anyone but he takes it from that woman.' In Piquet's opinion the Croatian was difficult, cold, loud and even inelegant. He could not understand his employer's interest but Ecclestone enjoyed the spirited fun offered by a powerful, tall woman.

The challenge was similar to winning the world championship for a second time and the odds became unexpectedly stacked in his favour after Balestre rejected complaints about the water ruse by suspicious rivals. Ecclestone was truly blessed by his new friendship with Balestre. Although Formula One was mired in wars about all kinds of technicalities, Ecclestone and Balestre had grown to share a special understanding about FIA's powers to control speed and safety. Playing to Balestre's vanity, Ecclestone negotiated around the sanctions, appeals and hearings in Paris to win an advantage while Piquet and Alain Prost, a French driver in a Renault, fought ferociously on the track. Towards the end of the season, Prost was in the lead but at Monza in September Piquet snatched victory, electrifying the Brabham team. Few believed the victory was honest. Renault and Ferrari protested that Brabham was illegally adding chemicals to enhance the fuel's octane. 'Everyone knows that the fuel used by Piquet's Brabham was not legal,' Prost complained. Again Ecclestone avoided sanctions by persuading Balestre that the additives were not outlawed by FIA's regulations. 'He doesn't want to fight us,' Mosley told Ecclestone. 'Too many senior FIA members support us against him.'

In a thrilling finale, the world championship would be decided at the last race in Kyalami. Using the same fuel, Piquet was leading to win the world championship for the second time when Prost retired. Assured of the championship, Piquet slowed down and allowed his Brabham team mate, Riccardo Patrese, to pass and win. 'I don't pay drivers to lose races,' cursed Ecclestone. With the championship confirmed, all the protests were shunted aside except one from Gordon Murray. The designer wanted his reward for success. 'What's happened to the sale?' asked Murray, referring to his previous request for more money, spurned by Ecclestone's promise that they would divide the spoils after Brabham's imminent sale. 'Fell through,' replied Ecclestone. 'I want my money,' said Murray, demanding a huge pay hike to put him level with his rivals. Ecclestone hated being dependent on a designer but reluctantly agreed. He was after all on the threshold of a new bonanza.

Under the Concorde agreement FOCA controlled Formula One's television rights. In 1982, without consulting Balestre, Ecclestone established FOCA TV. Before the beginning of the following season, his contracts with the circuits included a new clause assigning the television rights for the Formula One race to FOCA. The same year, he also signed on behalf of Formula One a three-year deal with the European Broadcasting Union (EBU), a non-profit agency representing ninety-two national television broadcasters across the world including the BBC and the equivalent broadcasters in every European country. In return for the EBU's guarantee that every broadcaster buying Formula One would agree to show the entire race, Ecclestone pledged that all the teams would compete. With the certainty that the advertisements on the cars and the hoardings would appear on the television screens for at least two hours, Formula One had reached a turning point. Sponsors were guaranteed lengthy exposure and the public's awareness of Formula One would grow, multiplying the sponsors' fees to the teams.

Ecclestone did not appreciate the full potential spin-off from the EBU agreement until the BBC refused to broadcast the poor-quality pictures offered by some national television companies, including those from Spa in Belgium. Ecclestone's remedy was to build his own television production area at Chessington. FOCA TV planned to transmit pictures from Ecclestone's own trackside cameras from the Spa circuit to the EBU for dispatch to their members. The next step, Ecclestone gradually realised, would be to eliminate the EBU and directly supply Chessington's pictures to the broadcasters. His tactics, throwing up problems but potentially profitable solutions, were almost by chance producing a strategy to transform a minority sport into a global attraction. Under the EBU contract, advertisements were not allowed between the camera and the cars. Ecclestone approved that rule. The advertisers' tarpaulins hanging over the trackside fences had always upset him. Formula One, he was convinced, needed the sleek image associated with organised entertainment. Although he had no patience for marketing executives – he would never employ a public relations representative – he was inspired by Mark McCormack's success at Wimbledon. He wanted to offer the circuit owners better-quality advertising, provided by the sponsors, matching his passion for perfection. His idea coincided with an approach by Paddy McNally, a smooth forty-two-year-old Englishman employed over the previous ten years by John Hogan at Philip Morris. McNally suggested to Ecclestone that he leave Philip Morris and, as the circuits' agent, sell the advertising and provide hospitality for the sponsors.

McNally was not Ecclestone's natural soulmate. A middle-class boy, McNally's motor experience was limited to working in the scrap car business and as a rally driver. After school he had abandoned training as an accountant to sell vacuum cleaners on hire purchase door-to-door in Blackpool and Wigan, traded bric-a-brac off a stall in the Portobello Road and was then employed as a journalist on *Autosport* magazine in 1963. As a lucrative sideline at the magazine he had exploited the opportunity to study before the readers the 'motors for sale' columns, picking the best deals to trade cars across Europe. After ten years he had earned a substantial amount and, seeking prestige and comfort, he briefly joined Firestone in Rome before he was hired in 1973 by Philip Morris in Switzerland to promote Marlboro cigarettes. For nine years he had travelled around the race circuits and become dismayed by the crude environment. The solution, he told Ecclestone, was for the circuits to adopt the model used by FIFA for the football World Cup. He wanted to buy from the circuits the exclusive rights to sell their advertising and hospitality and resell both at a higher price. The hospitality would be similar to the enclosures at Ascot, Henley and Wimbledon. The attraction for Ecclestone was not only McNally's ambition to improve the circuits' appearance but the chance of absolute control. In 1983 McNally offered a share in his new company, Allsport Management, based at Geneva airport, to some FOCA teams. In unison they declined. Ecclestone was delighted. He would retain control by forging an arrangement between his company, Formula One Management (FOM) and Allsport. McNally would pay Ecclestone a fee for the right to sell advertising and hospitality at Formula One events contracted by Ecclestone on behalf of FOCA.

McNally's concept first took shape in March 1984 as the 'Paddock Club' at the races in France, Belgium and Austria. During the first year McNally lost credibility. 'What's that sign doing there?' Ecclestone screamed about an unattractive advertisement at the first race. 'Get Williams's double-decker bus out of the circuit,' he cursed, meaning the team's traditional hospitality centre. 'This isn't Ascot,' Frank Williams protested to Ecclestone. 'It needs to be,' was the reply. McNally, some observed, was being 'treated like dirt' by Ecclestone. 'It's lucky,' they were reminded, 'Bernie doesn't control the air we breathe.' At the end of the first year McNally announced he was quitting. 'I've lost too much money,' he told Ecclestone. 'I'd go on a bit longer,' Ecclestone advised. 'It's cost so much already and you've put a lot into it, so try harder.' The mild-mannered McNally obeyed. During 1985 his fortunes turned. Sponsors were attracted by the hospitality and advertising increased.

McNally's operation gave Ecclestone the chance personally to govern access to the Paddock and the pits, rejecting applications from those he disliked, especially critical journalists. 'Bernard likes to encourage the view that he's controlling everything,' grumbled Frank Williams, 'and that a leaf doesn't fall in Abyssinia without his approval.'

Supervising access to the Paddock personified Ecclestone's creeping monopolisation of the contracts and personalities within Formula One. Nothing and nobody was allowed to impede his will, even in death. In August 1984, just before the Austrian Grand Prix, Herbie Blash told Ecclestone that David Yorke, a sixty-year-old who had brokered Brabham's contract with Martini, had died in a local hotel. Soon after, Blash confided to Brabham's transport manager that Ecclestone, fearful of Yorke's death complicating the team's departure, had ordered, 'Stick Yorke in the transporter and we'll take him home after the race.' The driver, obviously worried by the order but equally fearful of displeasing Ecclestone, asked incredulously, 'In the back of the transporter?' 'Either in the back or in the front with you and when you get to Dover you can say he's asleep.' 'But if he's in the back, he's not on the carnet,' said the driver searching for an escape. 'He's covered in the carnet,' replied Blash, 'under "bodywork".' Eventually, the driver realised it was a joke but Ecclestone's black humour encouraged widespread fear of him. In 'Bernie's Kingdom' he was the fulcrum on which every move turned – both physically and legally. His unwillingness to delegate irritated Phil Lines, his television producer, who resigned. Inevitably there was a dispute about severance pay. After repeated protests, Ecclestone paid his debt with an Alfa Romeo saloon car and promptly forgot another questioning employee.

Ecclestone's perfectionism and McNally's success provoked the teams at the end of 1985 to complain about the Paddock's prices and the restrictions on access. Keen for a fight to confirm his supremacy, Ecclestone countered that the Paddock Club would be closed. As he anticipated, the teams protested that Paddock hospitality must be kept open for their sponsors despite prices rising to $500 for the race day. The steep prices matched Ecclestone's image of the sport as the ultimate choice of entertainment for Hollywood's stars including, among the new visitors to the Paddock and Ecclestone's motorhome, George Harrison, the Beatle. Formula One was edging towards a professional business but a major obstacle remained.

In Ecclestone's world, there were celebrities, friends and deals. If any three came together, profit was always the priority, as McNally discovered after Ecclestone decided that his junior partner should not pocket all his new earnings. Instead, he was ordered to become the promoter of the unprofitable Dutch, Austrian and French Grand Prix. All three risked closure, as Ecclestone announced. His initiative to threaten the French Grand Prix was calculated to instigate a new conflict with Balestre to resolve one critical uncertainty – the legal ownership of Formula One. Ecclestone now realised that without legal ownership his plans and potential fortune were at risk. In the absence of a binding contract entrusting indisputable possession of Formula One to Ecclestone, Balestre assumed that FIA owned the Grand Prix, an opinion shared by all the teams, circuits and broadcasters, with the sole exception of Ecclestone. Rather than confront Balestre, Ecclestone silently exploited the uncertainties by acting as Formula One's legal owner, especially during his negotiations with the circuits. Offended by that posture Balestre protested, only to be squeezed by Ecclestone's casual mention about the possibility of the FOCA teams not racing in France, or the likely closure of the French Grand Prix. The ultimate threat, Ecclestone knew, was intolerable for FIA's president who enjoyed parading around the event with friends and national politicians.

To pacify the Frenchman's outrage about this latest challenge, Ecclestone simultaneously fed Balestre's passion for an ermine lifestyle including private planes and chauffeured limousines. Together they enjoyed the mutually profitable stand-off until a major difference erupted in 1985. To stymie Ecclestone's progress, Balestre reintroduced the ban on skirts. Intentionally, his edict coincided with the expiry of FOCA's television contract with FIA. Ecclestone wanted the television agreement renewed for five years in return for a total payment of 11.2 million Swiss francs. Balestre offered a comprehensive deal if FOCA's latest threat to boycott the French Grand Prix was lifted. Ecclestone agreed. The race was won by Nelson Piquet, Brabham's only victory that year in a season dominated as in 1984 by McLaren. The following day Ecclestone met Balestre in Marseille to seal the deal. Ecclestone was reassured by Balestre's cheerful acceptance of all his proposals and by his promise of better cooperation between FOCA and FIA. Soon after leaving Marseille, Ecclestone discovered he had been duped. The Marseille agreement to permit skirts, Balestre announced, was dead. But in compensation Balestre renewed the television contract. 'Don't get mad, get even,' Ecclestone consoled himself. No one understood just how profitable the television rights had become.

6

Coup

'Marriage', Ecclestone frequently told his friends, 'is like going to the nick. Not very exciting.' He enjoyed repeating his mantra, 'If it flies, floats or fucks, rent it.' Despite his reservations, in 1985 Slavica Malic demanded that Ecclestone commit himself to her. The pressure had started the previous year, one month before she was due to give birth to a child in June 1984. The circumstances were not romantic.

In the aftermath of their affair in Brazil, Ecclestone had returned to his penthouse in London to continue his normal life with Tuana. Their seventeen-year relationship appeared untroubled but in May 1984 everything changed. 'I have to tell you something,' said Ecclestone soon after returning home. Over the next minutes he revealed his affair and mentioned that the Croatian woman was pregnant. 'She says that if I do not live with her, she will go back to Croatia and I won't see the child,' explained Ecclestone and burst into tears. Tuana, also in tears, sobbed stoically, 'You cannot have been happy with me. So go away and be happy with her. I wish you all the happiness.' Ecclestone cried loudly, 'She told me that she couldn't have children.' Tuana finally abandoned her demure manner. In an impassioned outburst based on anguish rather than any facts, she cried out, 'She's blackmailing you. Do you think she would be pregnant if you were Herbie Blash?' she asked referring to Brabham's loyal engineer. Eventually some calm was restored. Ecclestone got up and straightened the paintings and curtains, as he always did. 'I didn't know you wanted children,' she sobbed. Ecclestone was silent. He hoped to have a son, she believed. Over the following days, until he flew to the Grand Prix in America, the two continued to live together.

While in America Ecclestone heard that Slavica had given birth to a daughter, who would be called Tamara. He flew directly to Italy. In the hospital in Milan Slavica made it clear that either they set up home together in London or she would take her daughter to Croatia, beyond Ecclestone's reach. Looking at the highly strung woman, Ecclestone recognised a tough game of poker. He tried not to reveal his feelings but he did not want to lose contact with his new child. He was reluctant to upset his comfortable arrangement in London but, while regretting not having children with Tuana, consoled himself, 'She didn't ask and I was too busy.'

On other hand, he was attracted to the challenge of the strong, opinionated woman, remembering his mother's strict control over their home and his father. One reservation might have been how little he knew about the fiery woman's past. Because she spoke no English, he only knew that Slavica Malic had been born into comparative poverty in Rijeka on 25 May 1958 and that her father, a docker, had abandoned the family in her childhood. He was unaware that during her teenage years she had been imprisoned for stealing and that, after her release, she had posed for nude photographs. 'I did some stupid things,' she would later explain. 'You know how it goes. You are in a photographer's studio and he says, "Can you just undo that button?" But I needed the money.' Monty Shadow, with his knowledge of Malic, could have told Ecclestone the stories but was not asked. Some of Ecclestone's oldest friends including Ron Shaw would believe that Shadow supported Malic's demand that Ecclestone set up home with her in London. Ecclestone would only admit to his friends, 'I wasn't very happy with the idea.'

Still unable to decide between Tuana and Slavica, Ecclestone telephoned Ann Jones. Clearly worried, he explained that Slavica was reluctant to allow him access to the child unless they lived together. Jones was in hospital recovering from a hysterectomy but despite this, realising that he was relying on her, she replied that the relationship might be a good idea. Ecclestone was persuaded. He flew to London and ended his relationship with Tuana. He decided to abandon all his collections, including the valuable Japanese artworks because 'it wasn't good for me to take them'. With just a suitcase and his black briefcase, he crossed the river to a newly purchased flat in Chelsea. Days later Ecclestone and Slavica arrived at Ann Jones's hospital bed with their baby and some flowers. While they were talking, Jones noticed that Tuana was arriving. When she saw the other visitors, Tuana silently and sadly retreated.

Ecclestone's new home with Slavica and their baby was a flat at Pier House in Oakley Street. After buying an adjoining flat Ecclestone applied for permission to merge the two. The application was denied but the party wall mysteriously disintegrated and, after repairs, the three lived in the large apartment. At the same time, in May 1985, Ecclestone bought a nine-storey black glass-fronted block in Princes Gate, opposite Hyde Park, from Adnan Khashoggi, the flamboyant Saudi arms dealer famous for his sex orgies. Initially Ecclestone denied to enquiring journalists that he had any connection with the house and the reports that he was paying contractors in cash to rip out evidence of Khashoggi's hedonism – a sliding roof above Khashoggi's bed which opened the bedroom to the stars, marble bathrooms and mirrors.

Slavica Malic enjoyed her new lifestyle. In May 1985 they had flown in Ecclestone's plane with Ron Shaw to Monaco for the Grand Prix. Preoccupied with business, Ecclestone did not seem happy until he crossed the square from the Hôtel de Paris to the casino. And he was not unhappy, even when he lost about £250,000 playing roulette. The following day he sat in his motorhome and, long before the race ended and before Piquet's Brabham pulled out of the race, he urged his party to head for the helicopters to return to Nice airport. Clutching his briefcase he herded Sean Connery, Gordon Murray, Shaw and Slavica towards the helipad. After two fully laden helicopters had departed, Ecclestone was at the front of the queue. As the third helicopter was about to be filled, the dispatcher said to two people who had just arrived, 'You're next.' 'Hang on,' said Ecclestone, 'we've been waiting longer than these people.' 'Yes,' replied the woman, 'but you're not the king of Sweden.' In future, Ecclestone resolved, he would hire his own helicopter.

Ron Shaw's report to the Saturday crowd of Ecclestone'a friends, the car dealers, bookies and the shirtmaker – which was now meeting at Fortnum & Mason on Piccadilly – reflected on his bewilderment about their friend's relationship with Slavica. Every night Ecclestone telephoned Tuana and, in tears, confessed his unhappiness. 'Bernard has a problem,' Tony Morris volunteered, 'and Tuana's worried.' Tuana had called, he explained, and revealed her visit to a clairvoyant on the Kings Road to explain her concern. The psychic described images of crashing heavy metal, tears and a man's death if he did not stop crying. Morris relayed Tuana's story to Ecclestone, who suppressed his feelings. Slavica Malic was unable to control hers. Volatile and occasionally tearful, their arguments continued in spite of the birth of their daughter. She seemed to have smitten a man who instinctively crushed any opposition, but who appeared to be unable to resist her particular potency. He had even stopped buying shirts from Frank after Slavica protested, 'Shit shirts, darling,' and refused to iron them. Her aggression, others assumed, was a veneer for insecurity. She telephoned Ann Jones repeatedly to ask about Ecclestone's relationship with female employees. She was particularly suspicious about a secretary who had flown with Ecclestone in his private plane. 'Are they having an affair?' she asked. 'Not as far as I know,' Ann Jones replied. But that did not protect the woman from dismissal. As Slavica's complaints increased and her demand for security grew, Ecclestone relented and agreed to marry.

The two arrived at 11.30 a.m. on 17 July 1985 at the Chelsea and Kensington Register Office on the Kings Road. One week earlier Ecclestone had asked Max Mosley to be a witness. 'I couldn't find anyone else,' he later explained, 'and Max wasn't doing anything.' Mosley arrived with his Colombian housekeeper to be the second witness. Discovering that she did not understand English, the registrar declared that she was disqualified. 'You'll have to wait for a few minutes,' Ecclestone told the registrar. 'Max is calling his secretary to get over here fast.' After the ceremony the four stood on the street. No photographer had been hired and Ecclestone naturally had avoided any thought of a party. 'We should have lunch to celebrate,' said the thirty-two-year-old bride standing in perilously high-heeled shoes and a skimpy miniskirt. 'OK,' agreed Ecclestone morosely, 'we'll try Langan's.' Jumping out of his car as they reached the Piccadilly restaurant, Ecclestone was told no tables were available. 'Right, I'm off to the office,' he told his new wife. 'See you later. Take a cab home.' The wedding was not a treasured moment.

At home on her own the new Mrs Ecclestone cursed her husband's work ethic – and his simple tastes. There were no fine wines in their cellar, just Beck's beer in the fridge. There were no delicacies from London's great food shops because her husband was happiest with egg and toast covered with brown sauce. She had seen how he quietly cared for employees, photographers, mechanics and any others he knew had fallen on hard times, paying for doctors or to mitigate unexpected poverty – all given without a fuss. But for her there was no demonstrable love. His modesty was tormenting. The Saturday circle was also puzzled, not about the absence of an invitation to the wedding of a private man, but that such a hard-headed dealer should succumb to a mid-life crisis and decide to marry. The two of them seemed so different. Over a bottle of champagne they ribbed Ecclestone, 'You're the one who always said: "If it flies, floats or fucks, rent it." ' Ecclestone tolerated the cynics who quipped that he and Slavica were the same height once Bernie was standing on his wallet. In his own way, he loved Slavica and was thrilled to be a father again with another chance to build a home life. 'She's good-hearted and calls the shots as they are,' he said in a moment of self-indulgence before switching back to business.

To sever his relationship with Tuana, he had bought a house for her in Kensington. Jeffrey Archer, the novelist, living in a flat below theirs on the Albert Embankment, heard that the penthouse was for sale. Realising that if he made a bid, Ecclestone would push the price above £3 million, Archer called in a favour owed to him by Ron Shaw. Five years earlier Archer had, at the last moment, rescued Shaw by agreeing to speak at a charity dinner organised by Shaw. 'I owe you a favour, big time,' Shaw had said afterwards, 'and we Cockneys keep our word.'

'I'm calling in that favour,' Archer told Shaw in a telephone call. 'I want you to buy the flat from Bernie, probably for about £2 million and then sell it to me. I'll save a lot of money.' 'He'll kill me,' exclaimed Shaw with obvious fear.

'He'll cut my legs off.' Archer insisted. Shaw made the offer and then panicked. Ecclestone smelled a rat. 'You're sharp,' Ecclestone told Archer who explained the background to the deception.

'It's yours for £2.2 million,' offered Ecclestone. 'Done,' said Archer, benefiting from a rare moment of commercial weakness. (The apartment is now worth over £20 million.)

In Ecclestone's world, to recognise any talent or express gratitude, especially to a driver, was destructive. It could expose weakness. In the eternal power struggle, his permanent truculence against society affected his attitude towards everyone, including Nelson Piquet. In 1985 Piquet was ambitious to win another world championship but was disgruntled with the Brabham and disenchanted with Ecclestone. The fault was partly Murray's but also the new BMW engine which Ecclestone admitted 'has blown up so many times that I can't count. It's a shambles to say the least.' In Piquet's opinion Ecclestone was no longer interested in developing his cars. He had lost Michelin's sponsorship but had struck a good deal with Pirelli, even though he believed the Italian tyres were inferior. Ecclestone's execution of the deal had been clever: while keeping the loss of Michelin's sponsorship secret, he had told the Italian corporation, 'I'm unhappy with Michelin, would you be interested in sponsoring Brabham?' Pirelli agreed to supply free tyres.

The sponsorship pleased Ecclestone, but the result undermined Piquet's chance of winning races. Early leads were lost as his Brabham broke down and, even when he passed the chequered flag for victory in Canada, he felt scorching pain as burning oil dripped on to his foot. The short-term cure while continuing to race had been to wrap his foot with ice. He blamed Gordon Murray, who was away, travelling with George Harrison on meditation holidays. 'Brabham', complained Piquet, 'is falling apart.' 'Gordon is being strange,' Ecclestone agreed. The remedy was to spend more money but, regardless of Brabham's value and Piquet's importance, Ecclestone complained that his annual losses were already £1 million and declared, 'I'm not wasting any more money.' Negotiations to settle Piquet's demand for a pay increase were stalled by Ecclestone's refusal to concede even a small amount. No matter how much he needed Piquet, he could not tolerate someone squeezing a better deal. Piquet was, at the same time, secretly negotiating a contract with Frank Williams but loyalty required an amicable divorce and even Ecclestone's blessing. At the last race of the season in Austria, Piquet suggested that he was being lured by Ron Dennis and McLaren. Quickly, Ecclestone persuaded Dennis that under no circumstances could Piquet be offered more than Ecclestone was paying. Satisfied that he had trounced Piquet, Ecclestone gave his approval for his driver to leave Brabham. To Ecclestone's surprise, Piquet walked straight into Williams's pit. 'You get paid so little by Bernie', commented Piquet, 'that you have to get something else out of it – and I wanted the world championship.'

The following year, 1986, Ecclestone arrived in Brazil for the year's first race and watched Piquet win in a Williams, the start of a ferociously competitive season between the Brazilian, Prost and Nigel Mansell. Ecclestone ignored the impact of Piquet's departure on the Brabham team and cast around for a replacement. His sponsors, BMW, Pirelli and Olivetti, demanded an international star and the best available was Niki Lauda. The Austrian had retired for the third time after winning his third world championship in 1984 for McLaren because of unhappiness with Ron Dennis who, he believed, was 'a grumpy man on the point of making a lifelong enemy'. Lauda was tempted by Ecclestone's $6 million offer to drive for one season, although Ecclestone would say that he refused Lauda's demand for £5.5 million. The contradictions after the event obscured the reason for their disagreement: 'Bernie', said Lauda, 'left the follow-up of being nice and friendly too late.' Finally, he chose Elio de Angelis, the twenty-seven-year-old Italian and former Lotus driver.

Fending off Ecclestone's bickering comments, Murray was redesigning the Brabham to remedy recent disappointments. Ever since Ecclestone had responded to Colin Chapman's criticism that the Brabham was 'too long' and had unilaterally chopped one foot off the car while Murray was on holiday, their mutual trust had slowly withered. In Ecclestone's opinion Murray's talent was fading and his self-confidence was low. Murray was still uncertain about his work when he took the car and driver in May 1986 to the Paul Ricard circuit near Marseille for tests. De Angelis, lying in an unusually near-horizontal position, was navigating around a bend at 180 miles an hour when a wing broke off. He lost control and crashed. He died instantly. Ecclestone was shocked.

'In retrospect it was totally my fault,' admitted Murray. 'It was a very, very radical car.' Murray was not only distraught but also disenchanted. Ecclestone had lost a good driver and now lost BMW's sponsorship. Without finding a replacement, there was insufficient money to develop the team. 'I was pissed off,' said Murray, 'and I could see he was pissed off.' 'He's gone off,' Ecclestone exclaimed, dissatisfied because he backed winners and Murray's latest ideas were duds. Their fourteen-year relationship crumbled. 'I said I was going to stop,' explained Murray, 'and he said, "Fine".'

Negotiating his departure package was the type of battle which Ecclestone never lost – even if there were ambiguities. Unwisely Murray had never secured a signed contract from Ecclestone. He had relied on Ecclestone's handshake. 'You own half the company,' Murray recalled Ecclestone saying, 'so you don't need cash now.' Ecclestone had promised Murray 'a share' in the company but disputed that he had quantified the size of the 'share'. Nor could they agree on Brabham's value. Not surprisingly, Ecclestone minimised its worth. Beating Ecclestone in negotiations was way beyond Murray's ability and, losing his patience, he finally accepted a pay-off of £30,000, far less than he thought reasonable. Minutes after his success, Ecclestone's memory about the details faded. By his credo, two grown men had reached a deal and it would be impolitic to mention the minutiae of the negotiations. Instead Ecclestone simply presented himself as generous by allowing Murray to take the Brabham car in which Piquet had won the 1982 world championship. 'What I've done I've done honestly and correctly,' said Ecclestone after Murray complained. 'I've never done anything bad to anyone in my life. I've never cheated anybody. If I do a deal, I don't need to write it down on paper. Everybody knows I won't go back.'

Murray was immediately hired by McLaren who, over the next two years, 1987 to 1989, won twenty-eight Grand Prix races.

Without Murray, a good driver and a reliable car, Ecclestone was becoming disillusioned. Balancing the requirements of drivers, engineers and sponsors required time and money. 'If a driver blows an engine,' Ecclestone complained, 'that was another sixty grand down the drain.' Life in the pits was also no longer fun. Colin Chapman was dead, Teddy Mayer had gone and was replaced by Ron Dennis, who irritated Ecclestone, and Frank Williams had just suffered appalling spinal injuries in a car crash in France causing permanent paralysis. Ecclestone also missed the charismatic drivers like Jochen Rindt and Carlos Pace. He liked some of the new 'fighting' drivers like Ayrton Senna and Nigel Mansell but the aura and romance of their dead predecessors was missing. 'Maybe', he speculated, 'it's the pressure or the money. Maybe it's my fault too. There is no room for failure. It's all about the quick and the dead.' Without his daily, twenty-four-hour attention to detail, Brabham's decline accelerated. In 1987 the team nearly came last in the championship and other sponsors announced their departure. He had reached a crossroads. Having been a racing driver, a team manager and the organiser of the FOCA teams, he was Formula One's unchallengeable expert. Developing Formula One as a global business was more profitable and interesting than caring about Brabham. He decided to sell the team. The eventual buyer, for over £5 million, in 1988 was Alfa Romeo, his tenants in south London. They quickly resold the team to Joachim Luthi, an investment manager who soon after was jailed in Switzerland for fraud. Chessington remained the centre of his Formula One television operation but Ecclestone's office moved to his black glass tower in Princes Gate.

The sale coincided with Max Mosley's return to Formula One. In 1986, unable to overcome the burden of his father Oswald's reputation, Mosley abandoned his political ambitions in the Conservative party and began searching for an alternative life. His quest coincided with Ecclestone's new ambitions. The timing was fortuitous. Mosley, the Oxford graduate and lawyer, understood institutions and was intrigued by political power, while Ecclestone was the unbeatable master of commercial deals. In conversations they agreed that by combining their talents they could change Formula One. 'The teams are not a good power base,' Mosley told Ecclestone. 'Ken Tyrrell's breaking of the strike at Imola showed that.' The boycott at Imola as part of the battle to control Formula One had nevertheless confirmed Ecclestone's authority and the circuit owners' weakness. Mosley suggested that their strategy should be to sideline the teams and oust Balestre. The two started to plot how they could grab control of FIA. They had to exploit Balestre's weaknesses.

'Max is kicking his heels and doing nothing,' Ecclestone told Balestre. 'You need someone who's not a clown. Why not hire him?' Balestre was suspicious. Ecclestone's advocacy of the general good always seemed to equate with his own self-interest. Eventually Balestre agreed that the two should fly to join him at his home in the south of France. To both visitors, their host at dinner was a risible sight. Bombastic self-importance clouded any rational judgement. Unlike his visitors who genuinely loved the sport, Balestre resembled a police chief interested in the power and perks of office. Stroking his vanity, his visitors knew, would inflate his vulnerability to Ecclestone's that Mosley should be appointed his accomplice in FIA. Eventually, holding his head in his hands and grumbling, 'It's wrong', Balestre conceded. 'Max should be the president of FIA's Manufacturer's Commission,' suggested Ecclestone, suppressing a smile. 'Yes,' replied Balestre. FIA's members, he knew, would oppose the nomination but democracy could be ignored, even when the vote against Mosley was overwhelming. Balestre simply appointed Mosley and used his relationships to placate the opposition.

Silkily, Mosley ingratiated himself with Balestre as a confidant. Unburdening himself, Balestre admitted to Mosley that Ecclestone was uncontrollable. Formula One, he feared, might break away from FIA. 'What can I do?' he asked. 'Let me think about that,' replied Mosley, 'and find a solution.' After consulting Ecclestone, Mosley suggested that Balestre should adopt the traditional British Establishment's method of neutralising its critics. Ecclestone should be appointed head of FIA's promotions. '*Bonne idée*,' roared Balestre, oblivious to the Trojan horse sitting opposite. Two other former Brabham employees – Charlie Whiting and Herbie Blash – were also infiltrated into FIA. With added bravado, Ecclestone and Mosley arrived by helicopter at Silverstone for the Grand Prix. As they landed they wrecked tents and caused mayhem. This was now their turf. Complainants would be ignored.

Although appointed by Balestre to be responsible for promoting all of the world's motor sports, Ecclestone was only interested in the development of Formula One. His ambition was clear: to turn an enthusiast's sport into a global business. While speaking about 'The Show' and adopting the jargon of the entertainment business, conjuring images to excite television viewers to sigh 'I'd love to be there' as the cameras panned over Monaco's yachts or the Barcelona waterfront, the reality remained undefined. The show, spectacular for spectators at some tracks, was less impressive on television screens. Some organisers refused to match his demands. The circuits in France, Belgium and Britain were ordered to improve. Only the British refused. Ecclestone wanted the RAC to choose between Brands Hatch and Silverstone – and remove the dirt. The RAC, disdainful of Ecclestone, refused. Like the FOCA teams and the circuit organisers, the RAC's executives did not understand Ecclestone's vision, not least because he failed to volunteer much information.

Ecclestone needed sixteen races to fulfil his contract with the EBU. In Austria, Argentina, Brazil and the USA race organisers reported that financial problems threatened their race. Ecclestone's solution was a personal investment in return for a share of any profits. Gambling without knowing whether 1,000 or 100,000 spectators would turn up, he demanded in return that the advertising and hospitality rights were assigned to Allsport. The Nürburgring managers refused so Ecclestone moved the race to Hockenheim. At the Spa circuit in Belgium, Ecclestone had negotiated 'ownership' of the Formula One race for ten years at no cost, and kept the income from the gate receipts, the catering and even the lavatories. His offer of relief from financial disaster to other circuits was conditional. As the television audiences grew, he received requests from circuits across the globe to stage Formula One races. Loss-makers like Holland and Austria were only briefly tolerated. There was little warning about the ultimate sanction of terminating an agreement. In Ecclestone's lexicon, talk was pointless. 'The trouble with people in our business', he explained at the time, 'is that they'll never face up to reality. They're all chasing bloody dreams and myths. There ain't nothing special about our business. Nothing at all. It's all facts.' Those seeking a meeting were told, 'I don't need to see you, I only need to talk to you.' Those seeking to procrastinate were given an ultimatum, 'Let's not have a meeting, let's have a decision.'

Ecclestone's skills were proven by the success of the Australian Grand Prix in Adelaide in 1985. He had decided to move the race from Melbourne after John Bannon, the premier of South Australia, had flown to England in 1984 to meet Ecclestone over lunch at the Star pub in Chessington. The deal was quickly concluded: the centre of Adelaide would be temporarily transformed into a race track. The result – a four-day street party for over 300,000 people – was to be spectacular.

Next in the queue seeking a Formula One race were communist-bloc countries. Leonid Brezhnev, Russia's leader, was an enthusiastic collector of western cars, including a Ferrari and a Rolls-Royce. Officials in the Kremlin suggested to Ecclestone that a Grand Prix could be staged in Moscow. Nothing was concluded before Brezhnev's death in 1982. 'Then the city's mayor', said Ecclestone, laughing as he remembered, 'wanted us to race across the cobblestones in Red Square and put the whole deal through his wife's bank accounts.' Instead, Ecclestone spent three years negotiating with Hungary's communist government. Initiated by Tamas Rohonyi, the Hungarian-born organiser of the Brazilian Grand Prix, the negotiations reached their climax on a Danube steamer. Over lunch the minister responsible whispered to Rohonyi, 'Are you sure it will work?' 'Yes, why?' asked Rohonyi. 'Because if it doesn't, I'll be shot.' Despite freezing snow, the circuit in Budapest was completed by May 1986. From across eastern Europe 240,000 spectators arrived to experience western culture in a communist country, three years before the fall of the Berlin Wall. During that visit, Ecclestone heard of a silver auction in Budapest. The beautifully crafted artefacts were cheap for dollars. As the auction progressed, Ecclestone was tugged from behind. 'Please stop bidding,' beseeched a wizened rabbi. 'All that silver you're bidding for was stolen from synagogues during the Holocaust.' Ecclestone let the rabbi bid unchallenged. The following day, as usual, he did not wait for the end of the Grand Prix. Before the last lap, he pushed everything into his briefcase and dashed with Mosley towards a helicopter. 'The only real luxury I afford myself', he would later say, 'is to chopper away straight after a race.' He missed Nelson Piquet win the race driving a Williams. The event's political and sporting success inevitably attracted criticism.

In a sport of unusual envy and rivalry, purists complained that the raw courage of a gladiatorial contest was being replaced by commercial packaging. Although the majority knew that no driver could survive at nearly 200 miles an hour without skill, daring and nerves of steel, Ecclestone's omnipotence spurred his enemies to spread rumours about the source of his fortune. Anti-Semites called him 'Ecclestein' and others accused him of pocketing FOCA's cash. This provoked him to sue successfully for libel, although seven years later he would forgetfully tell *The Times*, 'I never sue. It's because I'm religious. I was always taught to turn the other cheek.'

Few disputed that Formula One had benefited from his deals but the truth eluding the Formula One community was understanding precisely how Ecclestone had accumulated his power and wealth. Entrepreneurs used other people's money to finance their original ideas usually, but Ecclestone was using his own money to effect other people's ideas and no one could accurately assess how much he was earning. During the Cold War Kremlinologists were hired to interpret the sparse words spoken by Russia's leaders. Now, Formula One could have similarly analysed an Ecclestone riddle published by *The Times* in February 1988: 'The only obstacle to getting it right is people. Lots of people are frightened that they will lose power they think they have but probably don't have anyway.' Exploiting his opponents' weakness was the source of Ecclestone's fortune. One downside of his success was public interest about incidents which previously would have passed unnoticed.

In 1988 Balestre refused to penalise Ayrton Senna for deliberately crashing into Alain Prost in Japan in retaliation for an incident the previous year. Thanks to that deliberate shunt, the Brazilian would win the world championship. The link between FIA's 'justice', celebrities, speed, death and big money fed curiosity about the mastermind of the melodrama. Those seeking an explanation watched their target prowling around the Paddock with a briefcase supposedly stuffed with dollars until he disappeared into his new motorhome, the symbol of his power and dubbed 'The Kremlin'. Access to the grey, seemingly windowless, bus was electronically triggered from inside and only a few were invited to enter, not least because the owner resented visitors disturbing his office. Those who smoked were particularly unwelcome. The few admitted received no hospitality other than soft drinks. The rare interviewer inside the coach was presented with an enigma: a custodian who cajoled and threatened. 'I suppose I'm a bit like a headmaster,' he said. 'Problems happen and they have to be dealt with on the spot.' He aspired to present himself as a modern businessman espousing old-fashioned values. 'I carry out my business in a very unusual way. I don't like contracts. I like to be able to look someone in the eye and then shake them by the hand rather than do it the American way with ninety-two-page contracts that no one reads or understands. If I say I'll do something, I'll do it.' Yet somehow one newspaper interviewer, from the *Independent*, emerged with the distinct impression that Ecclestone had a degree in chemical engineering, and a strange quotation about his age: 'I am forty-seven, fourteen years older than my sister who says she is thirty-one.' In reality, he was fifty-eight. Few peered beyond the verbiage to understand that Formula One's development into a global business owed everything to two events: first, Ecclestone had soundly beaten Balestre and, second, he had halted the fragmentation of the sport, whereby each country presented a different spectacle. His new financial model in Europe and Australia compelled circuit owners to accept his standards and pay for everything, and, critically, receive no income except from the entry tickets.

'I would have taken the entry ticket money too if they'd let me,' said Ecclestone. The only major exception to the universality of his all-embracing suzerainty was America where, even at its best, Formula One was a minority attraction compared to the Indy and NASCAR (National Association for Stock Car Auto Racing) races. Denied any government support, circuit owners resisted Ecclestone's model because without profits they faced bankruptcy. He was strangely ambivalent about his inability to satisfy their requirements.

Watkins Glen, a successful venue since 1961, had expanded to keep pace with Ecclestone's demands but went bankrupt in 1981. His move to Las Vegas was unsuccessful. Under pressure from the teams and sponsors to succeed in the world's most lucrative market, he had signed contracts in Detroit and Dallas. Each race was handicapped by poor facilities and each circuit owner accused Ecclestone of greed, complaining that he creamed off the profits, a charge he did not convincingly deny. Unsympathetic to their complaints, he wanted the races to look better and earn more profits. To prove his argument, he moved the venue to Phoenix, Arizona. The inhabitants, he discovered, preferred to remain in their air-conditioned homes rather than sit in the blazing desert. On the race day, the circuit's stands were empty. He blamed the organisers for his financial losses. 'The people who do business in America seem to have failed to understand what a contract is and [to] respect it.' The FOCA teams were equally difficult. He lost interest. Formula One, he insisted, should not become Americanised. 'We're too sophisticated for American audiences. Their television coverage is like all-in wrestling.' The sport's expansion, he predicted, would be in the Far East. They have 'lots of money but they don't know what to do with it'. There was an unexpected symmetry as Ecclestone set out his vision of the future in the face of universal scepticism. Just at this time, the old order was passing away.

On Sunday 14 August 1988 Ecclestone was at his new house in Sardinia with Herbie Blash. Marco Piccinini called with the news that Enzo Ferrari had died. On Ferrari's own orders, he was to be buried before any public announcement but he had ordained that a few, including Ecclestone, were to be told immediately. Ecclestone was unusually sad about the Old Man's passing. For an hour he reminisced with Blash about what had been, in his opinion, a father-and-son relationship. In the evening he drove across to Silvio Berlusconi, a neighbour, for dinner. To Ecclestone's pleasure Italy's media magnate had clearly not been on Ferrari's shortlist.

Ecclestone's relationship with Berlusconi was critical to his next step. Formula One's worldwide popularity owed much to television but, he realised, he had sold the television rights to the EBU too cheap. In anticipation of signing the renewal of the Concorde agreement and on the expiry of the second EBU contract in 1990, he needed to recover control of the television rights. The EBU's managers had warned Ecclestone that their contract was the only one available. None of their members, they insisted, would negotiate separate agreements. Jonathan Martin, the BBC's head of sport, contradicted that self-interest of remaining united. Not only would the BBC break the EBU's monopoly but he was prepared to start the programmes thirty minutes before the race to allow Formula One's sponsors more exposure. Armed with the BBC's support, Ecclestone could negotiate separate agreements with every broadcaster. His good fortune was Balestre's ignorance about the value of the television rights and his knowledge was unlikely to improve. Since suffering a heart attack in November 1986, his grip over FIA had weakened.

Ecclestone himself did not fully understand the world of television beyond the EBU. He just knew that tycoons like Berlusconi had established networks to rival the state broadcasters and would pay more for popular programmes to attract viewers. His expert to navigate him into this new territory was Christian Vogt, a Swiss formerly employed by the EBU. Through his experience with them, Vogt enjoyed personal relationships that allowed him to negotiate television contracts with the three key countries – France, Italy and Germany. If he could secure exclusive deals, he believed, the rest of the world's broadcasters would follow. His selling pitch was not the race but the platform for advertisers – the chance of, incredibly, a potential 26 billion viewers. With that massive exposure, the value of the sponsorship was also certain to increase. To show the advertisements, the broadcasters were required by Ecclestone to transmit the complete Grand Prix live in peak time. Two hours of non-stop live television was offered as an magnet to broadcasters and advertisers. The organisation and energy required to complete the negotiations was impressive. This was no time for Warren Street-style short cuts. Even he did not anticipate what the deals would eventually unleash. In later years Ecclestone would quip, 'First get on, then get rich, then get honest.' He was still groping his way out of the first stage.

At the end of October 1990 Ecclestone was sixty. His staff at Chessington organised a surprise birthday party. He did not hide his disdain. At home his wife and their two daughters – Petra had been born in December 1988 – were ordered to ignore the anniversary. A few days later Sidney Ecclestone died, aged eighty-seven, of a heart attack. He had been sitting on a sofa holding his wife's hand and slipped away. Ecclestone went to the funeral service near St Albans with Slavica but did not enter the crematorium's chapel. Instead he walked around the grounds in an agitated state. His daughter Debbie believed that her father simply disliked funerals, an idea he fostered in order to conceal Slavica's demand that he did not sit with his eldest daughter.

Until two years earlier, Debbie and Slavica had enjoyed a good relationship. Debbie's regular visits and meals with her father and Tuana had continued with his new wife, and their children had played together in Chelsea or Debbie's home in Chislehurst. Debbie's husband had even ferried Slavica between Chelsea and Chislehurst. But soon after Petra's birth, Debbie had arrived unexpectedly at the Chelsea house. Without provocation Slavica had burst into a rage, screaming that Debbie was never to return. Thereafter she forbade her husband to meet his first daughter and, with little protest, Ecclestone agreed. It was as a result of that feud that Ecclestone had obeyed his wife's order that he shouldn't go into the crematorium. In a letter to Ann Jones two months later, Bertha Ecclestone revealed that her son and Slavica had nevertheless called at her house soon after.

'I was surprised that Bernard took his death so deeply,' she wrote, 'but I suppose seeing him in fairly good health it was a shock it came so quick.' Bertha added how her son 'has been so kind to me'. Ecclestone's failure to display emotion openly belied his sense of responsibility for his parents. He took his widowed mother to visit friends regularly and later paid for her care at home. His soft side may not have been visible to the Formula One fraternity, but he was always kind to his mother. In contrast, in business only his harshness was apparent as he manoeuvred towards the irresistible fortunes of television.

Max Mosley, a motoring enthusiast, criticised Ecclestone for his lack of interest in any motor sport other than Formula One. 'You've done well out of Formula One,' Mosley admonished, 'but you're the head of FIA's promotions. Now let's make rallying work.' The sponsors and car manufacturers, especially Renault, Mercedes, Ford and Porsche, were keen on saloon car races across Europe and Africa and the large television audiences confirmed their popularity but Ecclestone was unenthusiastic. 'It might be fun for the participants,' he niggled, 'but there are no spectators.' Undaunted, Mosley insisted that they watch a rally in Portugal. 'Bernie took one look at the mud,' recalled Mosley, 'one look at his shoes and said "I'm not going out there", closed the door and drove off.' Television coverage of rally races declined noticeably. Even enthusiasm for the annual Le Mans 24-hour race, attracting at its peak over fifty cars and a world-wide audience, diminished. Automatically, fewer contestants and less advertising were attracted to subsequent races.

With Formula One dominating television, the manufacturers had to commit themselves to that form of racing or nothing. Some organisers accused Ecclestone of suppressing any competition and sued. Although they won limited damages, Ecclestone was the victor. 'Anyone who says we tried to kill it off is just talking rubbish,' he said, brushing aside the dispute as 'unimportant'. Balestre was unsympathetic to the complainants. 'You mustn't blame it all on Bernie Ecclestone and try to say that he wants to compete against other championships and kill them off . . . Mr Ecclestone has his own ideas – he prefers Formula One which is his God-given right.'

Balestre's support did not surprise Ecclestone. Focused on his re-election in 1991, the president relied on Ecclestone and Ecclestone in turn said nothing to disabuse Balestre of his sympathies while he contemplated the renewal of the Concorde agreement, due in 1992. His critical requirement was Balestre's approval to reassign Formula One's television rights to FOCA. Since the 1987 agreement FIA had received 30 per cent of the EBU's payment while Ecclestone and the teams received the remainder. The FIA's actual annual income had been no more than $1 million. Ecclestone did not intend to alert Balestre to his plans for aggressive expansion. Instead he would allow the president to underestimate the value of the television rights. To obscure his objective, he arranged that Paddy McNally should negotiate the new Concorde agreement with Balestre. Speaking French with an engagingly honest demeanour, McNally encouraged Balestre's conviction that he was negotiating with an ally. 'I used Paddy', Ecclestone admitted, 'because Balestre would not be suspicious.'

By then McNally's business was flourishing. Although Ecclestone insisted that McNally finance some loss-making

Grand Prix races and the construction of new buildings at Hockenheim and other circuits, McNally was reasonably sure that he would recover his investment by providing over 80 per cent of most circuits' hospitality and advertising. He approached Balestre as a director of Allsopp, Parker & Marsh (APM), a company registered in Ireland so as to pay even less tax than in Switzerland. Besides McNally, APM's other named director was Luc Jean Argand, the Swiss lawyer introduced to Ecclestone by Jochen Rindt and, ever since, an important adviser. APM's other shareholders were unknown nominees registered in Guernsey. Although representing APM, McNally's approach to Balestre was crafted by Ecclestone.

In their conversations McNally did nothing to reassure Balestre about Formula One's future television revenues after the termination of the EBU contract. On the contrary, there was, McNally suggested, some uncertainty and the president might consider the prudence of an alternative arrangement. Namely, in exchange for granting APM the television revenue for the next three years, APM would guarantee FIA $5.6 million in 1992 rising to $9 million by 1996 and more if certain targets were met. Convinced of his genius — a prejudice encouraged by McNally and Ecclestone – Balestre saw the advantage of securing a guaranteed sum which could be converted from dollars, a weakening currency, into French francs. The president was also persuaded of his own cunning. On the grapevine, Balestre had heard that Canal 5, the French broadcaster and one of the EBU's biggest contributors to Ecclestone's package, was on the verge of insolvency. He assumed that McNally and Ecclestone were unaware of Canal 5's predicament and that he would secure the advantage of a guaranteed income at Ecclestone's expense. In reality, Ecclestone was negotiating a contract with another French broadcaster and Christian Vogt was concluding television agreements across the world for nearly ten times more than the EBU had paid. Despite misgivings among his staff, Balestre signed the agreement with McNally, losing the automatic right to 30 per cent of the income. Ecclestone would subsequently claim that he had advised Balestre not to accept the APM offer. Critics would say Ecclestone's lament was a smokescreen to justify millions of dollars cascading into his coffers.

Under the old Concorde agreement, Ecclestone received 23 per cent of the television income, the teams received 47 per cent and FIA 30 per cent. But with FIA's agreement to take a fixed amount, Ecclestone's share notionally rose to 53 per cent of the fixed amount while the FOCA teams divided 47 per cent of the income and 30 per cent of the prize fund among themselves. Doing the sums, the teams would claim that they were receiving just 23 per cent of Formula One's income. On the surface, little seemed to have changed but, with the prospect of unlimited income, Ecclestone modestly proposed a mere technical alteration to the contracts. He suggested to the teams that they transfer the management of their commercial rights from FOCA to Formula One Promotions Administration (FOPA), a company owned by Ecclestone. The broadcasters would sign agreements with FOCA but, in a back-to-back contract, FOPA was the real beneficiary. Nothing, he reassured the teams, would change. Ecclestone would continue to negotiate and collect their income from television and the circuits and bear the expenses and risks of all the Grand Prix races, including the loss-makers. The difference was that while FOCA was a loose, non-legal group, FOPA was owned by Ecclestone. All the teams agreed, with the exception of Frank Williams, Ron Dennis and Ken Tyrrell. Over the years, all three had tolerated Ecclestone's way of getting things done. All were aware of his tactic: if a meeting was veering off into an unhelpful direction, he would cause confusion by throwing out a ridiculous suggestion. 'He's gone off piste again,' Williams would say as Ecclestone disregarded procedures. But this time, they agreed, they would not be diverted by any of his ruses.

Ecclestone would say that he was the victim of his own success. Formula One had become a successful British industry clustered around the M25 motorway north-west of London, in an area now known as Britain's 'Motor Sport Valley'. During that development, all three team owners had risen from poverty to financial comfort. Their gratitude to Ecclestone was tempered by irritation about his creeping supremacy.

Frank Williams, grateful for Ecclestone's support since his accident – the helicopter sent by Ecclestone to bring Williams to the Grand Prix at Brands Hatch soon after the accident had flown past a vast hoarding bearing the message, 'Welcome Back Frank' – objected but could be pacified. Ron Dennis was more tricky. Under his exacting management, McLaren had developed into a world-class team capable of trouncing Ferrari. Unlike Ecclestone he had attracted Lauda to return from retirement for a $4 million contract and retained Philip Morris's support. But Dennis and Ecclestone spoke a different language. The man's style, Ecclestone complained, grated. At FOCA meetings, the former mechanic appeared obsessed by details, oblivious to the big picture and always wanting to fight. At least, Ecclestone consoled himself, he could eventually manipulate Dennis's weaknesses to secure his support but Ken Tyrrell was not so malleable. The aggressive timber merchant, whose team still beat Ferrari and McLaren, rejected the offer outright. Ecclestone's response was curt: 'Well, you invest in the loss-making circuits. Take the risk with me.' Tyrrell bad-temperedly refused and, with Dennis's support, made a counter-demand. The two wanted Ecclestone to sign an undertaking that when he died they should inherit his commercial agreements. Dennis, struggling with vocabulary, had intended to say they should be Ecclestone's 'successor' but instead blurted out his request for a 'death agreement'. Surprised by the insensitivity, Ecclestone replied simply, 'No,' but even a Warren Street dealer was unaccustomed to such naked avarice. When Ecclestone told McNally about the demand, his partner was shocked. 'Ron's become arrogant because he's winning the championship. He's always complaining about the money I'm earning.' In the midst of a savage recession, none of the three would have wanted to resolve the latest problem. Elf, the French oil company, was supplying a special fuel to Williams placing other teams at a disadvantage. 'In my opinion,' said Ecclestone, 'Formula One needs special cars, engines and drivers – what it doesn't need is special fuel.' Solving those problems, Ecclestone believed, justified his income.

Stonewalled by Ecclestone's obstinacy and unable to suggest an alternative, Dennis and Tyrrell finally and ungraciously accepted Ecclestone's offer. But neither were allowed to read the contracts between FOCA and the television companies; nor did they understand how Balestre's agreement to forsake the 30 per cent stake had enhanced Ecclestone's income. Subsequently, Ecclestone's critics would say that between 1992 and 1995 his 53 per cent share would deliver $341 million from television to his personal account, while FIA, having forsaken its 30 per cent share, received $37 million instead of $65 million. In reality, after 1992, Ecclestone was taking 73 per cent of the television income and the twelve teams divided the remaining 27 per cent. McLaren received 2 per cent. McNally would admit to friends about 'an amazing windfall' and 'more revenue than I'd expected'. Ecclestone's justification to the teams would be succinct: 'I offered you the chance to take the risk, and you refused. So I got the money.' An unforeseen twist to the new agreement would transform Ecclestone's wealth.

Balestre's approval of the 1992 Concorde agreement – signed in 1990 – was also his death warrant. Without Ecclestone's approval, Max Mosley decided to challenge Balestre for the presidency in the 1991 elections. Balestre was unaware that Mosley's polite charm concealed burning ambition. Although his career as a barrister and racing car manufacturer had been unspectacular, his calm demeanour, articulate intelligence and diplomatic proffering of advice appealed to those disillusioned by Balestre's bellowing gesticulations and chaotic mismanagement. Balestre's search for the spotlight to arbitrate on controversies during races had exhausted their sympathy as much as his refusal to consult members. The Frenchman, however, was convinced

Coup

that he enjoyed loyal support among all the affiliated national automobile organisations, especially because most clubs in Africa and Asia lacked any interest in racing. Their executives' allegiance, he reassured himself, would be secured as usual by promising that FIA would continue to fund their first-class air travel, five-star hotels and gourmet meals. He was blind to the attractions of the alternative: a quintessential Englishman, fluent in German and French, whose unflamboyant style promised to enhance the sport.

In public Ecclestone offered Mosley no support. Motor organisations who sought Ecclestone's opinion were not steered to vote against Balestre and occasionally Ecclestone speculated that Mosley would not win. Mosley tolerated Ecclestone's neutrality. Recalling Harold Wilson's quip, 'If you can't ride two horses you shouldn't be in the circus,' he understood Ecclestone's monochrome approach to politics. He was a dealer with limited understanding of institutions and history. Ecclestone's motives for engagement with FIA were entirely different from his own. 'Bernie', Mosley would say, 'is in it for money, sometimes like a disease, while my family had money but no reputation. So the presidency gave me a chance to restore my family's reputation.' Ecclestone was equally blunt: 'Max had nothing to lose by standing and at the beginning even Max did not know if he could win.'

On the eve of the election, Ecclestone's attitude changed. 'Brother Mosley,' Ecclestone greeted the candidate as he took his telephone call. By assiduously courting the motoring clubs outside Europe, particularly in Japan, North and South America, and some smaller countries disillusioned by Balestre's blustering style, Mosley had won exceptional support. His guarantee to protect all the perks, and his pledge to stand for re-election after twelve months, had undermined Balestre's accusation that Mosley was disloyal and 'indulging in a campaign aimed at destabilising FIA and brainwashing the member countries with false truths'. At the last moment, Ecclestone arrived at a realistic conclusion: 'Balestre had become a bit of a handful and even an unguided missile, so I pushed for Max when he needed it.'

157

Early on the morning of the election, 9 October 1991, Ecclestone telephoned Balestre. 'Jean-Marie,' he said, 'you're going to lose the election. Do a deal with Max. Offer him a power-sharing agreement if he withdraws.' The Frenchman scoffed. 'Don't call me with bad news so early,' he protested and explained his possession of a list of personally pledged votes. 'I will win,' he insisted. He never imagined that the delegates' promises would be ignored in the secrecy of the ballot. After all, he calculated, the delegates knew that the ballot papers were marked and anyone who voted against him risked not only losing his perks, but he could withdraw their country's right to host Formula One and other races. His threat was ineffectual. Mosley's own list of promised supporters was nearly identical to Balestre's. His twelve years in office was ended by forty-three votes to twenty-nine.

Ecclestone was delighted that his staunchest ally had won the other most influential position in the sport. But, naturally, he would care for the requirements of his second most staunch ally too. In FIA's arcane world, Balestre still retained an obscure office so, the following year, after successfully standing for re-election, Mosley adopted Ecclestone's idea and made Balestre 'president of the Senate', a powerless position but blessed with all the financial comforts. More important, Ecclestone became a member of the Senate and kept his vice-presidency of FIA, enjoying the conflicts of interest.

Together Mosley and Ecclestone consolidated their control of FIA, Formula One and all motor racing. The rebels had become the establishment. In Ecclestone's opinion, Mosley was transformed by victory – 'Getting self-belief in what he wanted to do.' An Oxford graduate of physics and trained barrister, Mosley was able to master all the technicalities of the sport. His new self-confidence made him slightly wary of Ecclestone: 'You never knew with Bernie. I couldn't take any risks.' Others would say the opposite. Without the need for an interpreter and speaking in shorthand, the two became indistinguishable and inseparable.

* * *

Satellite television was transforming Formula One. Celebrities – kings, presidents, actors, models and pop stars – appeared at races, adding glamour to the daring and heroism. Serious personalities, pampered by the promise of exclusive hospitality, became 'wired' once they tangled with the heady atmosphere of speed, glamour and the chance of death. Ecclestone met heads of state regularly, both in the countries hosting the Grand Prix or those anxious to entice Formula One to their countries. Formula One had become a global extravaganza. Ecclestone's edict to 'stop pimping in my Paddock' gave those admitted to the area the pride of exclusivity. Each televised race, seen, according to propagandists, by up to 500 million viewers (an exaggeration in fact), increased the sponsors' appetite. Honda was the latest to rejoin Formula One to promote a new range of cars in America. Other manufacturers began competing for the best teams. The television broadcasters were jubilant. Sponsorship of a team by a corporation was followed by the purchase of advertising time on television during the races, repaying the television broadcaster's fees to Ecclestone. Satisfied with the increasing income from the sponsors, the team managers were unaware of the growing gap between their income and Ecclestone's.

The glow lasted one season. In July 1993 there was disarray and even talk of a crisis at Princes Gate. An average of 200 million viewers were watching each race but the sting was the unexpected scrutiny of races that television brought. Maps of race tracks lay on the floor of Ecclestone's office. Faxes were strewn over his desk. Telephones were constantly ringing. The scrupulous tidiness was abandoned. Wearily, Ecclestone engaged in endless telephone calls to stem controversies. The results of five of the last eight races were disputed and technology was dividing the sport. Ecclestone insisted that Formula One remained a competition between drivers while the manufacturers wanted computers installed on the cars to enhance the drivers' skills. Formula One, the commentators chimed, was losing its sparkle by becoming excessively technical.

Ferrari was not performing well and, ever since Enzo's death, was failing against McLaren's and Williams's superiority in aerodynamics, composite materials, wind-tunnel testing and electronic suspension. Buffeted by the car industry's worst crisis, Ferrari's survival was in doubt. Luca Montezemolo, the young and inexperienced interim replacement for Piccinini, was struggling to regain Ferrari's supremacy, vital to Formula One's legend. The ideal candidate to lead Ferrari, Ecclestone believed, was Jean Todt, the French manager of Peugeot's sporting team. His inclusion in the fraternity would be unusual: he had a reputation for being straightforward, either telling the truth or remaining silent. His honesty was not the factor that aroused Ecclestone's support, though. Rather, in 1986, he had watched as Todt and Peugeot had taken Balestre to court over a dispute and won. FIA appealed and won. To resolve the tension, Ecclestone had invited the two men to meet at the Hôtel de Crillon and after a brief conversation left them to agree the peace. Ever since, he had been watching Todt's steady progress. So in 1992 he called Todt and suggested that he fly to meet Montezemolo in Bologna. Montezemolo, who regarded Ecclestone as 'a point of reference' with indispensable advice, was grateful. Todt joined Ferrari knowing that rebuilding the team's expertise to challenge Williams and the British would require at least five years. His placement played, Todt knew, to Ecclestone's love of being Formula One's broker-in-chief. Later, he realised, Ecclestone would occasionally describe himself as the go-between despite playing no role at all but, amid the constant rancour, someone had to keep the show together and at that moment a technical argument was dividing the sport.

The lightning rod was Nigel Mansell, a popular British world champion. In 1992 Mansell had romped to victory winning nine out of the sixteen races for Williams and scoring double the points of the runner up. His success owed much to a new electrical control system guiding the car's suspension. Ron Dennis was committed to copying the innovation for the 1993 season. Mosley wanted to ban the developments. Harking back to the days when Williams and Dennis, like all the competitors, prepared cars for racing in driving rain and searched for nuts and bolts in the mud, Mosley complained that excessive expenditure and computers were destroying racing. The grumbles that Mosley's dictatorial tendencies ignored Formula One's transition to a technical race between designers was drowned by the shock that the relationship between Mansell and Williams had collapsed. Mansell had refused Williams's new contract and after his deadline passed, Williams lowered his offer. Not realising that Formula One's doors swing both ways, Mansell was embarrassed and publicly abandoned Formula One. Ecclestone sympathised with Williams. 'Drivers', he said, 'are overpaid and there are lots of new drivers.' Mansell, he thought, should know that it was the car that won the championship. 'When you play poker,' he added, 'you ask yourself two questions: How strong is my hand? How much am I prepared to risk? If you have a mediocre hand, you'd better be careful.'

Mansell departed for America and the British media searched for a scapegoat to blame for the loss of a hero. Since Williams was struggling to survive in a wheelchair, the blame for the sporting disaster was heaped on Ecclestone. The media's problem was, as ever, the mystery. Facts about Ecclestone's background, his family or his control over Formula One were still sparse. Even his age remained unknown. Although dozens of men in the pits knew some answers, none dared to speak. Formula One's finances were equally opaque. Protecting himself behind a network of similarly named corporations registered in London and the Channel Islands, Ecclestone was relieved that no journalist discovered the filings in Companies House showing that in 1993 he had paid himself £29.7 million, a British record. Even Ron Dennis, who had furiously denounced Ecclestone's wealth during a wild evening at a night club hosted by Philip Morris, remained unaware of the truth.

Ron Dennis did not appreciate Ecclestone's hunger for deals.

Earlier in the year, John Surtees had sat at a formal dinner with Kevin Schwantz, who was beginning his career as a motorbike champion. At a neighbouring table Ecclestone overheard Schwantz say to Surtees, 'I need a Manx Norton.' Within seconds Ecclestone had dashed across and announced, 'I can get one of those.' Later in the year he had suggested to the teams that, to add some excitement, there should be additional refuelling stops during the race. His idea was rejected as expensive. 'I'll supply the equipment,' Ecclestone told the teams. His idea was accepted and the rigs were installed. Then each team received an invoice from Ecclestone. Challenged about his offer by Dennis, Frank Williams and Ken Tyrrell, Ecclestone replied 'I said I was going to supply them, I didn't say I was going to pay for them.' The lesson was to listen to Ecclestone's precise words and analyse the full meaning. 'People', Ecclestone concluded, 'don't know what they want; they only know what they don't want.' The raw homily was borne out by Mosley's victory in limiting computers in the cars; and Mansell faded from the headlines.

Ecclestone felt newly emboldened against the three English teams. An unexpected ally had appeared on the grid. Under his guidance, Flavio Briatore had, since 1989, successfully transformed the Benetton team. Briatore's route into Formula One was unusual. Born in 1950, Briatore had enjoyed a colourful career in Italy until his partner in a paint-manufacturing business was arrested for fraud and killed by a car bomb. The firm collapsed and Briatore was convicted *in absentia* for fraudulent bankruptcy with a custodial sentence of four and a half years. By then Briatore was living in America and, following his marriage to a US citizen, became Benetton's North American manager in 1982. Under his supervision, Benetton expanded from ten to 800 shops and Briatore began a partnership with Regine nightclubs. As his celebrity grew, the gossip was not only about Briatore's relationships with beautiful women, including Elle Macpherson, but also his frequent flights from New York to the Virgin Islands and the Cayman Islands. Although he had secured an amnesty for the alleged crime from the Italian government, he anticipated staying in America until he received an order from Luciano Benetton in 1989.

Luciano Benetton had called Ecclestone. He had entered Formula One by purchasing Toleman Motorsport, which he renamed Benetton Formula for the 1986 season, but the team was failing; to secure one more chance, Benetton said, he intended to appoint Briatore as the team manager. 'Would you look after him?' he asked Ecclestone.

Briatore and Ecclestone met at the Dorchester Hotel. 'I know nothing about Formula One,' Briatore confessed and added that he was unsure whether he was even interested. Although they appeared an incongruous couple, they were united by a passion for business and intrigue. Ecclestone volunteered to provide an education starting at the next Italian Grand Prix in Imola, a race track surrounded by attractive countryside and restaurants serving good food. 'Soon after I walked with Flavio in Imola,' Ecclestone later admitted, 'I got a call from John Hogan who said, "You should not be seen with him." I told John, I'll be the judge.' Briatore was captivated by the atmosphere. The flamboyant showman with an affection for beautiful women soon appreciated the Formula One fizz. Dubbed by Ken Tyrrell and other traditionalists as 'The T-shirt salesman', Briatore admitted, 'We start from the bottom,' albeit with Ecclestone's help. At 3 a.m. on 5 September 1991 at the Villa d'Este, a grand hotel on Lake Como, Eddie Jordan, the forty-three-year-old Irish owner of a small Formula One racing team, was paid quite legally to approve, reluctantly, the transfer of Michael Schumacher to Benetton. The young German had driven brilliantly in Belgium and would, in Ecclestone's opinion, attract viewers in Germany. 'I persuaded Flavio Briatore to take Michael. I arranged the original deal,' Ecclestone declared.

Briatore's energy and showmanship appealed to Ecclestone.

He was amusing, inventive and had found some serious sponsors. Unlike the English team principals, Briatore shared Ecclestone's fear in 1993 that the Grand Prix was becoming boring. To promote Benetton as the in-crowd's car, he spoke of the sport as entertainment not technology, arranging music, models and glamorous parties: 'Noise and lifestyle is what Formula One is about. The mix of power, speed, human beings fighting together.' Max Mosley was impressed. 'He's hiring good people, bringing a breath of fresh air into Formula One – and he's good company.'

At the beginning of the 1994 season in Brazil, Ecclestone was confident about Formula One's future. Schumacher was seriously challenging Ayrton Senna driving for Williams; and Senna's recruitment to drive in the same team as Alain Prost who had convincingly won the 1993 season had provoked the Frenchman, the winner of four world championships, to retire. The angry rivalries among the drivers added to tension on the circuit and spontaneously attracted the media.

Seven months earlier, just after Alain Prost had announced his retirement, Ecclestone had met two British journalists in his motorhome at the Portuguese Grand Prix for his first published interview since 1990. Unguarded about expressing honest sentiments, he replied to the journalists' questions about the consequence of Prost's departure. Convinced that no single driver was important, Ecclestone answered that Prost, regarded as a boring character compared to Senna and Mansell, would soon be forgotten just like all the drivers who had died on the track. The conversation continued until Ecclestone recalled 'the old days' of frequent tragedies. Drivers' deaths, he said, were 'a form of natural culling'. The publication of that opinion provoked outrage. Ecclestone appeared to be monumentally tactless. 'That's gone down like a lead Zeppelin,' said Mosley. In Ecclestone's defence, considering the awful effect upon him of drivers' deaths, he had probably misrepresented himself. But Ecclestone, a man who never read a book, relied on the *Daily*

Express for news, the newspaper read by his father, and only enjoyed James Bond and action films, was insensitive to the effect his words would have. To make amends, he later told another British newspaper, 'I would prefer to see them retire than be killed.' In truth, he believed that drivers were paid hugely to risk their lives, so any sympathy ought to be measured. 'Bernie has a genius for getting out of trouble,' observed a trusted lawyer. 'But he normally gets himself into trouble in the first place.' The clumsiness would have been forgotten if Schumacher's ruthless ambition had not changed Formula One's atmosphere.

The first two races of the season, won by Schumacher, were marked by crashes and accusations. The strange sound of Schumacher's Benetton car and his speed aroused suspicions. Frank Williams was convinced that Briatore had fixed both races. Investigation would show that Briatore's car did possess an illegal traction control. His defence would be that the device, although installed, was not used. The argument heightened the excitement when the teams met for the third race at the Imola track in San Marino. Ecclestone was not particularly concerned about the intense debate regarding unrestricted speed although he would hear later that Senna had complained about the risk of accidents on that track.

Over the previous years, Ecclestone's relationship with Senna had become close. He liked the Brazilian's gentle charm and regularly invited him for meals to his Chelsea home where Slavica and their daughters became attached to a man who was generous and charming despite his fame as the world champion. Like his rivals, Senna had been accused of skulduggery and no one could forget his collision with Prost in 1990 that clinched his title. But in Ecclestone's world cheating was unexceptional. In any case, resolving those problems was FIA's responsibility.

Mosley, preoccupied by safety, judged the Imola track to be particularly dangerous. Ever since he had raced against Jim Clark at Hockenheim in 1968 and witnessed the carnage after the English champion's fatal crash, he had unsuccessfully tried to persuade Formula One's enthusiasts that better safety would not ruin the sport. His own crash in a Lotus the following year at the Nürburgring had reinforced his conviction.

In the preliminary races at Imola, there was a bad crash in the practice session and then Roland Ratzenberger crashed during the qualifying session and was killed. His death cast a pall over the drivers and strengthened their commitment to improve safety at all the circuits. Senna started the race on 1 May seemingly preoccupied. At the seventh lap, he lost control and crashed at 131 miles an hour. Metal pierced his helmet and he was dead, the first death during a Grand Prix in twelve years, and the first on television.

Ecclestone was not unnerved by the news. Deaths on the track had been part of his life. He quickly shepherded Senna's family into his motorhome. A telephone call delivered the bad news. His brother, he told Leonardo Senna, was 'dead'. Minutes later, as he helplessly watched Leonardo's hysteria, there was another telephone call. Ecclestone corrected himself. There had been a misunderstanding, he apologised, Ayrton was injured 'in his head'. Leonardo no longer understood or believed Ecclestone. In reality Senna *was* dead but to avoid the complexities of Italian law the formal declaration had to be made beyond the track, preferably in a hospital.

Outside Ecclestone's motorhome, the calamity was unfolding in real time on television. Cameras showed the chaos and live coverage from a helicopter following the ambulance carrying Senna's body added to the drama. After the track had been cleared, the race restarted and was won by Schumacher. To escape the hysteria, Ecclestone flew to his wife and children in Croatia. Like Ecclestone, they were depressed. 'It didn't seem possible for him to die in a race car,' Ecclestone said later about Senna. 'He had always seemed so indestructible. It was total disbelief when I found out he was dead. I was just numb.' He added, 'I suppose the one thing you can say is that when a driver gets killed while he's racing, he at least goes out doing exactly what he wanted to do. I don't find that at all depressing.' This was bravado talk to conceal genuine sadness.

Across the world, there was blanket coverage of what Ecclestone would call, 'a public death – like crucifying Jesus Christ on television'. There were complaints for allowing the race to be completed and also questions about whether Formula One was too dangerous. There was also embarrassment because, after flying with Slavica to São Paulo for the funeral, Ecclestone was forbidden to attend the ceremony by Senna's family. The misunderstanding in the motorhome had been distorted. Thousands gathered on the streets for a 'state' funeral while Ecclestone watched Slavica accompany the city's mayor on television from his bedroom in the Intercontinental Hotel. Ecclestone returned to Britain dismissive about those forecasting the end of Formula One but the crisis was serious. The death stoked the drivers' demands for new safety rules.

Max Mosley propelled himself into the spotlight. 'They were driving at 170 mph in an unprotected petrol bath,' Mosley told journalists, 'without even a safety belt as protection. Make a mistake and all you had was two yards of grass before you started collecting pine trees.' Before Senna's death, drivers relied on their guts to be quick. Now Mosley rose to the occasion. Dangerous corners were removed, kerbs were lowered and chicanes or barriers were installed across the track to slow the cars' speed. Overnight the limitations made racing safer. Mosley's performance astonished Ron Dennis. 'What they are saying is that we have to spend a lot of money to go slower,' Dennis said perceptively. 'I have a real problem with that.' Ecclestone was also surprised, but avoided a public argument. On some issues, he knew, caution was advisable to avoid a collision with Mosley's conviction of always being right. Their differences melted away when the teams arrived for the next race in Monaco. To their relief, the television audience would soar by 20 per cent. 'I always said Formula One is bigger than any one person,' Ecclestone told journalists. 'It proved it truly is.'

A near-fatal cash at Monaco guaranteed even more viewers at the next race in Barcelona.

With the championship thrown open, Michael Schumacher in the Benetton car became a favourite, but to increase Formula One's popularity Ecclestone needed a rival to compensate for Senna's absence. He brokered the deal for Nigel Mansell to return from America and drive for Frank Williams at the French Grand Prix in July. Williams was reluctant but Ecclestone appealed for support from Renault who supplied the Williams engine. Williams surrendered and Mansell received £2 million to drive in four races starting in July. 'We're looking good,' Ecclestone told visitors, delighted that a bitter rivalry had developed between Damon Hill and Schumacher. Hill, driving alongside Mansell in a Williams car, was determined to match his father Graham Hill and become the world champion. Only Schumacher stood in his way. With Teutonic precision, the driver who would win seven world championships described his personal experience on the track as he sought the prize for the first time: 'Messages are coming at your brain all the time – sights, sensations, feelings, changes – all the time steering the car, changing gear and watching competitors at 200 mph. I'm super-fit to cope with G-forces as I chase to carve milliseconds from the lap times.' Schumacher was more than the driver – he was effectively the team's manager orchestrating his own success.

Ecclestone knew that Schumacher's burning ambition was eclipsed only by Briatore's. Neither questioned their own unforgiving ruthlessness because that was the essence of winning. Basking in the spotlight with Heidi Klum, a German supermodel promoting Victoria's Secret underwear, Briatore featured as regularly in the gossip columns of celebrity magazines as in the sports pages. 'It takes the same amount of effort to get a beautiful woman as it does to get an ugly one,' he would frequently say, 'so you might as well have a beautiful one.' His fame in Italy was fed by his lust for Benetton's victory and a $300 million prize. In the season's first two races, Senna and other drivers had been suspicious of Schumacher's engine, and that distrust was increased on 3 July at the French Grand Prix as Schumacher surged in front of the Williams cars. To Briatore's relief, Mosley ruled that there was no proof that the 'driver aid' in the car's computer had actually been used. Schumacher could retain his winning points. Some of the drivers complained that justice had been tilted to favour the show.

The German driver, well ahead of the field on points, was hungry for victory but in the qualifying sessions one week later at Silverstone, he lost the key pole position for the race to Damon Hill by three-thousandths of a second. Truculent, he was black-flagged during the actual race by the stewards but instead of returning to the pits, disobediently roared around the circuit while Briatore argued his case. Damon Hill won the race. For the next two weeks, in the build-up to the German Grand Prix, motor sport's politics spilled into the mainstream news. Schumacher was threatened with fines and a ban from two races. German fans threatened to incinerate the forests around Hockenheim if their hero was not allowed to race. Amid death threats, Hill arrived at Hockenheim with a police escort.

In his motorhome, Ecclestone was delighted about a tragedy with a happy ending. Schumacher's disqualification after Silverstone, he heard from Mosley, 'is a bonanza. Everyone's talking about it in the pub.' Germany versus Britain was guaranteed to score record television audiences. Ecclestone was fielding calls about safety, Schumacher's arrogance and appeals from Silvio Berlusconi to save Italy's Grand Prix, the next fixture. After Senna's death, the callous would say the tragedy had not been wasted.

Live television had complicated Ecclestone's life. In the early days, the media had entirely focused on the drivers. But since the television cameras entered the Paddock and the cable channels' insatiable appetite needed to be fed, the drivers and team managers spilled out on the airwaves. Fans were no longer fed just long-distance shots of cars but became familiar with the fractious personalities along the grid. To energise the soap opera,

Ecclestone encouraged Todt, Dennis and Briatore to squabble on television, and when that palled, he enjoyed watching Briatore's reticence when questioned about his past. The mystery added spice to Formula One. To increase excitement at Hockenheim, Ecclestone had added an extra refuelling stop. The drama in the pits, he told the teams' business managers, also exposed the sponsors' logos longer on television.

Soon after the race started, there was a succession of collisions. Good television, some thought. But Ecclestone had not anticipated that during the stop of Benetton's second car, fuel would spill on to the bodywork and catch fire, destroying the car and injuring a mechanic. After the race – a succession of crashes and mechanical failures forced Hill and Schumacher to retire – an investigation by FIA's stewards discovered that Benetton had removed a compulsory filter from the refuelling rig to speed up Schumacher's pit stop by one second. Benetton and Briatore were publicly accused of cheating, an offence compounded by their earlier indictment for their use of illegal software. Although Mosley had allowed Briatore to escape punishment for the 'non-use' of the computers, the evidence about the filter was irrefutable. Conviction by Mosley and FIA would have banned Schumacher from the championship. 'The refuelling accident', said Ecclestone, 'does not worry me more than any accident happening on the circuit. We have not had any problems with it this season. It does not make me rethink refuelling. You saw how quickly the fire was put out.' As usual, Ecclestone had not asked Briatore for any explanation. 'I never ask people questions that could embarrass them,' Ecclestone explained. Taking their lead from Ecclestone, neither Schumacher nor Briatore regarded the risk of FIA's 'justice' too seriously. Adding to the drama, hundreds of millions of television viewers also saw Damon Hill and Schumacher end weeks of feuding on the podium. 'Oh you've missed it,' Ecclestone was told as he emerged from his motorhome. 'Schumacher and Hill have just shaken hands up there.' 'I know,' replied Ecclestone, 'I arranged it.'

Two days later, on 18 October 1994, Ecclestone arrived in Paris. Fourteen of the sixteen races had been completed and Schumacher, despite being banned from two races because of his conduct at Silverstone, was still five points ahead of Hill. The championship was wide open, a lucrative position for the business. The following day, Max Mosley, as FIA's president, would judge at the end of a trial whether Briatore had broken the rules by removing the filter from the refuelling rig at Hockenheim. Conviction would end Benetton's chance of winning the championship and ruin the season's climax. Ecclestone arranged for Briatore to be represented by George Carman, a skilful English lawyer enjoying a deadly reputation with juries in the libel courts.

By then, Ecclestone and Briatore had become good friends. They flew together to races, played poker occasionally, sometimes with Schumacher, and met socially in Ecclestone's new Georgian-style house in Chelsea Square bought in 1992 and rebuilt by 1994. In turn, Briatore had bought Ecclestone's flat in Oakley Street. In Briatore's opinion, their friendship rested on their mutual passion for punctuality and his admiration for Ecclestone's commercial genius. Others suspected that Ecclestone's self-protection had been undermined by Briatore's charm and exhibitionism, surrounding himself with beautiful women and even covering the walls of his home and office with photographs of himself.

The Italian was less enamoured with Mosley. 'You don't choose your parents but you choose your friends,' he said. Mosley had become ambivalent towards Briatore. The Italian had brought valuable colour to Formula One but two allegations of cheating in one season seemed excessive. Nevertheless, Mosley was amenable to confessions.

Ecclestone had arranged for Carman to arrive the night before the hearing and stay at the Crillon. On that evening, Ecclestone called on Carman in his bedroom and, over two hours, explained to the lawyer how justice worked in Formula One. 'He's guilty, that's decided,' said Ecclestone. 'We're not looking for any change to the verdict. All that's left is the press release. We're looking for changes to the words in Flavio's appeal for sympathy.' To reduce the punishment, continued Ecclestone, Briatore needed to admit his guilt. 'I see,' said Carman. 'I need a drink.' Going down to the bar, Ecclestone telephoned Mosley and suggested that he cross the road to the hotel. In that convivial atmosphere, the famous advocate entertained his hosts with scandalous stories about life at the Bar. As a fellow lawyer, Mosley was noticeably impressed and responded positively when Ecclestone suggested, 'I think they want to do a plea bargain.' Mosley was pleased. FIA's judicial status, he believed, was weak, especially if Benetton later appealed to a national court. To avoid the mess, two members of the English Bar could amicably settle the case by agreeing that Benetton would plead guilty and pay a fine but would not suffer a ban on either Schumacher or the team from competing in the next race in Japan. Carman, intrigued by the novel scenario, agreed. With that settled, Briatore was grateful to Ecclestone for influencing Mosley in his favour although the Italian resented Mosley personally. 'Mosley', Briatore said, 'did not like Benetton winning.' The evidence suggested the opposite but there was undoubtedly a clash of values between the roguish Italian and the aesthetic Englishman. 'Our relationship', said Briatore, 'deteriorated after the Paris judgement.'

Briatore's disdain for Mosley was reinforced by Ron Dennis. Mosley, said Dennis, suffered from a 'damaging ego'. The previous year the two had argued about Mosley's new regulations banning electronic driving systems to help the less successful teams. Dennis also disliked Mosley's safety crusade. If the choice was between attrition and elimination, he favoured blood sports. Dennis spoke for many Formula One fans who equated the gladiatorial contest of Formula One with Ben Hur's chariot race. In his personal battle to make McLaren the champion, Dennis wanted his rivals to be crushed, even if the consequence would be to race against himself. 'There are no miracles in motor racing,' he observed. 'Nobody can wave a magic wand over the back eight cars on the grid and suddenly have them at the front. If they are not capable, they will die.' The Lotus team had just collapsed amid debts.

Ecclestone sided with the teams against Mosley's campaign. He ridiculed Mosley's condemnation of 'Ben Hur wheel-to-wheel banging'. 'That's part of overtaking, Max,' he said, misty-eyed about the old era. The final contest of 1994 in Australia challenged that opinion. At the start of the race around the Adelaide street circuit, Schumacher was just one point ahead of Hill. Their public reconciliation in Germany had not lasted long. On the eve of the previous race, Schumacher had suggested that Hill was not a truly world-class driver. The headlines around the globe promised attrition rather than competition. The two high-profile deaths earlier in the season appeared to be forgotten. At least 300 million viewers watched the two men roar from the starting line ahead of a packed field. On lap 35 Schumacher glanced off a wall and, as he slowed down, Hill came from behind to overtake. As Hill passed the German, Schumacher turned his steering wheel and drove the Benetton straight into Hill's car. Suspicious observers did not believe the crash was accidental. Both retired from the race and Schumacher became the world champion. The year's excitement had been watched by 6.1 billion viewers, a record. 'Schumacher', Ecclestone reflected, 'is a ruthless, brutal driver who'd do anything to win. If he can live with what he did, that's it. So many others have done worse. What can you do? I wasn't surprised. Often people do things in life which are like them and not nice.'

Few realised that most of the season's television coverage had been produced by Ecclestone's personal company. In a hangar at Biggin Hill, the Battle of Britain airport he leased in 1994, Eddie Baker had developed a television production and broadcasting centre, alias 'Bakersville', transmitting images across the world via satellite. For races in Europe Baker dispatched twenty-eight identical silver Mercedes transporters with over thirty cameras and production equipment to spread around the circuit. The same 300 tonnes of equipment was dispatched beyond Europe in three Boeing 747s followed by 280 staff flown in the company's jets to erect vast air-conditioned hangars in three days, powered by their own generators. The sight of those trucks at the circuits, precisely aligned according to their sequential number plates, was the testament of Ecclestone's pernicketiness to create the world's biggest mobile broadcast unit. Attention to detail was the foundation of Ecclestone's control.

The growing audience convinced Ecclestone that his income could be magnified by selling a subscription service which allowed fans the personal choice to enjoy each race. Viewers, he imagined, would be willing to pay to become a studio director in their homes by personally selecting the view from any of FOCA TV's cameras positioned around the track and on most of the cars. After discussing the idea with Rupert Murdoch, whose investment in the Premier League had transformed Sky TV's finances, Ecclestone was convinced that the £36 million he had personally invested since 1993 to supply pictures to Murdoch and other European broadcasters would become a new bonanza.

None of the teams or the wider world realised the enormous return Ecclestone was earning from his investment in television. Rather, they focused on the tangible evidence of Formula One as an important British business. Some spoke about 'Motor Sport Valley' – 2,000 companies employing about 20,000 skilled staff with revenue of over $6 billion stretching from Norfolk to Southampton. Each team employed small armies of highly skilled designers to produce over six months the 3,500 drawings to hand-build a single car which, after testing in a wind tunnel, would move accurately over the track. Others noted the transition from the 'mates together' in the early 1970s to a global sport which was paying drivers $12 million a year. Once again, there was limited interest in Ecclestone, who did not even feature in 'Who's Who'. When his salary of £29,750,000 was finally revealed, his reply to questions about his wealth was crisp:

'You'll never get me to discuss last night or money.' His attitude towards money was unambivalent: 'The teams know that if I'm making a buck, they are making a buck and then everyone is happy. People trust me.' The few newspaper profiles were coloured by descriptions about his 'cult of mystery and menace', reinforced by his own secrecy and presentation of himself as a recluse like Enzo Ferrari. 'I don't give a damn what people think of me to be honest,' he later said. 'I'm doing a job the best way I can. So maybe I upset a few people on the way. Make a few people happy, a few unhappy, but that's how it is.' He was unapologetic about his unpalatable truths. A man who had risen from the bottom was prone to honesty, even if offensive, especially defending his attitude towards drivers' deaths. 'I remember when François Cevert was killed at Watkins Glen,' he explained. 'I was sitting on a crate with Carlos Reutemann and he asked, "What happened?" "Oh, he went under the guard rail and was more or less cut in half." "Christ, why did he go off?" "Well he just lost it." "Oh. What engine are we using this afternoon?" '

There was no weariness of age in his voice but his sentiments, based on challenging experiences, were expressed in terms which younger people, unaware of his background, could find offensive. The cultural gap between himself and those seeking the story behind Formula One's success could only widen. In 1995 Ecclestone was sixty-five, the age when most men retired. New commercial opportunities were continuously solicited but few materialising that year were as interesting as that of Ron Walker, an Australian businessman.

In 1993 Walker had approached Ecclestone proposing that the Grand Prix be moved from Adelaide back to Melbourne. He offered a ten-year contract paying about A$12 million a year instead of Adelaide's A$9 million. Walker explained that the finances of his offer were guaranteed by the Victoria state government. This was the breakthrough which Ecclestone sought.

New circuits were expected to subsidise the sport and expand the television audience. Ecclestone did not promise Walker any profits: 'I tell them up front, "You are going to lose money running this event." I know how many people are going to be there. There is no bullshit. I would not ever tell them that this is fantastic, that they are going to make a fortune.' Walker and his political supporters partially disagreed. Melbourne's reputation, they believed, would be transformed by the city's repeated mention in the world's sport's pages. Having secured Ecclestone's agreement stipulating that the terms were commercially confidential, the Victoria government revealed that the race would be run through Albert Park, Melbourne's principal garden in the city centre. Every year the circuit would be built and then demolished, costing about A\$65 million. Legislation was enacted to protect the government from any financial claims for damages and authorising hundreds of trees to be felled. Protestors were told that the cost would be outweighed by the financial benefits to the city. They were not reassured. Yet in 1995 over 300,000 spectators flocked to the first Grand Prix, spending an estimated US\$150 million at the season's last race. This was won by Damon Hill after Schumacher, that year's world champion, withdrew. After Walker and the city's politicians congratulated themselves, the businessman suggested to John Major, the British prime minister, that Ecclestone should be offered a knighthood. Walker obtained endorsements from Nelson Mandela, Silvio Berlusconi, Bob Hawke and Max Mosley. Ecclestone believed there was a chance after an invitation for lunch with Major at Chequers. In the company of thirteen others, he was seated near the prime minister and acknowledged as a successful businessman and a Tory supporter who had helped the party financially. His contribution had not been paid directly to Lord Harris, or 'Phil the Carpet' as Ecclestone called the party treasurer, but by Ecclestone's friends to maintain deniability. Ecclestone's nomination was nevertheless rejected. There were too many questions. Not only were his encounters with the Inland Revenue and the judges' criticism unhelpful, but there was no support from the political Establishment. Whatever the truth, Whitehall was unprepared to embrace an apparently hard man steeped in mystery. Instead he was offered a CBE, which he rejected.

After his father's death, Ecclestone regularly visited his mother, now crippled, admired her paintings and drawings of birds and pushed her wheelchair on outings. In the summer he took her at the weekends to Court Lodge in Kent, a sixteenth-century house owned by Ron Shaw, who regularly invited his old gang to congratulate themselves for escaping from Dartford. While Ecclestone swam in the pool, rode Shaw's horses and played cards, he enjoyed the fact that his mother could witness his status as the emperor among friends.

In 1995 Bertha Ecclestone died, aged ninety-one years. Her son planned to attend the small funeral near St Albans. His plans were once again upset by Slavica. His wife heard that Debbie would also be in the church, aggravating Slavica's unease about her husband's past relationships. Ever since Slavica had raged that Debbie was never to return to their Chelsea home, Ecclestone had only once secretly met his daughter. Slavica had also forbidden her husband to meet Tony Morris, his oldest friend. He had not been completely obedient. Now she heard that Tuana Tan also intended to attend his mother's funeral. Confronted by his wife's fury, Ecclestone hid in the bedroom to avoid her wrath. Seeking consolation he telephoned Tuana, the first time for years.

'Why do you allow her to do this?' Tuana asked. In reply, he expressed guilt about the past and feared Slavica would leave, taking their daughters. He was, Tuana believed, 'not happy'. 'There is', she confided, 'enormous compassion in his heart. He has a soft heart. He wanted to be the strong one in the family. He was desperate.' On the day of the funeral, without Slavica's knowledge, he drove to the church but did not dare enter. Instead, he telephoned Ann Jones, his former secretary who had retired four years earlier. 'My mother's funeral is happening right now,' he said, 'and Slavica won't let me go. She doesn't want me to meet Tuana and Debbie.' Jones was not surprised but offered no solution. Inside, the congregation was less than a dozen people, but included Debbie's husband Paul Marks.

Many believed that Ecclestone had not attended his daughter's wedding some years earlier because he disapproved of his son-in-law, and for the same reason had not seen his grandson, born in 1980. But most blamed Slavica's jealousy. 'I'm staying with Slavica', he later told Tuana, 'for peace and quiet.' In later years Ecclestone portrayed himself in interviews as heartless and unwilling to go to funerals because he despised double standards. 'If somebody is dead,' he said, 'they're dead. It has nothing to do with respect. Half the time the people who go to funerals didn't respect the people when they are alive. Better to look after them when they are alive and don't worry when they are dead. And I don't believe in this after-life.' When he died, he added, he would prefer no mourners at his funeral. 'If it's cheaper, I'll be happy.' He liked to appear as a hard man, but a handful of insiders knew that his brutal facade was sometimes phoney.

On 13 December 1995 Ecclestone got an anguished telephone call from Jonathan Martin, the BBC head of sport. Now he really did seem heartless. Over the years, Martin's skills had created a hugely popular following for Formula One on BBC television. The relationship between Martin and Ecclestone had been strictly commercial. They only met at Princes Gate to settle contracts and had never eaten a meal together. On that day Martin received mortifying news. Without warning, Ecclestone had switched the contract for the Formula One races from the BBC to ITV. The five-year contract, which was to start in 1997, was for £65 million, compared with £7 million paid by the BBC.

'Bernie,' said Martin, 'it would have been nice to have been allowed to put in a competitive bid.'

'Unless you've been cheating me all these years, Jonathan,' replied Ecclestone, 'there is no way you could possibly pay what

they're paying so there was no point in talking to you about it.'
'Well, it's a great deal, Bernie,' concluded Martin. ''Bye.'

Martin's only consolation was that four years later, when ITV
showed the qualifying sessions of the race in France, Ecclestone
objected. ITV's lawyers, he pointed out, had not read the small
print properly. Their contract was limited to the races. The
qualifying sessions would cost extra. Ecclestone was on a roll,
but for high stakes. He had made a huge personal investment
in digital television, which was in its infancy at this point: it
was estimated for the first year he had spent about £40 million,
and he needed returns. He was negotiating a £50 million deal
to supply digital television in 1996 to Kirch TV in Germany, to
Berlusconi in Italy and to a French television broadcaster. But
nothing had yet been agreed. Nevertheless, he intended to pay
himself £54 million for the last year, becoming Britain's highest-
salaried executive. Fifty years earlier, he had earned pennies
selling motorbike parts using the Gas Board's telephone. Now,
few could guess the value of Formula One's television rights.

7

Billionaire

No one was more suspicious of Bernie Ecclestone's wealth and ambitions than Ron Dennis. In one way, Dennis was similar to Ecclestone: he believed in winning. Restless, meticulous, obsessive and aggressive, Dennis admitted, 'The pain I feel of failure is such an incentive to succeed. I am just a terrible loser.' Rarely satisfied, he was steadily transforming McLaren into a potent challenger. Volatile and prone to explosions of rage, he dismissed his critics as those who recognised that 'I have higher standards than they have achieved'.

Dennis's description of himself was derided by Ecclestone. 'Dennis has an inferiority complex because he is inferior,' he told his staff. His ambition to inherit the capo's mantle, Ecclestone scoffed, was a risible quest for a man with limited savvy to understand the magic of juggling four competing interests – the teams, the sponsors, the broadcasters and the circuits – with a myriad of different nationalities and ultimately produce a seamless package sixteen times every year. In Ecclestone's opinion, Dennis owed him gratitude for having vaulted from a Brabham 'grease monkey' to a life of a multimillionaire. 'Bernie doesn't love me,' retorted Dennis, 'because he doesn't like to sleep with the enemy.' Dennis's resentment coloured his reaction to a sequence of events which gradually emerged during 1995, not least because they had occurred in secret.

At the end of 1996 the Concorde agreement between the teams and FIA would expire. Mosley would need to negotiate new terms. The FIA was certainly vulnerable. Balestre had been fairly outwitted by Ecclestone's skilful negotiation of the 1992 agreement and FIA had lost approximately $65 million from the television rights. By contrast Ecclestone and McNally had earned over $200 million. Tilting the scales back to FIA's advantage depended on Mosley's ability to extract a better deal from his friend, but he suspected that Ecclestone would play a blinder.

In Mosley's opinion Ecclestone had transformed an amateur's sport into a global business and, regardless of his short cuts, had become indispensable. Once digital television was profitably established – an inevitability, he assumed – Formula One would be a gold mine. The sport, he believed, belonged to FIA although Balestre had failed to establish its legal ownership firmly. At any stage, Mosley feared, Ecclestone could exploit that ambiguity and say to FIA, 'I'm taking the teams away into the sunset and I'm going to set up a rival Formula One' – a possibility because FIA had never signed an agreement with Ecclestone personally. In Mosley's imagination 'Bernie could have said "I won't pay anything" and what could I have done?'

The uncertainty had been compounded by Ecclestone's musings to Mosley during their frequent journeys to Biggin Hill in 1995: 'I'm thinking about selling Formula One to the teams.' Ever since Ron Dennis had demanded a 'death agreement', Ecclestone had challenged the teams to buy his business but they had refused, not least because some disputed Ecclestone's ownership. 'I'm offering to sell it at a 30 per cent discount,' Ecclestone told Mosley to conjure the prospect of future negotiations with Ron Dennis, Flavio Briatore, Frank Williams and Ken Tyrrell. To avoid that horrific scenario, Mosley wanted to cement a deal with Ecclestone alone but during their conversations Ecclestone responded with ambiguity. 'The teams have no right to Formula One,' Mosley urged Ecclestone. 'You should do a deal with FIA because it will be longer term and more secure.' 'I'll think about it,' replied Ecclestone. The more Mosley urged an agreement, the more Ecclestone spun out their tortured negotiations. Playing poker with Mosley was so much easier than haggling on Warren Street.

Ecclestone nevertheless needed security. His mental calculator reckoned that after negotiating television deals covering nearly 125 countries Formula One would be earning gross profits of about $225 million every year, just from the television rights. In addition there was the income from sixteen circuits and the share of McNally's profits. In total, he could pocket over $300 million annually before paying their share to the teams. Only Mosley could protect or challenge that cash machine. Instead of vagaries about his commercial rights, Ecclestone wanted a cast-iron contract granting him unchallengeable ownership of Formula One across the world. The moment to strike, he decided, was after Mosley had committed himself exclusively to Ecclestone. So he spoke with total clarity – 'I own Formula One.' Mosley did not agree, although with hindsight he admitted, 'I didn't realise how questionable the ownership of Formula One was. But I knew that I needed to legitimise the business back under FIA's control.' In that uncertainty, Ecclestone's claim to the ownership of Formula One could not be dismissed outright. Unaccustomed to trading, Mosley felt 'weak' about his position: 'You can always trust Bernie to act in his own interests. He held the cards in the short term.'

Ecclestone denied there was any legal confusion. Mosley, he insisted, should recognise his unchallenged 'total ownership'. At the end of one journey to Biggin Hill, Mosley expostulated, 'Bernie, you're not a liar but your concept of the truth is different from other people's.' To settle the dispute, Mosley finally offered Ecclestone the rights to Formula One for fifteen years. On expiry the rights would return to FIA. Ecclestone liked the idea. Fifteen years was a long time and, if he was still alive, there was ample scope for renegotiation. So, capitalising on Mosley's concession, Ecclestone stipulated that he would pay FIA just $9 million a year for that exclusivity and no percentage of the television income. More important, he would not sign the new agreement on behalf of FOCA, the organisation representing all the teams. Instead, he would sign on behalf of FOCA Administration Ltd, a company owned by himself. 'An ace deal,' Mosley said after the contract was signed in December 1995. Mosley left Ecclestone to complete a separate deal with the teams.

The fifteen-year agreement was a remarkable Christmas present for Ecclestone. His personal annual income from the television rights in 1996 was already fixed at $103 million. Under the original agreement, FIA's 30 per cent share would have been worth $67 million. Instead, FIA received $9 million. In his own defence Mosley would say that the teams would not have tolerated FIA receiving such huge sums; that FIA had secured a guaranteed income without any financial risk; that there was no alternative because Ecclestone was irreplaceable; and, finally, that Ecclestone needed security to promote digital television, which would enhance Formula One's global success. Mosley did not fear accusations of wrongdoing despite FIA buying a private plane from Ecclestone for his use. The sale, like their cooperation in minor property deals, was founded on a long relationship between a street-fighter and a politician united to suffocate any complaints from the teams. Everyone knew that Mosley enjoyed an enviably luxurious lifestyle financed by FIA but no one questioned the regulator's accounts.

The teams' mood when Ecclestone flew to Melbourne in March for the opening race of the 1996 season was mixed. Damon Hill was sure that Williams would dominate the field; Ron Dennis believed McLaren was on the verge of winning the world championship; Ken Tyrrell ungraciously acknowledged that his glory days were past; and Flavio Briatore was grim because Michael Schumacher had been lured by Jean Todt to Ferrari with some key engineers. The move fatally damaged Benetton's prospects and Briatore would be fired in 1997, though he departed with a fortune. Ecclestone himself was recovering from surgery on facial injuries inflicted by a German shepherd guard dog while staying as Steve Wynn's guest in Las Vegas. 'I was sitting with Steve in his office,' Ecclestone told those enquiring in the Paddock, 'and was about to pat the dog and he jumped up at my face and bit my nose off.' After a bodyguard pulled the dog off, Ecclestone was rushed to Wynn's plastic surgeon. Two hours later, Ecclestone returned to Wynn's palatial home still wearing his bloodstained clothes. 'Hi, Bernie,' said Wynn, standing in the garden with the same dog by his side. 'Sorry about that, but don't blame the dog. That's what he's trained to do.' Ecclestone assumed that his ordeal would evoke some unsympathetic comments.

Although rivals on the track, the team principals were angered by the spread of Ecclestone's financial tentacles. Reading the draft of the new ten-year Concorde agreement which would start in 1997, Dennis had noticed the modifications indicating Ecclestone's enrichment. With Williams's and Tyrrell's support, he objected to the deal that Mosley had made assigning the rights to Formula One for fifteen years to Ecclestone personally. 'I assigned the Formula One rights to FOCA not to FOCA Limited,' said Dennis. 'You've done a double.' 'Bernard, I don't think this is fair,' added Frank Williams, who with hindsight realised that during the 1970s he and the others had been 'there for the taking'. Williams glanced at Dennis who, he acknowledged, had 'seen much further down the line' than himself. Dennis objected to Ecclestone's squeezing too hard. 'I agree with Frank,' said Dennis in his curmudgeonly tone. 'It's greedy. It's not right.' 'What's not right?' Ecclestone asked, feigning bewilderment about Dennis's smouldering language. The teams, he knew, were angry that 'anyone should earn the money I was earning. But I'd offered to sell the business to them at a discount and they'd refused.'

'There's no Queensberry rules here,' Dennis told Ecclestone. 'It's all about money.' Glancing at Ken Tyrrell, Ecclestone saw a disappointed man whose team had slipped down the grid and won nothing since 1983. He would successfully encourage Tyrrell to sell his team and brokered a good deal with British American Tobacco. 'Tyrrell never thanked me, never said anything,' said Ecclestone. Even that kindness aroused Dennis's suspicion. In his opinion,

Ecclestone was rarely helpful but perpetually searching for revenge. 'Bernie carries a grudge and waits for the moment to strike.'

In April 1995 all the teams except Tyrrell, Williams and McLaren (the 'Three') had signed the 1997 Concorde agreement but the Three, Ecclestone had heard, had spoken about 'staying united' and 'not allowing Bernie get up to his old tricks of playing us off against each other'. To repeat his trick, Ecclestone encouraged Eddie Jordan, praised by some as 'a rough diamond', to ask awkward questions at the successive meetings. Grateful for Ecclestone's previous help in staving off his team's bankruptcy, Jordan obliged, repeatedly diverting the Three's attacks into the grass. Ecclestone was begrudging in gratitude: 'Eddie Jordan is as honest as he can afford to be. I bailed him out a few times. He took advice. I gave him what he wanted.' Dennis scoffed about the tactic. 'Eddie's an empty box making a lot of noise.' Uncharitably Ecclestone agreed: 'There's no need to wind Eddie up. He winds himself up.' Jordan's ceaseless gabbling sidelined the immediate danger until Dennis and Luca Montezemolo met at a Heathrow hotel in spring 1996 to discuss the renewal of Concorde. It would be impossible, they agreed, to recover the rights to Formula One from Ecclestone but they revived the idea of a 'death agreement'. At the next FOCA meeting, Dennis challenged Ecclestone, saying that the rights should eventually revert to the teams. Ecclestone was no longer shocked by Dennis's bulldozer manner. 'The rights never belonged to the teams,' replied Ecclestone. 'They belonged to FIA and now they belong to me.' The succession was not on his agenda. And, he added, his control over motor sports had expanded. Mosley had just granted ISC, a company owned by Ecclestone, the television rights for fifteen years to every major motor sport including Le Mans, the Paris–Dakar rally and the international truck competition. All had loyal if diminishing television audiences. The contract, Mosley was confident, would be approved by the 120 delegates of the General Assembly. Ecclestone's monopoly of television coverage of all motor sports was complete. Together with Mosley, he could dictate the agenda to the teams. Frank Williams was philosophical: 'We were more keen about pissing on our competitors', he conceded, 'than arguing with Bernie. The end game was to win the race.' The meeting ended sourly – except for Ecclestone.

On leaving the office at six o'clock every day, Ecclestone tried to forget the day's business problems. For years he had enjoyed returning to his Chelsea home and Slavica's good cooking, to spend the evening watching action films and wildlife documentaries. His preference for home life irritated his wife. Considering her husband's millions, she wanted to show off her expensive clothes and jewels in London's celebrity haunts. Although Ecclestone was complaining of heart pains, he sometimes reluctantly agreed. On 4 July 1996 he went to Harry's Bar, a members-only restaurant in Mayfair. Returning home, he approached his front door and two men appeared. 'What do you want?' he asked. As he put his hand in his pocket, a fist struck his head and he fell to the ground. Lying on the pavement, the repeated kicks to his body and face fractured his cheek bone and broke his nose. Blood gushed from his mouth. A diamond ring on Slavica's finger, said to be worth £600,000, was pulled off and the muggers fled. For a moment Slavica thought her husband was dead. The medical attention could not cover up the heavily bruised face photographed in the hospital. 'It was all so unnecessary,' he told newspapers two days later. 'I was not putting up a fight.' Over the following day, his self-pity turned to anger. 'I'm not intending to die,' he told another enquirer, 'and I don't advise anyone to try to kill me unless they come well equipped . . . The only reason they have not done it is probably they're the real fat cats and they have been sitting on their arses.' He would thereafter carry the photograph of his bruised face in his briefcase as proof of his suffering. 'They took a brain scan in the hospital,' he quipped, 'and found that I've got one.'
That was his only joke about the experience. He wanted

revenge. On the basis of 'Don't get mad, get even', Ecclestone asked John Bloom, the former washing-machine tycoon, to find a reliable criminal investigator. Since their meeting in the mid-1960s on his yacht in Monaco, Bloom's star had collapsed. In 1969 he was declared bankrupt after prosecution at the Old Bailey and thereafter had tried to rebuild his fortune, occasionally with Ecclestone's financial help. In return Bloom was pleased to ask Tony Schneider, a violent London gangster renowned as a loan shark, to recommend an investigator. Schneider suggested John O'Connor, a former commander of the Flying Squad at Scotland Yard, employed by Kroll. O'Connor had come across Ecclestone during an investigation in 1976 about FOCA's purchase of stolen British Airways tickets. A BA employee was convicted and jailed for the crime; Ecclestone's explanation that he honestly assumed that the tickets were genuine had been irrefutable, but left O'Connor regarding Ecclestone as 'cocky'. His judgement did not change when he met him again and examined his injuries. In O'Connor's experience, the muggers had been trained how to punch. His only suspects were two black amateur boxers but with insufficient proof, he refused to disclose the names out of fear that Ecclestone might not pass on the names to the police but execute summary justice 'on the quiet'. Although there was no evidence that Ecclestone had ever commissioned violence, he was not averse to that lingering image by telling journalists that he was given the names soon after the incident and offered to buy the ring back, but decided not to get involved. O'Connor was doubtful. Ecclestone certainly wanted the world to know that his attackers had not escaped. Extracting revenge was his trademark. 'I'm a very good friend and a bloody bad enemy. You cross me and sooner or later I'll get you,' he told an interviewer, choosing how he wanted to be seen. 'I may not get you beaten up or chopped up, but one day I'll level the score.' He implied that his assailants had been dealt with. 'I did some enquiries myself and found out who they were – but they have not been arrested.' Ludicrous rumours suggested that two bodies had been found in the River Thames. 'I've never killed anybody,' he told subsequent enquirers. 'You'd hear about it if I had.' He wanted the public to know that his fearsome reputation was justified. 'I don't cultivate it. It's a matter of fact.' Since O'Connor refused to reveal the names and the police never arrested any suspects, the investigator was not paid.

Nine days after the attack, the bruising had still not disappeared and Ecclestone was at Silverstone for the British Grand Prix. He decided not to abandon a prank he had dreamed up against Karl-Heinz Zimmerman. The Austrian, born in 1948 in Lech, a skiing resort, enjoyed firing a cannon that he kept in his motorhome at the end of the British race. On the day before the race, a group of police surrounded the motorhome that resembled an ersatz Viennese coffee house and demanded access with their dogs to satisfy a tip-off about explosives. Around the motorhome, uniformed policemen had taped off the area and mentioned the severity of the sentence on conviction. Zimmerman became seriously alarmed. 'I told you there would be a problem,' said Ecclestone gravely, knowing that the only ones unaware of the hoax were Zimmerman and the dogs sniffing in Zimmerman's cupboards. Zimmerman's panic didn't pass until he was taken for questioning to Ecclestone's motorhome, though by then he had told his Austrian cook in his local dialect to take the hold-all containing the cannon and gunpowder out of the bus. With the cannon removed he could enjoy what he gradually realised was another poker-faced prank by Ecclestone.

Silverstone always attracted celebrities and their access had been improved by the introduction of swipe cards into the Paddock. Among those invited by Max Mosley was Tony Blair, the leader of the Labour party, expected to be elected as prime minister the following year.

Mosley's involvement in Blair's invitation had begun in February 1996 when Ecclestone had featured in the *Sunday Times* Rich List as Britain's highest-paid businessman. Jonathan

Powell, Blair's chief of staff, telephoned David Ward, a former Labour party official employed by Mosley at FIA, and asked whether Ecclestone might become a donor to the Labour party. Ward was certain that Ecclestone had never voted Labour and was a Conservative. Ecclestone, he mentioned, had met Margaret Thatcher in 1981 at the launch in the Albert Hall of Colin Chapman's Lotus cars and again in 1987 at a party in Downing Street on the eve of Mark Thatcher's wedding. More recently, he recalled, he had heard the rumours about Ron Walker and donations to the Conservatives that had not provided the anticipated honours. Ecclestone's possible ambivalence was balanced by the certainty that Mosley, Ward's new employer, contributed money to Labour through the Thousand Club. 'Do you know how we can contact Ecclestone?' Powell asked Ward. 'Blair has already been invited to visit Silverstone in July,' replied Ward, 'and we can arrange for him to meet Bernie.' On the day, at Mosley's request, Ecclestone welcomed Blair into his motorhome and, together with Ward and Bernd Pischetsrieder, the chairman of BMW, discussed Britain's adoption of the Euro currency. Despite the fact that they didn't see eye-to-eye about Europe, Ecclestone liked Blair. Unknown to the future prime minister, he had been welcomed at Ecclestone's motorhome because the RAC committee refused to admit a Labour party member into their club house. Subsequently Jonathan Powell was reassured by Ward that Mosley would speak to Ecclestone about a donation at an appropriate moment.

On the track, Frank Williams's car won the race, driven by Jacques Villeneuve, the son of Gilles Villeneuve. Williams cars were dominating the season and Damon Hill seemed destined to become the world champion. Ecclestone had a particular interest in the outcome. To help Frank Williams and to reintroduce American interest into Formula One, he had brokered Villeneuve's recruitment as Hill's team mate and was surprised by his poor performance, especially in Australia where he ceded the lead to Hill, blaming an oil leak. 'It seems',

Ecclestone confided just before Silverstone, 'as though someone at Rothmans, Williams or Renault said, "We could be in trouble here." They would prefer to have an English world champion I suppose. You wouldn't want a French Canadian coming in. It causes problems elsewhere.'

Allegations about fixing the race did not trouble Frank Williams, whose restored self-confidence encouraged Ron Dennis and Ken Tyrrell to reconvene and agree to reject the proposed 1997 Concorde agreement. By then, to mollify the teams, Ecclestone had offered to increase his payments to them. For the Three, the amount was insufficient and Ecclestone's refusal to consult them about Formula One's ownership and his successor was, they believed, insolent. A meeting was arranged for all the teams on 7 August 1996 at Heathrow. After speaking to Montezemolo, Dennis arrived confident of unity while Ecclestone had precisely calculated how to undermine the Three. His telephone call to Maranello had promised Montezemolo a special deal – to share among the remaining teams the extra money which the three British teams would have earned if they had signed Concorde. 'Ferrari must stay legalist,' Montezemolo told his staff. 'We need the competition to succeed. I didn't want to do deals with the Three under the table.' At the meeting to Dennis's surprise, Montezemolo and the other teams accepted Ecclestone's offer to take effect in January 1997. Dennis conceded defeat but still refused to sign the agreement. Ecclestone got up and walked out with a blank face. 'He can't express happiness about anything,' observed John Hogan.

'I did the deal with Bernie,' Montezemolo said after, 'because he gave me what I wanted. He is very good at pitting Ferrari against McLaren. He is the champion of the world in dividing the teams, but Bernie is very good for Ferrari.' After returning to Maranello, Montezemolo telephoned Ecclestone. 'Bernie, this is the last time I'll sign to help you,' he warned. After ending the conversation Montezemolo doubted whether Ecclestone understood. He rightly gauged that Ecclestone's only interest was getting the best deal.

To Ecclestone, Montezemolo's sentiments were irrelevant, as were everyone's. 'I feel betrayed by Luca,' Dennis admitted. 'They put me on a white horse and say, "Charge, we're with you." Then I get to the top of the hill and no one else is there.' Unlike Montezemolo, he fought for all the teams, not just for himself but, he consoled himself, 'you fight or you die'. Even Ecclestone was displeased. Formula One's finances had become unrealistic. Mechanics were earning £150,000 a year plus perks; Dennis had just signed Adrian Newey, the designer, for £2 million a year; Frank Williams and Dennis were travelling in their own jets and each had banked over £50 million; and the circuits which had paid £500,000 in 1981 for a Formula One race now paid £10 million. All that was thanks to Ecclestone and in gratitude Dennis accused him of 'greed'. Nevertheless, his granite performance destabilised Dennis. Four weeks later, the Three surrendered. Meekly they conceded their willingness to sign Concorde after all. To their dismay, the other teams, meeting in Maranello in September, refused to allow the Three to receive the increased payments for twelve months. They would be allowed to continue racing, but only on the old rates. The Three were incensed. 'Dissension in the ranks,' quipped Ecclestone untroubled by the stand-off. 'The biggest problem is that we've all come up together. When there's no money involved the family's united. As soon as there's money, members of the family think, "I should have more." I've tried to help struggling teams over the years, but it's like somebody drowning. You throw them a lifebelt, then when they get to the shore, they say, "You idiot, you hit me on the head with the lifebelt." '

The day before the teams had met in Italy, Christian Purslow, a thirty-one-year-old banker, started work at Salomon Brothers, then the world's biggest bank. Purslow was proud that Salomon's had hired him at top rates to develop its media interests. Within his first hour at the London office, Purslow was ordered: 'Cold-call Bernie Ecclestone. A contact in Australia has said that he's thinking about floating Formula One.'

During September Purslow met Ecclestone three times and returned to his office bemused by Ecclestone's secret. Formula One, the banker understood, was a phenomenal profit machine but lacked any recognisable machinery to appeal to investors. The uncertainties were unique. The familiar operational chart for corporations placing the chairman at the top with descending lines of delegation was instead a circle with Ecclestone, a sixty-six-year-old man permanently carrying a briefcase, controlling everything from the centre. Remarkably, there were also no physical assets. There was no land, one building and only a few vehicles. Ecclestone's fortune relied upon juggling fractious interests and unpublished contracts in English with a multitude of nationalities. 'If they can't speak English,' Ecclestone had said, 'they aren't worth knowing.' Around the clock, Ecclestone was either outsmarting or sweet-talking the teams to comply with a Concorde agreement which would expire in 2007, and that was a major problem. In ten years there would be nothing except Ecclestone's genius to reassemble all the parts. Ecclestone understood but would never admit one crucial fact: he had exploited the haphazard growth of the business, snatching out of the chaos the legal ownership of Formula One without any formal agreement or purchase. Would anyone, Purslow wondered, want to invest in that risk? On the other hand, he mused, 'I've just met a man sitting on a gold mine which the world doesn't know about.' In the banker's opinion Ecclestone was an agent but, unlike Mark McCormack earning a 10 per cent commission, Ecclestone was a super agent taking about 70 per cent of the $330 million net profits every year by balancing glory and grief. And unlike any other business, he could forecast the minimum profits over the next seven years. 'It's got a lot of hair on it,' Purslow reported enthusiastically. 'It's worth anything between £1.5 billion and £3 billion.'

Purslow compiled an inventory of Ecclestone's empire. Through contracts and relationships, Ecclestone controlled companies owning the television production sales of all the races, a company transporting Formula One around the world, he brokered the sponsorship for the teams, took fees from McNally's hospitality and advertising company, and received up to $35 million from each of the race circuits. In later years, that sort of business would be classified as 'intellectual property' and valued for a fortune but in 1996, in the absence of solid assets, ignorance bred suspicion.

Ecclestone appeared to be keen on a flotation but in truth had been persuaded to adopt that course after a medical examination; an angiogram following a high cholesterol reading had revealed blockages in his arteries. A stent had failed and the only remedy was a heart bypass. The operation could be delayed but always carried a risk.

Facing the possibility of death, Ecclestone spoke to a solicitor about his will. To his surprise, Ecclestone was told that his wife, although living in Britain for over seven years, could not benefit from a tax-free inheritance in the event of his death because she was not domiciled in the country. Instead, his business would be broken up and sold to pay 40 per cent death duties. To prevent that catastrophe, he needed to transfer all his wealth to an offshore trust owned by his wife and hope that he survive for another seven years. Unaware of any tax expert in London and too secretive to confide in someone else, he consulted Luc Argand, the Swiss lawyer introduced to him by Jochen Rindt. Argand suggested that Ecclestone consult Stephen Mullens, a tax specialist operating from a small solicitor's practice in London.

Mullens realised that the introduction to Ecclestone was a career-making break. Swiftly, the intelligent lawyer ingratiated himself with the master-dealer who was uneducated about the complications of finance, tax laws and trusts. Mullens suggested that Ecclestone should divest his ownership of Formula One to offshore trusts so his family could avoid paying British taxes. To execute the plan and avoid the Inland Revenue's sanctions required certain formalities, which lawyers and accountants could organise. The most important rule, Mullens emphasised, was that following the transfer to the trusts, Ecclestone could exercise no influence over the fate of his fortune. If he disobeyed the rule, he was warned, and sought to contact Luc Argand and his wife, who would be appointed as trustees, the Inland Revenue would declare the transfer void and demand the payment of taxes. Fearful that the transition of ownership could be jeopardised before he died, Ecclestone felt obliged to obey Mullens's orders. In February 1996 FOCA Administration Ltd and Formula One Administration (FOA) was gifted by Ecclestone to Petara Ltd, a Jersey company owned by Slavica.

Emboldened by Ecclestone's trust in him, Mullens suggested that the only way for Slavica and their daughters to enjoy his wealth after his death was to sell Formula One and pocket the cash. The best route, said Mullens, was a flotation. Ecclestone was unsure, but the message, initiated by Mullens, was eventually delivered to Purslow. To the banker's bemusement, Ecclestone spoke a lot about the succession. 'I don't want the teams fighting like in ancient Rome,' he said, basing his comparison on Hollywood films. A public company, he hoped, would squash the squabbling. Purslow, like everyone else, was unaware of a doctor's sombre verdict on Ecclestone's medical complications. 'I don't want a bun fight when I keel over,' Ecclestone added, 'with all the vultures swirling around. I want to protect the interests of my family.' Purslow nodded in sympathy but did not reply that all Ecclestone's recent talk about revenge, death and a life of mystery had created an assumption that he had something to hide which would not comfort potential investors. Purslow also pondered the requirements to secure the flotation of Formula One Holdings (FOH): the mass of documents and professional reports verifying an honest and profitable business. Reputable City lawyers and accountants would need to certify that a recognisable infrastructure would care for investors' money. Ecclestone could provide none of those assurances. Within Princes Gate there were a few in-house lawyers who

1 With his slicked-back hair and immaculate suits, the young Bernie Ecclestone (left) loved big American cars, although this Studebaker was owned by Fred Compton (right), his first business partner.

2 The partnership started with Ecclestone renting Compton's forecourt to sell motorbikes. Eventually, Ecclestone's success forced Compton to sell him the business.

3 Winning at any price – here at Crystal Palace in 1950 – was the principal source of Ecclestone's happiness, not only in racing but in business.

LEFT: 4 As a Warren Street car dealer, Ecclestone haggled with spivs and criminals. Here, he adopted his lifetime's credo, 'No profit, no fun'.
5 High stakes gambling and formal dinners with his first wife, Ivy (left) were the focus of his social life during the 1950s. Occasionally he met Jack Brabham (centre) whose Formula One racing team Ecclestone bought in 1974.
6 & 7 Ecclestone's parents: Bertha Ecclestone, holding her grand-daughter Debbie, and Sidney Ecclestone a reserved man, he inspired his son's interest in motors and racing but they appeared to have little else in common.

ABOVE: 8 & 9 Ecclestone met Tuana Tan (above, right and below, with friends) gambling at Crockfords in 1967 and left Ivy for the Singaporean carrying just a suitcase. Their seventeen-year relationship ended abruptly: 'I didn't know you wanted children,' she said tearfully as Ecclestone departed carrying just a suitcase.

10 Gordon Murray, the car designer and owner of Brabham cars, was critical to Ecclestone's victorious Formula One career but as with most of Ecclestone's relationships, Murray departed angry about money.

11 Patrick Duffeler, with Ecclestone and a 'pit popsie', failed to prevent Ecclestone taking over Formula One after a bitter struggle. 'I don't approve of Bernie's approach to business,' said Duffeler. 'Bernie's God is money.'

12 Niki Lauda and Ecclestone at the Austrian Grand Prix in 1978. Lauda, an
exceptionally courageous and intelligent Formula One driver, was one of the
few to outsmart Ecclestone in negotiations.

13 Nelson Piquet won the World Championship driving for Ecclestone but
was not surprised when his employer refused to celebrate. 'All he did was
do the job he was paid for,' said Ecclestone. 'Bernie can lick my arse,' Piquet
shouted during a drivers' strike shortly after.

14 The conspiracy between Ecclestone and Max Mosley (left) to outwit Jean-
Marie Balestre (right), the pompous and greedy French president of FIA,
ended in Ecclestone's profitable ownership of Formula One.

15 Enzo Ferrari – the man Ecclestone called his mentor.
16 Michael Schumacher kisses Ecclestone while Damon Hill looks on. 'Schumacher is a ruthless, brutal driver,' said Ecclestone admiringly.
17 Few Formula One principals are more critical of Ecclestone than Ron Dennis. 'Bernie doesn't give things,' he said. 'You have to fight for them.'
18 The crash between Ayrton Senna and Alain Prost in 1990 was a familiar 'shunt' to decide the fate of the race. Ecclestone described the frequent Formula One tragedies as 'a form of natural culling'.

19 In 1997, Ecclestone's Christmas card celebrated his notoriety following
the exposure of his £1 million donation to the Labour party.
20 Luca Montezemolo, the head of Ferrari, constantly challenged
Ecclestone's control. 'You've earned too much,' Montezemolo said. 'You're
eating too much cake. You've got indigestion.'
21 Few of Ecclestone's relationships arouse more bewilderment than his
friendship with Flavio Briatore. 'People say I shouldn't be associated with
Flavio and people who cheat,' Ecclestone said. 'I couldn't care.'

22 Ecclestone's tumultuous marriage with Slavica puzzled his friends although he loyally said, 'She's a super mum.' Shocked when she divorced him, he said, 'I would never have left her . . . I've never walked out on anything.'

23 Vladmir Putin's agreement to pay $40 million a year for a Formula One race did not surprise Ecclestone. After a fifteen-minute private conversation in Sochi in October 2010, Ecclestone commented 'He's learning to speak good English.'

24 Hollywood stars and businessmen want to be associated with Formula One. Sir Philip Green escorts Jennifer Lopez and her husband Marc Anthony around the track in Monaco, while Ecclestone looks on.

scrutinised the contracts, while Ecclestone's auditor was not one of the City giants but Brian Shepherd, a kindly man raised like Ecclestone in south London with an interest in miniature china owls. 'We need a corporate governance framework,' announced Purslow. 'We need a board of directors and a finance director.' Ecclestone was appalled. 'I don't like men in suits pretending to run the business. We don't need a finance director. Here are the contracts, add the profits up, and you've got your sums. What's the problem?' 'The media analysts won't accept that,' replied Purslow. 'A finance director will cost £30,000 and that's a small price for respectability.' 'OK,' agreed Ecclestone reluctantly.

To prepare the prospectus for the flotation, teams of lawyers arrived to scrutinise his contracts and sleek accountants clutching computers tramped through his offices seeking the truth. A lifetime of secrecy was threatened. Brian Shepherd watched the invasion and recognised Ecclestone's torment. 'Bernie doesn't like telling people things, especially strangers. They're pestering the life out of him, driving him mad by asking loads of personal questions.' Ecclestone had always espoused organised chaos and making decisions on the hoof. The Concorde agreements were rated 'cosmic secret', guarded better than any state secret. Only a handful of people knew the truth about the prize money and the television income. 'If two people know something it isn't secret any more,' Ecclestone believed. Purslow assumed that the process was not painful for Ecclestone because he wanted to sell his business. He did not guess the truth. 'No documents or copies of documents can leave the building,' Ecclestone ordered. The thought of lawyers and accountants taking over from him was incredible. 'I don't think it's right and I think eventually the business will suffer. You need someone to fly by the seat of their pants and hopefully get it right. I would rather they were a little like me.' Increasingly disenchanted by the process, he visited Salomon's headquarters with Eddie Jordan for a briefing. After listening to a ten-minute speech, Ecclestone looked at the female banker and announced, 'This isn't what I want. Jordan, are you coming or staying?' He blamed Stephen Mullens, the lawyer in charge of the family trusts in the Channel Islands. 'The float was his idea,' he thought. 'Everyone thinks I'm about to die. I could make the flotation work if I want to, but I'm not so sure any more.' Purslow remained unaware of his change of heart.

The 1996 season ended in mid-October. Damon Hill was the outright champion and both McLaren and Benetton nursed their disappointment at not winning a single race. Despite his success, Hill was 'astonished' to have read a newspaper report before his final victory that Williams would not renew his contract. He did not discover the true reason at the time. Ecclestone was more focused on his own and Formula One's finances than the Grand Prix results. To execute the plan to avoid inheritance taxes and cash-in still required Herculean work which the bankers, lawyers and accountants were organising.

He saw no irony when in October, snatching an interlude between listening to professional advisers, he drove to the House of Commons to meet Tony Blair. The previous month, Jonathan Powell had telephoned David Ward to ask whether Ecclestone's meeting with Blair had produced a donor. 'Nowadays,' continued Powell, 'we don't consider anything less than £1 million.' 'Are you serious?' asked Ward incredulously. Both knew New Labour had set a sliding scale for honours and access depending on an individual's wealth and importance to the party but this new level was quite special. At Ward's request Mosley spoke to Ecclestone, who agreed to consider the proposition. His reply triggered a smooth progression. Michael Levy, a former pop promoter employed by Blair as a fund-raiser, arranged a meeting with Blair in the House of Commons. After speaking alone with Blair for twenty minutes, Ecclestone emerged with little recall about the conversation and was taken by Levy to another office. 'We would be grateful', said Levy, 'if you could make a significant contribution, something around £1 million.' Ecclestone listened, said nothing and left after five minutes. 'Bernie wasn't impressed,'

Mosley told Ward soon after. 'He said there wasn't a fat chance of giving any money.' Soon after Levy appeared at Ecclestone's office. 'He's amateurish,' Ecclestone told Ward.

Ecclestone returned to the business of arranging the 1997 season with an additional race, while Purslow was struggling to compose a draft prospectus for the flotation of Formula One Holdings. Working in secrecy, Purslow assumed that he would produce a document in the summer. There was, he told Ecclestone, one problem requiring a solution. The EU wanted to ban tobacco sponsorship of sport and that would affect Formula One, not in Britain where the link had been voluntarily broken in 1992, but in Europe and beyond. Something, said Purslow, needed to be sorted out. A coincidental telephone call from David Ward to Mosley brought the strands together. 'If you can get Bernie to give Labour some money,' said Ward, 'we will get enormous access.'

There was no coincidence that early in January 1997 Michael Levy telephoned Mosley. The Labour party was about to launch its most expensive election campaign and Levy still hoped to tap Ecclestone for £1 million. Mosley was sympathetic and thought he had a lever. Newspapers had just reported Tony Blair's order to Gordon Brown to limit tax income rates at 40 per cent and to resist raising the tax to 50 per cent. Mosley called Ecclestone. 'Look what your friend Tony has done,' said Mosley. 'He's helping business and saving you tax.' Paying 40 per cent rather than 50 per cent on £54.9 million, said Mosley, would save Ecclestone millions of pounds. Ecclestone was unimpressed. He was a Tory without any interest in helping Labour. 'One million pounds will give us access,' said Mosley switching gear, 'and help us on tobacco.' The tobacco companies, especially Philip Morris, were agitating against the ban.

The relationship between Ecclestone and Philip Morris was close. About 30 per cent of the circuits' advertisements and 30 per cent of the teams' sponsorship – notably Ferrari and McLaren – was paid by tobacco companies. Ecclestone did not forget that

Aleardo Buzzi, the retired European president of Philip Morris, had brokered the peace in Lausanne in 1981. Formula One's dependence on tobacco involved regular meetings between Philip Morris executives and Ecclestone to discuss the industry's continuous campaign to resist government restrictions. Their conversations invariably returned to the 'irritants' deployed by governments against tobacco and the industry's ability to exploit inconsistent national laws, a topic which was even discussed when Ecclestone appeared at the corporation's annual party at the Monaco Grand Prix. The sensitive relations between Philip Morris and the governments was firmly entrusted to the corporate affairs department, known unaffectionately within the corporation as 'the skunk works'.

In 1997 Walter Thoma, Philip Morris's new European president, expected Ecclestone to help the industry whenever possible. After all, a healthy proportion of the billions of dollars Philip Morris had invested in Formula One was in Ecclestone's bank account. 'There had been ample discussions with Bernie and Max to keep anti-tobacco laws out of the business,' Thoma volunteered. Ecclestone was sympathetic. 'I believe that it would be difficult to replace the amount of money put into the sport by tobacco companies,' Ecclestone said at the time, 'but having said that, I think that everyone knows that it will happen sooner or later. I don't know why it should happen, because I don't believe that people start smoking because they see advertisements.'

Mosley's suggestion of buying access to Blair suited Thoma's agenda but even then, Ecclestone was still not keen to help his political enemies. Accordingly, Mosley ratcheted up the pressure. 'It would be a great favour to me, Bernie,' said Mosley. As a frustrated politician, Mosley mentioned that £1 million would not only give him access to Blair to lobby on Formula One's behalf but also provide an opportunity to present himself as a prospective Labour politician. In Ecclestone's opinion, Mosley's new pitch tilted the reason for a donation. Giving money to Labour, Ecclestone believed, could now be justified. 'I want Max to be in a good position to get a Labour seat,' Ecclestone said. 'I want to help Max look good in front of Blair.' The notion that Blair would promote Mosley's political ambitions when the Tory party itself had rejected Oswald Mosley's son did not apparently faze Ecclestone. 'Max's father was Labour,' explained Ecclestone. Oswald Mosley's rapid journey from Labour to fascism was easily ignored by Ecclestone's later explanation, 'Max didn't care if he was Tory or Labour.' In that unlikely scenario, Ecclestone simply recognised Mosley 'as the man who made things happen'. He also knew that Philip Morris, in the past, had a natural interest in tobacco's relationship with politicians. In 1992 the corporation had retained Margaret Thatcher for an annual fee of £500,000 to argue on their behalf against a ban on tobacco sponsorship. He assumed that a similar campaign would not be repeated in 1997. Philip Morris did not want their fingerprints on any political deal. Mixed in with helping the tobacco company was also Ecclestone's appreciation of Mosley's love of politics. He finally agreed to pay Labour £1 million.

Ward passed on the news to Jonathan Powell with a caveat: 'I will support Bernie Ecclestone's contribution so long as I can talk to Tony and outline the sensitive issues around Formula One.' Powell agreed. Soon after, Ward was seated in Blair's living room at his Islington home. Powell and Peter Mandelson, who had welcomed Ward, remained outside. 'You're getting £1 million from Ecclestone,' Ward told Blair in the clearest terms, 'but you must understand that the issue of tobacco sponsorship will arise in a European directive and we believe that there are better ways to achieve the same by a voluntary global agreement.' The EU's draft directive, explained Ward, banned tobacco sponsorship across the whole EU but that was beyond the competence of the EU powers. Under EU law, sponsorship was a subsidiary issue for each member country to decide, so the directive would be illegal. In any event, emphasised Ward, Formula One was not opposing a ban. Tobacco sponsorship of the British Grand Prix had been voluntarily stopped but the draft European directive would ban tobacco sponsorship in other countries. 'We just want a transition period,' continued Ward. The problem was, he added, the officials in Brussels were stubbornly uninterested in transition. 'There is no need for controversy, but we will want your help.' At the end of twenty minutes, Ward was convinced that Blair understood the link between Ecclestone's £1 million, tobacco sponsorship and the fact that Formula One supported gradual transition. 'I understand,' said Blair. Ecclestone, an admirer of the Tories who intended to vote Tory in the election, handed Ward his personal cheque although Labour remained pledged in its 1997 manifesto to ban tobacco sponsorship of all sports. For Ecclestone the gambler, the £1 million was the same as pushing his chips on to red at the casino – red for Labour and red for Ferrari, sponsored by Philip Morris.

At the beginning of March 1997, in anticipation of a successful flotation, Ecclestone indulged in legal theatrics lasting for several weeks. A series of documents was laid on a table in Jersey for signature to formally divest Slavica of control over Formula One. Ecclestone had already gifted FOCA Administration Ltd and Formula One Administration (FOA) to Petara. Now Petara, renamed Formula One Management (FOM), was transferred by Slavica to SLEC Holdings (named after Slavica Ecclestone), another company registered in Jersey. Then she was directed to the final stage, signing documents to transfer the same SLEC shares to Bambino Holdings, a Jersey company which became the legal owner of Formula One. Luc Argand, a long-term associate of Ecclestone, was a director of Bambino while Stephen Mullens was an adviser. Bambino Holdings was itself owned by a trust based in Liechtenstein over which none of the Ecclestones had any legal control. To protect the fortune from the Inland Revenue, time had been allowed to lapse between Ecclestone transferring the shares to Slavica, and his wife divesting herself of the shares to the trust. Consequently the trustees entirely controlled Formula One while Slavica and her two daughters would only enjoy the financial benefits after Formula One was floated and the shares sold to the public. To confirm that Ecclestone had completely divested himself of any legal ownership of Formula One, an announcement would be made hailing Slavica as Britain's richest woman. 'No one in the world believes that I would have given all that I had to my wife,' said Ecclestone, 'but that is actually what I did. I wanted to make sure that she and the children were well looked after if anything happened to me.' Under British law, Slavica's new wealth would completely escape inheritance taxes if Ecclestone survived seven years. Slavica was rich but powerless. The transfer of the shares to Bambino and the Liechtenstein trust excluded Slavica from any influence over Formula One.

With the housekeeping completed, Ecclestone flew to Melbourne for the opening race of the season. By then, each race was watched in about 130 countries by over 330 million fans. The gossip was still about Frank Williams dismissing Damon Hill, the world champion who was scrambling to find another team.

On the day of the race, 9 March 1997, Ecclestone's life changed. The London *Sunday Times* reported the proposed flotation for £2.5 billion. The leak took Ecclestone by surprise and shocked the entire Formula One community. Until then, Ecclestone was valued by the media at about £275 million. The newspaper report created not only a new billionaire but incredulity. Few could imagine how a sport steeped in secrecy, offshore funds, a complex web of relationships and internecine fighting could attract investors at such a huge price. The mood in the Paddock in Melbourne was incendiary. None were more angry than Ron Dennis. £2.5 billion was far beyond his imagination. To prevent an explosion of his anger, he avoided Ecclestone: 'I felt Bernie was being greedy and not respectful of the teams' contribution. We were the actors and we should have had an equitable share.' Over twenty-three years, he had watched Ecclestone increase his involvement from a 2 per cent commission for negotiating the transport and organisers' money, but had never conceived how he could eventually pocket billions of pounds. When they finally met later that day, Dennis said stiffly, 'Bernie, you're not being honourable.' Ecclestone sensed the anger but remained cool. The master of the struggle, usually one step ahead of the posse, he rarely lost his temper. The best tactic was to doubt the newspaper's accuracy. Later he was more succinct. 'My feeling is to wait and see,' he told a journalist. 'Whatever we put on the market will be valued at that figure so I may as well wait for the revenue stream from pay-television which will bring in enormous profit and give Formula One its full worth. Salomon Brothers is telling me this is a stupid attitude and the market is good at the moment. The more they talk the less interested I am.'

In London Purslow was fretting. The leak – and he would never discover the source – was nothing less than disastrous. 'The breach of secrecy', he told a colleague, 'is an absolute shock. This is a no-go moment.' Bankers hated losing control of their agenda and new valuations of Formula One were sprouting like crazy in the media – anything between £1 billion and £5 billion depending on the income from digital television. He had not even started to value the company accurately because the obstacles remained formidable. Ecclestone's secrecy had created ambiguities about his deals and the flow of money between Britain, the Channel Islands and Switzerland. In the absence of clarity Purslow could only justify floating at just over £1 billion, making the newspaper's value of £2.5 billion an albatross for his untested proposed board of directors. None of the three – Marco Piccinini, the former Ferrari team manager as the proposed deputy chief executive, Helmut Werner, a former chief executive of Mercedes as the chairman and Davis Wilson, formerly of Ladbrokes, as the finance director – were familiar in the City. The sniggers from rival banks about a lack-lustre board controlling a maverick were mild compared to the raw emotion in the Paddock.

Ron Dennis and Frank Williams had been prepared to sign the new Concorde agreement but only on the original terms accepted by the other seven teams, and threatened to sue Ecclestone if he refused. Now they demanded 20 per cent of the shares in the flotation and more of the television money. 'They want a share of my business,' said Ecclestone contemptuously. 'I made them rich, why don't they give me a share of their business?' Recognising reality, Ecclestone decided on a partial retreat. He counter-offered 10 per cent of the shares to be divided among the teams but in return wanted the Concorde agreement extended. He also offered FIA 10 per cent of the shares or $100 million from the flotation. That offer won Mosley's support in arranging two crucial approvals. First, Luca Montezemolo agreed that he would not change sides again but support Ecclestone against the Three; and second, Mosley arranged that FIA's World Council would support the flotation and ignore the Three's protests. 'It's Bernie's and Max's' game,' said Dennis, exasperated by the stitch-up. He decided to muddy the waters. Purslow was asked whether Ecclestone, the invisible trustees or even FIA actually owned Formula One. Whatever the answer, said Dennis, it raised doubts about the validity of the television contracts. Destabilised by the new uncertainties, the banker confessed that his timetable was wrecked. No formal flotation prospectus could be ready before the summer 'launch window' and the next opportunity, the following year, could be too late. Ecclestone was unsympathetic. 'Let's get the job done,' he urged, accustomed to getting his way. Purslow's solution was to dispatch Ecclestone to meet potential investors in road shows. Ecclestone was to be introduced as the head of 'England's most profitable and successful company'.

After the first meeting in London, Ecclestone's disenchantment revived: 'I'll be damned if I'm going to do their job for them when they are being paid to market the company. I'm busy running this year's competition and after that I will be busy setting up next year's. I'm in no hurry and it will happen when I'm ready.' One newspaper called him 'the client from hell' but the serious criticism included questions about his honesty. Tom Rubython devoted a whole issue of *Formula One Business* magazine to the cover story, 'Is this man fit to run a public company?'. Ecclestone issued a writ for defamation and Rubython apologised. The Lex column in the *Financial Times* warned that if Ecclestone was selling, investors should be wary. 'I don't want to stand up in front of the shareholders,' Ecclestone told his banker. On the other hand, Ecclestone was not about to brush aside £2.5 billion. He wanted the cash and was resigned to give some to the teams, even to Ron Dennis, if that overcame the hurdles. Finding solutions was Purslow's problem.

On a sunny day in May, the banker welcomed the team principals to Salomon Brothers' boardroom for a presentation. Although Ecclestone slipped in and out of the meeting to take telephone calls, there were no voices of disapproval and, Purslow thought, the mood was positive. He was wrong. Dennis didn't like Purslow and didn't like the plan. 'No team thought the flotation was the right thing,' he said, 'and I was as emotional as everyone else.' So much of Ecclestone's business was shrouded in Jersey trusts. 'It's the peanut under the cup trick,' he complained, mentioning the Roebuck trust as a mysterious ingredient in the Ecclestone family's constantly changing offshore empire which even Ecclestone claimed to find baffling. 'It's all so complex,' said Dennis.

Since Ecclestone seemed perplexed, especially about the trusts, Dennis hired Tim Shacklock of Dresdner Kleinwort for advice. The banker reported that a flotation was not viable. Dennis raised the stakes: 'We're being dictated to about life in the future and I had strong feelings.' The exchange of recriminations came to a new climax at a meeting with Ecclestone on 6 June 1997. The Three had finally signed the Concorde agreement but demanded a stake in the proposed publicly owned corporation. The belligerence became heated. 'You never told us about the huge profits you were making from TV contracts,' said Dennis, belatedly grasping that television rather than the teams controlled the Formula One 'show'. 'The teams owned those rights, Bernie, not you.' Frank Williams agreed. 'It's not right, Bernard,' said Williams. Quick to lose his temper, Ken Tyrrell rose, began screaming obscenities and violently uttered one of the most memorable lines in Formula One's history: 'Bernie, you've stolen Formula One from the teams. You never owned it.' Williams looked at Tyrrell with admiration. 'Ken's gone ballistic,' he thought. 'But it was reasoned and he was right.' Ecclestone started clapping, deriding the anger as grubby comedy. 'Well done, Ken. Have you finished? Now sit down.' Then Ecclestone became unusually belligerent. 'Formula One', he told them, 'is bigger than all of you. We'll do fine if you all pull out. I can float without you and without giving you any shares.' He stormed out of the meeting. 'The teams can go to hell,' he cursed. 'Some of them think they have me by the balls but their hands aren't big enough.' Tyrrell was scathing about the man. 'Even Napoleon had a Bernie complex,' he would say. Frank Williams would praise Tyrrell as 'a real racer. A pillar. You could anchor yourself to him.' Eddie Jordan looked around at the men left behind. 'If there's a war,' he thought, 'I want to be in the trench with Bernie, because there'll only be one winner.'

On reflection, Ecclestone was disappointed to have betrayed his customary cool but his anger was genuine. 'Their behaviour was hurtful and the most hurtful was Tyrrell. He was disappointing. I was also disappointed with Frank because I had helped him. But I never called Frank to say, "You're ungrateful." ' He was not disillusioned by Ron Dennis. 'Ron was not disloyal because you can only be disloyal if you're loyal in the first place. I have never much trusted Ron.' Dennis, he recalled, had started in business with just £2,000 and had paid himself the previous year over £1 million. 'Ron will never be grateful for what I did.' Ecclestone's perennial self-justification was to ask, 'Where were they at the beginning? They didn't make the investment at the time. They signed away their rights in 1992. They weren't entitled to it later.' Benevolent dictators were better than democratic ownership: 'If the teams owned it, they'd destroy it. They can't agree on anything, not even on how to share their money out. They think they can run the business – I know they can't.' Reflecting later,

Ecclestone reminded himself that, as in poker, 'You must know the hand you play.' Abiding by that rule, he decided 'it was better to let them play because if I went to them I would have had to compromise. So it was best to wait because they couldn't win.' Ron Dennis was convinced by his advisers that he could.

The flotation, destabilised by the publicity, was rocked by Ecclestone's misplaced faith in digital television. Success depended on the broadcasters promoting the new service but, he complained, they had failed. Fans in Europe were not buying the service but preferred the free terrestrial show. In turn, the sponsors warned that they would not tolerate smaller audiences on digital. Ecclestone realised that he had gone a step too far. Worst of all, in June 1997 Kirch TV, the biggest Formula One digital television service, was racked by a cash crisis. Fewer than 10,000 Germans had subscribed to Kirch's digital service for Formula One and he could no longer afford to pay Ecclestone. Digital had also failed in Italy, France and Britain. Ecclestone's personal losses were considerable. His hand was weak. Rushing from one meeting to another, he was confronted by a myriad of proposals and, he confessed, was unsure what to do. On the verge of folding, his plight worsened. Ecclestone's advisers belatedly realised that the flotation required clearance by the EU in Brussels. In particular, his plan required a formal declaration from Karl van Miert, the European competition commissioner, that Formula One's operations did not offend the EU's competition rules. Ecclestone's lawyers began the arduous chore of compiling a formal application to the EU to obtain the declaration. In many ways, it was academic. In July Purslow admitted defeat. Three hurdles prevented the flotation getting started: the EU, the teams and tobacco. 'I'll sort it out,' said Ecclestone, unwilling to lose any fight, even one he had come to resent.

To some, Ecclestone appeared only as a winner. Newspapers still reported that he would receive £2 billion from the flotation and that he had just bought a chalet in Gstaad, the ski resort of the super-rich, and also Olden, a fifteen-bedroom hotel, for £4 million with plans to spend £17 million on its redevelopment. He had also sold his house in Sardinia. 'I knew that if I got kidnapped my wife would not pay to get me back,' he explained.

Amid the frantic activity, Tony Blair won the general election and was appointed prime minister. Soon after, Michael Levy invited Ecclestone to meet him in the House of Commons. In a brief conversation, Levy expressed his hope that Ecclestone would agree to 'loan' the party £800,000 every year for three years. Of course, Levy explained, the loan would not be repaid. Ecclestone's expressionless reaction persuaded Levy to add, 'For two and a half million pounds you will have the key to Downing Street.' Quick as a flash Ecclestone replied, 'I've got the keys to the whole of Rio and it's done me no good.' Although Ecclestone departed with a glacial smile, Levy was undeterred and invited David Ward to visit his home in north London. Mistakenly, Levy thought that Ward was employed by Ecclestone. Sitting in the garden, Levy asked, 'Is Bernie thinking of giving more money to Labour? We wondered if he would commit himself to giving Labour £1 million every year for the life of the current parliament.' 'There are problems,' Ward replied. On 15 May Frank Dobson, the new health minister, had announced in the House of Commons that the government intended to ban tobacco sponsorship of all sports. Soon after, Tessa Jowell, a junior health minister, announced the same policy in Brussels. 'We must arrange another meeting with Tony,' Levy soothed. In Ward's mind that meant that he and Mosley would explain their problems to Blair. Ecclestone left all the issues about the EU directive to Mosley and Ward, just as he relied on Mosley to sort out the problems raised in Brussels about the flotation, and they had increased.

Nine months earlier, in November 1996, Wolfgang Eisele, a German television producer from Heidelberg, had visited Princes Gate. He presented Ecclestone with a problem and asked for a solution. Since 1983 Eisele had owned a television production company providing broadcasters with coverage of various motor sports including rallies, drag racing and truck racing. His small but profitable business faced ruin in 1995 after ISC, Ecclestone's company, was granted the television rights to all motor sports by FIA. Since then, Ecclestone appeared to have minimised the broadcasts of all non-Formula One motor sports on television. In Ecclestone's opinion only Formula One captured meaningful audiences. Eisele ranked among the small broadcasters and race organisers who were complaining that ISC was behaving like a monopoly. For two hours Eisele explained to Ecclestone that his business should be allowed to survive. He mentioned that European laws forbade Ecclestone crushing any competition but he hit a brick wall. Ecclestone assumed that no one could challenge his cast-iron agreement with Mosley and refused to seek more airtime for truck racing at Formula One's expense. They parted on bad terms.

Eisele returned to Germany determined to win. He filed complaints in the German courts and then submitted a complaint under the competition laws to the European Commission in Brussels. Articles 85 and 86 of the European Treaty forbade cartels or businesses abusing their dominating position. While Eisele's complaint was investigated by Karl van Miert, in Germany he won a quick victory. On 4 June 1997 a court ruled that FIA, by granting the television rights for truck races to Ecclestone and denying Eisele his rights, had violated European competition laws. Ecclestone had cause to be fearful. If the German court's decision was supported by van Miert, Ecclestone's control of television coverage over all motor sports was illegal and the value of Formula One would be slashed. After consulting Ecclestone, Mosley chose the nuclear option: FIA announced the permanent termination of European Truck Racing. In quick response, Eisele's lawyers returned to the German court and obtained a ruling that FIA's decision was illegal and, if implemented, FIA would be punished by a hefty fine. Mosley retreated. Eisele's creeping success infuriated

Ecclestone. 'I'm sure Mercedes is financing this,' said Mosley. 'No way,' insisted Ecclestone, convinced that Jurgen Schremp, the chief executive, would not be so disloyal.

Ecclestone's problems in Brussels and Karl van Miert's sympathy to complaints were not ignored by Ron Dennis, undoubtedly prodded by Ken Tyrrell. Ecclestone's plans, in Dennis's opinion, were 'something none of us could swallow'. Bound, he thought, by a 'certain honour', the Three employed lawyers to challenge Ecclestone in Brussels. In a lengthy submission to the EU commissioner, Dennis accused Ecclestone of dangerous conflicts of interest. Namely, he was simultaneously negotiating with the circuits and broadcasters as FOCA's representative and on FOH's (Formula One Holdings) behalf; and, while representing FOCA and FOH, he was also a member of FIA's council which regulated the sport; and, he had assumed rights which really belonged to the teams as FOCA members; and now Mosley, the supposed independent regulator, was representing Ecclestone's commercial interests in Brussels instead of those of the teams.

'Ron has left it too late to get any ownership of Formula One,' said Ecclestone, 'and he now sees the EU Commission as a way to up the ante.' The proposed flotation had worsened relations and, although the idea was effectively dead, Ecclestone talked angrily about withdrawing the offer of shares to the teams. At the same time, on 5 September 1997, his submission seeking the declaration to allow his flotation arrived in van Miert's office. To Ecclestone's distress, the application was accompanied by copies of all the contracts between himself, FIA, the teams and the television companies, all of which had hitherto been kept secret. 'He's a big dickhead,' Ecclestone cursed van Miert. 'Why is the EU interfering in sport?' Concerned about the breakdown in relations and the continuing failure to sign the Concorde agreement, Mosley wrote to the teams before they met at the Nürburgring in October urging, 'I feel we should make one final effort to move things forward.'

8

Tobacco

'He'll see us on 16 October,' said Max Mosley. The news of a meeting with Tony Blair did not particularly excite Ecclestone. Meeting kings, presidents and prime ministers was normal in his life. He knew, however, that his donation had paid for access into Downing Street.

Blair's agreement to meet Ecclestone, David Ward reassured Mosley, was directly connected to their conversation in his Islington home before the election, linking the donation and tobacco sponsorship. Ward assumed that Michael Levy had told Jonathan Powell about his latest request for annual £1 million donations. Ecclestone had not committed himself but the chance of more money had not harmed Formula One's influence.

Ecclestone did not intend to rely solely on Blair to prevent an immediate ban on tobacco sponsorship. Helmut Kohl, the German chancellor, was a friend and a Formula One fan. Ecclestone and Mosley had met the politician at the Grand Prix in Nürburgring on 27 July 1997. While walking around the circuit and later in his motorhome, Mosley had mentioned the sponsorship problem. The chancellor had agreed to become involved. Now they needed his help and the two flew to Bonn. During a short meeting in the chancellor's office, Mosley mentioned that if the EU directive was not dropped, Formula One would move to Asia. He reminded Kohl about the threat to end the French Grand Prix in 1992 after Frank Williams had been fined for French television's transmission of his cars covered with tobacco advertisements racing in the Japanese Grand Prix. The fine had been squashed by rushed legislation after Ecclestone's warning. Ecclestone hoped that they were not destined for a repetition of the French experience. Kohl, a big man at least three times Ecclestone's weight, assured his guests that Germany would repeat its previous veto of the EU directive and he would tell Blair about his position. The chancellor, Ecclestone knew, would be as good as his word. Tony Blair would hear from Bonn before their Downing Street meeting.

The short walk up Downing Street with Max Mosley was familiar to both men. Three days earlier both had been photographed on the same pavement as they headed towards a charity reception. On this occasion, though, no one witnessed their arrival.

Seated in a circle in a small ground-floor room with Powell and Ward listening, Mosley addressed the prime minister, as he would later say, 'lawyer-to-lawyer'. Eloquent and precise, Mosley's argument appeared irrefutable. The sponsorship ban, said Mosley, would be pointless because pictures of Grand Prix races transmitted from non-EU countries would display tobacco advertisements. All FIA wanted, explained Mosley, was a global solution. 'We don't oppose the end of tobacco advertising but we just want gradual elimination so that alternative sponsors could be found.' Blair nodded. If phased reduction was denied, Mosley quietly explained, 50,000 British jobs and digital television could easily be relocated outside the EU. Blair looked towards Ecclestone. Personalities at that moment, the businessman knew, were irrelevant, but Ecclestone was annoyed by Frank Dobson's portrayal of him as a representative of the tobacco industry. He had never smoked, he occasionally drank a single glass of beer and he did not care who sponsored Formula One but, he wanted Blair to know, there was no contest between a left-wing health minister and himself. With the snap of his fingers Britain could lose the Grand Prix and Motor Sport Valley. Those who ignored his warnings were always surprised that he did what he said. But, deliberately, he made his brief contribution unmemorable. He carefully did not mention tobacco or his need for a favour. He allowed Mosley to deliver what he believed to be the killer blow. 'Under European laws', said Mosley, 'the proposed EU directive is illegal.' On health issues, he explained, Brussels had no powers to impose directives on the UK or any member country. Blair nodded his understanding, and in 2000 Mosley's interpretation would be endorsed by the European Court of Justice. In conclusion, said Mosley, Formula One did not want an exclusive exemption from the ban, but merely a timetable for phasing out tobacco sponsorship. 'Let's keep in touch about this,' said Blair after thirty-five minutes. The three visitors departed convinced that there was an understanding. Shortly after, Mosley bumped into Peter Mandelson at a reception in Lancaster House. 'How's it going?' Mosley asked. 'The whole of Whitehall is reverberating to the sound of grinding gears,' smiled Mandelson, implying that Formula One's request was being granted.

By the following Monday, Ward heard that Blair had given an order to 'sort out the Formula One problem'. Jonathan Powell explained that the government was seeking an exemption in Brussels for Formula One from the directive. Shortly after, Tessa Jowell, the junior minister of health, called Mosley. Tony Blair, she said, had directed that Formula One should be given special exemption until October 2006. Mosley was displeased. He did not want special treatment for Formula One. He had argued for the abandonment of an illegal directive. Blair had ordered something he had never requested.

The next day, Ecclestone and Mosley flew to Spain for the European Grand Prix at Jerez, the last race of the season. Once again, the world championship was a cliff-hanger. Schumacher was leading by one point over Jacques Villeneuve driving for Williams. Schumacher could win the championship if Villeneuve did not finish the race. Frank Williams feared a repetition of the 1994 championship when Schumacher had shunted into Damon Hill. The 320 million television viewers who watched the race monitored the tense rivalry. At a corner on the forty-eighth lap, Villeneuve began to overtake Schumacher on the inside. As he eased ahead, Schumacher turned his car into Villeneuve's. To the German's surprise, after hitting the Williams his Ferrari bounced off the track into gravel while Villeneuve's car, damaged but still moving, came third after two McLarens. The stewards declared the incident to be accidental but Mosley disagreed and summoned Schumacher to a formal hearing.

On 6 November, five days before the 'trial', Mosley and Ecclestone met for dinner at San Lorenzo in London. 'Schumi hasn't done anything he should be punished for,' Ecclestone told Mosley in the course of a customary pre-trial discussion. 'He's innocent.' Schumacher's fame, Ecclestone knew, transcended Formula One and magnified the sport's income. By then, a small patch on the superstar's overalls cost the sponsor at least £500,000. More than money, Schumacher was 'magic on another planet' with 'remarkable ability to read and pace the race'. As a driver, Ecclestone knew, he was even better than Ayrton Senna but he was also cold-bloodedly ruthless and reckless. Banning or fining him would not expunge his passion to win and the sport needed his presence for the championship. Mosley agreed to reconsider the case.

Ecclestone was feeling particularly emboldened. FIA had just hosted a party in Monaco to celebrate his '50 years of service to the motor sport industry'. There had been tributes from Luca Montezemolo, racing drivers, team managers, Prince Albert of Monaco and a clutch of presidents and prime ministers. Flushed with those congratulations, Ecclestone was pleased that an amicable solution had been found to the tobacco sponsorship ban. The success reconfirmed his importance to the teams. On 4 November, Tessa Jowell announced that Britain would require exemption from the EU directive for Formula One and the problem appeared to be terminated.

Two days later, David Hill, Blair's trusted spokesman in Downing Street, was asked by a journalist if Ecclestone had made a large donation to the Labour party. 'Good God, I've no idea,' replied the director of communications. Soon after, Hill emphatically denied that Ecclestone had made a donation or that there was a link with Formula One's exemption. The same question was put to Ecclestone. Ecclestone was agitated. 'I wanted nothing to do with this,' he cursed in a mild voice. On his own initiative, he directed Herbert Smith, the City solicitors, to issue a statement that ' . . . Mr Ecclestone had not given a donation to the Labour party . . .' combined with a threat to start libel proceedings if the allegation was published. Mosley was appalled. 'That's a mistake,' he told Ecclestone. 'You should have said nothing.' Some urgent fire-fighting, Mosley decided, was required.

After lunch with Mosley in Chelsea, David Ward rushed to Downing Street to meet Jonathan Powell and Alastair Campbell, the prime minister's trusted media supremo. His instructions from Mosley were to urge the politicians to remain silent 'so that the problem goes away'. On his return Ward reported, 'It's total chaos.' Neither official wanted to admit that Hill, on their orders, had made a mistake. 'They didn't want to listen to me,' he told Mosley, sensing that Powell and Campbell, anxious to protect the prime minister, would cast Ecclestone as a villain and encourage Blair, if necessary, to lie. 'You could be in trouble,' Mosley told Ecclestone. 'It's no one's business,' Ecclestone retorted, unaware that funding a political party was a public, not a private, issue.

As his disquiet grew, Ecclestone was relieved that Mosley had discovered a legal escape route. Under the official rules, donations over £5,000 did not need to be listed until the party's accounts were published the following year. The crux was to refuse any comment. 'I said to those clowns,' recalled Ecclestone, 'if someone puts me up against the wall with a machine gun, I will not confirm or deny anything about the donation. They said, "OK, OK, we'll do the same." ' Ward telephoned Powell and again urged that the government stay silent about the donation.

In Ecclestone's confined circle of like-minded businessmen, a conspiracy of silence was effortlessly executed but he had entered into a foreign world. He was playing with Alastair Campbell, criticised by his enemies as an unprincipled thug, and a prime minister preening himself about his pledge to behave 'whiter than white' by eradicating sleaze. A conspiracy with Ecclestone to suppress the truth hardly appealed to Blair's entourage. On the contrary, ignoring Ecclestone's interests, Blair had already asked Derry Irvine, the Lord Chancellor, to limit the damage.

Britain's most senior lawyer believed that any confession of the truth was 'utterly absurd'. Instead, he advised that the government should create a smoke screen, ignoring Ecclestone. Acting on Irvine's advice, Blair concocted with Gordon Brown, the chancellor of the exchequer, a ruse. They would order Tom Sawyer, the party's general secretary, to write a letter to Sir Patrick Neill, the commissioner of standards in public life, based on a falsehood. Sawyer's letter, referring to the new code of conduct for party funding, mentioned that the Labour party had accepted a donation from Ecclestone while in opposition, and that 'Mr Ecclestone has since the election offered a further donation'. Sawyer expressed his concern to Neill about Ecclestone's offer of a second donation. So far, wrote Sawyer, the second offer had been refused out of fear of a potential conflict of interest because of the tobacco exemption. Neill was asked whether the party's concern was justified. Ecclestone would never discover whether Sawyer or Blair knew that he had ignored Levy's request for a second donation but he did realise that the letter was 'catastrophic because it was an implicit admission that the original donation was questionable'. Sawyer's letter was sent on 7 November. Ecclestone sensed the chaos. 'I've dealt with a lot of politicians,' he told David Ward, amazed by Blair's naivety, 'and I've never had any problems before. I like to think I can trust people – and he's the prime minister – but Labour are like boy scouts and the Tories are like hardened criminals. The Tories would have known how to stop this.' On the same day, David

Hill began prevaricating. He discovered the truth but, he would later admit, used evasions and menaces to deflect the journalists' questions.

The *Sunday Telegraph*'s scoop on 9 November reported Ecclestone's donation and the link to the government's political somersault in Brussels. So far, no one knew the amount Ecclestone had given and in the guessing game, there were estimates between £100,000 and £1.5 million. The money, it was reported, was a crude bribe for help because Ecclestone had always voted Tory and, according to Tory officials, had previously contributed to their party. Overnight Ecclestone's anonymity evaporated. By breakfast time on Sunday, Ecclestone was equated in the media with buying access. 'They've got me hooking up the government,' he said in a cool tone to Mosley. 'There's nothing I can do and I don't care. I'm not fazed out.' Since few facts about Ecclestone were publicly known, the old myths were repeated – the menace, mystery, manipulation and the omnipotent office shredder were all laid bare. His dislike of publicity had bequeathed an image of a sinister businessman who unscrupulously destroyed his competitors while married to a woman twenty-eight years younger and a foot taller. Across the world, he found himself in the middle of a storm, depicted as a villain guilty of bribing the government. To illustrate the 'corruption' reports, the television news programmes broadcast pictures of Ecclestone and Mosley walking up Downing Street. Viewers would assume they were watching the historic moment after Formula One had paid cash for access but in reality the images were those recorded earlier in the week at the charity event.

By the end of Sunday, everyone was running for cover. The following morning, 10 November, Gordon Brown appeared on the BBC's *Today* radio programme. Asked about the donation, he unconvincingly prevaricated, denying any knowledge about Ecclestone's money. Events had moved beyond the government's and Ecclestone's control. Patrick Neill replied with remarkable speed. Regardless of the truth, he wrote later that day, the appearance of taking Ecclestone's money had raised questions of honesty and offended the rules. Therefore, he concluded, not only should the second donation be refused but Ecclestone's first donation should be returned. In Downing Street there was panic. No one had anticipated that interpretation. The so-called 'spin doctors' spoke about limiting the damage by admitting some limited truth. So Hill told enquiring journalists that Ecclestone had given the party 'over £5,000'. Downing Street's admission contradicted Herbert Smith's denial and Ecclestone's position rapidly deteriorated. Another Downing Street spokesman was authorised by Hill to say that during their Downing Street meeting 'no request was made regarding policy' by Ecclestone. In synchronisation, Ecclestone issued a statement, drafted by Ward and Mosley, admitting he made a donation but adding, 'I never sought any favour from New Labour or any member of the government, nor has any been given.' When he looked at the television news that night and saw the newspapers the following morning, Ecclestone was 'pissed off'. No one believed any of the denials. The conspiracy to deceive had unravelled. Labour, he moaned, should have stuck to their agreement not to mention his donation.

Ecclestone found himself like flotsam on the high seas – helpless to control his destiny. Adrift from Downing Street, he could only rely on Mosley. 'What are they up to?' he asked. 'Find out what's happening,' ordered the man accustomed to controlling rather than reacting to events. Mosley sent Ward back to Downing Street asking the prime minister to exonerate Ecclestone publicly – and put him in the clear. By midday there was no reply and, fatefully, Ecclestone and Mosley were conducting an FIA disciplinary hearing in Colnbrook, Berkshire, about Schumacher's crash into Villeneuve at Jerez. Until then, Ecclestone had never contemplated drawing comparisons between the simplicity of cheating in Formula One and the contorted dishonesty in Westminster, but the hearing about a simple crash turned out to be enmeshed in conspiracies.

The night before the Schumacher hearing, Ecclestone had met the driver and Jean Todt, the Ferrari team manager, in a London hotel. Over dinner Ecclestone was told that during the Jerez race the Ferrari team had been eavesdropping on the radio conversations between the Williams team managers and Villeneuve. One manager could be heard telling Villeneuve that Mika Hakkinen of McLaren was just behind him and should be allowed to pass. 'Hakkinen has been very helpful,' Villeneuve was told. 'Don't let me down, Jacques. We discussed this.' Soon after, Villeneuve allowed Hakkinen to pass and win. There was clear evidence, said Todt, that the Williams team had conspired with McLaren to fix the race. To put pressure on Mosley, the transcript of the conversations had been given to *The Times* for publication just before the hearing. Ferrari's argument, presented by the newspaper, was that Schumacher had been provoked to crash to overcome the conspiracy. In reply Frank Williams and Ron Dennis expressed their 'disappointment' that Ferrari were secretly listening to their conversations. Some believed Ferrari had concocted the smoke screen to divert attention from Schumacher's malevolence, while others mentioned a link to Williams's and McLaren's dispute about the Concorde agreement. Ecclestone told Todt that the tapes would not influence the outcome of the trial. 'I've told Max that Schumi's innocent,' said Ecclestone. 'I'm sure he'll agree if Michael says the right things.' Schumacher nodded his understanding.

During the actual hearing, Schumacher gradually conceded a point to Mosley. 'I saw him coming past,' he admitted, 'and I just thought, "I must stop him." ' In deliberating his judgement, Mosley changed his position. 'I must decide what's in the overall interest of the sport,' he told Ecclestone, 'and it's no use banning Schumacher, or fining him a huge amount. The fans won't like it.' Accordingly, Mosley declared that Schumacher's swerve had been 'instinctive' and 'not made with malice or premeditation. It was just a serious error.' Instead of a ban he took away Schumacher's second position, knowing that it was a meaningless gesture, and ordered him to teach road safety for seven days. Villeneuve was confirmed as the world champion. FIA's justice was completed.

Before leaving the building with Mosley, Ecclestone heard 'by accident' that Alastair Campbell, in conversations with selected journalists, was portraying Ecclestone's donation to the party as an attempt to change Labour policy. 'Tony Blair has started talking,' Ecclestone cursed. 'It's third-rate behaviour.' As he emerged from the building, a group of journalists approached. Blair, they exclaimed, had admitted the donation. 'Well, if Mr Blair said that, he wouldn't lie, would he?' Ecclestone replied. 'How much did you give?' he was asked. '£1 million,' he said. His sensational disclosure was explosive. On the front pages was Ecclestone's admission and on the back page was Schumacher's conviction for a deliberate crash. Ecclestone had become a byword for sleaze in Britain's political history. Wags dubbed £1 million 'a Bernie' and politicians renamed 10 Downing Street 'Bernie's Inn', a reference to the popular restaurants of the 1960s and '70s. Off-message, Jack Straw, the home secretary, publicly admitted that Blair had 'been aware of the second offer from Mr Ecclestone when they met at Downing Street' and then promptly disappeared. To close down the horror, Campbell arranged Blair's first post-election television interview. The prime minister's words were carefully rehearsed to place all the blame on Ecclestone. Even 'before any journalist had been in touch' with Downing Street, Blair told his audience, the Labour party had notified Ecclestone that, despite his 'firm commitment' of paying another £1 million, 'We couldn't accept further donations.' Only then, said Blair, had the government asked Neill about the probity of the first donation and, as a result, it would of course be repaid. To tilt the balance further in his favour against a used-car dealer, Blair concluded, 'I'm a pretty straight sort of guy.' The lies saved Blair but left Ecclestone's reputation damaged.

'I've been hung out to dry,' he complained. In the past he had not cared what was said about him but now every word risked a fortune. The flotation was jeopardised by his association with sleaze. 'I'm pissed off that they have been trying to dig up dirt,' Ecclestone complained about journalists. 'But people will be buying shares in a company that makes money and that is what counts.' To restore his reputation, Mosley drafted a letter on his behalf to *The Times*: 'I made the donation to the Labour party because I believe Mr Blair to be a person of exceptional ability who, if free to act, would do an outstanding job for our country.' Explaining that he wanted to free Labour from dependence on trade unions, he continued 'There were no strings attached.' He had, he wrote, paid £27 million income tax the previous year 'for the simple privilege of living in England rather than a tax haven'. In return for paying taxes, Ecclestone insisted that he had the right to 'enjoy the same rights as everyone else' and make a donation to 'any political party I choose. Anything less implies that I have done something wrong and is a gross, insulting and irrational restriction of my freedom.' In an interview with *The Times*, Ecclestone explained that Blair was 'anti-European' like himself and he had contributed out of anger about the Conservative 'demon eyes' advertising campaign in the 1997 election smearing Blair. To others he was more candid. His integrity was in doubt: 'I just hope that my reputation is of someone who is straightforward and honest, and not of someone who is going to screw people, because I haven't done that. My reputation is worth more to me than money. I'd like to be remembered as "the handshake guy", the one who did it all on a handshake.' In the City of London, a member of the Rothschild family wryly recalled the Square Mile's traditional assurance, 'My word is my bond', and his own response, 'I'd prefer to take the bond.' Trusting politicians revealed remarkable naivety.

Ecclestone's expectation that his explanation would be accepted revealed that he was at best simplistic about the electorate's genuine cynicism. At worst, few believed his summary of the dilemma: 'Being nice to people to gain something is not in my nature . . . I am a deliverer. I like the business to be done fair

and square. I am not interested in what other people think of me
. . . I have enough money not to be corrupt . . . All I've done I've
done honestly. I'm just a bloke doing a job. I've never cheated
anybody.' Asserting his honesty was critical to the flotation.
The business had never been healthier. Christian Vogt had just
concluded a ten-year deal with Canal Plus, the French television
station, for about $500 million.

The hope that a letter to *The Times* would repair Ecclestone's
reputation was dented by Ron Dennis. 'I don't believe that Bernie,
a cheapskate who counts every penny, gave £1 million out of his
own pocket,' he said. In Dennis's opinion, the argument showed
how Ecclestone was 'crossing to the dark side', a reference to the
film *Star Wars*. Later that same day the two met to settle their
differences. 'You know where you are with Bernie,' Dennis said.
'You know he'll do anything to extract money. He won't feel good
tomorrow morning unless he thinks that I'll wake up and feel
screwed by the deal.' Although the flotation was dead, Ecclestone
refused to admit defeat, and repeated his offer of 10 per cent of
the shares to the teams and 10 per cent to FIA. 'Bernie doesn't
give things,' Dennis reminded himself. 'You have to fight for
them.' The offer was rejected. Dennis was enjoying Ecclestone's
discomfort and was anticipating that more difficulties would
either wreck the flotation or give him a bigger share.

As he emerged from the meeting with Dennis, a stream of
telephone messages was waiting. Among them was an anguished summons to call Slavica in Croatia. Clearly upset, his wife
revealed that a local newspaper had published an extensive report
describing her wild teenage years illustrated by nude photographs.
The reporter, Momir Blagojević, a former boyfriend and the
photographer, described how Slavica, working as a prostitute,
had been employed by the local secret service to target Ecclestone.
Ecclestone was convinced that these allegations were outrageous
and untrue. He had known she had posed in the nude and
accepted her vehement denials. He repeated his mantra: 'I never
worry about what people were, I care only what people are.'

Blagojević's blackmail and Ron Dennis's obduracy, Ecclestone realised, were linked to the notoriety of the £1 million donation. 'I wish to God Labour had accepted the £1 million I gave them,' he told the *Sunday Mirror*, 'because since they returned it every nutter in the world wants a piece.' As the storm passed, Ecclestone realised that Blair was a better dealer than himself, and Westminster was infinitely tougher than Warren Street. 'Blair played with chips,' he thought, 'I played with money. Blair played a crooked hand. These people did the best they can for themselves and then tried to bury me.' On reflection, if anyone was to blame, it was Mosley and he was more upset than Ecclestone. His partner's trust in Labour had exploded in his face. 'I'd done it to help Max and he felt bad,' Ecclestone lamented. The Establishment, both agreed, could not be trusted. Ecclestone had not broken the law or done anything wrong while the politicians had lied and reneged on their promises. He refused to be questioned by Sir Patrick Neill's inquiry about what he expected for £1 million. 'If you appear you get yourself involved,' he explained. Except that the dust never quite settled. His name and Formula One became a metaphor among politicians and the media for buying influence. To Slavica's distress, at their daughters' school, one pupil read out an essay at assembly about Ecclestone's apparent corruption of the Labour party. 'Blair is hateful,' said his wife. A cheque for £1 million was sent to Ecclestone who kept it until the last day before cashing it. Over the next five years, he cancelled races because of bans on tobacco advertising and threatened others unless proposed bans were dropped.

Ecclestone's embarrassment in London galvanised the bureaucrats in Brussels. After scrutinising Formula One's documents, van Miert's lawyers discovered an interlocking web of agreements facilitating Ecclestone's control of a business which excluded competitors. In his formal letter to Ecclestone, van Miert asserted that Formula One Holdings was 'abusing its dominant position to favour Formula One'. The company's restrictive clauses in its contracts with the circuits prevented any non-Formula One races and limited the televising of other events. Lacking any transparency, the arrangement was criticised as a stitch-up made worse by the Concorde agreement, damned as 'a serious restriction of competition'. The most offensive document in the EU bureaucrat's opinion was the 'excessive' fifteen-year contract with FIA. Under EU rules, any agreement lasting more than five years was 'a serious infringement of EU competition rules' which could be punished by fines. In summary, wrote van Miert, FOH did not qualify for flotation nor, fatally, could it even continue in business without change.

Looking for an explanation for van Miert's prejudice, Ecclestone alighted on the row about the Belgian Grand Prix at Spa-Francorchamps. On 1 December 1997 Belgium's national government, ruled by the Flemish socialists, had banned tobacco sponsorship of Formula One. Ecclestone retaliated by cancelling the 1998 Grand Prix located in the French-speaking part of Belgium. His decision, said Ecclestone, would only be revoked if the tobacco ban was lifted. Appalled by the risk of losing $27 million income, the local French government pledged to repeal the law. Van Miert, a Flemish Belgian, retaliated. Breaking the confidentiality rules, he listed his criticisms of Formula One to the *Wall Street Journal* and divulged his confidential letters to Mosley and Ecclestone. By exposing his bias, the commissioner undermined the EU's credibility. Delighting in the chance of a fight, Mosley filed a complaint in the European court for an apology and costs, describing van Miert's formal letter as riddled with 'errors of fact'.

Negotiating a resolution, Ecclestone knew, could take years. To force the pace, he and Mosley deployed what they anticipated would coerce the Commission in the same manner as they had originally persuaded Tony Blair. Mosley revealed that if the European commission sought to dictate how Formula One conducted its business, then Formula One would leave Europe. The 'Exit Option', Mosley believed, was reinforced by statistics. Only fifteen out of FIA's 113 member countries were in the EU and only one-fifth of the television audience was in the EU. Moving the headquarters of the sport would cause more damage to Europe than to the organisers, said Mosley. In public Ecclestone supported his friend but was unsure about the cost and the teams' support. Most doubted his ability to arrange races in South Korea, Malaysia and China. 'The Asian dream', an insider told newspapers, 'has been scuppered by the financial crisis.' Ecclestone's influence, he speculated, 'will never be the same again'. Ron Dennis was particularly caustic. Jubilant that he had pocketed $200 million in 1998 from Mercedes for a 40 per cent share of McLaren, he was convinced that he would receive more cash once van Miert compelled Ecclestone and Mosley to release their grip over Formula One.

Unaccustomed to surrender, even Ecclestone sensed it was time for compromises. Knowing that the flotation was dead, he could painlessly offer the teams 10 per cent of the proposed public company – each team would get 1 per cent – and sugar his offer with 50 per cent of the television revenue. But in return he insisted the 1997 Concorde agreement, finally signed in May 1998 in Monaco by ten out of the eleven team principals, should be extended to ten years, despite the EU Commission. Only Ecclestone did not sign the thirty-sixth and final draft. Dealing with van Miert, he knew, would be harder. Removing Eisele's complaint would be a beginning. 'Some people you can't reason with,' said Ecclestone. 'We'll just have to get on and settle with him.'

Ecclestone had met Eisele through an intermediary in July 1997 in Germany. If Eisele withdrew his complaint, said Ecclestone, they could form a partnership in a television programme covering all non-Formula One motor sports. Eisele refused. 'Do you think you're going to win against me?' asked Ecclestone. Eisele nodded. One month later, in his hotel in Gstaad, the two met again. In the course of their conversation the two agreed that the German would withdraw his complaint if Ecclestone paid him $5 million. Ecclestone set out the terms. To ensure he got value for his money, Ecclestone said the payments should be staggered. He would pay $500,000 immediately and the remainder in two payments: the first after Eisele withdrew his complaint, and the second after Formula One's flotation. Ecclestone also wanted the names of those financing Eisele's lawyers. Eisele refused to divulge the names but agreed to the rest and wrote down the account where the money should be deposited. Ecclestone noted that the money was destined for a private account in Switzerland. 'He should pick on someone his own size,' he told his lawyer. Eisele received the first payment and thereafter, in Ecclestone's opinion, was in trouble.

By then, Ecclestone's vulnerability was spotted by others. Patrick Peter, a French race organiser, wanted the television rights to GT car races and lodged complaints in Brussels that he was being locked out of circuits. Privately he approached Ecclestone for damages of about £14 million to be paid to a Panamanian corporation. Another vulture emerged from the European Commission. Panayotis 'Panos' Adamopoulos, a Greek official describing himself as 'a spear-carrier for van Miert', warned Mosley, 'You don't know what you're up against.' Formula One's case, he explained, would be improved if he could personally visit the Monaco Grand Prix. Mosley agreed. Adamopoulos added that his family should also receive tickets. Four people received the $16,000 hospitality package but Mosley had not calculated that Adamopoulos would leave the town without paying any bill. 'He's a man who can be bought,' said Ecclestone about an official who would in 2006 be accused in Greece of blackmail and subsequently imprisoned. Van Miert, Ecclestone suspected, was equally dishonest for helping the production of a BBC *Panorama* television programme denouncing Ecclestone for murky finances and his £1 million donation to Labour. Mosley wanted to sue the BBC. 'Don't bother,' said Ecclestone who no longer cared about criticism. His focus was on business and finding an alternative to flotation.

In his search for cash, Karl Essig, a Morgan Stanley banker, offered a solution. Instead of flotation, said Essig, 'You could do a debt deal.' Formula One Group would sell $2 billion in bonds to banks, giving Ecclestone the cash while the business, Formula One Administration, repaid the loan from its earnings. The major hurdle was to reassure potential investors that Formula One was sound. By any measure, there was no safer business. In 1998 Ecclestone's companies reported £122 million profits on sales of £244 million. Supporting that extraordinary revenue annually were 4.9 billion viewers in 131 countries. Ecclestone's earnings were guaranteed by the television contracts, some lasting ten years. The only twist was Essig's pitch to Ecclestone that the bonds would be repaid out of a future flotation, a scheme which required the banks to take a lot on trust. Salomon Brothers, the world's biggest bond dealer, said Christian Purslow, would refuse to participate. 'Tobacco and the EU make it tough sledding,' he warned, not mentioning that mutual disdain between himself and some team owners was an insuperable obstacle.

To convince investors, Ecclestone appealed to Mosley for help. FIA's president was chaffing. He wanted to help Ecclestone but also feared that 'the entrepreneurial side of racing has almost been taken to the limit'. Everyone in Formula One had become seriously rich, including even Eddie Jordan. The Irish businessman had persuaded a director from Warburg Pincus, the investment fund, whom he had met in the directors' box at Coventry City football club, to invest in his faltering team. 'The banker didn't seem to have a clue,' said Jordan after pocketing £40 million. Jordan would laugh again when he repurchased the 40 per cent share from the bank for a fraction of its original price, and resold the team to another bank. He would be less amused in May 2001 when Mr Justice Langley, hearing Jordan's suit against Vodafone for allegedly breaking a three-year sponsorship agreement worth $150 million, stated, 'It is readily apparent from the documents that [Mr Jordan's] evidence was untrue' and that Jordan's written statements submitted to the court were 'known to Mr Jordan to be false'. Despite their wealth, Mosley cursed, the teams constantly argued. No one irritated him more than Ron Dennis whom he regarded as a self-important money-grabber renowned for paying contractors to wash the gravel outside his home every six months. Dennis's ambition for the teams to run Formula One was, in Mosley's opinion, nonsensical. Nevertheless, to help Ecclestone, he invited Dennis for dinner to the Poissonnerie, a traditional fish restaurant in South Kensington. Dennis accepted, though he considered Mosley effeminate and untrustworthy even if sharply intellectual.

To seduce his guest, Mosley praised McLaren's success as a championship team. 'You should relax,' said Mosley. 'You're rich and married to a beautiful woman. There's no need to continuously fight.' Mosley's sermon irritated Dennis. 'I was being lectured about how lucky I was to receive everything, and I thought, I've got it all because of my hard work. And it benefited all the teams.' As Mosley continued, Dennis recalled how his host and Ecclestone had in the past laughed at him, challenging his dignity. 'I couldn't understand Mosley's motives. He was head of FIA and yet he was supporting Formula One's threat to leave Europe. I suspected collusion between Mosley and Ecclestone.' Dennis wanted the teams to control Formula One, or at least receive a far greater share of the profits. Nothing less would satisfy him. At first he replied to Mosley in strangulated sentences, which Mosley attributed to his struggling to assert his importance, but eventually Dennis cut through the fog. 'I scuppered Bernie's float,' he boasted, delighted to have prevented Ecclestone from reaping a windfall. Mosley was mindful of Ecclestone's quip, 'If I gave the teams 1 per cent of the business they would be angry that someone else has 99 per cent.' The dinner ended on a sour note. Mosley wondered if Dennis required psychiatric help. 'I feel sorry for him,' Mosley told Ecclestone without conviction. Dennis was equally uncharitable towards Mosley. Nevertheless, Mosley and Ecclestone persuaded Dennis that the flotation would eventually be rejuvenated and he would finally receive his reward. To secure those extra millions, said Ecclestone, he needed Dennis's support for Morgan Stanley's £2 million bond.

On 16 November 1998 Ecclestone, flanked by Dennis, Luca Montezemolo and Marco Piccinini, appeared at Essig's first road show in London. Dennis agreed to be present because 'Bernie gave me assurances that the teams would benefit from the bond.'

'I asked Ron for a favour,' Ecclestone would say. 'He did a better job than I did.' Montezemolo was present because 'Bernie promised us a share in the cake.' All four pledged that they were working together in a sound business. The banker himself hoped to overcome 'the ill-informed and misleading background noise'. The worst part was van Miert's complaints. Normally, the Commission sought to resolve issues by private negotiation and on that basis Ecclestone issued a statement at the meeting to the City professionals pledging that 'all concerns raised by the Commission have now been, or can be, dealt with'. He was repeating Stephen Mullens's assurances to the *Financial Times* about 'just a few minor issues to resolve'. Ecclestone's guarantee annoyed van Miert. The commissioner, wanting a public fight, told enquiring journalists with some relish that Ecclestone was mistaken. There were unresolved issues, said van Miert, knowing that his declaration would trigger the London Stock Exchange's refusal to approve the bonds. In the same week as Long Term Capital Management, a New York hedge fund, lost a record $1.6 billion, the rating agencies also refused to bless the bond. The City's verdict was delivered to Ecclestone in his office by Robin Saunders, an attractive American banker employed by the Westdeutsche Landesbank, a state-owned German bank, who had been asked by Essig to subscribe to the bonds. 'This deal will never happen,' declared Saunders. Ecclestone's credibility was damaged. His advisers, criticised for poor housekeeping, had failed to persuade the City that Formula One was a sound business worth $2 billion. Days later, Morgan Stanley's salesmen reported, 'There's been too much noise. It's too hot.' Essig admitted defeat.

Ecclestone was flummoxed. Bankers' promises were repeatedly broken. 'It seems to be difficult for them', he reflected, 'to understand all the businesses they get involved in. The strange thing is that they seem to want to see how a business works, to find out what a company is really like and then the first thing they want to do is change it.' Ron Walker suggested that Ecclestone contact Brian Powers, the chairman of John Fairfax, an Australian media corporation, and a director of Hellman & Friedman, an investment fund in San Francisco. 'Powers is known as "The Vulture",' Walker added to convince Ecclestone he was dealing with a serious player. Powers, Ecclestone discovered, understood Formula One's virtues. It was a simple business with fixed sources of income – the circuit races, McNally's Allsport, sponsorship and television – producing about $400 million profit every year. The complication was relying on Ecclestone to juggle the conflicts among the erratic teams. 'What sort of investor are you looking for?' Powers asked in early 1999. 'Deaf, dumb and blind,' replied Ecclestone. 'Well,' replied Powers somewhat nonplussed, 'would two out of three be OK?' 'We could do business,' replied Ecclestone. Eight meetings with Powers proved Ecclestone's mastery of the details but equally the absence of a budget or a reliable prediction of profits. After 'arm-twisting' about the price, Powers told Ecclestone that the $1.4 billion he required was 'too high, and we're spooked about the EU investigation'. Reluctantly, Ecclestone returned to the bankers, pleased at least that Morgan Stanley was trapped. Before committing itself, Ecclestone had extracted a written undertaking from the bank to find $2 billion. Without a clean exit from its liability, the bank needed a saviour. The lifebelt was offered by Robin Saunders. Finally, Ecclestone had found a banker who believed in his business. 'Can we get rid of Morgan Stanley?' Ecclestone asked. 'No,' replied Saunders. 'They've done one year's work. You won't want to go through all that again.' Ecclestone's refusal – unusual at that time – to allow any documents to be taken from Princes Gate, or even copied, was an added burden for the bankers.

As she trawled through the accounts of Formula One Administration Ltd, Saunders noted that FOA had received about $150 million a year from the circuits and $219 million in 1997 from television revenues. Mosley had just released viewing figures for 1996 showing that 40.99 billion people in 202 countries had watched part of Formula One's races, more than watched football and the Olympic Games. In 1999 FOA would earn $241 million and the company was anticipated to receive a further $1.5 billion by 2004. More than half of that money went directly to Ecclestone. Beyond that period FOA's gross revenues for the following five years, 2005 to 2010, could be guessed at around $2.3 billion. In Saunders's opinion, the first tranche was 'watertight'. The stumbling block was Ecclestone's credibility. No City investor could believe he was earning such huge profits without concealed glitches. To reassure herself, Saunders needed to check Ecclestone's contracts with broadcasters, circuits, sponsors and the teams. Each contract needed to be vetted to ensure that the rights did belong to Ecclestone and not to FIA, and that Mosley formally agreed to Ecclestone's ownership. Whenever there were doubts, Mosley's signature was needed to confirm Ecclestone's ownership. 'Max has been extremely helpful,' she told Ecclestone.

To secure City approval and limit her risk, Saunders reduced the loan to $1.4 billion and guaranteed that the Westdeutsche Landesbank and Morgan Stanley would repay the bond holders. Ecclestone agreed to immediately repay $400 million to the bankers and pay 8 per cent interest on the remaining $1 billion until the loan was completely repaid in November 2010. The high interest rates would stimulate Ecclestone to repay the debt swiftly. For the bond issue Formula One Administration Ltd was renamed Formula One Management (FOM). The bankers' signatures finalised the deal on 28 May 1999 and they celebrated at a London restaurant but without Ecclestone. Impatient throughout the process, he nevertheless praised Saunders: 'She was the one kicking arse all down the line and making things happen.' She did more. She bestowed financial credibility on the ex-Warren Street dealer. It was his breakthrough.

The following morning, Ecclestone telephoned Saunders. 'I've been a naughty boy,' he told the banker. 'What is it?' she asked. 'I have to have a triple heart bypass,' he said. 'When?' 'Today,' he replied. 'I want to jump out of the window,' she exclaimed, later admitting that it was the 'worst day of my life'. Despite the exhaustive financial diligence, she had assumed that the 'key man insurance' had scrutinised whether the sixty-nine-year-old was healthy. If his operation failed, someone would be legally liable.

Coincidentally, on the same morning Ecclestone received an unexpected call from Tuana Tan, the first for many months. 'What's wrong?' she asked, sensing fear in the voice of the man she still loved. After explaining his predicament and his apprehension of death at the very moment he had realised real wealth, she promised 'I'll pray for you.' In the afternoon, Saunders was reassured that the operation was a success but she would be unaware of the internal bleeding he suffered during the night. 'I'll only stop working,' he would say three weeks later, 'when they're lowering me into the ground, and that's a long way off.'

Ecclestone was recovering from the surgery when, on 30 June 1999, van Miert formally issued his judgement: 'We have found evidence of serious infringements of EU competition rules which could result in substantial fines.' FIA and Ecclestone were accused of creating a monopoly which excluded others in order to pocket unreasonable profits. FIA, said van Miert, was 'abusing its power' in favour of Ecclestone and could no longer assign the television rights of any international motor event to Ecclestone. On the contrary, all the rights which Ecclestone had obtained by agreement with FIA, declared van Miert, were worthless. The investors who had pledged $1.4 billion had good reason to be concerned that the Ecclestone's 'few minor issues' could wreck Formula One. Ecclestone was consoled by Mosley's scathing riposte that the Commission's 'hopelessly flawed' judgement was 'riddled with errors and mistaken assumptions'. Mosley was in his element. He loved a fight and the Commission, he believed, was vulnerable. His first victory was van Miert's apology for leaking documents to the *Wall Street Journal*.

More eager than ever to raise cash before the end of the tax year, Ecclestone asked Saunders, 'Do you want to buy 50 per cent of Formula One?' 'No,' she replied, 'but I know someone who does.' Her candidate was Robert Tschenguiz, a London entrepreneur. The two met. Ecclestone's price was high. He valued Formula One at $3.5 billion and wanted $1.1 billion for 50 per cent of the shares plus the buyer's liability to repay the $1.4 billion bond. Tschenguiz bowed out but Saunders offered a replacement – Scott Lanphere of Morgan Grenfell Private Equity.

Lanphere was a Formula One fan. He had already met Ecclestone while considering whether to invest in Tom Walkinshaw's Formula One team. 'He does whatever he can get away with,' Ecclestone had commented about Walkinshaw, describing an inspired team manager. 'The trouble with Tom is that he cheats and gets caught,' continued Ecclestone who respected bankers much less. Trusting Ecclestone's judgement, Lanphere bought 12.5 per cent of Formula One in October 1999 for $325 million (£275 million) with an option to buy a further 37.5 per cent share for $975 million by 1 February 2000. At those prices, Formula One was worth $2.6 billion.

Although he negotiated the deal with Ecclestone, Lanphere formally negotiated the purchase from Stephen Mullens. To fulfil his ambition to raise sufficient finance to buy the 37.5 per cent stake, Lanphere arranged a weekend summit in Mustique to entice potential partners. His guests included the Bronfmans, the American drinks family, Leo Kirch, the German television tycoon, Mansour Ojjeh, a part-owner of TAG Heuer, the Swiss watch company, and a shareholder in McLaren, a director of Lehman Brothers and Tommy Hilfiger, the clothing designer. In Lanphere's opinion, they were 'all rich, flaky and wanted to get into the deal without letting Bernie get the best of the deal'. Before flying to the Caribbean, Lanphere demanded more information 'for my lawyers' from Ecclestone and Mullens, representing the family trusts. Ecclestone was, as usual, resistant. He hated giving away secrets, especially about the contracts and the Concorde agreements. The banker's request was irritating, especially his demand for a comfort letter that Ecclestone's submissions to van Miert were true. 'You don't know who you're playing with, boy,' Ecclestone told Lanphere, who was seen standing outside Harvey Nichols, the Knightsbridge store, arguing with Ecclestone on his mobile telephone. 'You're playing me,' shouted Lanphere. Eventually Ecclestone agreed to disclose some information and Lanphere flew to what he called 'the rich atmosphere of Mustique' to 'bait and switch' the potential investors, which translated as 'hooking them into something different to what they expected'. Lanphere's scheme was to sell the 37.5 per cent stake but personally keep control of Formula One. He returned to London empty-handed.

Ecclestone began to doubt Lanphere's judgement. After buying the Formula One stake, Morgan Grenfell had paid £40 million for a 25 per cent stake in the Arrows team owned by Tom Walkinshaw in collaboration with an obscure Nigerian 'prince'. Unknown to Ecclestone and Lanphere, the Arrows finances soon after rapidly declined as the 'prince' remained invisible and Walkinshaw diverted funds to his private company in the British Virgin Islands. Eventually Walkinshaw would be sued by Morgan Grenfell and the businessman would be called 'downright dishonest' by Mr Justice Lightman. So long as he did not lose personally, Ecclestone was tolerant of skulduggery, so he bailed out Walkinshaw for about £3.2 million, albeit backed by securities – but he judged all players by their deals and Lanphere was failing the test.

Fearful of not selling the 37.5 per cent stake before the end of the tax year, Ecclestone suggested to Lanphere that he could find a partnership for the $975 million purchase with Thomas

Haffa, the forty-seven-year-old chief executive of EM.TV, a fast expanding German media company with close links to Leo Kirch. 'But your option will expire at 5 p.m. Geneva time on 9 February 2000,' Ecclestone warned.

In legal terms, Lanphere was negotiating with Mullens as the representative of the family trusts. The tax lawyer had early on become sceptical of Lanphere after Morgan Grenfell had bought outright only 12.5 per cent of the shares rather than 37.5 per cent. Mullens was 'disappointed' and to protect his interests had included a clause in the contract with the bank empowering the family trusts to issue new shares to sell to another buyer if Lanphere failed to meet the deadline. Mullens wondered whether he or his advisers fully understood the implications of that clause.

As the deadline approached, Lanphere and Haffa were still arguing but Lanphere was convinced that the closing date would be extended. Normally, Ecclestone assumed he could get on with anyone and was indifferent about relationships unless he was deceived, but as the deadline neared, he exclaimed, 'Lanphere's an idiot. He's a madman.' Lanphere understandably resented the criticism. In the banker's opinion, he was blamed for conflicts created by Ecclestone himself but was sanguine about the deadline. The banker and Haffa believed Ecclestone would be flexible. Neither had yet learnt to remember Robin Saunders's observation, 'Bernie always does what he says.'

Without Lanphere's knowledge, Mullens had been simultaneously negotiating to sell the newly issued shares to Brian Powers. Early on 9 February 2000, the day Lanphere's option would expire at 5 p.m., Ecclestone telephoned Powers. Ecclestone chortled that Lanphere and Haffa were in his office disputing the final terms. 'Out of my office,' Ecclestone ordered. After the door was closed, Ecclestone told Powers, 'They've messed up a bit. They're pushing the envelope a little too far.' Then he told Powers, 'If they don't meet the deadline the stake's yours for $712 million.' This was less than Lanphere because Powers was not charged for a proportion of the debt. At one minute past five, Lanphere and Haffa were still bickering. Ecclestone telephoned Powers, 'I've got bad news for you,' he said, 'we're partners.' While they spoke, Lanphere entered Ecclestone's office to declare that he had a deal with Haffa. 'You're too late,' said Ecclestone who, although the family trusts had lost about $263 million, would stick to the deal with Powers. Lanphere was shocked. Ecclestone, he believed, had been 'unethical' to muddy the ownership between himself and the trusts. 'You know what you did was wrong,' Lanphere told Mullens, but recriminations were pointless. More bewildering was the remarkable deal Powers sealed. Only about $400 million was paid by his fund and the remainder was borrowed from Ecclestone's family trust. Formula One was valued at £1.7 billion and Ecclestone still held 50 per cent of the shares. The sale was a relief. Out of the carnage, Ecclestone had pocketed about $2 billion. He could now look in the eye those City slickers who had simultaneously chastised him while pouring money into suspect dot.com businesses sold by goofy nobodies, and those of the same breed who had compelled him, after a failed court case, to buy the Formula One.com website for $10 million from a California company that had registered the domain before he understood the internet. To many, Ecclestone appeared to be cashing in and getting out. He proclaimed the opposite: 'Money doesn't drive me. Money is the by-product, not my ambition, although my success is judged by money.'

Brian Powers was hungry for more. He wanted to buy Allsport. Patrick McNally's mobile telephone rang just as a covey of partridges was heading in his direction while he was shooting with Guy Sangster, the racehorse owner. The birds flew unthreatened overhead as McNally heard a voice say, 'I want to make you a very rich man.' Three days later Luca Montezemolo mentioned that many of the Formula One teams were displeased by Ecclestone's sell-off and would break away from Formula One. Powers took fright and abandoned any interest to expand his investment.

On reflection, Ecclestone was unhappy about the sale. Powers's deal was unattractive but there seemed to be no alternative. If he died, the company's value would immediately drop and the trustees could be vulnerable. 'Think about this for two minutes,' he told an enquirer. 'I'm gone, Slavica marries a strapping young guy who can do all the things I can no longer do . . . he comes along and says, "Darling, what's happened with Formula One? The value's fallen. It's completely mad. You should sue the trustees." And if she's passionately in love, and it's no aggravation to her, he would go to a lawyer and they'd sue the trust.' Distinguishing between fiction and facts about trustees was irrelevant to Powers and Lanphere who together still owned 50 per cent of Formula One. Neither had yet understood that ownership of the shares did not mean control of Formula One. In Ecclestone's mind, 'Their 50 per cent is like 5 per cent. The trust, not the shareholders, controls Formula One.'

In the small print of his agreement with Lanphere and Powers, Ecclestone had added a seemingly benign clause which in reality was financial dynamite, namely, that regardless of the profits – and the Formula One cash machine would spew out about $400 million that year – no money would be paid to the shareholders unless Bambino's trustees agreed. In normal companies, directors would always approve a dividend to reward the shareholders but Ecclestone had other plans. Bambino was allowed to withhold dividends so long as the $1.4 billion bond had not been repaid. Quite legally, he anticipated using the 'Dividend Clause' to avoid paying any dividends to the shareholders until the bond was repaid.

Powers was not concerned by that clause. His own share-holder's agreement with Ecclestone, he believed, gave him sufficient influence, but he had no time to exercise it. Just one month after his purchase of the shares, Powers was told by Ecclestone that Haffa would pay 'a good price' for his stake. Haffa, a former car dealer who had been introduced into the media world by Leo Kirch, bore some similarities to Ecclestone but their differences were the German's fatal flaws. Driven by his love of publicity and ambition to create the Disney of Europe, the deal junkie yearned to strut in Formula One's spotlight but, like the others, he never realised that the shares entitled him only to Formula One's merchandising rights but not to control of the company itself. Notoriously, Haffa rarely scrutinised contracts. His filing cabinets were full of completed contracts for the purchase of films and other artistic ventures which he had never quite understood. Exploiting that chaos, Powers persuaded Haffa in March 2000 to pay in cash and EM.TV shares three times more for the shares than he had paid Ecclestone one month earlier. Lanphere also agreed to sell 12.5 per cent of his stake to Haffa but only in exchange for EM.TV shares. In total Haffa paid $712.5 million in cash and $880 million in shares for his 50 per cent stake. Overnight, Formula One increased in value from $2.6 billion to $3.4 billion. In the lightly regulated Neuer Markt, Germany's new alternative stock market, EM.TV's share price also soared to 3,000 per cent higher than when it was launched. In his lackadaisical manner, Haffa failed to commission lawyers to scrutinise the conditions of his ownership of the 50 per cent stake. Instead, he assumed that he could rely on the due diligence executed by Powers and Lanphere.

Spotting that folly, Ecclestone offered Haffa more shares from the half of the company still owned by the family trusts. Ecclestone's price was based on the increased value negotiated by Powers. Excitedly, Haffa accepted Ecclestone's offer and committed himself to buy an option on a 25 per cent stake for just under $1 billion. Ecclestone naturally did not celebrate his success but the wodge of folded £50 notes permanently in his pocket represented his established status as a billionaire. His new wealth refuelled his anger about the snobs managing the British Grand Prix race at Silverstone.

Ecclestone had little affection for Silverstone, an 800-acre plot owned by the British Racing Drivers Club (BRDC) where Grands

Prix have been held since the first competition year, 1950, and every year since 1987. The dilapidated buildings, the shabby environment and the poor road access were in Ecclestone's opinion an indictment of the club's management, but his relations with Silverstone were amicable until Tom Walkinshaw was elected the club's chairman in 1992. Walkinshaw's bid to revolutionise the club's finances was opposed by the majority of members, led by Ken Tyrrell. After shrugging off accusations of misconduct for persuading the board to invest £5.3 million of the BRDC's money in his own failing business, Walkinshaw was deposed along with the entire committee. Ecclestone was disappointed by Walkinshaw's demise, which ended the chance to rebuild Silverstone, and never fully understood the reasons behind Walkinshaw's removal. 'I don't ask questions where I don't want to know the answers,' he said. 'In Formula One people make promises and do things to keep their teams running and think, "Tomorrow it'll be fine." But they don't keep their promises. Their eyes get in the way of reality.'

The committee's replacements were rich enthusiasts unsympathetic to Ecclestone's transformation of their amateur sport into a global business and unwilling to remedy his intolerance of Silverstone's shoddiness because of the club's poverty. Unlike other Grand Prix circuits across the world, Silverstone received no government finance and Ecclestone's success had killed any prospect of British politicians approving a subsidy which would ultimately enrich Ecclestone even more. Those excuses were of no interest to Ecclestone. The BRDC managers were expected to raise more money to pay Ecclestone and the teams, and to improve their facilities regardless of their income. He had little truck with win–win scenarios, just the maximum win for himself. The endless argument between the two sides ended with an abrupt refusal by the BRDC and RAC to upgrade Silverstone to international standards. Ecclestone's threat was heartfelt: 'If you don't want to play, I can take the Grand Prix somewhere else.'

One target of his anger was Jackie Stewart, the British champion embraced by the BRDC as the trusted ambassador of British motor car racing. Their frosty relationship since the mid-1960s had deteriorated with Ecclestone's success. Undoubtedly influenced by Ken Tyrrell, Stewart resented Ecclestone earning from the sport more than anyone else in the world. Stewart was especially sore because he believed he had contributed to Ecclestone's prosperity by introducing him to the ruler of Malaysia who wanted to host a Grand Prix. Then, in the early 1990s, Stewart had introduced Ecclestone to the Crown Prince of Bahrain, which also led to a Grand Prix in that country. Stewart's expectation of gratitude was mistaken. 'Bernie's deals are his deals and no one else's,' rued Stewart. The personal animosity was incurable. When Max Mosley spoke of Jackie Stewart as 'a twit in a flat cap', Ecclestone was less charitable. Their mutual dislike had been aggravated in 1997 after Ecclestone arranged for Jackie Stewart's team in Monaco to be parked inconveniently on the fringes of the Paddock. 'I just thought he would like to be a little a bit nearer the palace,' said Ecclestone in a slight to remind the Scotsman who was boss. 'He'd like to be a prince,' added Ecclestone. 'What's there to like about him?' Stewart had also not enjoyed Ecclestone's prank introducing John Bloom under a pseudonym as a potential sponsor offering $35 million. For several weeks, Stewart had negotiated with the supposed billionaire, who frustratingly cancelled their 'final' meetings to sign the sponsorship contract to fulfil another 'unexpected' obligation required for an orthodox Jew. Stewart may have felt he had evened the score when he made some ungenerous comments, both during the Labour donation scandal and after Ecclestone threatened to terminate the British Grand Prix. Their mutual antagonism aggravated the fate of the British Grand Prix.

Ecclestone's hostility to the BRDC and Silverstone, he insisted, was purely commercial. Foreign governments were pleading to host a Grand Prix despite the certainty that in return for paying Ecclestone up to $30 million annually for a ten-year contract they could lose millions of dollars. On those terms Malaysia bought into Formula One because no other international event could similarly promote the country across the world. The Singapore government wanted the same deal and other countries were lining up to pay to become famous. All were required to meet Ecclestone's expectations precisely. Dubai failed to host a Grand Prix because, after Ecclestone arrived as agreed at the Carlton Tower Hotel in London, he was kept waiting for many hours by the Maktoums, the ruling family. Ecclestone only travelled to complete the deal and not to waste his time, and their eventual offer that he should finance the construction of a circuit was, he replied, nonsensical. Formula One's popularity was his message to the BRDC. The context, as Jackie Stewart knew, was that the teams would only race sixteen times in one year and one fixture would be dropped to accommodate a new Asian venue. The French Grand Prix, Ecclestone announced, was to be cancelled (although in 1999 he had bought the Paul Ricard circuit) and the next to disappear might be Silverstone.

Although the BRDC's membership was classless, a few dismissed Ecclestone as a mere working-class boy. In public someone close to Lord Hesketh, its president, had openly cursed the 'second-hand-car dealers running the sport' and at a packed meeting when the club was financially strapped after the Walkinshaw era, Ecclestone's offer of help was publicly rejected by snipes from the back of the hall, 'We don't want your money, you dirty little sod,' and, 'Stand up, dwarf.' Ecclestone walked out trying to feign disinterest but dismissed some of their leaders as rotten, lazy, greedy, incompetent, self-important snobs obsessed by their traditions. Instead of praising his creation of Formula One as Britain's success, they delighted in back-stabbing feuds in a public goldfish bowl. 'The people running Silverstone are "old school tie" and not businessmen,' he said, complaining about their inability to build a decent race circuit. 'If Silverstone does not match up, it should not be on the calendar.'

Ever since his first five-year agreement in May 1986 to

hold the British Grand Prix at Silverstone, there had been constant discussions about whether the Grand Prix should be permanently relocated to a reconstructed site at Donnington or Brands Hatch. In 1999 the argument was resurrected. Twenty-three-year-old Nicola Foulston had inherited Brands Hatch and was plotting to transfer the Grand Prix to her modernised circuit after buying and closing down Silverstone. After being thwarted by the BRDC, she approached Ecclestone. In his view, it was the annual 'let's play games with someone' and if Silverstone was the plaything, he would fight to score a better deal, not least because Jackie Stewart opposed Foulston's plan. In return for her paying $10 million a year for ten years to stage the Grand Prix, Ecclestone agreed to move the race from Silverstone to Brands Hatch in 2002. And the price would rise by 5 per cent every year. Foulston had no intention of spending $60 million to rebuild the circuit. Instead, she found a buyer. Octagon, a sports marketing group based in New York, was headed by Sir Frank Lowe, a keen Formula One supporter. Foulston's company was worth $13.2 million and produced annual profits of $9 million but with the prospect of staging the Grand Prix, she wanted $192 million. Notwithstanding the fact that Foulston had loaded her company with unenforceable contracts, Lowe expressed his interest if Ecclestone supported the move and if planning permission was granted to rebuild Brands Hatch.

Before Ecclestone signed the deal, he was visited by Sir Tommy Sopwith, the BRDC's chairman, and Denys Rohan, Silverstone's chief executive. Both urged Ecclestone against the move to Brands Hatch. 'I'll stay at Silverstone,' replied Ecclestone, 'if you pay me the same – $10 million plus 5 per cent.' 'But that's double what we're paying now,' replied Rohan. 'Well, that's the deal,' stated Ecclestone. 'That's too rich for us,' they said. On 14 May 1999 Ecclestone signed a contract with Foulston to switch to Brands Hatch in July 2002. 'It was an offer I could not refuse,' he explained. The British motor racing establishment was outraged. Kent council approved the redevelopment and early in December

1999 Lowe bought Brands Hatch for £120 million giving Foulston a clear £50 million profit.

Nature added another twist. The British Grand Prix was normally held in July but Ecclestone had changed the date to 23 April 2000. Predictably, the circuit was drenched by continuous rain. After the first cars arrived, the whole area became a soggy mud field. Thousands of spectators were stranded ankle deep in mud and their cars were immobilised. The disaster confirmed Ecclestone's criticisms about the BRDC's incompetence. 'He fitted us up with mischievous intent,' complained a club official. Ecclestone was still celebrating the BRDC's embarrassment when he flew five weeks later to the sunlit race in Monaco.

Thomas Haffa invited Ecclestone and Slavica to a party on his yacht moored near the Paddock. The German was in an expansive mood. His share price, he said, would double in the near future – they were €120 that week – and he would soon rival Disney. There was something endearing to Ecclestone about a German seeking to dominate the world's entertainment industry. 'He's flash, a lovely guy,' decided Ecclestone. Looking at the Grand Prix course snaking around Monaco harbour Haffa confided to Ecclestone, 'I've got the most expensive seat here.' Ecclestone smiled. Haffa was clearly on a roll. 'All he wants to do', thought Ecclestone, 'is to walk down to the pit with me. Nothing wrong with him.' Powers suspected the worst and quickly cashed in the EM.TV shares he owned, accepting that he had recouped only 100 per cent profit on his investment rather than a notional 300 per cent. Lanphere, trusting Haffa's prediction about EM.TV's share price doubling, decided to stay for the ride. The experience was brief. Shortly after the Monaco weekend, Haffa was accused of falsifying EM.TV's accounts and the share price collapsed. He was investigated but not prosecuted. Lanphere's $325 million investment shrank in value to $6 million. Just one year after being hailed 'private-equity house of the year', Morgan Grenfell Private Equity imploded. Lanphere was among the casualties. Ecclestone was surprised by Haffa's self-destruction and the fallout. Financial markets were beyond his experience and he did not foresee that Haffa's meltdown would cast doubt on Formula One's ownership, justifying the teams' dislike of Ecclestone selling off the shares. When an unexpected saviour appeared, their fears were substantiated.

Leo Kirch had always wanted to own Formula One. Like so many others, he was attracted by the profits, the glamour and the opportunities for his television empire. To get control, he paid $550 million for EM.TV's shares and overnight owned 50 per cent of Formula One. Ron Dennis and Luca Montezemolo were outraged. Both had been angered by Ecclestone's original sale without consultation. Dennis's hostility had not been new but Montezemolo had been converted to the opposition after meeting Thomas Haffa in Maranello. 'I thought he was only good to buy a car from the showroom but not Formula One,' Montezemolo said about his turning point. 'I could not take him seriously. He was a joke.' The amusement disappeared once the shares were transferred to Kirch whose intention to switch Formula One entirely from free television to pay-television was alarming. Even Ecclestone became rattled by the prospect of the taciturn and partially blind non-English-speaking recluse deterring sponsors by broadcasting to smaller audiences.

His concern grew after the introduction of Dieter Hahn as Kirch's representative to run the sport. 'He has a steamroller approach to get what he wants,' noted one of Ecclestone's lawyers, 'so Bernie won't give him what he wants, especially anywhere near the business.' 'You should visit the teams,' Ecclestone told Hahn as a prank. 'Let them meet you.' Hahn telephoned the team principals. 'I'm the owner of 50 per cent of the business,' he introduced himself, 'and I'd like to tell you my plans.' Ecclestone was amused to hear that Hahn's calls were met with a common reply, 'Call back in six months.' Hahn suggested that his brother Wolfgang become involved in the sport's management. 'Formula One looks like fun,' Wolfgang told Ecclestone, 'and I'm a fun sort of guy.' Believing that the German wanted a job without doing any work, Ecclestone remained silent. He would manage the business, ignore the flak and not return the Hahns' telephone calls. He agreed, however, that Alexander Ritvay, a lawyer employed by Kirch, could move into Princes Gate to monitor his investment, but he would languish in the building, frustrated by Ecclestone's reluctance to cooperate. Montezemolo also succumbed to the Hahn brothers' insistence on meeting him in Lugano. The Ferrari chief was horrified. 'When I realised that they are part of the business,' Montezemolo later told Ecclestone, 'I became upset. You are doing very well but it's our business too. It's time to open a new page, discuss the management and cutting the cake.' Other team principals complained that their investment was unsafe in the hands of a sick old man. And Ecclestone was younger and less sick than Kirch. Negotiating the ownership and management of Formula One between the fractious interests became hectic. 'I'll find a solution,' Ecclestone replied, 'let me do it.' Off the top of his head, he suggested that Formula One should be owned 45 per cent by manufacturers, 45 per cent by Kirch and 10 per cent by him. 'I don't care who owns the shares. It would make no difference to what I do,' he said. The glibness challenged his credibility.

One complication had been removed. Amid accusations of financial misappropriation in March 1999, van Miert and all the EU Commissioners resigned. Mario Monti, a serious Italian professor of economics, succeeded the Flemish nationalist. Mosley already knew that Monti was a fan of Formula One. As a nine-year-old child, Monti had previously told Mosley, he had been taken by his parents to watch the Grand Prix at Monza. The great Juan Fangio had won and his parents had driven the legendary Argentinian in their car to Milan with Mario Monti in the back seat holding the winner's trophy. Relieved, and encouraged by that pedigree, Mosley approached Monti on 25 January 2000 to consider a settlement. He was helped by Alan Donnelly, a Labour MEP, who would become a highly paid FIA official. Together they persuaded Monti that if he dared to defend his predecessor's prejudices he would be humiliated by a catalogue of van Miert's transgressions. Unwilling to engage in the public brawl, Monti was amenable to retreat, leaving Ecclestone's and FIA's empire largely untouched. Among the conditions was that Ecclestone should negotiate a settlement with Patrick Peter, the French race organiser. Ecclestone paid Peter under £2 million. Mosley's success barely registered amid the eruption of a bitter argument about the ownership of Formula One.

Kirch's ownership of 50 per cent of the shares triggered a dispute between Ecclestone and the teams whether FIA, Ecclestone, the teams or Kirch was Formula One's legal owner. Having failed to foresee how 50 per cent of the shares could drift into the hands of a stranger, Ecclestone could not offer a palatable solution. At that moment, Paolo Cantarella, the chief executive of Fiat and owner of Ferrari, announced a breakaway to counter Kirch's involvement. Since the manufacturers financed Formula One, explained Cantarella, they, rather than Kirch, would organise their own season of races and pocket the profits. Terrified that he might lose his investment when Ecclestone's agreement with FIA expired in 2010, Kirch awaited Ecclestone's move, while Ecclestone held back to see how Mosley reacted.

For his part Mosley feared that FIA was losing control over the sport and met Ecclestone in Paris to discuss Formula One's ownership. The sport, Mosley believed, belonged either to FIA or to Ecclestone but certainly not to the teams or to Kirch. Unusually, his conversation with Ecclestone ended in a heated argument. 'I took all the risks,' said Ecclestone, 'I built the business up and I own it.' He denied that FIA had any rights other than to designate an event as official. 'You must allow me to buy Formula One outright.' 'No,' replied Mosley, 'that's our Crown Jewels. It will never be approved by the members.' Ecclestone packed his papers and prepared to leave. 'If anyone tries to grab Formula One,' he warned, 'I'll do a "scorched earth". I'll make sure there's nothing left after I've gone.' Mosley had every reason to believe Ecclestone's threat. 'Even the EU commission agrees that we own the Formula One licence,' Mosley replied in a quiet voice. 'But I agree we need certainty.' Ecclestone nodded. He wanted the same.

Mosley could not persuade FIA's members to sell the trade mark to Ecclestone but after brain-storming he produced a novel solution. Just as the freehold owners of property in Britain frequently leased their buildings for 100 years, he proposed that FIA extend the fifteen-year contract with Ecclestone to a licence of rights for 100 years. Ecclestone refused. 'We've got enough cards,' he impulsively replied but then reconsidered. As the owner of a 100-year licence, he realised, he could more easily fight the Association des Constructeurs Européens d'Automobiles (ACEA), Cantarella's breakaway group, and with Mosley's help he could out-face the teams. He relented. 'It'll need Monti's approval,' said Mosley. The EU commissioner was intrigued. 'A lease is not an infringement of the competition laws,' explained Mosley, 'and the alternative risks FIA losing control over Formula One.' Monti adopted Mosley's suggestion that the idea was justified to protect the 'very high-risk and expensive investment' for new technologies. In return the purchaser of the 100-year lease would have to recognise FIA as the sport's regulator. 'You'll have to pay,' Mosley told Ecclestone. 'You're trying to sell me my own business,' Ecclestone countered, calculating that others including Kirch would seize the opportunity to buy the 100-year licence. 'It's worth $500 million,' said Mosley. 'Then sell it for that,' said Ecclestone offering in April 2000 just $50 million and some additional payments, grumbling that Mosley only helped when it suited him.

To distance himself from the negotiations, Mosley appointed a four-man team to meet Ecclestone, who finally agreed on 11 May to pay $360 million. 'I'd pay $360 million just to get rid of FIA,' said Ecclestone in another burst of anger. 'I really don't need to buy this.' 'Well, I'll find someone else,' replied Mosley. On 20 June 2000 Paolo Cantarella told Mosley that ACEA was about to send a rival bid. Displeased, because any deal with Cantarella would lead to endless litigation with Ecclestone, Mosley replied that ACEA's bid would have to be received by 28 June and match Ecclestone's $360 million. 'Max has done us no favours as president,' complained Ecclestone. That view was not shared by Cantarella: 'Mosley has been Ecclestone's ally ever since they both owned a team.' His own bluff was called. He did not bid.

On 28 June Ecclestone was in Warsaw to watch FIA's members unanimously approve the sale of a 100-year licence to Bambino Holdings, confirming FOM's exclusive right to negotiate and collect fees from organisers and sell the television rights to broadcasters. 'Nice to have but not worth the money,' said Ecclestone. To comply with the EU's requirements, he also agreed to resign as FIA's promotional director, to sell the television rights of other motor races to Dave Richards, a successful Formula One investor, and to limit future television contracts to five years. Despite their arguments, Ecclestone and Mosley had spoken the same language to produce a mutually satisfying decision.

The turbulence and the agreement reawakened the teams' suspicions about Mosley's relationship with Ecclestone. 'We thought a 100-year deal was very naughty,' said Frank Williams. The critics compared Sky TV's purchase in 1997 of a four-year contract with the British Premier League for $743 million to Formula One's deal of $3.6 million for each year. At best, thought one team principal, Mosley was akin to the Provisional wing of the IRA, always running an organisation parallel to the formal FIA. At worst there were unfounded rumours about an undefined dishonest relationship with Ecclestone for which there was absolutely no evidence and which was vehemently denied by both men. Accustomed to criticism, Mosley brushed aside the ridiculous idea of taking back-handers from a former second-hand-car salesman. 'We need a Don King clause,' Mosley told his critics, meaning that the long 'lease' would prevent the sport falling into the wrong hands. Pleasing the teams, he sighed, was always difficult because, having spent so much money, they resented his indifference to ruffling feathers and the unanimous approval he received from FIA's members. Ron Dennis particularly disliked Mosley's condescending comment when he also mentioned the possibility of a breakaway. 'Ron', said Mosley, 'has no role in the FIA Formula One world championship apart from that granted to him in common with other teams by the Concorde agreement. Unfortunately he finds all this rather difficult to understand.' But Mosley's fluent vilification could not smother Dennis or Montezemolo.

The rapid changes in ownership, Ecclestone's £1 million donation to Labour, the battle about Silverstone and the secrecy of Formula One's finances prompted *The Economist* magazine to assign an investigative journalist to delve into Ecclestone's reputation. The known facts appeared at first to justify their concerns. The City had rejected the flotation; the $1.4 billion bond arranged by Saunders had been rejected by the City leaving her bank (the Westdeutsche Landesbank) with most of the debt; half of FOM's shares were owned by an unfriendly German; and van Miert's criticism had not been assuaged. By June the sport's internal critics had provided the magazine with sufficient evidence to justify doubts about the constant metamorphosis of Ecclestone's network of private offshore companies. Denied Ecclestone's guidance, the magazine in particular picked on APM, an Irish company whose directors included McNally, Stephen Mullens, Luc Argand and unknown nominees, considering it mysterious and enormously important. Subsequently Ecclestone would say that APM was McNally's agency used to negotiate the rights to Formula One's trade marks on umbrellas, T-shirts and other unimportant merchandise with Disney, and was by 1998 a commercial and legal mess. Only then, Ecclestone explained, did he realise the importance of registering himself as the licensed owner of the 'Formula One' trade mark and, after buying APM from McNally, his lawyers began to register the Formula One trade mark across the world. In 2000, in Ecclestone's opinion, that manoeuvre was too sensitive to reveal to outsiders. His secrecy aroused suspicion. Focusing on the consequences of it, the magazine highlighted three damning court judgements. In December 1971 Mr Justice Goff had criticised Ecclestone's tax affairs in his early career which 'showed a talent for financial trickery'. A later judge described Ecclestone's control of Formula One from his motorhome as 'similar to a tent of a medieval king in the battlefield. There are the equivalent of courtiers who control access to the presence.' Worst was Mr Justice Longmore's criticism in 2000 about Ecclestone's business methods involving a Korean corporation contracted to create a Formula One circuit: 'He conducts his business by way of meetings without making notes and his memory of what occurred at such meetings is somewhat hazy.' More critically, the judge declared, 'I do have to record that Mr Ecclestone has not been a man of his word . . . [and] . . . I have some reservations about any evidence from him that is not supported by other evidence in the case.' In his defence Ecclestone said that he had successfully defended the case and was relieved when the Koreans were eventually prosecuted in Korea.

The Economist's conclusion, published on 15 July 2000, claimed to have 'uncovered several disturbing features' about the 'secrecy' of Formula One finances, Ecclestone's close relationship with Mosley and his conflicts of interest between his own companies and FIA: 'Nearly all of Formula One's affairs are shrouded in secrecy; not only are the terms of all agreements "commercially confidential" but even the existence of some agreements is a secret. Nobody inside Formula One is seriously able to question how it is run. That is what happens when one man is allowed to establish such a financial stranglehold on a sport.' *The Economist* judged that politicians, the sponsors and the world's major car manufacturers risked being 'tainted' by Formula One's 'murkiness'. The editorial concluded, 'When the odour that surrounds a sport becomes too overpowering the worst danger of all looms: that it will switch off the interest of the general public.'

Others in London would have been outraged by the damnation and considered an action for defamation but Ecclestone had become immune to criticism. He shrugged off the demand for 'greater transparency and accountability'. Stubbornly he decided, 'I have a position which I think is right and I'll defend. I won't run away from a fight.' Eventually, he knew, every attacker fell by the wayside. Wolfgang Eisele was the latest. Although he had failed to recover his $500,000 from Eisele, the German's threat had evaporated and in victory Ecclestone was magnanimous. Eisele was given a pass to the German Grand Prix and entertained for lunch. 'Another Redskin bites the dust,' Ecclestone sang. Ecclestone's artfulness was to head off potential defeats by playing for time, dividing his opponents, or singly emerging from an impenetrable morass with a profitable deal. He grasped that opportunity over the fate of the Grand Prix at Silverstone.

Ecclestone's commitment to stage the British Grand Prix at Brands Hatch in 2002 was opposed by Jackie Stewart, newly elected as the BRDC's president. To prevent the transfer from Silverstone, the former world champion lobbied John Prescott, the minister responsible for the environment and transport. To Stewart's delight, on 8 September 2000 the government withdrew Kent council's power to grant planning permission for Brands Hatch's redevelopment. Frank Lowe, the founder and chief executive of Octagon, the company that had bought Brands Hatch, was shocked. Stewart's finesse threatened his company with huge losses from its irrevocable ten-year commitment to Ecclestone to stage the Grand Prix. Nor could he escape financial disaster by declaring Octagon, a British subsidiary, bankrupt. Shrewdly, Ecclestone and Foulston had extracted a guarantee from Interpublic, the American advertising conglomerate and Octagon's parent company, for any debts. Lowe could only hope that Stewart's victory would still be stymied if Ecclestone abandoned the British Grand Prix. Ecclestone was willing to play the game. Once again Stewart and Ecclestone were head-to-head about Silverstone's shabbiness and snobs. 'Bernie,' said Stewart, 'I get $100,000 for a speech but if it's for a good cause I do it for much less. So you should also cut your cloth if necessary. You should cut the fees for England. Think of the national interest, the good of the industry and the outrage if you pull out.'

'You can talk,' countered Ecclestone. 'I pay taxes in Britain and you've lived for twenty years in Switzerland to avoid taxes. I don't owe Britain anything. I don't care about a British Grand Prix and I don't care if the media go after me.' There was a price to be paid, in Stewart's opinion, for such outspokenness, not least burying Ecclestone's chances of receiving a British honour. The rulers of many other countries had showered Ecclestone with praise and awards but his own government was silent. Ecclestone cared about that snub, but not enough to stop seeking the best deal long after others would have stopped. Sir Tommy Sopwith's old- money brigade fuelled his aggression. 'All they do is send down toffee-nosed public school types to see me, and I don't want to deal with them,' he said. Ecclestone's anger about the snobs, the condescending upper classes, was inflamed. The memory of the mockery in the Dartford school playground sixty years earlier remained fresh, as were his forlorn attempts to overcome social barriers. Regardless of his fortune, appearances, especially size and class, always seemed to be pertinent. Sopwith acted the part. 'I would not underestimate the little man,' Sopwith commented later. 'I think Bernie only wants one thing. Bernie wants to be richer than he is. I can't imagine anyone being richer than he is, but Bernie can.' The club's secretary agreed: 'The BRDC is being arguably bled dry to keep a slot on the manic merry-go-round of the Formula One calendar.'

Frank Lowe knew nothing about racing or British honours but was concerned that his company's financial state was precarious. Ecclestone offered a solution but to allay suspicions arranged for Ron Dennis to propose the plan at a meeting in Princes Gate in

October 2000 to Lowe and Martin Brundle, the former racing driver and ITV commentator, who would become the BRDC's chairman.

Ecclestone's relationship with Brundle was prickly. As a contemporary of Ayrton Senna, the driver had clearly failed to make a serious impression on the sport but since most of his contemporaries were dead, he wielded authority as a survivor and television commentator. Naturally, he had only secured the job with Ecclestone's approval and on occasion, Brundle relied on Ecclestone to provide the celebrities to appear on his programme. His fame had secured his election to the BRDC's committee but that, in Ecclestone's judgement, did not prove his qualifications to deliver the promises which they had negotiated.

Ecclestone proposed that Lowe abandon Brands Hatch and buy the rights to stage the Grand Prix in Silverstone for fifteen years. In turn, the BRDC would be committed to spend $100 million to improve the circuit. To finance the redevelopment, Ecclestone would contribute $7 million a year and would commit Formula One to remain at Silverstone for ten years starting in 2001 for a payment of $1 million annually with a 10 per cent annual uplift. To offset his costs he would still receive the annual $10 million payment from Lowe who would also be liable to pay $14 million annually to the BRDC and towards Silverstone's reconstruction. In total Silverstone was receiving a windfall of $21 million a year. Before agreeing, Lowe asked Ecclestone to step outside. 'Bernie, I don't know much about motor racing, but is this the right deal? Do you think we could make money? Do you recommend it?' Ecclestone replied, 'Yes.' After its formal agreement, Ecclestone would say that the contract was 'a joke and uncommercial' and that he recommended Lowe not to go ahead. The deal was announced on 2 December 2000. Although Brundle was delighted by Silverstone's windfall, he criticised Ecclestone: 'It's clear for anyone to see that Bernie seems to have been trying hard to destabilise the British Grand Prix, Silverstone and the BRDC.' 'They still don't get it,' retorted Ecclestone.

9

Revolt

On Saturday 26 May 2001 Ecclestone hosted a party in Monaco's harbour to celebrate Slavica's forty-third birthday. In contrast to his modest lifestyle – usually coming home after six for dinner in the kitchen cooked by his wife – he had borrowed *Le Grand Bleu*, the recently launched private yacht with its crew of more than fifty, from American businessman John McCall. 'They'll ruin the new decks,' Ecclestone warned the American owner of the world's biggest private ship. 'Don't worry,' McCall replied generously. Early the following morning Ecclestone went on to the deck to find the pristine wood covered with red wine stains and holes from stiletto heels. While Slavica slept, he urged the crew to repair the damage. His fuss passed unnoticed by everyone except his wife. Even asleep she was conscious of his fastidiousness, a trait she disliked.

Inevitably, Ecclestone had not enjoyed the party. After detaching himself to vet the guests coming on board, he slunk towards the back of the reception and finally headed to his cabin. Left behind, Slavica placed herself firmly at the centre of attention. All were aware of their volatile relationship. Stubborn, jealous and uncompromising, Slavica preferred to launch into arguments with her husband rather than walk away from a fight. He had listened in silence to her frequent boast that her social popularity was the reason for his success. Often, he realised, her appetite for alcohol fuelled her brashness and her conviction that he was unfaithful to her. 'She shouts a lot,' he admitted to a newspaper, 'and sometimes she throws plates. I go and hide in the next room because she seems to love terrorising me.' As a joke he fixed a sign on the kitchen door, 'Never mind the dog, beware of the wife.' Slavica admitted that her brashness annoyed some but Ecclestone found the vulgarity attractive. 'Slavica is super company,' her husband volunteered, aware that at her birthday party she shunned some guests, especially those from Formula One. Surrounded by celebrities – the type her husband abhorred – she acknowledged only a handful of mutually acceptable guests, including Max Mosley and Flavio Briatore. 'Get out of Formula One,' she would scream at Ecclestone, 'or I'll leave you.'

Ecclestone was never quite sure whether his wife was serious. He was permanently enthralled by her zest, which marked a contrast with his former relationships and life with his parents. Among his many fond memories was their night in Rome just before her birthday party with a German motor executive. Over dinner Slavica and the German had enjoyed joyful banter. As they returned after midnight to the Hassler hotel, the executive attempted to pick up an attractive policewoman. He would spend the next four hours in jail until Ecclestone negotiated his release. The memory of those escapades balanced Ecclestone's complaint, 'Slavica can be a pain in the backside but she's still a bloody good mother and a very moral woman – a real Italian mama who won't have a dishwasher in the house and never had a nanny. She changed all the nappies.' That praise evoked her sarcasm: 'And I love you too, darlink. Even though you drive me crazy.' He failed, she complained, to understand her serious need for emotional support and her stated indifference to money. That was not surprising. Compared with Croatians, he was undemonstrative, but her supposed coolness towards his baubles lacked credibility for him. True, the yacht, the Gstaad hotel, the racehorses trained by Johnny Humphries and the private planes were rarely used for pleasure but he loved having them. She found this incomprehensible. 'It's a pain being married to a workaholic,' she complained. 'He doesn't give me enough time.' She was angry that he took so little enjoyment from his billions; his passivity at home and at her birthday party showed little evidence of the happiness he derived from his faith in ordinary life.

Prompted by a friend that the whispers about their arguments were unhelpful for his children and Formula One's image, they decided to give interviews to portray happiness. 'We do everything together,' he told one interviewer. 'On Saturday, we shop together at Waitrose.' After returning home, he continued, he enjoyed helping their daughters with their homework or spending the afternoon watching them play school sports. 'My girls are always with me,' he said with genuine affection. 'I give the best love.' Slavica praised her daughters because 'They know the value of money. I have taught them to be thrifty . . . They are not label heads, they don't want Gucci or Prada – that is a sickness.' No evening was better, she continued, than watching *Who wants to be a millionaire?* or listening to the Beatles. In perfect harmony, the daughter of a fireman chimed, 'One day, if I go back to Croatia, I will live on an island and catch small fish from my boat and be happy. I would never want to run Formula One.' To those who interpreted their self-portrayal of marital bliss as exaggerated, the syrup was stirred by Slavica's declaration, 'I just love being taller because I can cuddle him. He's so sweet.' Previous descriptions mentioned her height as 6 feet 2 inches compared to his 5 feet 2 inches, but to capture the new harmony, she volunteered that while she was 5 feet 9 inches, he was 5 feet 4 inches. His contribution was more earthy. 'I realised Slavica was special the third time I slept with her.'

The truce was short-lived. In her frustrated misunderstanding of business, London society and her husband's fear of his eventual dependence on others once old age and illness set in, she lashed out. Even to those who knew her well, she seemed to be permanently angry. As her threats to leave escalated into threats to call the police, Ecclestone occasionally called Ron Shaw for help. Shaw and Vee, his wife, rushed to Knightsbridge to calm the tirades. 'He got conned into something,' said his friend. 'He's been tucked up.' Those embarrassing arguments, some of his friends believed, were battles for his children. Others assumed that Ecclestone could not conceive of married life without abusive relationships, even when he arrived at his office, haunted and defensive, with a black eye. The injury, inflicted in Monza, had been Slavica's rebuke for Ecclestone parading with a beautiful model. 'Slav thought I was being serious with the young lady but I was joking,' Ecclestone explained. At those moments, he sympathised with his wife's outbursts. Ever since Momir Blagojević's attempted blackmail in a Croatian newspaper she had suffered depressive bouts and occasional panic attacks. With Ecclestone's help, the *Sunday Mirror* had exposed Blagojević's dishonesty but other embarrassing details had emerged. *Bild*, the German tabloid newspaper, had been offered extremely compromising photographs of Slavica from another photographer and Ecclestone had been obliged to pay handsomely for their suppression. Other stories of her life in Croatia's hotels during the communist era strained their relationship. 'I admit that I was no angel when I was young,' she told him. 'I did crazy things but I was never a prostitute.'

On Slavica's insistence Blagojević and the newspaper were sued for libel. Pursuing the blackmailer proved in the short term to be disastrous. The repeated trips to Croatia, the delays and the humiliation were a torment. Eventually Ecclestone's quest compelled Blagojević to apologise and the newspaper was closed down. But even after the victory, Blagojević telephoned Slavica. 'He was', she said, 'like a loony, obsessed about me, mad like a stalker.' As therapy, she gave newspaper interviews to describe her personal problems, mentioning how Goran Ivanišević, the Croatian tennis star, was her friend and how he relied on her friendship to fight against adversity on the court. Unwittingly she discovered that, despite all their wealth, the only thing she could not buy was something free. Similarly Ecclestone sought to restore his reputation as a tough man who never suffered. He was pleased that after Blagojević's defeat, he had approached the blackmailer in the courtroom and, grabbing him by the lapels, warned him, 'I'm the midget, so watch out.'

As a diversion he bought, through an offshore trust, a mansion of 55,000 square feet at 18 and 19 Kensington Palace Gardens, a unique private road running along the west of Hyde Park. Two buildings, previously embassies, had been expansively converted into a single home by David Khalili, an Iranian developer, for a reputed total investment of £84 million. The Ecclestones' trust paid £50 million for a marbled palace with a huge ballroom, eleven bedroom suites and underground parking for twenty cars. On her first visit Slavica announced her refusal to move in. Two more visits did not change her mind. 'I bought it because it was cheap,' he would say and resold it in 2004 to Lakshmi Mittal, the Indian steel mill owner, for $105 million.

Slavica's mood had not improved by her husband's seventy-first birthday. She greeted his appearance in the kitchen to see his birthday cake, saying acidly: 'Why are you so miserable? It's a day of celebration. Get out of the kitchen if you're going to be so miserable, go to your office and do some work.' He worked hard and only wanted peace. Recent meals had often been acrimonious. While he ate in silence and drank a beer, Slavica talked with her daughters. On this occasion, he walked out of the room clearly upset. Left behind were Tamara, seventeen years old, and John Keterman, her twenty-two-year-old boyfriend. Keterman had proposed to Tamara four days after their meeting and had been accepted by the family. He had witnessed her parents' rages. Once, seated in the back seat while driving to the cinema with the Ecclestones, Keterman had heard Slavica scream without warning, 'Slow down. You drive too fast, you maniac.' Ecclestone had, in her opinion, taken a wrong turning. Suddenly, she grabbed his hair and knocked his head against the driver's window. Ecclestone pulled over while she got out and started crying. Eventually she calmed herself and they walked in silence to the cinema. The engagement eventually ended and Keterman sold the story of this and other experiences with the Ecclestone family to a Sunday newspaper. At the following Saturday coffee morning, Ecclestone's friends could not resist mentioning the sensational description of Slavica hitting her husband. 'Listen,' replied Ecclestone, 'some people pay for it. I get it free.'

There was no evidence of their fractious relationship on the day following Slavica's birthday party as he travelled from the yacht by launch across Monaco's harbour to his motorhome in the Paddock. As he sat ensconced in his sanctuary, the early visitors, including Karl-Heinz Zimmerman, the headquarters' manager, could not fathom his ambivalence towards his marriage. Ecclestone volunteered no clues. Even to his close staff, he deemed any admission of domestic troubles as weakness. Whatever Slavica did, he would never abandon the marriage, not least because he had become accustomed to conflict as the essence of his life.

From his leather armchair at the end of the motorhome, Ecclestone watched Formula One's world pass by on four monitors connected to concealed cameras. Entertainingly Flavio Briatore was prancing around the Paddock entrance seeking opportunities to speak to those who could influence his fate. Ecclestone enjoyed observing his friend's vanity when Renault, his new team, was stuck at fourth in the championship. Looking at the camera covering the entrance to the bus, he assessed his visitors. Besides those calling on genuine business were men who sought to use his name, those wanting to exploit their relationship and a few offering themselves as the 'son he never had'. Several callers represented the seven countries seeking to host a new Grand Prix in 2004 and replace the two unnamed circuits Ecclestone had announced would be abandoned. Some were willing to pay Ecclestone $40 million for one race and a 10 per cent annual increment instead of the $10 million paid by the traditional European circuits. Perceptively, he predicted, 'In the next ten years, Europe is going to become a third-world economy. There's no way Europe will be able to compete with

China, Korea, India.' Increasing the television audiences across Asia guaranteed new profits. To those supplicants he was the patriarch but others saw a man confined within a cage he had constructed, personally and professionally. Beyond his personal fortress, the teams inhabited their own communal camps, brutally visible to each other along the grid. Shuttling between the cages, Mosley smelled the friction and, like Ecclestone, identified the cause.

Luca Montezemolo had become particularly fractious. Outside his office in Maranello he had hung a huge, grainy black-and-white photograph of Niki Lauda winning the Spanish Grand Prix in 1974. Near the car and the chequered flag was a smudged figure waving frantically in celebration. That was Montezemolo, Ferrari's team manager, on the unforgettable occasion of his first Formula One victory. No one could deny his pedigree, especially Ecclestone. Since Jean Todt had joined the team, the self-assured Italian had reorganised Ferrari by recruiting Ross Brawn, the best manager-designer, and Rory Byrne, an outstanding aerodynamicist. Together they had ended twenty years of failure by responding to the demands of Michael Schumacher that had led to his victory as world champion in 2000. One year later Schumacher and Ferrari were dominating the season. 'It's a great shame there aren't a few more like Michael around because he races to win,' cheered Ecclestone, carping about his bland competitors. At Monaco there were few chances for McLaren and Williams to challenge Montezemolo's revived team in what most anticipated would be an unexciting race. Trumping the team leaders' egoism had been Ecclestone's skill but Montezemolo had suddenly become resistant to his cunning. The visit to Maranello of Dieter and Wolfgang Hahn, Leo Kirch's representatives, had outraged the Italian. 'They are not part of Formula One,' he told Ecclestone. 'They cannot improve Formula One.' After brief reflection, Montezemolo told Ecclestone, 'You have sold what you say is your business. But it is our business.' Ecclestone, he knew, had already pocketed over

$2 billion and was eagerly waiting for another $1 billion in cash from Kirch.

The German media tycoon was trapped. After taking over EM.TV's shares in Formula One, he owned a 50 per cent stake but was legally locked into buying for $1 billion a further 25 per cent stake from Ecclestone to which Haffa had unwisely committed himself. Naturally Kirch was a reluctant buyer but the alternative, as Ecclestone reminded him, was much more expensive. In effect, Ecclestone was playing poker. Having paid $60 million, he was refusing to pay the final $300 million to FIA for the 100-year agreement until he had received the $1 billion from Kirch. In the wake of an unusually bitter argument, Mosley became suspicious that Ecclestone was 'stringing us along and even might renege and embarrass me by not paying the $300 million'. Fearing the worst scenario, in February 2001 Mosley consulted Gordon Pollock QC, an eminent commercial lawyer in London, to find out whether FIA could challenge Ecclestone's claim to own Formula One and its trade marks. 'This isn't an argument you want to have,' advised Pollock. 'In a similar case, the parties spent 119 days in court just arguing a preliminary point. After that, not surprisingly they settled. You don't want to spend years in litigation with Bernie and then you won't win.' Mosley needed to break the vicious circle.

Kirch was being squeezed by Ecclestone. According to the agreements, if Ecclestone failed to pay $300 million to Mosley, Kirch's investment in Formula One would expire in 2010. Although he owned many interests, including the television rights to the football World Cup, his empire would collapse in bankruptcy if his Formula One rights expired as worthless in 2010. To stay solvent Kirch needed to float his company to raise $1 billion and, to achieve that, Ecclestone had to sign the 100-year agreement. To force Kirch to bring pressure on Ecclestone, Mosley flew to Turin to meet Paolo Cantarella, and encourage the Fiat executive to reactivate his breakaway plan. In October 2000 Cantarella had written to Ecclestone on behalf of the five manufacturers offering to buy 'a substantial stake' in Formula One. On their behalf, a Goldman Sachs banker had met Mullens in Paris in January 2001 with a detailed plan to take control of Formula One. Soon after, the negotiations collapsed. Mosley now wanted another attack. 'Will you renew your bid?' asked Mosley. 'We'll do Formula One after 2010,' replied the Italian. On 4 April Cantarella formally announced he would establish a new breakaway group of teams to rival Formula One. Days later, the managers of Renault, BMW and Mercedes pledged their support. They were followed by the chief executive of the new Jaguar Racing team. 'The prospect of a counter-bid will focus Bernie's attention,' thought Mosley. Hearing about the move, Ecclestone accused Mosley of 'extortion'.

'Pay up by 21 April,' replied Mosley, 'or we may make other arrangements.' Mosley then switched to Kirch. 'You risk', Mosley warned, 'losing everything if the 100-year deal is not signed.' Kirch agreed to pay $1 billion immediately. Next, Ecclestone reluctantly agreed to sign the 100-year agreement although he was only obliged to pay a quarter of the $300 million. The remainder was Kirch's money. After a massive signing session of seven different agreements, Kirch and Ecclestone paid $300 million to FIA. 'I want the interest because of the delay,' said Mosley. 'That's $13.6 million.' The final agreements were signed on 21 April 2001. FOM also agreed to pay $12 million annually for FIA's regulatory costs. On the day of the massive signing Ecclestone, unusually, betrayed his nerves. He telephoned Stephen Mullens repeatedly until he heard that $1 billion had been deposited in the trust's bank account. Without floating the company, Ecclestone had personally pocketed over $3 billion and still controlled the company with just 25 per cent of the shares.

The unnoticed time bomb was Kirch's $1 billion. At the last moment he had borrowed the money from three banks, principally from the Bayerische Landesbank, a German bank in Munich whose chairman, a friend of Kirch's, was the state's prime minister. In return for approving the loan, the politician and Kirch understood that his television stations would support the ruling Bavarian conservative party in the next elections. Remarkably, in the rush, the Bayerische Landesbank did not send any lawyers and accountants to examine Formula One's records in London. The bankers committed $1 billion after assuming that EM.TV's advisers had been asked to conduct the essential due diligence. They were unaware of the 'Dividend Clause' which could deny Kirch any income to pay the interest on his loan, let alone repay the loan itself, and severely curtailed his control of the business. So Kirch owned 75 per cent of Formula One yet Ecclestone acted as the sole owner taking all the profits.

The news of Ecclestone's fifth significant financial transaction incensed Luca Montezemolo. With hindsight he pinpointed that day as the beginning of 'my real fight with Bernie'. Six days later Ecclestone was in his motorhome in Monaco. Halfway through the Grand Prix, he was driven to the helicopter and flew from Nice to London without seeing Schumacher's victory in a Ferrari. Montezemolo was pleased for his team but unforgiving towards Ecclestone. Montezemolo and Cantarella's opening demand was for the teams to receive 100 per cent of the income from television, advertising and hospitality rather than allowing Ecclestone to pocket nearly 70 per cent.

'Paolo Cantarella dreams of owning Formula One,' Ecclestone noted after the dust settled. The Formula One show had become valuable for car manufacturers. Mercedes, Fiat, BMW, Toyota, Ford and Renault were using Formula One as an advertising platform in Russia, China, India, Brazil and other emerging markets. Renault had returned to Formula One to sell an extra two million cars by 2010. Toyota and Honda were pledged to launch new Formula One teams to spend vast sums on television advertising. 'We are entering a new era,' Montezemolo told Ecclestone. 'You are doing very well but it's our business too. We are the actors and without the actors there's no show.' Ecclestone scoffed. Actors were hired and fired and never owned the theatre. Yet Montezemolo speculated that his breakaway group could circumvent Ecclestone and conclude a direct deal with the banks, the circuits and the television stations. His pitch was that the teams should get the money rather than allow Ecclestone to use the profits to repay the Eurobond. Initially the group would demand 100 per cent of the income but they were prepared to settle for 85 per cent of Formula One's annual $700 million revenue.

In anticipation of Ecclestone refusing, Cantarella hired Gordon Diall, a Goldman Sachs banker, to plan the Grand Prix World Championship (GPWC) after the Concorde agreement expired in 2007. Not all the manufacturers were convinced that the complications of a breakaway could be overcome. FIA would not approve a breakaway, the circuits under contract to Ecclestone's FOM could refuse to give access to the GPWC, the television broadcasters would be bound by contracts with Ecclestone and the sponsors' support was uncertain. Regardless of the obstacles, their common cause was a dislike of Kirch.

To maintain the same mystery as Enzo Ferrari, Montezemolo rarely attended Grand Prix races and expected any meetings to take place in Maranello. But in November 2001 he flew to Geneva to speak at the first GPWC meeting about his mastery of the new media technologies, sponsorship and global marketing. His successful organisation of Italy's football World Cup competition in 1990, he said, equipped the GPWC to usurp Kirch. The report from Geneva did not alarm Ecclestone. 'Those muppets', he said pushing his chest out like a boxer, 'couldn't make ten bob together.' He intended to call their bluff but events denied him the opportunity.

Just before Christmas Deutsche Bank announced that Kirch's empire was no longer creditworthy. In February 2002 a representative of the three banks (the Bayerische Landesbank and also J. P. Morgan and Lehmans) which had loaned Kirch $1.55 billion to buy Formula One offered Cantarella and the GPWC manufacturers the opportunity to buy Kirch's 75 per cent share in Formula One. Ecclestone was not surprised when

Cantarella shunned the opportunity. Despite all his bravado, he wanted to run Fiat, not a racing company. Ignoring Cantarella's rejection of the offer, Montezemolo rushed to criticise Ecclestone for allowing Formula One's ownership to change for the fourth time in three years. Privately, Ecclestone was niggled. Financing from banks, he realised, had 'seemed a good idea but was a waste of time'. The absence of good professional advisers had bequeathed a mess. Although proud that 'I fly by the seat of my pants' he feared that few outsiders understood him. He publicly blamed the family trustees for selling his shares. 'Part of my life's work has ended up out of my control,' he pleaded with an eye to his critics. Stephen Mullens rather than himself, he suggested, had taken control.

Kirch's total default of $1.8 billion induced a political crisis in Bavaria. Ecclestone spotted the Bayerische Landesbank's problems as a golden opportunity to buy back Formula One cheap. 'If the banks try to control Formula One,' he told Brian Powers, 'they'll quickly run the business into the ground.' Fortunately Thomas Fischer, the Bayerische Landesbank's representative, was the sort he could do business with. Ecclestone noticed that the former boxer 'liked to hang loose and hang tough' and was blessed with an unhealthily large ego. Invited by Ecclestone to visit several races, Fischer was escorted around the Paddocks pulling ostentatiously on his braces as he met the famous. 'I'm the new chairman,' the German announced and nodding towards Ecclestone continued, 'and this is my CEO.' To Ecclestone's delight he sensed the banker's bewilderment as he learned the complications of managing Formula One. On his return to Munich Fischer announced that the bank was looking for a quick sale. Ecclestone offered $600 million and, without better offers, expected Fischer to trade. At the bank's headquarters Gerhard Gribkowsky, the forty-four-year-old risk officer, was appalled. 'That's a stupid way of trying to sell something,' he told Fischer. 'You're just getting offers ranging between the ridiculous and the unrealistic.' To Ecclestone's disappointment, in March 2003 Gribkowsky engineered Fischer's departure. Worse for Ecclestone, Gribkowsky told journalists, 'The bank controls Formula One and has decided not to sell its Formula One shares.' Ecclestone asked Powers to fly to Munich and negotiate the repurchase of the shares. 'I've been beaten by the Munich Mafia,' Powers reported. 'I'm going to see this guy and read him his fortune,' Ecclestone told Sacha Woodward-Hill, his in-house lawyer. The following day, Ecclestone telephoned Gribkowsky. 'This is Bernie. You don't control anything. If you want to speak come to London.' The banker's arrival at Princes Gate was, Gribkowsky admitted, 'a tense moment'. Sitting on the sofa in Ecclestone's office, he explained that he represented 75 per cent of the shares. 'You', he told Ecclestone, 'are just the CEO working on the shareholders' behalf.' Ecclestone smiled and abruptly bid Gribkowsky farewell. 'I told him the facts of life,' Ecclestone said to his staff. Gribkowsky got the message. Fighting Ecclestone would be bloody. 'We've got to avoid warfare,' he reported to his superiors in Munich.

In truth the banker was only just beginning to unravel Ecclestone's carefully constructed labyrinthine commercial structure. Bambino, the Ecclestone family trust in the Channel Islands, owned 25 per cent of Formula One but controlled the network of Formula One companies. 'The companies can't do a thing without Bambino's permission,' he recalled Ecclestone saying. Unspoken was Ecclestone's unique ability to construct new walls to prevent an outsider's entry and exit from the maze. As Martin Brundle would joke, 'Bernie attaches strings to the shares, sells them and then pulls it all back again.' Exploiting the banker's impotence was Ecclestone's next line of attack: 'The banks got a stake in something they didn't want and now they're trying to get out without losing too much money. If they had done anything like the due diligence they should have done when they lent Kirch the money, they would have realised that because of the way the shareholders' agreement is structured, they can't do a thing without Bambino's permission.'

One person key to Ecclestone's strategy was Stephen Mullens, the trustee of Bambino, who was given an office in Princes Gate. 'He's helpful and very bright,' attested Ecclestone. Without telling the bankers, Mullens had proposed that the company's [FOA] rules should be changed in 2002 to limit the number of directors on the board to three – himself as a representative of Bambino, Ecclestone as FOA's chief executive, and a representative of the three banks. Amid the disarray following Kirch's bankruptcy in April 2002, the banks and the German administrator failed to assert their rights and Mullens proposal was 'approved' by himself and Ecclestone in September 2002. Accordingly, the banks were in a permanent minority and could be outvoted by the board's majority – Ecclestone and Mullens.

Grasping that Ecclestone had organised a clever coup – the owners of 25 per cent of the shares effectively controlled Formula One – Gribkowsky approached the two American banks (which were owed much less than the German bank). Without recovering control of FOA and FOH, Ecclestone's two companies, Gribkowsky said, all three banks would lose their money. To his surprise both American banks refused to confront Ecclestone. Litigation, they feared, would fail and they would be harmed by bad publicity. Instead, both urged cooperation. The bankers' disunity re-energised Ecclestone's ploy to spread confusion. Telephoning the American bankers, he contradicted Gribkowsky, threatened to break up Formula One by decamping to GP2, a slightly smaller race, and mentioned a plan to refinance the whole business leaving the banks without any assets. The banks' failure to scrutinise the contracts, he emphasised, left them powerless to control a worthless investment without even a dividend from Bambino. Ecclestone's credibility was strengthened by the manufacturers' threat to establish the breakaway GPWC. In a final twist, he feigned his own powerlessness. Bambino, he said, was beyond his control. Gribkowsky, he suggested, should address his complaints to the trustees at the FOM board meetings which he did not attend. Stephen Mullens, he smiled, was the ideal antidote to complaining bankers. 'Mullens is an arsehole,' Gribkowsky cursed in a telephone call to Ecclestone. 'He's so difficult and playing his cards perfectly.' Mullens, Ecclestone knew, took the struggle against Gribkowsky personally. 'I agree,' replied Ecclestone sympathetically. 'I hate Mullens. I wish the banks could participate in the management but I've got no say.' Maintaining good personal relations with Gribkowsky was Ecclestone's way of defusing the banker's frustration that Formula One remained Ecclestone's business and no one could share it. Brian Powers and Robin Saunders were again dispatched to buy the banks' stake. 'You're offering a haircut,' scoffed Gribkowsky about the derisory amount. 'I want 100 per cent of my money back.'

Despite their arguments, Gribkowsky flew at Ecclestone's invitation to the races in Istanbul and Shanghai, and then visited other circuits. By hugging the banker, Ecclestone calculated, his enemy would be disarmed. If he chose, Ecclestone could endear himself to anyone. Walking through the Paddock, touching the German on his shoulder or arm and confiding indiscreet observations about Frank Williams, Ron Dennis, Luca Montezemolo, Max Mosley and the sponsors and drivers, Ecclestone hoped the banker would appreciate his genius in juggling the conflicting interests and the intimacies of everyone's lives. Gradually, Gribkowsky began speaking about peace and mutual understanding – working together to ensure Formula One's success. Ecclestone encouraged his sentiment. In Ecclestone's book, seeking peace showed weakness. But at the same time, by appearing alongside the banker, Ecclestone hoped that the team's owners would accept a fait accompli. Even if his enemies derided the folksy image, he needed to keep Gribkowsky onside by using the GPWC's existence to feed the banker's fear about Formula One's possible disintegration. Formula One was tipping into an unprecedentedly turbulent era.

Although Luca Montezemolo was committed to the rebellion, Ferrari's fate depended on Formula One. Michael Schumacher's world championship victory had spurred the sale in 2002 of 400 special editions of a Ferrari model for $600,000 each, earning about $240 million in revenue and healthy profits. Montezemolo was rewarded with a $19 million bonus. To maintain the team's winning profile, he budgeted to spend $295 million in 2003, compared to Minardi's $27 million, about the same as Ferrari costs in 1990. The financial race was matched by Ferrari's principal rivals – Patrick Head at Williams and Adrian Newey at McLaren – but neither anticipated Ferrari's stunts to remain supreme.

In 2001 Ferrari had contracted with Bridgestone to build better tyres than the Michelins used by their competitors. The company also hired 200 computer engineers to write software programmes to guide their cars over every metre of each circuit. To catch up, Ron Dennis hired 120 engineers. Williams, powered by a new BMW engine but in an inadequate body, was simply outclassed. If their rivalry was confined to technology and ingenuity, Montezemolo could have solidified the teams' alliance to challenge Ecclestone. Arrogance weakened his argument.

At the Austrian Grand Prix in May, Rubens Barrichello, Ferrari's second driver, was ordered in the last lap to let Schumacher pass to win the race. The spectators' boos increased as Schumacher, embarrassed by the arrangement, forced his defeated team mate during the televised ceremony on the podium to accept the winner's cup. Fans cursed 'an all-time low' and Stirling Moss wrote about 'a public-relations disaster'. Ecclestone, who as usual had left the stadium before the race ended, admitted, 'What happened on the podium was sheer stupidity.' Although Mosley fined Ferrari $1 million, Montezemolo was not embarrassed. In September, on course to win a record eleven races, Schumacher was again embroiled in race fixing. In the last seconds of the American Grand Prix in Indianapolis, Schumacher allowed Barrichello to pass and win. Television audiences dropped sharply and sponsors, including Orange and Deutsche Post, withdrew. 'Formula One is being damaged by Ferrari's dominance,' complained Ecclestone.

Formula One had hit a low point. 'The biggest problem', Ecclestone admitted in a forlorn attempt to repair the damage, 'is the perception with the viewers that it's fixed. People don't like that. If there was a race between Michael and Rubens, a real race every time, then nobody would be telling us that Grand Prix was boring.' Ecclestone's challenge was to rescue Formula One. Audiences wanted the excitement of the old days but he had no taste to return to the horrors of fatal crashes. 'I don't think reckless risk ever produced good racing,' he said. 'I never believed people go to watch accidents. It's like going to the circus and seeing a guy on the high wire. You don't want him to fall but, if he does, you want to be there when it happens. Nobody is hoping he falls . . . We have as many accidents today as we ever had, but they walk away. Which is good.'

Improved safety had been Mosley's achievement but he felt particularly aggrieved by the sport's vulnerability. Not only was Ferrari rigging races but teams were employing an army of experts to improve tyres, gearboxes, brakes and electronics to secure victory after a gruelling two-hour race at nearly 200 miles an hour by a mere one tenth of a second. Absurdly, it was costing $200 million a year to achieve a fractional increase in speed but for a mere $20,000 a car could be driven ten seconds faster with refinements that were against the rules. Unless the manufacturers were prevented from spending unlimited amounts of money, Mosley feared, new teams would be crippled and the sport would irreparably change. With limited consultation, he suddenly changed the rules to limit the introduction of new technology and to restrict the number of new tyres and engines teams could use. 'I've been changing engines on Saturday nights for forty years,' pleaded Frank Williams. 'Well, you'll change your habits then,' replied Mosley, impatient with the bygone era of oily hands and banging rivets into an aluminium chassis. The manufacturers, Williams knew, supported his protest. They wanted speed to win. Montezemolo led the reaction against

Mosley's restrictions, explaining that Ferrari's 'exotic cars' sold to the public depended upon technical innovation from Formula One. 'Research', he told Mosley, 'is crucial for Ferrari's sales and I can't separate my sales from Formula One.' His opposition was supported by Ron Dennis who was enjoying a seemingly unlimited budget from Mercedes. 'You're driving a coach and horses through the Concorde agreement,' he told Mosley. Mosley tried to broker a truce but to his distress Dennis and Williams accused him of being unreliable. 'We have invested millions in stuff that has now been washed down the drain by Max,' complained Dennis.

The entry of Toyota into Formula One in 2002 raised the stakes. The world's biggest motor manufacturer had decided to commit a huge budget to win the championship. John Howett, the British manager, was welcomed by Ecclestone to his first meeting of principals at the Hilton at Heathrow. Within minutes Howett was dismayed by the apparent chaos. The six-point agenda was summarised in twelve words. Ecclestone was 'charming but destructive', bantering about controversial costs and operations to divert everyone's attention. Howett emerged after a two-hour point-scoring meeting convinced that 'Bernie's welcomed me and made sure I'm uncomfortable'. At the end of the season Toyota had scored just two points compared to Ferrari's 221 points. To improve his team's performance, Howett was committed to spend at least $250 million the following season. Ferrari's official budget was raised to $302 million but some suspected it was higher. The incongruity for Ecclestone was the teams' refusal to increase the number of races – and there was the opportunity to stage about thirty Grands Prix every year – despite increasing their budgets and demanding more money.

FOM's income varied. The Grands Prix in Canada, Hungary, Malaysia and Austria were the biggest sporting events of the year and the governments each contributed up to $30 million to balance FOM's books. The race in Melbourne cost the local government about $60 million to stage but the loss was repaid by the 440,000 fans visiting the city. For supplying the faultless three-day circus, including the television production, trophies, hospitality, advèrtising and the races, FOM earned an average of $35 million per race which cost on average around $19 million to stage – the costs being considerably lower in Europe than elsewhere.

The key to Formula One's financial success was the television contracts. The races were broadcast live to over 125 countries. Formula One's annual revenue was about $700 million, of which about $400 million came from television and the circuits. The teams received, on a sliding scale, a total of 47 per cent of the television revenue and about $35 million in prize money – about 23 per cent of the sport's total revenue with the inclusion of Allsport. Most of that income was Ecclestone's pure profit because the costs of the circuits and teams' expenses were not paid by himself. In theory, three-quarters of the 77 per cent of the profits he received should have gone to the three banks, but Ecclestone – or the Bambino trust – was taking the lot: over $500 million. Unsurprisingly, that arrangement encouraged envy, including the fable that Ecclestone had arrived in his Learjet for a Grand Prix only to discover that his wife had forgotten to pack his underpants, so he sent the plane back to Biggin Hill to collect them rather than buy a pair locally. The invention was repeated by his critics to illustrate Ecclestone's excessive wealth, especially Montezemolo, although he remained unaware of the actual amount. 'Our share of the television money is unfair, Bernie,' carped Montezemolo. 'You've earned too much. You're eating too much cake. You've got indigestion.' Ecclestone remained expressionless. In his opinion, Montezemolo was an open book whose bombast was easily deflated. Ecclestone now began plotting how he could reduce Ferrari's domination on the track and the repeat of a procession behind Schumacher.

Ecclestone's priority was to improve the 'show'. He wanted more competition, more overtaking and drivers responding to the fans. To make it a truly global sport, he had signed contracts to build circuits in Bahrain and Shanghai and a circuit near Istanbul would follow. Each would pay FOM over $30 million and many costs would be borne by the organisers. The additional fees covered the cost of flying six Boeing 747s from Europe – three containing all the television equipment and three planes for the teams. He denied taking any cut from Hermann Tilke, who designed the new circuits. 'I'm not a guinea hunter,' he insisted, using a Warren Street expression. The new global exposure was worth a fortune to the teams and their sponsors. Montezemolo applauded Ecclestone's success but wanted even more. Within his gift, he knew, Ecclestone could grant special favours.

As an act of friendship in 2002, Ecclestone had granted Flavio Briatore the television rights in Spain, a franchise which the Spanish refused to allow Ecclestone to exploit. Briatore prised open the treasure by signing Fernando Alonso, a Spaniard, to drive for Renault (which had bought the Benetton team and hired Briatore) and arranging for Renault to pay premium rates for massive advertisements during the Spanish Grand Prix featuring Alonso. To help Briatore further, Ecclestone organised an additional race in Valencia. By contrast, and of little interest to Montezemolo, the collapse of Alain Prost's team contributed to a fall in French audiences, cutting TF1's payments to Ecclestone from $25.9 million to $13.2 million. Worse, digital television collapsed in December 2002, costing Ecclestone at least £50 million, the annual loss of $105 million from Canal Plus and Kirch, and the cost of firing 200 staff. 'I still don't understand why people won't pay what is asked of them,' Ecclestone said, genuinely perplexed by the failure. 'It's quite incredible that pay-TV doesn't work. It baffles me.' Immune from those gyrations, Montezemolo only saw that Schumacher's success had boosted German audiences and that ITV was negotiating to sign a new five-year deal until 2010 for £130 million. The profits were going to Ecclestone (and in theory the banks) while each team received only $400,000 from FOA for attending every race, compared to Ecclestone's receipts in Europe of about $8 million.

In Montezemolo's calculations, Ferrari would be rewarded with more money from television if the GPWC rather than Ecclestone ran the show. He tasted the potential at the Monza Grand Prix in 2002, which was excluded from FOM's contracts. The cliff-hanger race was watched by a quarter of all Italian homes – 13.3 million viewers – because Ferrari was fighting to capture the title. Barrichello won with Schumacher second, just a quarter of a second behind. If that exposure was replicated across Formula One, Montezemolo believed, the teams would be much richer. Ecclestone feigned indifference to his threat. The circuits and the broadcasters were locked into contracts compelling the breakaway teams to await their expiry before they could start. Beyond that was his 100-year agreement with FIA and his ownership of trade-mark licences in every country. Finally, he would suffocate any breakaway with litigation. Montezemolo was equally combative. 'We are not in a prison,' he replied. 'Just like the English football teams set up the Premier League, we will set up our own league.' His sword of Damocles, he warned, would fall at the end of 2007 when the ten-year Concorde agreement expired. With such a lengthy deadline, both sides could bluff and threaten while the racing continued.

The first three races of the 2003 season suggested that Mosley's reforms were working. In all three, Schumacher was defeated and McLaren was leading. Brazil's Grand Prix in São Paulo on 6 April attracted record television audiences – 4.4 million viewers in Britain alone. Four days later Montezemolo struck. Patrick Faure, the head of the Renault team, announced that all ten teams had signed an agreement to establish the GPWC formally and create a rival series to Formula One. 'We will not compromise,' said Faure. Diall, the Goldman Sachs banker, was searching for a successor to Ecclestone. 'Ecclestone has made huge amounts of money,' said Montezemolo, intending to generate embarrassment, 'becoming one of the richest men in Britain, but he wants too much for himself. It is his biggest mistake. It's a mistake that the sport is now 75 per cent owned by the banks and the teams only receive 47 per cent of the television money, and nothing from the other earnings. We said these things three years ago but unfortunately somebody has not understood.' In normal times, Ecclestone had little affection for Montezemolo who, he scoffed, 'tries to copy Enzo Ferrari but he's got no presence and speaks too much', but after the announcement Ecclestone's reply was pointed. 'Nobody has been greedy at all . . . If Luca's so clever, how come he hasn't solved the problems at Fiat?' (At that moment, Fiat was on the verge of bankruptcy and Montezemolo was the chairman.) Parodying Montezemolo as a tired actor who repeated the same lament every year, Ecclestone accused the teams of 'trying to steal my business. They want to get control of Formula One without paying for it and use it as a car showroom to sell their cars.'

He hated the manufacturers' unreliability – never committing themselves to stay for ten years but entering and exiting the competition depending on boom or bust in the economy, and using their financial muscle to tilt their advantage against the private teams. Their involvement in Formula One invariably ended in tears. Encumbered by bureaucrats at their headquarters delaying technical modifications and tactical changes, they wilted on the tracks against the private teams. The crisis at Jaguar Racing, the team Ford bought from Jackie Stewart in 1999 for $65 million, confirmed his prejudice. Niki Lauda, the manager, had been paid $17 million and departed amid criticism for a poorly designed engine and chassis. Some blamed the paint for being 'too heavy' and others the engine for tending to blow up after two laps. John Hogan, his successor, could not rectify the problems. Rick Parry-Jones, the supremo, was annually spending $125 million but was suffocating amid the chaos of four different management teams in four years and constant interference from Ford's headquarters in Detroit. Convinced that Formula One ran on cash and not petrol, Parry-Jones was leading the breakaway. 'He'll be gone soon,' Ecclestone accurately predicted. In this war, Ecclestone assured Mosley, his monopoly was carefully protected. Knowing from their own experience twenty-one years earlier the difficulty of organising a breakaway, Ecclestone and Mosley spotted critical flaws in the plan. Within the 100-year agreement Mosley had included a term which gave FIA the right to veto any change of control of Formula One and he would block the GPWC operating on race circuits contracted to Formula One. 'Writs will fall like autumn leaves if they try,' Ecclestone said.

Undeterred, Montezemolo and the manufacturers directed Goldman Sachs to threaten the three banks to sell their 75 per cent stake at a hefty discount or the breakaway would make their investment worthless. Gribkowsky's $1.8 billion price tag was rejected. Enjoying the deadlock, Ecclestone urged Gribkowsky to play poker against the teams. After all, he had four years to negotiate. Gribkowsky refused. Fearful of the threat, he wanted a deal with the manufacturers – promising a stable, transparent business which fairly shared the ownership, management and profits between the parties. Ecclestone jeered. The breakaway teams spoke about equality, said Ecclestone, but Montezemolo expected everything to be tilted in Ferrari's favour. Ferrari's success was assured by the car's 100 per cent reliability in seventeen races compared with McLaren's struggle with engine failures; Schumacher earned at least $22 million in 2003, about a quarter of the total of all the drivers' wages; and the new Bridgestone tyres were proving superior to Michelin. But, not content with winning races, Montezemolo sanctioned a surprise attack on his rivals.

Early in the 2003 season Ross Brawn began secretly photographing his competitors' Michelin tyres during races and calculated that they were expanding beyond the regulation 270 mm width. Montezemolo went into overdrive to demand justice. Mosley and Charlie Whiting, FIA's technical director, flew immediately in FIA's Learjet to Maranello. The microscope evidence, said Mosley, confirmed that Pierre Dupasquier, Michelin's tyre expert, had made a mistake. The French manufacturer was compelled to produce new tyres for the last three races and Ferrari swept the board, destabilising Williams and McLaren. 'Survival and success is like escaping from Colditz,' lashed out a member of the McLaren team outraged by Mosley's apparent prejudice that FIA stood for Ferrari International Assistance, 'and in the meantime you mustn't let the bastards get you down.'

Enjoying a spat between the teams, Ecclestone played his cards deftly. 'Ferrari are good at their job, manipulating better than others. Max always looks like favouring Ferrari.' That was exactly Ron Dennis's complaint against all Mosley's rulings, especially his new restrictions on qualifying and refuelling during races. 'I won't embarrass anyone by giving his name,' replied Mosley to a journalist, 'but let's just say he's not the sharpest knife in the box.' 'It's all horrible,' said Ecclestone about the public brawl, with a hint of insincerity. Mosley, he knew, loved a crisis and used Richard Woods, his British media spokesman, to stir controversy, yet he disapproved of the new rules and encouraged the teams to confront Mosley. Nevertheless, every evening he telephoned Paris with a soothing message: 'Max, I'm sure we can solve this problem.' Disorientating the teams, they agreed, would weaken the breakaway and undermine the manufacturers. Ecclestone deployed his trusted ritual by whispering that the teams should receive more money.

Nine months later, Gribkowsky believed he had brokered peace. At a meeting in Geneva on 19 December 2003, he proposed a new ten-year Concorde agreement, paying the teams an additional $240 million on top of their existing $174 million. Since FOA's revenues in 2004 would be $798 million with $450 million from television, Gribkowsky appeared to have broken the glass ceiling. Finally the teams would receive more than Ecclestone, although the distribution was unequal. According to the secret clauses, the small teams, including Jordan, BAR, Sauber, Toyota and Minardi, would not receive a bonus, while McLaren and Williams would receive an additional £12 million each. The important payment, Ecclestone noted, was Ferrari's extra £30 million. Buying off Ferrari was always his trump. Without Ferrari, no breakaway was possible and auspiciously Montezemolo declared himself satisfied. 'Bernie always does a special deal for Ferrari,' noted Mosley, 'but in his mind the only question is "How much?" – the maximum for himself and the minimum for Ferrari.' Gribkowsky congratulated himself that his new terms had broken the deadlock and threat of a breakaway. Ecclestone was not convinced. The teams had squeezed a greater share of the money but he knew they would still not be satisfied and the fight would inevitably resume.

The immediate backwash was renewed publicity. Journalists entering his office were rapidly assessed. Those who arrived to probe into his life without proper research were treated with contempt or at best flippancy to deflect the conversation from areas he wanted excluded. 'I do have parents, contrary to the general belief,' he told the journalist writing a profile for the *Observer*, 'but I don't see them much nowadays. I haven't the time. I saw my father a couple of years ago. I suppose I don't have anything in common with them. I don't get involved in normal domestic affairs.' His father had died fourteen years earlier. 'My mother', he said, 'was a mother.' The image was of a heartless, tough loner. No reader could have imagined that he had visited his parents regularly, had employed his father, organised a long holiday for them in Marbella, financed their homes and had pushed his mother's wheelchair. Nor that he permanently carried their photos in a folder in his briefcase. In the same interview, he also said that he did not employ a driver, that he bought his children few clothes and that he flew economy class. Only his close friends would have enjoyed the deliberate mischief, especially the description of his private jet.

On Thursday 4 March 2004 Ecclestone arrived in Melbourne for the opening race of the new season. Few doubted that Schumacher driving a Ferrari would win. On the eve of the race, Ecclestone hosted a dinner party for Gribkowsky, Brian

Powers and Ron Walker. At the end of the meal, Ecclestone announced, 'We're going to play. Anyone want to come?' 'Yes,' replied Powers and Gribkowsky. The three arrived on the top floor of the Crowne Plaza, walked through the main casino and were admitted by two guards into a secluded annexe for high rollers. Ecclestone was directed to a blackjack table. Six local multimillionaires had been invited by the manager to play against Ecclestone as banker. The bets were unlimited. Cards swept across the green baize and, expressionless, Ecclestone supervised hundreds of thousands of dollars changing hands. After fifty minutes the manager whispered to Ecclestone, 'Mr Ron Dennis is at the door and wants to enter with his wife.' Barely moving his lips or head to acknowledge the man standing expectantly twenty yards away, Ecclestone replied, 'I know the guy but he doesn't have enough money. No.' Dennis glowered. His loathing, Ecclestone assumed, would soon revert to appreciation. At the end of another forty minutes Ecclestone became bored. 'That's it,' he announced. His face betrayed no emotion. '$400,000 up,' he was told. If he had lost the same amount he would have appeared just as unaffected. Gribkowsky left the hotel, finally understanding Ecclestone's self-control. Over two years Ecclestone's smooch had gradually dulled his senses. Behind a smoke screen, he may have fuelled disagreements among the three bankers – telling each banker something different – but that was child's play compared to deflating the egos of Formula One's principal players. The legacy of those battles accentuated the sour taste from Melbourne's disastrous Grand Prix. Only 100,000 spectators had turned up to watch the procession behind Schumacher who, instead of racing, waved to the crowd. Just as Mosley had warned, the cars' new computers and technical refinements had diminished the drivers' skills. Ferrari was employing 1,000 people costing over $300 million annually to transform Formula One into a competition about money rather than talent. Overnight, Gribkowsky calculated, Formula One's value had declined.

During his return flight to Europe, Gribkowsky reassessed his relationship with Ecclestone. A new hazard had arisen. Germany's bank regulators were demanding precise accounts to value Formula One. The Bayerische Landesbank was unable to comply with German law because of obstruction by the former car dealer. For two years Gribkowsky's conference calls with Stephen Mullens and Sacha Woodward-Hill, SLEC's company secretary, had been farcical. Repeatedly both lawyers refused to provide a balance sheet and Woodward-Hill never summoned board meetings where the accounts could be scrutinised. Finding a route through Ecclestone's jungle was beyond any mortal. 'Our shareholder rights have been stolen,' Gribkowsky told Ecclestone's lawyer, adding 'I'm not going to lose my $1.8 billion.' Woodward-Hill, he decided, was a fatal obstruction. 'You're in my way,' he declared. 'Get out or get hurt.' He decided to launch warfare against her and so, indirectly, against Ecclestone. Ecclestone planned his defence. He would use his old protégé, Eddie Jordan.

At Imola on 23 April Jordan revealed the secret details of Gribkowsky's proposed ten-year deal. The three leading teams, said Jordan, would receive £54 million and the remaining seven teams would have £60 million to redistribute among themselves, leaving Jordan with practically nothing. 'The GPWC', said Jordan, 'have told us a complete lie because they promised we would get a bigger share of the pot.' Gribkowsky's agreement collapsed. Ecclestone was not unhappy about the twist. Soon after, unable to compete with the leaders, Jordan walked away from Formula One with an estimated $100 million profit, in spite of his mixed fortunes on the track.

In August 2004 Schumacher won his twelfth victory out of thirteen races. Montezemolo demanded an additional $100 million annually despite television audiences collapsing, bored by what Ecclestone called 'the Bland Prix'. Even the drivers, he mocked, were clones 'all dressed alike, behaving like gentlemen and frightened to death of saying anything in case it upsets their team bosses or sponsors'. He was bored by the absence of outspoken rogues who partied as 'in the good times' and the absence of figures who were sex sensations like James Hunt. He missed drivers like Nigel Mansell: 'He was magic, a brilliant driver and the public absolutely loved him.' Ecclestone's contempt was even occasionally directed at Mosley. 'What time is it?' he asked Mosley on the telephone. Mosley had spent some of Ecclestone's $373 million to lease expensive offices in Trafalgar Square with a glorious view towards Big Ben which, in Ecclestone's opinion, was wasting the money he was earning. But Mosley was equally frustrated. Montezemolo, Dennis and John Howett constantly criticised his proposals to develop safety, reduce costs and improve competitiveness. 'The cost of your changes is colossal,' Howett told Mosley, highlighting his draconian timetable for cuts, 'and you're only interested in your own opinions.' Fed up with being abused, Mosley thought, 'These Formula One people look me in the eye and tell bare-faced lies.' After a moment's reflection he exclaimed during a meeting in Paris in June 2004, 'I've just had enough. I'm resigning.' To his surprise, 'Bernie did not plead that I stay. He even seemed happy to see me go, but he was apprehensive who would follow.' Mosley's departure with the prospect of chaos was not welcome to Ecclestone, but even Mosley could not penetrate the lack of visible sentiment. Emotion was usually absent from Ecclestone's reckoning.

Identical cold calculations steered Ecclestone's attitude in his negotiations with Silverstone. Over the previous two years, the BRDC's amateur pace rankled. 'I go to other circuits around the world and I'm embarrassed when I go to Silverstone,' he told the BRDC's executives. If Silverstone was not rebuilt to match the new circuits, he warned, he would after all abandon their agreement. Martin Brundle retorted that Ecclestone was waging a vendetta. Negotiations were always frustrated, complained Brundle, by Ecclestone stonewalling and delaying his signature

of documents. Ecclestone was unapologetic. He had presented
the BRDC with a scale model of Silverstone's proposed
development but lacked confidence that Brundle would properly
use the £100 million windfall he had extracted from the ruins
of Frank Lowe's investment. To meet Ecclestone's demands, the
British government had partly financed the reconstruction of the
roads around the circuit but, in anticipation of failure to meet
the completion date, Mosley had in 2002 limited the number of
spectators to 60,000. Only 5,000 instead of the normal 30,000
hospitality packages had been sold and the financial burden was
aggravated by the mist over Silverstone on race day. Ecclestone's
helicopter had been diverted and his entry ticket was rejected
by a steward failing to recognise the paragon. 'A county fair
masquerading as a world event,' he cursed, blaming Rob Bain,
the organiser. As Bain sought to explain the problem in the
media centre, Ecclestone ordered him to leave and withdrew his
FIA accreditation to attend his own race. He resigned soon after.
'That's outrageously insulting,' complained Martin Colville, the
club's secretary. 'But it's the way he deals with everybody.'

Since that day in 2002, Ecclestone and Octagon had together
pledged $42 million for the so-called 'Masterplan' to rebuild the
circuit to match international standards. Under their plan, the
Paddock would be rebuilt first, then the car parks and finally the
club house. Instead, ignoring Ecclestone's priorities, Brundle had
built only a new club house, confirming Ecclestone's complaint
about Silverstone's mismanagement. 'Formula One', he told
Brundle, 'has done a lot more for England than England has
done for Formula One.' In reply Brundle and Jackie Stewart
bad-mouthed Ecclestone to the *Daily Telegraph*. Rarely walking
away from a fight, Ecclestone mischievously encouraged Ken
Livingstone, the mayor of London, to stage a trial for a Grand
Prix through Regent Street. More seriously, Jackie Stewart
was given until August 2003 to find a solution to Silverstone's
deficiencies. He personally appealed to Tony Blair for support. 'I
won't hold my breath,' said Ecclestone. 'If we have not got a firm

commitment from those people by the middle of August, then we will say "bye-bye" and get out of it. Simple as that.' 'I just do not understand why Mr Ecclestone and Mr Mosley are being so vicious about Silverstone,' retorted Stewart. 'What I do know is that it is not a fair and level playing field. What Mr Mosley and Ecclestone have been saying about Silverstone has gone out of all proportion and reality.'

In 2004, despite receiving $42 million from Ecclestone and Octagon, the BRDC had still failed to sell the surplus land around the circuit to raise £150 million and build, as agreed, new grandstands and the Paddock. Exhausted by the futile rows, Octagon paid Ecclestone (FOA) $93 million in April 2004 to take over its contractual obligations. In total Interpublic, Octagon's American owner, had lost nearly £500 million but Ecclestone was richer. 'Boy, was I wrong,' lamented Lowe. 'Ecclestone's a curious man beyond belief. He thinks of things ordinary mortals might not.' Phil Geier, Interpublic's chairman, described the investment in Formula One as 'the biggest mistake I ever made'. Ecclestone may have been richer but he shared Geier's disdain. In the same time and with less money Shanghai, Bahrain and Malaysia had constructed new tracks. But while he praised the circuits, the teams and spectators damned Tilke's bland designs for limiting speed, overtaking and exciting competition. The criticism was ignored by Ecclestone, more immediately interested in the business for which the moment of reckoning had been reached. In a season of nineteen races, to accommodate the new races in the Middle East and Asia he had dropped fixtures in Austria and Portugal, and threatened the future of one race in Germany and the USA. With plans for new races in South Korea, Abu Dhabi and India, two other circuits would be abandoned. Ecclestone mentioned Silverstone as a candidate.

The uproar at Silverstone was predictable. Aficionados criticised the absence of popular support for Formula One in the new countries. Their soulless, empty stadiums, carped the English traditionalists, required fabricated excitement to compensate for the absence of fans, but Ecclestone was dismissive. 'I don't care a stuff if people come to the track or not,' he told Ron Shaw. 'I've got it on TV.' Some would say that he would even paint images of people in the grandstands so long as the television pictures were acceptable. Ecclestone believed the critics would be nonplussed by Formula One's annual receipt of over $45 million each from Abu Dhabi, Singapore and Korea. Even Montezemolo, he thought, owed him gratitude because, thanks to his expansion, Ferrari was the brand emblazoned on a Disney-type theme park in Abu Dhabi, tempting inhabitants along the Gulf to enjoy the Ferrari experience. Money should have cemented his relationship with Montezemolo but even with grudging acknowledgement of Ecclestone's success, the Italian did not end his attachment to the GPWC breakaway. Clinging to the possibility of Ecclestone's eventual removal by Montezemolo, Jackie Stewart urged the BRDC to hold out against his demands. Even Ron Dennis thought the strategy was unbalanced and warned Stewart that Ecclestone would never go. To his surprise, Stewart 'went berserk'.

Jackie Stewart's dislike of Ecclestone split the BRDC's board and Stewart won. Given the power to confront Ecclestone, he rejected the offer of a seven-year contract at $16 million per annum and counter-offered $10 million for three years. Fed up with their internal wrangling, and what he perceived to be their unwillingness to meet their obligations to rebuild the circuit and their bad faith over the $42 million they had already received from himself and Octagon, Ecclestone suddenly cancelled the British Grand Prix in 2005. 'I regret that we can't have a British Grand Prix but this is a commercial deal and I have to be fair to everybody,' said Ecclestone at the end of September 2004. His deadline for a new deal was 10 October. 'How much do you want us to pay?' Damon Hill, by then a BRDC official, asked Ecclestone. 'I don't care,' he replied. 'You can have anything you like as long as you pay too much for it.'

Gribkowsky was nervous. Montezemolo was still agitating for

the GPWC and Ecclestone was speaking about executing his own breakaway by abandoning the Concorde agreements. However, two months after his own deadline, Ecclestone capitulated and accepted a five-year deal for £6.4 million per year. Unusually, his coolness deserted him. He sued Jackie Stewart for accusing him on BBC radio of reneging on promises to the minister for sport. The writ was a knee-jerk reaction to a flea bite. His real battle was to keep control of his business.

Alexandra Irrgang, Gribkowsky's legal assistant, was bombarding Sacha Woodward-Hill daily with demands for facts, figures and memoranda. Under orders to divulge as little as possible, Woodward-Hill was strained coping with the Blitzkrieg. In response to Woodward-Hill's prevarication, Irrgang sent streams of faxes to Ecclestone personally – because he did not use email – demanding information. As her demands increased, Ecclestone became tetchy. Every day he telephoned Gribkowsky but the banker diverted the calls to Irrgang. 'We're going to issue a writ unless you cooperate,' warned the lawyer, delighted that Ecclestone was providing perfect evidence about his obstruction of the bankers' rights. Ecclestone, they intended to show, was unlawfully using Formula One as his personal property. On 26 March 2004 the banks issued a writ in the High Court to recover control. 'The writ is nothing to do with me,' Ecclestone told enquirers. 'I haven't even bothered to find out what it's about.' His impassive reaction was calculated to separate himself publicly from the family trusts, which controlled the company. Meanwhile, the trust's lawyers used legitimate ruses to delay the trial.

Ecclestone rarely allowed business disputes to interfere with personal relationships and the writ increased his respect for the banker. Gribkowsky was therefore welcomed to the Belgian Grand Prix at Spa in August 2004. The circuit, winding through the Ardennes forest, was a particular favourite of Slavica's. The drivers enjoyed the challenge in front of excited spectators and were that year celebrating the Grand Prix's return after a ban on tobacco advertising had been dropped by the government. Ecclestone's pleasure that his wife agreed to come to the race evaporated as a group gathered in Karl-Heinz Zimmerman's motorhome on the day of the race. Around the table were Flavio Briatore, Marco Piccinini, Niki Lauda and Gribkowsky, with Ecclestone at one end and Slavica at the other. Slavica had long before overruled her husband's ban on alcohol in his motorhome and Zimmerman opened a bottle of red wine. 'Bastard,' Slavica unexpectedly shouted at her husband. Gribkowsky was stunned. Lauda and the others assumed she was joking. Ecclestone urged his wife to calm down. Without provocation, she replied, 'Motherfucker.' Ecclestone gazed calmly at his wife who was clearly jolly. 'She can be super company,' he often repeated. A week earlier, she had bought a handbag for €50,000. Even if she bought a similar handbag every day, and every designer dress she saw, she would not be able to spend even the interest accumulating on the billions of dollars deposited in Switzerland. Instead, his wife repaid the wealth his genius had produced with embarrassment. Their lives had become a battlefield. He was thankful that, unlike at her last outburst in Bahrain, their daughters were not present. In their parallel lives, there was limited respect, friendship and love. Only their two daughters received his unlimited love and, for their sakes, he would tolerate her abuse. 'For outsiders looking in,' he admitted, 'it's a strange relationship.' Slavica was too proud to apologise. Admitting mistakes was alien to her. Hurt, Ecclestone eventually rose and walked into the Paddock. Among the mechanics, drivers and principals he would find little love, limited friendship, mighty respect and some fear. Everyone knew that Formula One depended upon Ecclestone and even the most famous in the Paddock had relied upon him for a favour, a loan or a gift. He commanded deference but not always personal affection.

Entertaining Gribkowsky in Belgium had not helped his cause. On his return to London, Sacha Woodward-Hill appeared tearfully in his office to declare her resentment at being caught in the pincers of mutual abuse. 'I'm at breaking point, in despair,' she said. 'I'm isolated and alone.' Ecclestone showed limited sympathy. He could not understand, she realised, why she would be affected by aggressive letters. Hovering between fighting and resigning, Woodward-Hill demanded firm orders to resist the banks. 'Ignore the letters,' ordered Ecclestone. 'Forget about it. They can make their plans and I'll make mine.' In his battle against the banks, he would react rather than plan each move. With Mullens's assurance, Ecclestone believed his prevarication could continue.

Gribkowsky was turning the screw. He had hired head-hunters to find Ecclestone's replacement. Initially applicants were asked to work in a junior position to learn the business. When that failed to produce a candidate, the headhunter's scenario outlined Ecclestone's forced removal. Ecclestone's only consolation was that the job description mentioned that two people would be hired to inherit his job. Annoyed by the ruse, Ecclestone called Gribkowsky in Munich. 'You will see what happens if you carry on like this,' he warned. Gribkowsky was shocked. 'If anything happens to me,' replied Gribkowsky believing that he was the target of a threat, 'there will always be another Gerhard.' Ecclestone was not deterred. Being tough was not a game. 'This guy you want to send here is no good,' he said about a candidate who was being secretly considered. 'He's no good for anything. I won't have him in the building.'

To seal his veto, he arranged for Mosley to invite Gribkowsky for dinner. 'The shareholders refuse to be treated like this by Bernie,' said Gribkowsky. 'Of course,' said Mosley diplomatically, 'but as president of FIA I will have the final say on any replacement.'

Mosley delighted in behaving as the consummate broker. But he failed to deter the banks' claim. On 6 December 2004 Mr Justice Park rejected Ecclestone's argument that he was a neutral director and handed control of Formula One Holdings (FOH) to Gribkowsky. 'It changes nothing at all,' said Ecclestone. The German banker, he was sure, could not force the family trusts to comply. 'No one bloody knows what they're talking about,' he told the *Observer* two days after losing, 'or even which company they're talking about.' Judge Park, he said, 'is totally out of order talking about me being appointed by a company called Bambino, which I am not. We are just about to write to him to put him straight on that.' Not mentioned was Gribkowsky's mistake. The real power over the business resided in the company called Formula One Administration (FOA), not FOH. Taking a day off on her birthday in January 2005, Woodward-Hill decided that Ecclestone could not care less about her work as company secretary. The formalities did not interest him. By nightfall she had decided that to frustrate Gribkowsky's schemes and for her own sanity, she would resign as company secretary. It suited Ecclestone and Mullens not to appoint a replacement.

Unwilling to fight on two fronts, Ecclestone flew to Maranello. Dealing with Montezemolo was unavoidable. Two weeks after the Spa race he had spotted Montezemolo in the Paddock at Monza. As always, the Italian was posing – playing to the cameras and waving to fans. But Ecclestone could not dislike the man in spite of his ego and his desire to topple him. To finally break the GPWC, Ecclestone wanted Montezemolo to extend Ferrari's commitment to the Concorde agreement from 2007 to 2012. For those extra five years, he offered Ferrari an additional $55 million signing fee, annual $50 million payments and a veto over any future regulation changes by FIA. The total package for the ten teams would be an additional $500 million a year for five years. By the end of the day Montezemolo had agreed. 'I knew that Ferrari would see sense,' Ecclestone said later. 'I gave them what they wanted.' The revolt, Ecclestone believed, was finally suffocated. Without Ferrari the other GPWC teams would capitulate.

Ecclestone was mistaken. Ron Dennis wanted to end Ferrari's dominance. 'I can't stand the internal wrangling that has made Formula One resemble the sporting branch of the Mafia,' said Dennis. 'I want a level playing field.' If the GPWC was dead, Dennis intended to replace Ecclestone's dictatorship with a new breakaway group, agreed at a hotel near Munich airport among 'the Nine' (without Ferrari), called the Grand Prix Manufacturers Association (GPMA). Their adviser was Christina Booth, a former Goldman Sachs banker. Although he pretended not be concerned, Ecclestone was furious that Dennis and Frank Williams were again challenging him. Whereas he appreciated Montezemolo as a good negotiator, he had no respect for that duo's threats. Certain that Dennis's rebellion would fail, he issued a deadline threatening to withdraw his $500 million offer if it was not accepted before the season started in Melbourne at the end of February 2005. 'Don't stampede into Ecclestone's open arms,' Dennis urged the teams. In previous arguments Ecclestone's patient persuasion had been always victorious but on this occasion he was rebuffed. As the deadline passed, he withdrew his offer.

The teams' anger about Ecclestone for yet again setting Ferrari against the rest was intensified after Mosley withdrew his resignation. The reason, which he did not disclose, was his failure to stymie Ecclestone's manoeuvres. For some months, Mosley had been cultivating Jean Todt as his successor but unexpectedly the Frenchman had been promoted at Ferrari. Without an alternative as a preferred successor, Mosley feared that Michel Boeri of Monaco, Ecclestone's candidate, would take over. Boeri, Mosley believed, was malleable, especially against Mosley's new regulations. Like the teams, Boeri opposed Mosley's immediate cuts as too expensive and favoured gradual reductions. Mosley's decision to stay was not universally welcomed. 'The teams are saying this is crazy,' said Frank Williams, 'and that they are no longer going to live with it. The prevailing atmosphere in the sport at the moment stinks. It is very unhealthy.' Dennis echoed the complaint: 'Max has this Machiavellian streak. He's always trying to kill the weak. His only motive is sheer control.' Naturally, Ecclestone took the opposite position. With Mosley back on board, he clung to his old ally to resist the siege and keep Formula One under their control.

* * *

The next counter-coup surprised both men. Just before the race in Melbourne, the first fixture of the 2005 season, Mosley and his new technical regulations were challenged in a campaign orchestrated by Paul Stoddart, the owner of the marginal Minardi team. With the written support of all nine teams, Stoddart proposed to breach FIA's rules and race a 2004 car. The entry was opposed by Mosley and, in retaliation, Stoddart appealed to Australia's courts, arguing that Mosley was breaking the Concorde rules. Mosley played tough. Regardless of the Australian courts, he said, unless Stoddart backed down, all FIA officials would immediately leave Australia and the race would not count in the world championship. 'Paul's been a bit of a nuisance since day one,' said Ecclestone, 'but we have protected him. Regretfully, there is now no place in Formula One for someone like him.' Stoddart surrendered and the race was won by Fernando Alonso in a Renault.

This was to be the beginning of Flavio Briatore's resurrection, McLaren's renewed challenge – and the decline of Schumacher's Ferrari. No team could beat the cycle. A flush of winners was inevitably followed by defeat.

Soon after his return to London, Ecclestone welcomed Gribkowsky to his office. In Ecclestone's world, losing rarely caused a grudge. He moved on to fight the next battle. 'Am I dealing with Bambino or Bernie?' asked the German sceptically. 'Is it one face or two?' Regardless of his court defeat in December, Ecclestone told Gribkowsky, Bambino was beyond his control. His answer was meaningless. Politely, Gribkowsky assured Ecclestone that his game had destroyed their friendship. This was a battle he intended to win. In January 2005 the banks started new legal proceedings in London against Bambino for control of FOA. Three weeks later, Gribkowsky returned to Ecclestone's office. He did not intend to stay long. After brief pleasantries, Gribkowsky smiled, bid farewell and set off in his limousine towards Heathrow. Ecclestone's telephone call ten minutes later was not unexpected. 'What's this document?' asked Ecclestone in an unusual voice. 'Which document?' replied Gribkowsky cheerfully as his Mercedes raced along the M4. 'The one on my desk,' said Ecclestone. 'I can't imagine,' said Gribkowsky feigning bewilderment. 'Goodbye.'

Over the previous months, the German had learnt important lessons from Ecclestone, not least that your enemy's enemy is your friend. Wolfgang Eisele was a perfect example. Damaged by his struggle with Ecclestone, Eisele welcomed Gribkowsky's arrival at his home in Heidelberg as a chance for revenge. During their discussions, Eisele revealed that among his documents was a letter suggesting a close relationship between Ecclestone and Bambino, the supposedly independent family trust. 'Can we have it?' asked Gribkowsky excitedly. 'It'll cost €100,000,' replied Eisele. The banker was shocked. Buying evidence was beyond the pale yet one page might secure the bank's $1.8 billion. He hammered the price down to €20,000. Shortly after, during his brief meeting in Ecclestone's office, he had, unseen, slipped a copy of a letter on to Ecclestone's desk and escaped. The letter linked Luc Argand, the Swiss lawyer for the family trusts, with Ecclestone. Gribkowsky correctly gauged Ecclestone's reaction. Publication of the letter – a letter representing Ecclestone as the spokesman for Bambino – would be embarrassing and, pertinently, Gribkowsky had shown his adversary that he had not only done his homework but had learned how to deploy Ecclestone's own tactics. Among Ecclestone's favourite maxims was 'You don't know what you don't know.' Now Ecclestone did not know what else Gribkowsky, using his control of FOH, could produce. The parties were waiting for a preliminary judgement in a second High Court case, disputing the control of FOA, which raised the relationship between Ecclestone and Bambino. 'This is unhelpful,' Ecclestone admitted. 'It could show that I am Bambino's puppet.' To avoid its publication, Bambino settled the case with Gribkowsky on 23 March 2005. Ecclestone finally agreed to the appointment of a majority of directors by the banks. 'We now have the power to sack Ecclestone,' announced Gribkowsky. 'If I can't work in freedom,' Ecclestone replied, 'I'll walk. If they want to change, let them.' Gribkowsky, Ecclestone proclaimed, had won legal control but his shares were worthless without Ecclestone's management. 'I don't care who's on the board. I don't give a damn about the ownership. I'm arrogant enough to believe that what I do is right. Unless I run it the way I want, I'll leave.'

The next morning Ecclestone emerged from his house to discover that two wheels had been stolen from his custom-made silver Mercedes AMG, delivered by the manufacturers the previous day. Security cameras had failed to spot the thieves. 'It's a real nuisance,' he said. No, he volunteered, he would not report the theft to the police. 'I haven't seen them round here for years.' Among those offering their condolences was Flavio Briatore. 'They've got to send the wheels from Germany,' Ecclestone told his friend.

10

Cheating

In his manoeuvres to keep control of Formula One, Ecclestone believed that he could rely on Flavio Briatore. The glitzy celebrity parading in the spotlight with beautiful women on yachts and private planes had carved a niche in Formula One since his return in 2000. Under his management Renault had rebuilt the former Benetton team to win the world championship with Fernando Alonso in 2005. Unashamedly Briatore linked his own success with Formula One's. 'I know what people want,' he said. 'It is about the lifestyle because every car is the same. Nobody comes to me after the championship and says your gearbox was terrific or your suspension. I am part of the lifestyle.'

Travelling around the globe with Ecclestone, he understood better than others how constant juggling kept the circus moving. 'I have a lot to learn from Bernie,' he said, 'because Bernie is the kind of guy who is very, very quick.' Formula One had made Briatore rich. Not only from Renault but, unusually, by acting as the agent on a 20 per cent commission for his drivers, including Nelson Piquet and Fernando Alonso. Good drivers from his team who were not his clients had been fired. Ecclestone was not disturbed by Briatore's brash ambitions. During his fifty-five years in the sport, Ecclestone had encountered every type of character but ever since Colin Chapman's death he had lacked a friend in the Paddock. Briatore, recently photographed by *Hello* magazine in a G-string on his yacht with Naomi Campbell, filled a void. Looking along the Paddock, Ecclestone would struggle to find better company. Frank Williams still courageously survived but their conversations were limited, while Ron Dennis seemed no longer content flying around the globe on his own plane and enjoying luxuries which few other former grease mechanics could enjoy. 'It's not like it used to be,' Ecclestone complained to Niki Lauda, sitting as usual in Karl-Heinz Zimmerman's hospitality motorhome. 'I miss the old days.' To distract himself, he invited Zimmerman to play a few rounds of backgammon, a game he normally won and a competition at which many in the Paddock aspired to challenge him.

Staying with Slavica on Briatore's yacht in May 2005 for the Monaco Grand Prix was, as usual, amusing – except that Briatore was griping about McLaren's victory over Renault two weeks earlier in Spain, and that McLaren was favourite to win again in Monaco. Ecclestone's response was barely perceptible. He was rarely bothered by the outcome of a race – an exciting race was all he wanted – except that Ron Dennis was hungry not only to win the world championship but also still wanted to grab control of Formula One. Ecclestone suspected that Dennis had secured Frank Williams's support for the GPMA by assuring the icon, confined to his wheelchair, that he would care for his wife after he died. After all, in his opinion Williams had tolerated Dennis luring away lucrative commercial relationships and his vulnerability had increased as his fortunes on the circuit ebbed. 'How can you be such buddies with Ron,' Ecclestone had asked Williams, 'when he grabs everything you have?' Williams answered by combining with Dennis against Ecclestone's new agreement with Montezemolo. To outwit the latest breakaway bid, Ecclestone needed Briatore's friendship. 'In this game,' Ecclestone would say, 'you do what you want to do, not what others want you to do. You can't give up. You've got to win.'

Outsmarting Dennis always gave him pleasure. At the beginning of the season, Dennis had threatened that McLaren would not start in the first race unless Ecclestone paid more money. Dennis had persuaded Toyota to join his cause. 'If they pull the gun on me,' said Ecclestone, dismissive of threats without force, 'they'd better make sure they have bullets loaded.' His mobile telephone's ringtone was the theme tune from Clint Eastwood's western, *The Good, the Bad and the Ugly*. The showdown to end the strife with Dennis started in Ecclestone's motorhome in the Monaco Paddock. 'The Concorde agreement will not be signed,' Dennis told Ecclestone. 'I bet it will,' replied Ecclestone. 'Right, £100,000,' countered Dennis. 'Done,' said Ecclestone. 'How about £250,000?' said Dennis. 'Done,' replied Ecclestone. There was a short silence broken by Ecclestone: 'I'll sign it.' Dennis looked puzzled: 'But that's not what we bet.' 'It is,' said Ecclestone. 'We never said how many people had to sign it, only that it would not be signed.' Ecclestone did not expect Dennis to pay up. Winning was sufficient pleasure.

While he easily shrugged off the brutalities of business, it was less easy to ignore Slavica's particularly embarrassing behaviour that weekend. Despite the luxury of Monaco in the sun, his wife shouted at her husband in front of Formula One's royalty. Retreating to the motorhome, Ecclestone turned to Zimmerman for solace. Strangely, despite their past differences, even Niki Lauda was welcome to sit for hours at his round table. The two Austrians sympathised with his humiliation. His daughters were compensation for any discontent. Briatore was his soulmate to face the teams.

Max Mosley disliked Briatore's vanity, especially his ostentatious manner of parading through the Paddock, playing to the cameras. Team principals, he believed, should dedicate themselves to the sport's intricacies rather than indulge in trivialities and politics. Ecclestone's close association with a man who started life as a bank counter clerk was beyond Mosley's comprehension. The sentiments were reciprocated. Briatore disliked Mosley although Renault's success was partially due to Mosley's latest rule restricting tyre changes. By forcing the teams to choose between hard or soft tyres at the beginning of the weekend, he had deprived Ferrari of an advantage. Montezemolo had also failed to adapt to Mosley's new aerodynamics rules. In contrast, Renault and McLaren had observed the changes and were crushing Ferrari. Although Briatore had limited affection for engineering and regulations, he shared Mosley's curse against increasing costs. 'Formula One should be profitable,' said the Italian, also appearing to side with Ecclestone against Ron Dennis and Montezemolo.

All those conflicts were simmering four weeks later when the teams arrived in Indianapolis, the world's oldest racing track, for the American Grand Prix. Formula One's relaunch in America was founded on a deal signed in 1998 between Ecclestone and Tony George, the circuit owner, to expensively rebuild the track. George relied on Ecclestone to deliver a compelling race.

The competition between Renault and McLaren at that stage was tight, while Schumacher's Ferrari was panned as a certain loser. Drawn by the prospect of a thrilling competition, 130,000 fans had bought tickets. Ecclestone had arrived with little enthusiasm. Formula One was a minority sport in America and barely profitable. Compared to the popular NASCAR races on 1,200 circuits, Formula One would soon be restricted to just one competition. In his critics' eyes, Ecclestone had been negligent. To have allowed Formula One to dissolve over the previous twenty years in the world's biggest car market was, they complained, folly. Forthrightly, he replied that Americans were incapable of concentrating for a two-hour Formula One race and even the few who remained seated were discouraged by the absence of American drivers and the inconvenient times of the other races across the world. Financially, it was also unattractive. The Indy circuit, accustomed to low-cost NASCAR races, could not match the booty offered by the new Middle Eastern and Asian entrants. 'But if you're so sure,' challenged Ecclestone, 'do you want to put some cash into the Indy races?' Unanimously they refused. The Indy was a cross to bear. In June 2005 none foresaw how a routine incident could jeopardise Formula One's fragility in America and the precarious relationships among the rival principals.

Two days before the race, Charlie Whiting, FIA's race director, telephoned Mosley to report that during the test drive Ralf Schumacher's Toyota had crashed on turn 13 after a tyre burst. A quick inspection revealed that Michelin tyres were vulnerable on that particular turn. Initially, Michelin's staff were reassuring that replacements would be flown from France overnight. Further tests, however, showed that no Michelin tyre would be safe on turn 13. During the previous year, the tyre's sidewall had been rebuilt and tests on a simulation machine had failed to expose an inherent weakness after ten laps at 180 miles an hour around that bend.

Seven teams were using Michelin tyres. All the team principals telephoned Mosley, who was in Monaco, to approve a simple solution. To reduce speeds at turn 13, FIA should order a chicane or barrier to be placed across the track. Mosley was not disposed to help. Three teams including Ferrari were using Bridgestone tyres and he asked rhetorically, 'Why should I penalise them?' Before issuing his edict, he telephoned Jean Todt to ensure Ferrari's support for his opposition. Todt was delighted: 'We didn't have a good car and our tyres were not good enough, so I said that Max was right.' Satisfied that he would not be embarrassed by Ferrari, Mosley refused to install a chicane, explaining that the three teams should not lose their advantage. Effectively, he had excluded seven teams from the competition. Unable to drive at the same speed as Ferrari, they would have to withdraw. Throughout Saturday, Mosley was inundated by frantic calls from Ron Dennis, Flavio Briatore and Ecclestone urging him to reconsider. Briatore was especially irate. He blamed Mosley for causing the problem at the beginning of the season by foolishly introducing the new rule forbidding any change of tyres during the race.

'I'll fix it,' said Ecclestone, believing that he could persuade Mosley and Todt to agree to a chicane. But during Saturday, Ecclestone sensed his powerlessness. 'Max won't budge,' he told Briatore. In the Paddock he was asked by ITV's Martin Brundle,

'What's going on, Bernie?' 'I don't know,' replied Ecclestone, unusually vulnerable. 'What is going on?' Seven thousand miles from Indianapolis and unwilling to dash across the Atlantic, Mosley refused to yield. 'I suspected', said Mosley, 'that the tyre problem was not as grave as they represented. I felt the situation had been created artificially and deliberately.' Convinced of skulduggery, Mosley interpreted the pleas by Dennis and Briatore, two men he disliked, as a deliberate challenge to his authority to administer Formula One's safety and fairness rules. 'Ecclestone and the teams', he reflected, 'thought they could dictate what happened. And they couldn't.'

The race on Sunday 19 June was disastrous. All twenty cars drew up on the grid but, after the first lap, fourteen cars withdrew. The spectators, unaware of the reasons, booed and threw beer cans on to the track. In the uproar the sedate race between the Ferraris and the stragglers became a defining moment for the relationships of Formula One's powerbrokers. Mosley was universally reviled and blamed for adoring a crisis. Briatore spoke about Mosley's pleasure in embarrassing the teams rather than finding a solution, a suggestion which infuriated Mosley. Even Ecclestone was critical: 'Max had a strong argument but could have got around it. He wasn't very helpful. He didn't appear to care that it would be the end of Formula One in America.' 'This was stupid, really stupid,' wrote Mike Mulhern, a reporter from the *Winston Salom Journal*. 'It is arrogance and stupidity that has caused this. It shows no respect for the people watching in the grandstands and on television. It is a slap in the face for the US public.' Despite the uproar, Mosley was unrepentant. 'Bernie knows that I'm not good at backing down. I felt it was unfortunate but not a disaster.' To prove his potency, Mosley prosecuted the seven teams for 'acts prejudicial to the interests of the competition'. Shortly after, the convictions and fines were overturned. 'Secret evidence', Mosley said, 'excluded the grounds for punishment.' The surrender was too late. Mosley was accused of 'posturing' and fuelling the civil war, rupturing

Formula One. The teams, Ecclestone decided, 'want Max's head'. In reality, they were also eyeing his own head.

On reflection, Ecclestone admitted his responsibility for letting Formula One slip beyond his total control. If he had never sold the shares, he conceded, 'we wouldn't have had all this nonsense.' To deflect the impression of his weakness, he feigned ignorance about the teams' objectives: 'I don't know what they want to do and I don't think they know. I think it's one of those things where somebody said something and wished they hadn't and they don't know how to get out of it.' The suggestion of the teams' regret lacked the credibility of his candour to others: 'Before we had more or less a dictatorship – and I was the dictator. Now there is more of a democracy – and it hasn't seemed to work because there is too much freedom for people to say and do what they want.' When pushed, he blamed all the team bosses: 'I do get a bit tired of the squabbling and people trying to push their egos forward when they have come from nothing and think they are something they are not. I have seen it so many times. I say to these people, "Look, come with me to the cemetery and I will show you where we have buried quite a few people." ' He was particularly angry with those like Ron Dennis who had become rich thanks to him. 'They have not put one dollar in and they have taken plenty out. Now they're flying around in private planes, have yachts and three homes. Are these people a little ungrateful for what has happened to them?' Now was the time, he decided, to call their bluff.

Since Gribkowsky's victory, Ecclestone had contemplated a break from the banker whose scrupulous formalities undermined his deal-making. 'Unless I run it the way I want,' he repeated impatiently, 'I'll leave.' His inflexibility alarmed Gribkowsky. The German banker had won his court battles and had also removed the two American banks from the board, so ostensibly he was in full legal control of Formula One – except that ultimately he was powerless without Ecclestone. To establish his indispensability, Ecclestone conjured a drama. Gribkowsky, he knew, wanted to recover the bank's money, so he again encouraged the banker to sell the shares to the manufacturers – Ferrari, BMW, Ford and Renault – who had led the failed breakaway. 'I'm sure they'll want to buy Formula One,' Ecclestone told Gribkowsky, but did not add at the time, 'I would be surprised if they bought it, but I will not be surprised when they don't.'

Sceptical of Ecclestone's certainty, Gribkowsky set off to entice Rick Parry-Jones of Ford Jaguar, Burkhard Goeschel of BMW, Patrick Faure of Renault and Montezemolo. At each meeting Gribkowsky was greeted enthusiastically, and each man added in further conversation how 'over the years' Ecclestone had 'cheated' the teams, making his replacement critical, he claimed. Gribkowsky was intrigued. The bruising battles had aroused his own suspicions about Ecclestone's honesty and the Formula One manufacturers were more practised eyewitnesses to Ecclestone's doubtful integrity. Yet the more he probed, the more the hyperbole became evident. None of the accusers could produce an iota of evidence that Ecclestone had 'cheated' or that they had been victims of any dishonesty. Instead, Gribkowsky gradually realised, their allegations reflected only jealousy of Ecclestone's success. Moving on, Gribkowsky urged Montezemolo and the other manufacturers to take over Formula One by 2006. Since none of them declined, he reported his 'success' to Ecclestone. Ecclestone was unconvinced. 'They want 50 per cent of the income and 50 per cent of the shares, so they must commit to support Formula One for a minimum of five years,' he told Gribkowsky. He knew how the manufacturers dipped in and out of Formula One but would never contractually commit themselves to spending over $1 billion. If they lost races or there was a recession, their directors would instantly pull out. Gribkowsky resumed his tour and after further conversations admitted defeat. 'Unfortunately,' Ecclestone consoled him, 'these people have the mentality that 90 per cent of 50 is better than 70 per cent of a 100. It all stems from the fact that their arithmetic is not very good.'

With Gribkowsky adrift, Ecclestone wanted to bury the revolt once and for all. He asked Brian Powers for help. 'I'm willing to walk away,' he told Powers, 'if the teams take it over.' Powers was briefed to show the teams how, if they bought the banks' shares, they could own the business within five years for nil outlay. Ecclestone said he was even prepared to sell his own 25 per cent stake as part of a comprehensive settlement. Powers first approached Ron Dennis. The reply was negative. 'He's paranoid about someone outsmarting him,' Powers reported. 'Keep trying,' said Ecclestone. Powers's journey culminated at BMW's headquarters in Munich with Burkhard Goeschel, the spokesman for the GPMA. Powers showed the director responsible for motor sport how he could recover his investment within five years. Like all the team managers, Goeschel suspected that any offer from Ecclestone would outsmart him. 'I don't want to take on debt,' said Goeschel. 'There is no debt,' insisted Powers. 'You'll get all your money back in five years.' The German would not be convinced. 'We want to race, not be in the business of owning commercial rights.' Unsurprised by the rejection, Ecclestone feigned a confession, 'The whole thing has become a nightmare. We've offered them what they wanted.' And now they rejected the chance. In bluff and counter-bluff, no one played poker better than Ecclestone.

The teams' confusion was better than any previous split orchestrated by Ecclestone himself. First they wanted to break away without Ferrari as the newly formed GPMA. Then they accepted Ecclestone's offer of additional money in a new Concorde. But then they were stumped by Ferrari's rejection of the offer. 'We don't want a breakaway,' admitted John Howett of Toyota, 'we just want proper professional governance, not something resembling a 1960s second-hand-car business'. 'Bernie, you keep pretending not to understand me,' pleaded Howett, 'but we must have certainty.' Ecclestone interpreted requests for 'a dialogue' as weakness. Whenever Howett, Goeschel and Patrick Faure of Renault demanded certainty about a new Concorde agreement, Ecclestone did little to resolve the confusion. 'Howett', he told Mosley scathingly, 'is just an MoT guy. My car doesn't need an MoT, and I don't need him.' Mosley agreed. Without Ferrari, the new breakaways were losers.

In early September Ecclestone returned to London from Monza. As usual he had flown back before the race ended, pleased that the contest between Ron Dennis and Flavio Briatore was still fierce. McLaren had won the race but Alonso and Renault were leading the championship. The Italian crowds had been depressed by Ferrari's stumbles. The atmosphere in the Paddock had been dispirited. Naturally, he had spoken to Montezemolo, Dennis, Williams and all his other critics, but Formula One's instability would linger, he knew, until the banks' ownership was terminated. Two days after his return, an unexpected telephone call from Eric Hersman solved the dilemma. 'I've got a buyer for Formula One,' said Hersman, whom Ecclestone did not know. 'If it goes through I want a 1 per cent fee.' 'You'll get that from the buyer, not me,' Ecclestone told the cold-caller, whom he regarded as a hustler. He was introduced to Donald Mackenzie.

Donald Mackenzie, a Scottish law graduate, was the senior partner in London of CVC Capital Partners, an international equity investment fund with over $30 billion under management to invest in a successful mix of over 200 companies including the AA, Kwik-Fit, Debenhams, IG Index and Halfords. Accused of lacking sufficient social conscience in his hunger for profits, Mackenzie understood Formula One's value. Ever since his schooldays in Scotland following the career of Jim Clark, he had been a Formula One fan and passionate owner of the latest Ferrari. Formula One, Mackenzie knew, was a cash machine. In 2006 Ecclestone expected to repay the $1.4 billion bond from earnings, four years early, and in the meantime the bonds were trading at a healthy premium. Private equity groups only chose investments whose value would grow annually by about 20 per cent and could be sold within ten years at a huge profit. He needed that reassurance for Ecclestone. More, like all private equity managers, Mackenzie flourished only if he was smarter than the managers of the company he was buying. Aiming to outsmart Ecclestone was a mighty challenge.

Three days after the Monza race, Ecclestone spent an hour with Mackenzie in Spa and, after deciding he was serious, called Gribkowsky. 'Why don't you come and meet Donald?' Gribkowsky, at his country house in France, accepted Ecclestone's offer to send his plane from Belgium immediately. 'If he's interested,' added Ecclestone, 'you can sell Bambino's 25 per cent for the same price.' Within three hours, Gribkowsky, smoking a large cigar and wearing dark sunglasses, and Mackenzie had met. 'I want $2.2 billion,' said Gribkowsky. 'That's the full recovery price plus the lost interest over the past five years.' After a day's discussion Mackenzie agreed. Ecclestone was delighted. His remaining stake would be sold to CVC for $450 million and he would repurchase 10 per cent of the final entity for $100 million. Lehman's would buy 15 per cent of the new company and J. P. Morgan 3 per cent. Ecclestone was grateful that Mosley, abiding by his 'Don King' clause, approved CVC as a suitable owner.

Nothing was revealed during the last three races in Brazil, Japan and China. The battle between Dennis and Briatore came to a climax at the nineteenth race in Shanghai, won by Renault. Alonso was world champion and Briatore was a lot richer. Six weeks later, on 25 November 2005, CVC announced that it had bought Formula One from the Bayerische Landesbank and Ecclestone's stake for $2.5 billion.

Soon after, CVC bought the shares in Formula One from the other two banks and also bought Allsport from Paddy McNally. Although its annual profits were about $100 million, McNally only received about £370 million and the other co-owners over £30 million. McNally added to his property portfolio in Switzerland, where he has lived for forty years, and his two country homes in southern England with the purchase of a Scottish grouse moor. Ecclestone was pleased with the deal. He usually won. The reward for his tenacity was deposited in the family trust's Swiss bank account.

Ecclestone had profited from five changes of ownership since he first considered floating in 1996. His route to extract over $4 billion plus a personal income of about $1 billion might have been less troubled if he had not faced death. The heart bypass, as he would admit, had a profound influence on him. Now the ownership was beyond dispute and money was no longer his priority, his sole interest was to manage Formula One on CVC's behalf. His annual salary of £2.5 million plus £1 million bonus and expenses including fuel for his Falcon jet was of limited interest.

In anticipation of CVC's first board meeting in Jersey, Ecclestone was asked to provide the 'CEO's report'. 'Can I send it to you?' Ecclestone asked Gribkowsky, who remained on the board. One page came out of the fax machine in Munich stating: 'There is nothing special to report.' Gribkowsky telephoned London. 'Bernie, it might be a bit *too* short.'

Down the years, Ecclestone often showed concern about his adversaries. He had heard that Gribkowsky was about to undergo serious heart surgery. He telephoned with an offer of help. Gribkowsky was grateful but unmoved. After all the strife, he assumed that Ecclestone's solicitations were not motivated by friendship but a desire to be loved. The offer of advice, he harshly concluded, portrayed the familiar isolation of billionaires; namely, that no one dared be honest with him. Ecclestone would laugh about that impression. Montezemolo, Dennis and other team managers were blunt critics. Friendship was another issue. Such sentiments were irrelevant to proving to Mackenzie his ability to persuade the teams to end the arguments. 'I'll sort it out,' he assured the new owner.

The news of CVC's takeover had outraged the Formula One fraternity. 'Our sport is in the hands of an asset-stripper,' complained Patrick Head, the Williams team designer. Ron

Dennis and Luca Montezemolo led the protest chorus. Once again, they cursed, Ecclestone had profited from a change of ownership without their agreement. While he had pocketed $450 million from selling his final 25 per cent stake, they were again denied any shares in the business. Aggravating their anger was the news about the increase of Mackenzie's windfall. After paying $2.9 billion for the shares, Mackenzie sat in Ecclestone's office discussing his strategy for financing his purchase.

'You should talk to Fred Goodwin,' suggested Ecclestone, referring to the chief executive of the Royal Bank of Scotland (RBS). 'Get me Fred,' Ecclestone ordered his secretary. Moments later the secretary called back. 'Mr Goodwin's on holiday.' 'I didn't ask where he is,' snapped Ecclestone, 'I said I want to speak to him.' Within minutes, Goodwin was on the line from his holiday home in Phuket, Thailand. By the end of the conversation, the bank had offered to lend CVC $1.5 billion and later a further $1.4 billion. Mackenzie intended to repay the debt from Formula One's revenue by 2014. When the news broke, Montezemolo found that even Briatore was listening to his complaint about Formula One's income being used by a financier to repay his loans. For the moment, Briatore refused to join any campaign but relayed the gripes to Ecclestone. 'Bugger them,' he exclaimed. The teams had refused to buy Formula One from Gribkowsky yet they objected to anyone's else's ownership.

To repair relations, Ecclestone invited the teams to meet Mackenzie at the Hilton at Heathrow. Montezemolo arrived but refused to enter the room. 'He wants special treatment,' Gribkowsky told Ecclestone. 'He fears Ferrari won't get their extra payments any more.' Glancing at Dennis, Ecclestone saw that his old adversary was as usual scowling, obviously angered by Mackenzie's new wealth from Formula One. As Ecclestone moved towards Montezemolo to persuade him to enter the room, the Italian began shouting. 'We provide the show and the money and now we're being ripped off. There's going to be no solution. We're going to leave Formula One. It's all over.'

'Come in now,' Ecclestone urged the performer. With a show of reluctance, Montezemolo agreed. The meeting ended in disarray. The teams wanted 75 per cent of the annual income and CVC offered the teams 50 per cent. 'Don't worry,' Ecclestone told Mackenzie as they left. 'I'll sort it out.' To break the teams' unity, Ecclestone got to work on Frank Williams. In the cyclical nature of Formula One, his old friend's fortunes had declined. He was willing to abandon his opposition and for $20 million sign the latest Concorde agreement from 2008 to 2012. 'Frank's always a good soldier,' said Gribkowsky. Giancarlo Minardi agreed the same deal. The bigger hurdle was the manufacturers and Ron Dennis.

'Ron's arrogance has exploded,' John Surtees observed. 'Sometimes he speaks to me and sometimes he doesn't.' At Jody Scheckter's pheasant shoot in Hampshire in winter 2006, Dennis arrived in a custom-built, extended silver Mercedes four-wheel drive driven by his German loader. Dressed in a tailored tweed shooting suit, he opened the tailgate to reveal an immaculate wooden interior. On the left were his two guns, on the right a kennel for his chocolate brown Labrador. A special flap prevented the dog scratching the paint while jumping down. In the middle compartment was a bar with six bottles of cold Dom Perignon and six gold Theo Fennell goblets engraved 'Ron and Lisa'. These, as Dennis proudly whispered to Peter Warr, the former Lotus team manager, had cost £2,000 each. 'Hide them,' whispered Scheckter mischievously as they drained the goblets. 'Where are they?' asked Dennis as he sought to collect his expensive trophies. Only four were retrieved. Dennis had no doubt that his host had retained the last ones. Pointing his shotgun at Scheckter's own Mercedes, he threatened, 'I'll blast a hole if you don't give them back.' Scheckter relented. He had no doubt that Dennis would shoot.

Dennis's bad mood was aggravated by McLaren's failure to win a single race and the torrid finances suffered by all the teams during the 2006 season. As usual, they were all spending more than they earned and Ferrari's sales were sliding from 7,000 cars to 2,000 cars. The squeeze was aggravated by CVC's refusal to pay the annual revenue to those teams which had failed to sign the new but uncompleted Concorde agreement due to start in 2007. 'Concorde agreements are pointless,' said Ecclestone, also refusing to sign, 'and the teams can't agree.' Mosley concurred, Ecclestone suspected, 'because Max doesn't like peace'. The sight of Ecclestone and Mosley once again enjoying confusion infuriated Dennis.

Regardless of any agreement, Dennis was pursuing his claim for 1 per cent of the shares or $40 million at an arbitration hearing in Switzerland (which he would eventually lose, because his lawyers originally signed an agreement implicitly excluding an action with the Formula One company which eventually sold the shares) but, in the meantime, he needed money and Mackenzie wanted peace. Renault was dominating the season when Dennis, on the eve of the Grand Prix in Barcelona on 13 May 2006, met Ecclestone in Zimmerman's tent and motorhome for a succession of meetings in unusual heat with Donald Mackenzie and Sacha Woodward-Hill. Agreeing a 700-page Concorde agreement lasting until 2012 was no longer feasible so Dennis demanded that the teams agree a short Memorandum of Understanding on the basis of Ferrari's agreement in 2005. The financial terms had been agreed one week earlier in Jersey by Mackenzie. On a sliding scale, the teams would receive an additional $500 million, doubling their previous income from 23 per cent to 50 per cent of the revenue, which included 60 per cent of the prize fund compared to 30 per cent previously, a sharp retreat from their original demand of 75 per cent. The winning team would receive nearly $58 million and Ferrari was guaranteed to get $88 million out of the $750 million generated during 2006 from the circuits and television. In Dennis's opinion the agreement was the beginning of the breakthrough in undercutting Ecclestone. Others did not share his self-congratulatory interpretation. On

Ecclestone's insistence, those who delayed the longest would suffer, so Dennis lost about $50 million as 'punishment' for refusing to sign earlier while Ferrari, at CVC's expense, was rewarded by an extra 5 per cent of the prize fund. The signatures heralded a truce. There was a sense of relief and jubilation which even an outsider would have recognised when Ecclestone boarded Briatore's yacht in Monaco two weeks later to celebrate Slavica's birthday and Renault's triumphs.

'Wall-to-wall billionaires,' Mosley acknowledged. As usual Briatore had gathered a clutch of celebrities including Bono, the Crown Prince of Bahrain and the Duchess of York. Mohamed Al Fayed was sitting with Lakshmi Mittal and Mosley. Suddenly the three men heard Slavica roaring with laughter. 'She's laughing about your haircut,' Fayed told Mittal. 'I'm not surprised,' admitted Mittal, 'I had it done at Harrods.' Briatore had good reason to celebrate. The following day Alonso, in a Renault, won the Grand Prix and was heading towards winning his second world championship. Briatore was riding high.

Two weeks later Niki Lauda saw Ecclestone walking miserably through the Paddock in Silverstone. 'Bernie, what's wrong? Is she breaking your balls? Bernie, you've fixed so many things, so you're going to have to fix this too.' Ecclestone was silent. At the outset he had believed that his young wife could be educated but the drama queen was clearly frustrated. Her English remained poor and her education limited. 'She's out of her depth and does not understand the British way of life,' said Ron Shaw, an old friend. Walking alongside her husband in Brazil, Italy or Japan as her 'hero' was mobbed, said Shaw, she found herself virtually ignored. Travelling to successive Grands Prix had become a chore. Married to a billionaire should have meant a glamorous lifestyle in couture clothes and endless socialising with celebrities. Instead her husband really did enjoy shopping at Waitrose and eating in pubs or at home. 'He was proud that she ironed his shirts and cooked their meals but that was not her choice any more,' observed Shaw. 'For years Bernie believed that is what she also wanted but he was mistaken. She had changed. She hoped he would feel guilty.' At a dinner in the Monaco Automobile club, Slavica loudly asked her neighbour, Ron Dennis, 'Do have sex with your wife?' 'Yes,' he replied, puzzled. Going around the table, she asked each man the same question until she reached her husband. 'I get no sex,' she shouted. Even Ecclestone noticeably cringed. Earlier that day, the two of them had met Prince Albert with a woman. 'Are you having sex?' Slavica had asked the woman. Agitated by his non-stop work and unimpressed that he was managing one of the world's biggest sports, Slavica concluded to her audience, 'All he wants is money.'

Donald Mackenzie thought he had inadvertently witnessed that passion which Slavica disliked. Some weeks earlier, he had flown with Ecclestone to Geneva. 'Would you like to buy into Prada?' Ecclestone had asked. 'I could introduce you to them.' Together they had met Prada's chairman. After a few minutes Ecclestone announced, 'Right, I'm off. I've got some things to do.' Mackenzie's discussion continued until, glancing down, he noticed the large plastic bag Ecclestone had been carrying. 'Bernie's forgotten it,' he realised. Opening the bag in his chauffeured car, he saw bundles of £50 banknotes. There was, he calculated, at least £100,000. 'Thanks for the early Christmas present, Bernie,' he said on his mobile telephone. 'What are you talking about?' asked Ecclestone. 'The cash you left behind.' 'I don't know what you're talking about,' said Ecclestone. His deadpan refusal to acknowledge secrets or sentiments reinforced the enigma. Just who, Mackenzie wondered, is the real Bernie Ecclestone?

Formula One had hit a new peak. In the first months of the 2006 season, despite the teams' individual problems, the sport was producing record revenue, partly because of Ecclestone's improvement of the television coverage. Until that year the quality of the images varied and wherever the local television stations provided the pictures, as in Brazil, the bias in favour of the home team devalued the global coverage. Using the pay-television equipment, the new contracts in 2006 imposed Ecclestone's control over every Grand Prix. Before every race 120 tons of new light-weight equipment was loaded on to one Boeing 747. At the circuit 150 technicians and riggers set up twenty-four cameras around the track, two cameras on every car and an overhead camera fixed to a helicopter. All were linked by over fifty kilometres of cable to an air-conditioned temporary hangar powered by its own generators. Under Ecclestone's supervision, John Morrison, the controller, had perfected the production of high-definition pictures, maps, graphics, surround audio and the facility to replay highlights, all of which outclassed anything ever transmitted by the BBC or any other established broadcaster. The improved show attracted 154 million viewers for the final race in Brazil. Ferrari had produced an improved car and the competition between Schumacher and Alonso had intensified after the German driver announced his retirement at the end of the season. In the last laps Schumacher just failed to clinch the title from Briatore's Renault. Briatore's income soared but he knew the cycle was turning. There was a lesson to be learnt. Schumacher had earned well over $300 million from his career while Willi Weber, his manager, had pleaded guilty to bribing a witness to give false testimony and paid a €50,000 fine.

In the preparation for the 2007 season, McLaren rather than Renault would be Ferrari's challenger. Over a thousand engineers had perfected the new Ferrari but Dennis was hungry for victory and had lured Alonso, the world champion, to switch from Renault, a team now in trouble. In anticipation of success McLaren had also beaten Ferrari to win Vodafone's sponsorship and Montezemolo, having finally lost Marlboro's sponsorship, had failed to attract one of the many banks eager to replace tobacco sponsorship. Montezemolo had even asked Ecclestone for help by a special payment. Everything seemed set for McLaren's challenge after too many years in the doldrums. 'Hell is the feeling of not winning a Grand Prix,' admitted Ron Dennis. 'I have a belief that everything is important in life . . . I believe that at all times you should have the best, or at least try to have the best. This is not simply about money. It is mainly about commitment.'

Montezemolo ostensibly maintained his confidence in Ferrari's chances. The only niggle was the discovery in March 2007 of detergent near a refuelling machine in the Maranello workshop. Fearing a saboteur, technicians called the police but there were no clues or explanations. By June, after five races, Ferrari and McLaren were battling for an advantage with the balance in Ferrari's favour. In the middle of that month, Jean Todt heard that Gary Monteith, the manager of a specialist copy shop in England and a Formula One fan, had called Ferrari to report a startling event. The wife of Mike Coughlan, a senior McLaren technical expert, said Monteith, had brought Ferrari's 780-page manual for 2007 – its latest bible of technical, financial and personnel details – into his shop to be copied on to a computer disk. Monteith's confidential revelation had sparked an investigation providing the company with the evidence to obtain secretly a High Court order to raid Coughlan's home on 3 July. After recovering the disk, the investigators discovered that Coughlan's source was Nigel Stepney, Ferrari's race and test technical manager. Since March 2007 Stepney had been passing Ferrari's new designs, including those for a rear-wing flap-separator and braking components, to Coughlan by email and personal delivery. On the eve of Silverstone, Todt telephoned Mosley in Sicily with the news. 'Oh fuck, that's ruined the summer,' thought Mosley. Kimi Räikkönen in a Ferrari won the British race. Three days later, on 11 July, Coughlan admitted at the High Court in London receiving the secret material from Stepney, an accusation which Stepney denied.

Ron Dennis immediately understood the potential catastrophe. Mike Coughlan had previously complained of being 'unloved' by McLaren and, to ingratiate himself, had at the season's opening race in Melbourne offered information about Ferrari's refuelling strategy. Dennis accepted the information as normal pit gossip. He had, he would later say, even spoken to Todt about the danger of leaks. Now he realised Coughlan's activities would be viewed on an entirely different level as sinister. He immediately telephoned Todt and Mosley and insisted that none of his employees had seen any of Ferrari's documents. Todt was scathing. He was convinced that Coughlan's testimony about the manual being burnt in his garden after being copied on to the disk was untrue. The stolen manual, he was sure, had been taken to McLaren's headquarters. Ron Dennis's vehement denials merely inflamed the Ferrari team. Mosley did not need to be prompted by Todt to charge McLaren on 12 July with breach of the FIA's Code. The only person not noticeably excited by the allegations was Ecclestone. 'Nothing new,' he said. 'It's all been going on for years.' Cheating, Ecclestone knew, was common in Formula One. Key technical staff were constantly poached by teams from their rivals to obtain information. Reluctantly he agreed with Mosley that, with the police and courts involved, the accusations 'could not be brushed under the carpet' and FIA would hold a trial in Paris on 26 July.

Ferrari's grievance, Ecclestone knew, was greater than just another cheating episode. The personal relationships between all Formula One's leaders had been disrupted by the recent financial disputes, not least between Ferrari and McLaren. Todt's personal accusations nevertheless embittered Dennis who arrived in Paris to portray McLaren as the victim of a disgruntled employee's dishonesty. Dennis's defence was straightforward: there had been no 'spying' and there was no proof that McLaren had used Ferrari's expertise. Mosley was given a report by a senior lawyer commissioned by McLaren who had after a twenty-four-hour investigation exonerated Dennis of any knowledge about the rogue employee's misconduct. Coughlan's motives were explained by Nick Fry, the chief executive of Honda. Coughlan and Stepney, Fry explained, were applying for jobs and had presented Ferrari's secrets to prove their value to Honda. Finalising their contracts, said Fry, had only been delayed by the scale of their pay demands. Fry would not be officially criticised for failing to reveal their conduct. Retiring to consider the evidence, Mosley and the twenty-six members of the World Council, including Ecclestone, were unimpressed by the defence. 'Does anyone believe Dennis?' Ecclestone asked over lunch. Not a single voice supported McLaren. 'But we haven't got conclusive evidence,' said Mosley. Regardless of their suspicions, he explained, there was no proof that McLaren's technicians had seen or used Ferrari's documents to their advantage. 'We'll have to acquit.' Returning to his permanent suite at the Hôtel de Crillon, Mosley turned on the television to watch the news of the world's stock markets crashing. His telephone rang. Sergio Marchione, the chairman of Fiat, blasted Mosley for thirty minutes about the injustice. At least four McLaren executives, said Marchione, had seen the manual. 'Belief is not proof,' said Mosley who did not deny his own anger that Dennis, he suspected – though without evidence – had in 1998 given embarrassing documents about Formula One's finances to the BBC's *Panorama* television programme. His intention to sue the BBC for defamation had been restrained by Ecclestone. But he, like Marchione, harboured some unfinished business.

Jean Todt could not contain his anger and appealed citing circumstantial evidence. Before the Australian Grand Prix, Todt said, McLaren had asked Charlie Whiting to consider whether FIA would allow cars to be equipped with a moving-floor device to increase the down-force. Whiting ruled the device illegal without realising that Ferrari and not McLaren intended to use that concealed advantage. Only someone with access to Ferrari's 2007 manual, Todt argued, could have been aware of that secret mechanism. It was after Whiting's ruling was publicised that Ferrari became suspicious of Stepney. Investigations showed that the engineer had met Coughlan in Spain to discuss Ferrari's plans. 'Why Spain?' asked Mosley. 'The banks are more amenable there,' replied Todt mysteriously. At that point, the saga would have exhausted itself except that, unknown to Todt, raw passion had reignited Mosley's interest.

In mid-July at Silverstone Fernando Alonso had fought hard to come second, just ahead of Lewis Hamilton, his McLaren team mate. Lewis, nurtured by his father's support and money, was well known to be Ron Dennis's protégé as he won successive intermediate championships to reach Formula One. The special relationship fuelled unusual rivalry between the team mates. Alonso believed that his challenge to Kimi Räikkönen's Ferrari was being contaminated by Hamilton, despite the driver's occasionally fractious relationship with Dennis. As a result Alonso wanted to leave McLaren on financially advantageous terms. He called Flavio Briatore, his previous employer, to reveal that there were email exchanges between himself and a McLaren engineer on his computer suggesting that McLaren possessed Ferrari's manual. Briatore, not sad to see his former driver cause problems for Dennis, told Ecclestone, and Ecclestone repeated the story to Mosley. All three decided to do nothing. There was no point reopening the case and disturbing the sport. Shortly after that Alonso won the race at Nürburgring and was leading the championship.

Two weeks later in Hungary Alonso's hopes were dashed by Lewis Hamilton scoring advantages in the qualifying sessions. The aggrieved world champion approached Dennis on the morning of the race and urged his employer, 'I want you to run Hamilton out of fuel.' In Dennis's version Alonso then said, 'If you don't, I have information on my computer which shows that McLaren did know about Ferrari's manual.' Dennis was stunned by what he, amid considerable emotion, exaggeratedly called 'blackmail' and summoned Martin Whitmarsh, his chief executive. 'Tell Martin what you've just told me,' said Dennis. After Alonso had repeated his threat and departed, Dennis called Mosley on holiday in France. 'I've been blackmailed,' he said, describing Alonso's suggestions. 'What are you going to do?' asked Mosley. 'Fire him.' 'Calm down,' advised Mosley, doubtful about the 'blackmail' allegation. 'Let Alonso race and let him do what he likes.' 'OK,' Dennis agreed without realising that Mosley already knew about Alonso's emails. By the end of the month, Mosley had obtained copies of the emails and summoned the World Council to reconvene in September. At that stage, the saga took a savage twist which launched Formula One into a succession of unprecedented calamities lasting until 2010.

Four weeks later Alonso won the Italian Grand Prix and came to apologise to Dennis for his ultimatum, which Dennis accepted at face value. Dennis was unaware that his driver had already handed over the emails to Mosley, who in turn had just sent a letter to every driver offering an amnesty if they possessed any incriminating information about what had become dubbed 'Spygate'. In reply to his offer Mosley received from Alonso his personal computer containing an email exchange in Spanish about Ferrari's new braking system and the gas used to inflate tyres. Mosley could have ignored the evidence and the failure to find any substantive proof about Dennis's personal knowledge as sufficient to terminate the inquiry. But instead, after hearing from Ecclestone that Italian police had produced records of 323 SMS text messages over three months between Coughlan and Stepney, Mosley concluded that Dennis had not been totally candid. 'You don't get over 300 messages arranging a visit to Honda,' said Mosley to a journalist. After a protest from Dennis, Mosley 'agreed to fudge' his allegations about Dennis's honesty and proposed to pose for a 'reconciliation' photo with Dennis after the teams arrived in September for the season's fourteenth race at Spa in Belgium. The event, Dennis protested afterwards, was provocative. While he stood wearing a casual body-warmer in front of a crowd of photographers on the outside steps of the McLaren motorhome, Mosley, dressed in a suit, stood one step above smiling masterfully. In any event, no one was convinced by the show since even Dennis admitted that he was fighting for 'my integrity and the integrity of my company'. Dennis was outraged that he was disbelieved.

The atmosphere in Spa, Ecclestone noticed, was 'bad but no one expected the thing to blow up. The only people who really cared were the teams involved and the other teams were delighted that those two teams were out of the way.' Since Silverstone the competition between McLaren and Ferrari had stiffened. The championship would be decided in the last four races. On the eve of the Belgian race Alonso arrived in Mosley's office. 'He wants your assurance', Ecclestone had told Mosley, 'that he won't get into any personal trouble.' Of all the drivers Alonso ranked as one of the best but also as one of the most disliked. Some critical Spaniards blamed his father, an unpopular blast engineer at the village quarry, for influencing his son's mean spirit, the essence of his ambition. Mosley was uninterested in the driver's character. He simply gave his visitor the personal assurance he required. 'Max doesn't like Ron taking the piss,' Ecclestone told friends. 'Ron's a hands-on manager so he must have known something.' Mosley's briefing to journalists at Spa exceeded Dennis's fears. 'Until now,' Mosley said, 'I believed everything Ron told me. After all, I've known him for forty years. But now I don't believe that Ron has been completely truthful.'

In Mosley's opinion, Dennis had comprehensively lied to protect the cover-up. The antagonism between the two men had become part of the Paddock's legend but even Dennis was shocked when, moments later, journalists reported Mosley's accusation. 'Under Mosley, the teams always walk on tiptoe in case you're not the chosen one,' said Dennis. From personal experience, he feared becoming the next victim of 'Mosley's rapier tongue to humiliate people'. In motor sport's *Alice in Wonderland* judicial system, he feared conviction would come first, followed by the trial. Mosley, he alleged, was 'colouring the evidence because the more he went into it, the less he had'. Mosley's motive, Dennis speculated, was envy. 'Max has always been jealous', he told his advisers, 'that Frank, Ken and me were so successful and his own cars failed. He used to be one of the boys but after he became president, he attacked anyone he could. Power went to his head.' Hearing those accusations, Mosley demanded an independent investigation of McLaren's computer system. Over thirty experts, hired by Sidley Austin, an American law firm, minutely examined all the traffic and a barrister interrogated McLaren's engineers. Before they could report, Mosley and twenty-six members of FIA's World Council reconvened in Paris to hear Dennis's defence against the new evidence.

Before the hearing Ecclestone and Dennis spoke frequently on the telephone. 'Come to the hearing alone in a clean shirt,' Ecclestone advised, 'and confess.' 'But I'm innocent,' Dennis insisted, rejecting the advice of a man he regarded as 'heartless'.

'But Bernie,' said Dennis, 'Coughlan's one man. He couldn't influence 136 McLaren designers. It's not possible and all the evidence shows it didn't happen, I'm not going to roll over.' Playing the game was not Dennis's strength. He needed Ecclestone to broker a deal, just as Briatore had in Paris in 1994. But his relationship with Ecclestone and Mosley excluded the same 'chumminess'. 'Max is enjoying my trauma,' Dennis fumed. 'He regards honour as weakness.' Though he had considered pleas before the hearing in previous trials, Mosley refused to do so for Dennis. There seemed nothing to discuss. For his part, clutching at straws, in early September Dennis commissioned a psychological profile of Mosley from David McErlain. The report, describing Mosley in unflattering terms, defined his critic as possessing 'an abundance of charm but with flaws, who does not see people as friends but victims'. Dennis's own opinions were confirmed but it was worthless for the trial. Dennis also commissioned an investigation of Mosley's private finances. The agents produced only unsubstantiated rumours. 'It's so unjust,' complained Dennis. According to his friends, 'Ron's a bit too old, too rich and too straight to fight the battle.' In Ecclestone's opinion, Dennis refused to listen. 'He turned up with hundreds of people. Lawyers who wanted to fight. He could have got away with less if he had handled it better.' 'Dennis has lost all credibility,' Todt told Ecclestone. McLaren had exploited a crime. Mosley agreed.

During the three-hour trial in Paris, Dennis pleaded that McLaren's top managers were unaware of what Coughlan and others had done. There was, he insisted, no evidence of a conspiracy, except by Ferrari who planned something illegal. Accusing Ferrari from the dock boomeranged. Next Dennis was humiliated by the cross-examination. There was evidence, said Mosley, that McLaren had copied Ferrari's plans to change its braking system. 'We copied Ferrari from what we saw on TV,' answered Dennis. 'Ron thinks it's class war,' Mosley observed after Dennis left the room and waited for the verdict. No one, Mosley concluded, believed Ron Dennis. There was unanimity about McLaren's guilt. Mosley, as president of FIA, pronounced the sentence: 'McLaren is suspended for two years from Formula One.'

'Bit heavy,' said Ecclestone, speaking first. Alarmed by the prospect of Mosley's justice destroying Ferrari's only rival and ruining the championship, Ecclestone described two years' suspension as the equivalent of a death sentence. 'You've got to have a menu for punishments to fit the crime,' continued Ecclestone, 'not your personal prejudice based on how you feel when you get up in the morning.' In Ecclestone's opinion Formula One was about personalities rather than substance. While other managers tried to find solutions, Dennis always argued and then waited for either himself or Mosley to make a mistake. Now Mosley was veering towards that error. Ecclestone suggested a $100 million fine, by far FIA's heaviest punishment. After a discussion Mosley agreed to compromise. '$5 million for the offence,' he joked, 'and $95 million for Ron being a twat.' Summoned back into the room, Dennis was shattered by the indignity. The repercussions were to be awful, not least the reaction from Mercedes who owned 40 per cent of the team. The company disliked the relentless criticism in the media that they were 'linked to a bunch of cheats'. Knowing that Ecclestone and Mosley were discussing his fate with Mercedes, Dennis was outraged by the injustice. 'Just look what corporations get fined for manslaughter,' he said. 'One or two million pounds and you're fining McLaren fifty times that. It's mad.'

Ron Dennis felt victimised. Past cheating by other teams had been ignored. Renault had just pleaded guilty after stolen McLaren designs were discovered on Renault's computer system. On Ecclestone's suggestion Briatore fulsomely apologised and received no punishment from Mosley; Toyota had used technical material illegally supplied by an ex-Ferrari aerodynamicist to build their 2003 models and Mosley had done nothing; Honda was found to have built a car with a secret fuel tank – 'a diabolical cheat', in Ecclestone's opinion – which had been discovered by Renault after hiring a Honda employee. But the punishment was just exclusion from one race. Ross Brawn had moved from Benetton to Ferrari with all his designs. And Ferrari had just won the world championship with an illegal part – the floor device – that was ignored. 'It's daylight robbery by dying men,' cried a McLaren sympathiser. 'They'll have to be dead and buried before we can get change.' Dennis was defiant: 'No matter how beaten up I am, no matter how kicked around I am, the fact is I love Formula One.' Although his anger was directed at Mosley, he blamed Ecclestone for refusing to protect an honest critic: 'Bernie doesn't use a sledgehammer to crack a nut. He chooses the precise size to smash opposition – he never uses more force than necessary.'

Mosley's sentence was widely condemned, not least by Jackie Stewart, as 'unfair and unjustifiable'. Mosley hated 'thoroughly irresponsible' criticism from those who ignored the huge problems of maintaining Formula One's balance. 'Stewart never stops talking,' he said, 'he never has a chance to listen – so he doesn't know what's going on. He's a figure of fun among drivers, going around dressed up as a 1930s music-hall man. He's a certified half-wit.' Stewart was unaware that shortly after the trial Sidley Austin submitted their report to

Mosley. The lawyers had scrutinised 1.3 terabits of information in McLaren's computers, the equivalent of 80 million pages, and found one exchange between McLaren's chief engineers referring to McLaren's 'mole in Ferrari'. To reopen the case for a second time, Mosley and Ecclestone agreed, would have destroyed McLaren and Formula One. Instead, both called Mercedes and suggested that Dennis be removed. 'They'd gone looking for trouble,' explained Ecclestone unconcerned, 'and there was no need. I don't care what happens to Ron.'

11

Scandal

The disgrace heaped upon Ron Dennis left Mosley with a bittersweet after-taste. Saving Formula One from its leaders' vices was a thankless task, but asserting himself was important in order to complete the supreme challenge. Besides safety, Mosley believed, nothing was more important than cutting the teams' costs. If he did not achieve this, he believed, Formula One could not survive. Ecclestone disagreed. Trying to control teams' spending was pointless, he believed, because the manufacturers could effortlessly conceal what they spent. Darwinism was best: let the fittest survive. 'You can't stop people spending money,' Ecclestone told Mosley, knowing that it was pointless arguing with a man convinced he was clever and right. Mosley's passion and his refusal to wrap his proposals in tissue, Ecclestone suspected, would soon erupt into another dispute.

Mosley was nostalgic for the 1970s when his March team, run by fourteen people, supported Niki Lauda. Just four mechanics had pioneered revolutionary designs for the whole of Formula One. Now Ferrari, Toyota and McLaren each employed nearly a thousand experts. McLaren employed 120 engineers with doctorates solely to scrutinise volumes of FIA's rules, mastering the technical vocabulary to discover semantic loopholes to modify legitimately a car's aerodynamics. In that cat-and-mouse game, Mosley's staff were at a disadvantage against elite designers reputedly earning up to $10 million a year to increase a car's speed by one tenth of a second. Mosley wanted to restore some sanity to Formula One's costly muddle. 'Budgets are heading towards $400 million,' he explained, 'and a wind tunnel costs $40 million. It's got to end.' He wanted a cap of $64 million.

To enforce his cost cuts Mosley called a summit meeting of team principals in Paris on 11 January 2008. The FIA's inspectors, he suggested, should be given the power to scrutinise every team's accounts. Mosley ended the meeting convinced that, with the exception of Ferrari, every team was committed to his plan. Ecclestone, however, was non-committal. 'You should support this,' Mosley said. 'The less the teams spend, the less money they'll want from you.' Ecclestone said little. Beyond Mosley's hearing, some team managers were expressing their outrage about his proposed intrusion into their financial secrets. The prospect of another disagreement suited Ecclestone and Mackenzie of CVC although neither foresaw its influence on Formula One. The prospect of a new argument coincided with Ecclestone hearing that one of Mosley's enemies in Paris had paid 'a large sum' to investigators to find 'dirt' among his finances. 'Good luck,' Ecclestone told his informant, 'because they won't find anything.'

The dislike of Mosley's authoritarianism reignited interest in the GPMA breakaway. Even Montezemolo was drawn back to the idea of establishing an alternative to Formula One and spoke about winning support from major sponsors. Ecclestone was unconcerned. The 2008 season promised to be better than ever. There would be a new night-time race through Singapore's streets and Valencia's new Grand Prix track would also pass across the city, a spectacular event attracting more high spenders and visitors than the remote tracks. Despite the recession Formula One was rolling in cash, not least from television. In a quickly negotiated move with Michael Grade, Ecclestone had switched ITV's broadcasting rights back to the BBC – naturally at a profit for himself. Grade wanted to use the Formula One money to finance a bid for the European football rights. 'I'll take them back,' Ecclestone had told Grade, 'if you sign the contract by the end of today and pay a fee.' In the late afternoon, the receptionist at ITV's headquarters told Grade, 'Mr Ecclestone's assistant is here with the contract and is waiting for your cheque.' 'You could have sent an invoice, Bernie,' Grade roared down the telephone, laughing at how Ecclestone expected to pocket his profit instantly. Viewers were promised a fiercely competitive season after the opening races in Melbourne and Kuala Lumpur had been won by McLaren and then Ferrari. Poignantly, Jean-Marie Balestre had just died aged eighty-six, thirty-six years after his defeat had laid the foundation of Ecclestone's fortune. Managing the prospects and conflicts appeared to be similar to all those previous years until Ecclestone's stability was rocked on Sunday 30 March 2008.

An early-morning call to Ecclestone from Ed Gorman, motor racing correspondent of *The Times*, revealed that the *News of the World* was reporting over seven pages that Max Mosley had been filmed with five prostitutes in a London basement flat during a long sado-masochistic session. The justification for the invasion of Mosley's privacy was that the women were dressed in Nazi uniforms and were mocking the victims of the Holocaust, a particularly serious allegation considering the war-time sympathies of his father, Oswald Mosley. 'Fuck, fuck, fuck,' said Ecclestone, 'if anyone else did that he would be taken out and shot.' Gorman assumed Ecclestone meant that Mosley would be shot by Ecclestone. In reality Ecclestone was amazed to hear about Mosley's sexual preferences. 'Not my sort of thing,' he said. He immediately called his friend. Mosley had first heard about the exposé during the night. The newspaper had telephoned him for a comment, carefully timing the revelation until after the publication of its first edition to prevent Mosley appealing to a judge for an injunction. Early that morning he had bought the newspaper and decided to show a copy to Jean, his wife. 'Is that a joke specially printed for the children?' she asked. In Mosley's opinion, after a fifty-year relationship, they could survive 'a joint disaster'.

'Someone has set me up,' Mosley told Ecclestone, incensed that his private life had been invaded. 'I'll get even with him.' Ecclestone shared Mosley's suspicions. The rumour that people were digging up dirt about Mosley in Paris a month earlier, he thought, now made sense. 'It's Wapping Filth,' Ecclestone replied, 'and you should ignore it. So what?' James Hunt's wild sex life had been applauded by the same newspaper that was now castigating Mosley's. During the day Ecclestone consistently supported Mosley. 'If only he had been photographed in bed with two hookers,' he joked to the dozens of callers, 'he would have escaped.' While he was defending Mosley, he listened to his friend's speculation about the traitor's identity. 'Max is lashing out at everyone,' Ecclestone realised. To mitigate his plight, Mosley immediately wrote to all FIA's members denying any Nazi connection to the dominatrix sessions.

By the following day Ecclestone was neither joking nor discounting the international sensation. The teams were about to fly to Bahrain for the following Sunday's race. The theme from *The Good, the Bad and the Ugly* was ceaselessly ringing on his mobile. Every caller described Mosley's position as untenable. 'I don't see what this has got to do with FIA,' Ecclestone replied. The chief executives of the teams linked with manufacturers disagreed. 'He should resign anyway,' said the chief executive of Mercedes. The news from Bahrain was especially grim. The ruler's representative had already called Jackie Stewart. 'What's going on?' Stewart asked Ecclestone. 'Are you out of your mind?' The Muslim Crown Prince, Ecclestone was told, would ban Mosley from the Grand Prix. Not because of the alleged Nazi theme 'but because of the hookers'. The hypocrisy was breathtaking. Then came calls from a Toyota executive anticipating that Mosley would commit hara-kiri. Next was Fred Goodwin, the chief executive of RBS bank and a major sponsor. He expected Mosley's resignation, while the king of Spain urged, 'Max must go.' The king's message was particularly poignant. 'I won't stand on the podium with Max or shake his hand if he comes to Spain,' he warned, referring to the Barcelona race to be held after Bahrain. The following morning Ed Gorman called Ecclestone again for a comment. He tape-recorded Ecclestone's reply: 'Yeh, he's a great friend of mine but he can't continue.' An hour later Ecclestone called Gorman. 'What are you writing?' he asked. 'That Ecclestone says "Mosley must go",' replied Gorman. 'But I didn't say that,' said Ecclestone. 'But Bernie, I've got your quote on tape.' 'I didn't say that,' insisted Ecclestone. 'It's not on the tape.'

The conflict of interests and loyalties was tormenting Ecclestone. He owed Mosley, his best ally for forty years, an incalculable debt. For a dealer whose handshake was a pledge of trustworthiness, the thought of deserting his partner seemed unconscionable. That was especially true after Mosley began speculating that his privacy had been invaded by an agent employed by a Formula One enemy. 'I'm going to sue the bastards,' said Mosley. Ecclestone agreed to stay loyal but urged Mosley to stay away from the races.

By coincidence, Mosley had previously consulted John Stevens, the former commissioner of Scotland Yard who had been recently appointed the head of Quest, a firm of private investigators. During the course of their lunch in February about Formula One's security, Stevens had mentioned that a rival agency was checking whether Mosley had received bribes from Ecclestone. Without any evidence, Mosley guessed that the investigation was connected to an enemy in Switzerland who was seeking revenge. But mindful of his own secret sexual life, he also paid Quest to provide lessons in counter-surveillance. After the *News of the World* exposure he believed that his enemy had hired one of the prostitutes. The threat had been from within rather than from outside.

Forty-eight hours after the exposure, Quest was questioning 'Woman A' who organised Mosley's regular sessions after 2006. She revealed that the *News of the World* had already threatened her with exposure and a full-frontal photograph in the following

Sunday's issue unless she gave an interview. Outraged, she pledged to help Mosley. By then Mosley had deduced from the newspaper's own photographs that 'Michelle', known as 'Woman E', was their source. The tiny camera used to record the sex session had been supplied by the *News of the World*. Quest's investigators had also discovered that 'Michelle' was married to an MI5 surveillance expert. 'Woman A' and 'Woman E' were well known in a Milton Keynes pub and the MI5 officer, according to 'Woman A', knew about his wife's sessions with Mosley. Remarkably, 'Jason's' superior officers at MI5 were also aware of his wife's sexual activities. Mosley speculated that he had possibly become a British government target, as well as a target of a Swiss national. His outrage about the invasion of his privacy and the blatant distortion by the *News of the World* was shared by Ecclestone and, to his consolation, by the majority of FIA clubs.

By mid-May Mosley had stayed away from three races but the approaching Monaco Grand Prix was different. Not only did he live in the principality, but the race was the jewel in Formula One's social calendar. Mosley was stubborn. He had decided to enter the lions' den and accelerate a writ in the High Court against News International, the owners of the *News of the World*, for the invasion of his privacy. Considering the circumstances, his strategy risked expensive self-destruction but a trial, he believed, was his only chance to mitigate what he perceived as an injustice.

Ecclestone arrived in Monaco on Wednesday, 21 May, four days before the race. One highlight would be the usual celebration of Slavica's birthday on Flavio Briatore's yacht on the Saturday night, a special anniversary because Slavica would be fifty. Newspapers already reported that her daughter Petra had bought her mother a Pucci dress and Terry de Havilland shoes with her date of birth written in crystal on the soles.

The party had been planned for weeks. Among the invited guests was Mosley. Before that party, Mosley's professional fate would be discussed by all FIA's clubs at the automobile club in the principality. Mosley knew that representatives of 85 per cent of the clubs had written demanding his resignation but since they represented only 25 per cent of the vote he was certain of getting the majority's support. Less easy to ignore were Donald Mackenzie and Martin Sorrell, the CVC directors. Both had been urging Ecclestone to demand Mosley's resignation. Sorrell, a Jew, was particularly concerned by the alleged Nazi context. The two cornered Ecclestone in his motorhome. Claiming to have the support of Montezemolo, Briatore, Ron Dennis and John Howett, they badgered Ecclestone for Mosley's resignation.

Two weeks earlier, at a team principals' meeting in Barcelona, Ecclestone had supported Briatore's suggestion of a letter signed by everyone urging Mosley to resign. There had been unity until Adam Parr, representing Williams, objected. 'Why don't you circulate a draft and then when it gets to me I'll see what I'll do.' Briatore exploded, followed by Ecclestone. 'You fucking amateur,' shouted Ecclestone, 'you're trying to do what I used to do when I was sixteen.' The letter was never circulated, Parr suspected, because Ecclestone felt 'conflicted'.

Two weeks later, Ecclestone was resenting Sorrell's pressure. He had recommended Sorrell's appointment to CVC's board for Formula One because the owner of the world's biggest advertising agency was a Formula One fan, proud to have been Jackie Stewart's bag-carrier. Now, Sorrell was openly accusing him of anti-Semitism. Nevertheless, he succumbed. Together with Mackenzie and Sorrell, he headed down the Paddock to Jean Todt in the Ferrari motorhome. 'We've got to get rid of Max,' said Sorrell. 'No we won't,' replied Todt. Hookers were not strangers in Formula One and nor were Nazis. Todt would not be pushed into moral judgements. Ecclestone shifted and became uncommitted about the issue. 'Max is welcome in the Paddock,' Ecclestone told BBC television soon after and stood by his friend for a brief photo call, allowing Mosley to thank FIA members for their support until his term expired.

As Ecclestone walked back to his motorhome, he bumped

into Briatore. Two weeks earlier, during the Turkish Grand Prix, Ecclestone had not been well and Briatore had called so solicitously that Ecclestone became suspicious. Briatore's antagonism towards Mosley was, Ecclestone knew, not motivated by outraged morality. After all, there were innumerable newspaper revelations of Briatore's un-angelic sexual and commercial life. Briatore's agenda, Ecclestone suspected, was his own personal fate. Renault was performing badly in the 2008 championship, unable to match McLaren's convincing challenge against Ferrari. Briatore's additional problem was financial. The Renault team's debts were spiralling and, although Ecclestone had lent Briatore $30 million against his future income from CVC once the Concorde agreement was signed, Briatore blamed Mosley's expensive 'cost reductions' and rule changes for his embarrassment within Renault. Mosley opposed the new Concorde agreement, Briatore believed, because he and FIA would be stripped of his powers.

Compared to his overt opposition to Mosley, Briatore's attitude towards Ecclestone was friendly. He had reason to be grateful. The combination of owning the Spanish television rights for Formula One since 2002 and Alonso having won the world championships in 2005 and 2006 had added millions of dollars to Briatore's wealth, estimated by some as $100 million. Nevertheless he was dissatisfied. Unlike other team principals, Briatore was not a mechanic but a businessman. His seventy-eight-year-old friend could not last forever and some insiders considered him to be an ideal successor. Ecclestone had not recognised that possibility until he encountered Briatore on his return from Todt's motorhome.

'Max can't come to the party,' said Briatore, referring to Slavica's birthday celebration. 'You must tell him he can't come. If he comes, Carlos Ghosn won't come and Renault will pull out and that's impossible.' Ghosn was the chairman of Renault. Ecclestone stared at Briatore. 'What do you want me to do?' 'You tell him,' said Briatore. 'I don't know about that,' replied

Ecclestone, who did not know which was worse – telling Mosley or telling Slavica.

In Zimmerman's motorhome Niki Lauda watched Ecclestone enter and approach his wife. 'Flavio says I've got to tell Max he can't come,' said Ecclestone and explained the reasons. 'You're mad,' shouted Slavica. 'I won't do that to Max. It's my party. I do the inviting.' As tempers soared, Lauda watched the woman who sincerely thought of herself as stronger than her husband, dismantle the reputation of Briatore, her host. 'Flavio will stab you in the back,' she shouted. She was particularly upset about his recent magazine interview promoting his supreme contribution to Formula One. Her husband, she knew, had also been stung. Briatore had become too involved in Formula One's politics and worse. As she had told Ecclestone, Briatore had once told her that if her husband died, he could be trusted to look after the business. Ecclestone did not appreciate that solicitude and nor did Slavica. 'Don't you see that Flavio will always screw you?' Slavica screamed. 'No, he wouldn't,' replied Ecclestone, 'He's part of Formula One and he's got a business case.' Slavica was unconvinced. 'He says he's your friend,' she said, with what Ecclestone would later acknowledge to be perceptive sarcasm. Ecclestone was unconvinced about treachery. He instinctively compartmentalised his business and personal relations. 'Flavio hasn't got the balls to finish the job,' Ecclestone told his wife reassuringly. 'You should stop all this, give up work, or I'll leave you,' she shouted.

Slavica's anger prompted Ecclestone to make himself more available to the media but first he undertook one unpleasant chore. He telephoned Mosley with the news. To be uninvited from the birthday party – and in your own town – was painful for Mosley but Slavica's subsequent telephone call and apology did alleviate his hurt pride somewhat, though in reality he was not disappointed to miss Slavica dancing on the table, cheered on by Briatore's celebrities and billionaires. Slavica, however, refused to forgive Briatore. Ecclestone was subsequently forbidden to travel to Rome for Briatore's wedding on 14 June to Elisabetta Gregoraci. 'She's in one of her "I don't like Flavio" moods,' Ecclestone told his friend, 'and I'm not going to fight.' Not least because he disliked weddings.

By Sunday night, after Ecclestone had returned to London, the constant calls, messages and faxes demanding Mosley's resignation became irresistible. Mosley, he realised, was dead meat. 'You'll have to go,' Ecclestone told Mosley on the telephone that night. 'No way, I won't,' Mosley replied. To relieve the pressure, Ecclestone agreed to an interview with the *Daily Telegraph*. Mosley, he said, was under pressure from all sides. The Formula One community could not understand why he had not resigned within the first twenty-four hours. 'It is regretful he has not made that decision,' he said, because 'no one wants to deal with him'. In mitigation, Ecclestone added that 'Max is being punished for the wrong reasons'. After the publication on 31 May Ecclestone was hurt that Mosley refused to take his calls. Mosley was unfair, he thought. In the balance of their friendship, Mosley had benefited more from being close to him than the other way around. Helping Ecclestone had suited Mosley, and now he refused to understand the pressures. Mosley naturally held the opposite point of view.

The next race was in Montreal and Ecclestone flew via New York to meet Montezemolo. The world championship was attracting big audiences. Ferrari's dominance was being challenged by Lewis Hamilton in a McLaren. The British driver's victory in Monaco had partially repaired Ron Dennis's reputation. Meeting in the bar of the St Regis Hotel to discuss the fate of Formula One's finances, they also discussed Mosley's fate. 'We must persuade Max to leave,' Ecclestone told Montezemolo. The Ferrari chief was noticeably ambivalent. 'I've got no vote to kill or save Max,' he replied, 'and I don't want to be a moral judge, so it's his decision.' That was not what Ecclestone wanted to hear. He flew on to Montreal and an argument. Formula

One was Canada's most important sporting fixture, attracting 300,000 spectators and earning over $50 million for the city, but it had failed three times to pay the second instalment of the fees. If they failed to pay their debts of $30 million, Ecclestone warned the organisers, there would be no race in 2009. By then, Ecclestone was known among the Canadians as 'The Kidney', as in 'the painful kidney stone'. The Canadians were given an October deadline. Ecclestone could see that some doubted that he did what he said. The other deadline was delivered to Mosley by telephone. 'Luca says you'll have to resign,' Ecclestone said. Mosley was furious. Frank Williams, he had heard, had told Ecclestone, 'What Max does is nothing to do with us.' Now he telephoned Montezemolo's aide. The Italian denied any agreement with Ecclestone regarding Mosley's departure. Mosley chose to believe Montezemolo. 'You must resign,' Ecclestone told Mosley again. 'I'll leave it to the members of FIA,' replied Mosley. 'You'll lose the vote and be humiliated,' countered Ecclestone. 'No, it's up to them. They'll vote.' The general assembly was due to meet on 3 June in Paris. 'Bernie doesn't believe in absolute loyalty,' Mosley concluded mournfully. That day, Mosley believed, marked the end of their unbreakable partnership. They did not speak to each other for several weeks but Ecclestone could not ignore Mosley's influence. On 3 June he won the vote of FIA's World Council by 103 to 55. Now it was Mosley's turn to prove his power.

Emboldened, Mosley ordered immediate cost reductions and changes to some technical regulations. Montezemolo was the first to declare war. 'This is the breaking point. Max has gone into space. He's mad.' His sentiments were shared by all the teams. Hookers and Nazis had not annoyed most of the fraternity but there was anger that Mosley dared not only to tell rich corporations how to spend their money but to threaten to send forensic accountants into their plants to scrutinise their expenditure. 'You're destroying the Formula One dream. Your cuts are brutal,' Montezemolo told Mosley. Ecclestone was torn.

Until March Montezemolo had never suspected that Ecclestone's and Mosley's relationship could be in any way financially dubious but he had become suspicious about their 'strategic relationship'. Normally Ecclestone's management of Formula One was eased by the teams' squabbles to promote their favourite regulations, but now, Montezemolo believed, Mosley's agenda was actually opposed by Ecclestone as 'unclear and unstable'. Resentful of that criticism, Mosley approved without notice the launch of a Formula Two series supported by the Williams team in competition to a similar GP2 series that Briatore had created with Ecclestone's support and sold to CVC. Formula Two cars are slightly smaller but much cheaper than Formula One models. They are used for practice by Formula One drivers and by those aspiring to reach Grand Prix championships. Under Briatore's scheme, the drivers racing in the GP2 series would be paying about €1.5 million that year, but the Williams cars provided by Adam Parr cost about €300,000. Ecclestone did not hide his anger: 'He did that to damage me and ruin a good business.' Mosley was unrepentant. Interfering with Briatore's profits was not painful.

Ecclestone was struggling to resolve a dilemma. Initially he wanted to placate Mosley. In an unusual step he summoned Ed Gorman to deny the rumours about his involvement in the *News of the World* exposé. 'It's nothing to do with me at all. You must be joking. Secondly, this sort of thing is not my style – not the sort of way I would operate. Thirdly, there is no way in the world that I would want to destroy Max.' But then rumours started to spread about Mosley's further plan to change the distribution of Formula One's money to Ecclestone's detriment. Unable to reach Mosley, who cut off calls whenever he heard Ecclestone's voice, Ecclestone declared, 'The FIA has a clear, clear, clear agreement and signed agreement with the European Commission that they are the regulators of the sport. They are not anything to do with money. If Max comes back and says we should give more money to teams, I will tell him to mind his own bloody business.' But even in his anger, Ecclestone suspected a conspiracy against his old friend. 'The Jewish community controls an awful lot of the finance which comes into Formula 1, directly or indirectly,' he told *The Times*. 'They say FIA shouldn't let somebody like Max represent them.'

The apparent 'divorce' between Ecclestone and Mosley provoked intense gossip. Mosley's many enemies saw an opportunity to damage Ecclestone at the same time. The loudest was John Howett. Toyota's team manager had joined Ron Dennis and the other teams to urge Ecclestone and Mosley to translate the Barcelona Memorandum of Understanding into a new Concorde agreement. Howett disliked Mosley for 'constantly rewriting the technical rules' and disapproved of Ecclestone for fostering confusion. 'Ever since Barcelona,' Howett told Mosley, 'we've only had evasion from Bernie. We're getting tired of this.' He wanted the chaos replaced by structured governance. 'I'm under pressure to get money from Formula One,' he said, 'but whenever I see Bernie nothing happens.' Mosley openly blamed Ecclestone. To stir the pot, Ecclestone blamed Mosley. 'I don't want to have a war with Max,' he told Howett, 'and I hope he does not want one with me, but if war is declared we'll defend ourselves.'

A catch-22 situation had developed. CVC was refusing to pay the money owed to the teams until the Concorde agreements were finalised; and although the teams had signed, Mosley was refusing to sign because it would strip FIA of its control over costs and his power to change the technical regulations arbitrarily. Simultaneously Ecclestone refused to sign because he didn't want an agreement at all, but if there was to be one, he demanded that it last until 2015. The three sides blamed each other for the deadlock. Without a new Concorde agreement, the unreformed FIA remained in charge. Discipline and loyalties were breaking down, especially among the manufacturers.

In Tokyo, Toyota's directors were disappointed that Ecclestone had made little effort to forge a close relationship with their corporation and they completely lacked confidence in Mosley. His dictates over Spygate, the Indy race and other controversies involving Benetton, Ferrari and Renault had undermined their enthusiasm for Formula One. His reaction to the *News of the World* sensation tested their entire commitment. The directors were also dismayed by Ecclestone's ambivalence towards the manufacturers, a sentiment which Ecclestone effortlessly ignored. Toyota, he thought, was spending $350 million that year and yet none of its drivers had ever stood on the podium, let alone won a single race. Honda and BMW were equally failing. None employed managers able to shape a winning team. Consistent failure, he knew, was depriving all three teams of the positive media coverage to increase sales. He was unconcerned. If Honda, as gossip suggested, followed Ford Jaguar and departed, his distaste for the manufacturers' unreliability would be reinforced. However, his sangfroid was for once disturbed by the unusually united antagonism of the remaining teams towards himself and Mosley. He could not defeat that unity without Mosley.

For twenty-seven years Ecclestone had fought countless battles to grab and hold on to Formula One and throughout he had relied on Mosley's support. On reflection, Ecclestone realised that advocating Mosley's resignation had been a mistake. His own career had been built on loyalty and he had betrayed his principles. The cost was a unified revolt by the teams. To reassert himself, he wrote to all FIA club presidents praising Mosley's work and pledging his loyalty to 'my friend for the past forty years'. The public somersault restored relations with Mosley who, in turn, stoked Ecclestone's suspicions. 'All the teams want to destroy FIA,' Mosley told Ecclestone, 'and set up their own championship. There's no point for us in all this. We must protect ourselves.' The personal and commercial stakes, Ecclestone suddenly realised, had rarely been higher. 'There are a lot of balls in the air,' Ecclestone said, 'and two of them are mine. I want to be protected.'

The antagonism towards Ecclestone when the teams arrived at Silverstone on 6 July 2008 had grown. Dietrich Mateschitz, the Austrian owner of Red Bull, had abandoned his previous neutrality about Formula One's politics to side with Howett against the new finances. Since his entry into Formula One in 1994, the sales of his drink had soared, especially as the sport spread into the Middle East and Asia where sales in 2008 had increased by 79 per cent. The price of racing was high. The Red Bull team cost Mateschitz about $400 million a year yet his direct return from CVC was barely 15 per cent of that investment. The gap was bridged by Red Bull's massive media exposure but he was still aggravated by CVC's plan to earn $6 billion profit over ten years. Silently Mateschitz joined those seeking to wrest control from Ecclestone and Mosley and share the ownership with CVC. The most flamboyant protester was Flavio Briatore. Mosley was more than ever disenchanted by the Italian. He had capitalised on Ron Dennis's difficulties by luring Fernando Alonso back to Renault but instead of remedying his car's defects, he had begun to meddle in Formula One's politics. His complaint of being under pressure from his corporate chiefs to get more money from Formula One was, Mosley believed, a fig-leaf for a power-bid. Donald Mackenzie was also alarmed. The CVC partner warned Mosley to retreat and urged Ecclestone to forestall yet another breakaway.

During a heated meeting in his motorhome at Silverstone, Ecclestone suggested that all the teams meet on Tuesday 29 July at Maranello before heading to Budapest. In front of all the managers he called Montezemolo and settled that everyone would gather at Ferrari's headquarters. With Montezemolo's help he hoped to coerce the teams back into line without a Concorde agreement. Before he flew to Italy, he spoke to Jean Todt. 'Make a specific agreement with Luca beforehand,' Todt advised Ecclestone, 'and give him more than the others.' Ecclestone called Montezemolo. 'Don't talk about money,' he suggested, 'because that will just make the teams want more.'

The strained personal relationship between Montezemolo and Ecclestone and Mosley's estrangement from Ferrari over costs thwarted discussions to arrange the final agreement in advance of the meeting. Ecclestone's lack of foresight could be directly attributed to the absence of Mosley's advice. During those days Mosley was in high court fighting his case against the *News of the World* on the grounds of an invasion of his privacy. He was gradually exposing the newspaper's journalists as charlatans. On 24 July Mosley won his case and an award of £60,000 in damages. Mosley felt elated. Ecclestone was pleased. Four days later Ecclestone flew with the team managers to Italy.

During the days before the flight, Ron Dennis had been thinking hard. Since 1966 106 teams had gone out of business. Only two – McLaren and Ferrari – had stayed in the game all that time. 'You fight or you die,' he knew. He desperately wanted victory, not so much against Ecclestone as Mosley. One morning he awoke with a brainwave: 'I must give an olive branch to Ferrari.' He telephoned Montezemolo. 'We need to put the history of enmity between our two teams behind us,' he started. Ferrari, he continued, needed to reconsider its special treatment. 'You have the benefit of hindsight, Luca. Look at the sums. You took $50 million from Bernie but didn't realise how much was at stake. You can get a lot more.' Much could depend, he emphasised, on the summit at Maranello. He spoke about 'my strong feeling that Bernie is going to hostage the meeting' and urged Montezemolo to pre-empt Ecclestone's familiar method of controlling the teams.

Ecclestone had expected to chair the meeting but arrived late to discover Montezemolo in his place. Just hearing Montezemolo's theatrical speech about money reminded Ecclestone of a cartoon character. By lunchtime Ecclestone's obvious disdain prompted Montezemolo's retaliation. During earlier conversations with Briatore, Dennis and Howett, he had pledged to curtail Ecclestone's old trick of divide-and-rule and present a new breakaway group called the Formula One Team Association

(FOTA). He envisaged a triangular agreement between the teams, FIA and CVC with Ecclestone. Little progress had been made before lunch when Dennis approached Montezemolo. 'Spygate' still rankled but Dennis's argument for the teams to speak with a single voice was persuasive. 'When we start again,' Dennis said to Montezemolo, 'you should ask Bernie to leave.' Montezemolo recollected being 'surprised' when Dennis said 'get rid of Bernie'. For his part, Dennis was certain that Briatore had suggested 'Bernie should go out'. In retrospect no one wanted to take responsibility for suggesting Ecclestone's exclusion. 'Bernie is simpatico,' recalled Montezemolo, 'but he's always telling everyone something different. We have left too much room for him. *Basta* [Enough].' Then Dennis delivered his ace. 'Luca, why don't you become FOTA's chairman?' 'The clincher,' he told an aide, pleased by his pandering to the Italian's vanity.

When the meeting resumed, Montezemolo began criticising Ecclestone and ended: 'Bernie, you've been very important and we are grateful for everything you've done, but we now want to meet alone.' Some believe Ecclestone was angry about Montezemolo's rudeness, a suggestion he denied. But as he left the room with Mackenzie he could not ignore the new alliance against him. 'They threw us out,' Ecclestone told Mosley in a telephone call minutes later. Even for a man energised by aggravation, Montezemolo's ambush was a surprise. 'Well,' replied Mosley, 'you know Luca. He attacks you in public and apologises in private.' Inside the room Howett was relieved that Montezemolo had finally abandoned his special deals with Ecclestone. The teams had crystallised their demands for 80 per cent of all the income, crushing CVC's investment. In anticipation of the breakaway, the chores were divided up. Briatore would be responsible for negotiating the crucial commercial contracts for the breakaway group. 'They both speak Italian and Luca's very clever,' said Ecclestone, spotting a conspiracy. 'Luca's political. He gives Flavio things to say which he doesn't want attributed to him.' Briatore's overt ambition amused Ecclestone.

'The breakaway is good for Flavio,' he thought. 'He desperately wants to do it.' He so trusted Briatore that the previous year he had invested about £25 million as a co-owner in Queens Park Rangers, the struggling West London football club. Briatore had promised riches but so far the losses were greater than he had anticipated. While he focused on Briatore's loyalties, Ecclestone strangely did not spot Ron Dennis's influence. 'Luca has made life difficult for Bernie,' Todt observed when told about the showdown, 'but Bernie could have made it easier. Bernie was mean. He should have been more generous earlier. Bernie's looking for a fight when he should be searching for a solution.'

'It's all bluff,' Ecclestone assured Mackenzie, convinced that Montezemolo could not be taken in by flattery to orchestrate the crumbling of his own financial interests. 'They want everything to change,' continued Ecclestone, 'so nothing will change. Luca doesn't think things through.' Nevertheless Mackenzie fretted. Any extra money they finally squeezed out of CVC, Ecclestone consoled the financier, would be 'peanuts'. Watching the scene unfold four days later in Budapest, Niki Lauda mentioned to Ecclestone, 'You look as if you might lose.' FOTA, Lauda continued, posed a strong challenge and Ecclestone's relationship with Mosley appeared to be in tatters. Ecclestone betrayed no anxiety. His 'moles' in the FOTA camp encouraged his conviction that he could outplay any plot. As always, a breakaway would be stymied by his contracts with the television broadcasters and the circuits; and without television there would be no sponsors. Taking on his critics, even on Montezemolo's home stage at the Monza Grand Prix after Montezemolo joined the battle by openly criticising Ecclestone and Mosley, was a pleasure. 'At every Monza', Ecclestone told Montezemolo, 'you stand up and say the teams should get more and I should get less. You shouldn't bother to come here but send a recording.'

The revolution in Formula One was strangely being matched by a change in Slavica's behaviour. 'All of a sudden the wheels changed at fifty,' Ecclestone noted. Her anger multiplied. When having dinner with John Coomb, she suddenly turned on her husband. 'He thinks he's a big man but he's a dwarf,' she screeched. Coomb was shattered. 'Poor little bugger,' he thought. 'He can never make her happy.' Coomb was more surprised by Ecclestone's reciprocation. 'John says you've given him the worst dinner he's ever had.' Ecclestone had come to believe that abusive relationships were normal.

To placate her anger, Ecclestone agreed to spend some days during the summer off the Croatian coast with his wife, daughters and their boyfriends on *Petara*, his 198-foot yacht. He telephoned Niki Lauda: 'Would you like to come for a few days?' The driver was surprised. A few weeks earlier, walking on crutches following a hip operation, he had asked Ecclestone for a second pass for his son to help him in the Paddock. He arrived to discover that Ecclestone had refused to authorise an additional pass. 'Bernie,' said Lauda leaning on his crutches, 'I'm off. I don't need this aggravation.' Ecclestone called Pasquale Lattuneddu. 'Didn't you get my SMS about Niki? Why didn't you give Niki his extra pass?' Lauda smiled. Ecclestone, he knew, had never sent a text message in his life. Tiffs were never a reason to decline Ecclestone's company, so Lauda accepted the invitation and arranged to travel with Karl-Heinz Zimmerman. The two Austrians waited for Ecclestone to collect them by a church in a harbour. After hours of waiting, Ecclestone telephoned. 'Where are you?' he asked. 'I've been looking for you for three hours and I'm seasick.' Soon after, Ecclestone appeared in a rubber dinghy. Another ten minutes later they were by the yacht, just outside the harbour. Lauda could only imagine that his punctilious host had been delayed by a domestic storm. Nevertheless, over the following days, to Lauda's surprise, Ecclestone was in a good mood, and even Slavica was joyously making sure that everyone was happy. 'She's an excellent host,' Ecclestone thought, assuming that normality had resumed.

During a stop at a port Ecclestone was snapped by a local photographer with a beautiful girl. He reported Ecclestone saying, 'I'm looking for a new wife because Slavica doesn't make me happy.' The report and photographs were printed in Croatia and Italy. Slavica fumed to Monty Shadow, 'I've given him my life, I've been so faithful, I've given him incredible children and now this. And he doesn't want to give me any time. That's it.'

'It was just a joke,' Ecclestone later told his wife. 'If it was something serious I wouldn't have said anything.' The domestic turmoil was reflected in the relationships in his office. Ecclestone had tired of Stephen Mullens's presence. 'He's manipulative, a bit slippery and difficult to keep to what he says he'll do,' complained Ecclestone, 'and we need his office.' The solicitor was asked to leave. Ecclestone was unaware of any adverse consequences.

In late September, the teams arrived for the first Grand Prix in Singapore, a triumph of organisation for Ecclestone. The densely populated peninsula had pitched to stage the first night-time race around Marina Bay. In the Paddock Flavio Briatore was fretting. Over the previous fourteen races, the two Renault drivers had consistently failed to reach the podium. Nearby he watched Ron Dennis thrill that Lewis Hamilton was leading the close competition with Ferrari and that Alonso had not won a single race since rejoining Renault, while Nelson Piquet Junior, a novice, was struggling to match his father's legend. After the qualifying sessions in Singapore, both Renault cars were way down in the grid. In Renault's motorhome Briatore was bristling.

On the eve of the race, somewhere in the Renault camp, a plan was hatched to fix the race. Piquet, it was agreed, would crash his car at a precise place on lap fourteen. The crash would automatically force the safety car to emerge and stall the competition. According to the conspirators, just before the crash Alonso would unexpectedly enter the pits to refuel his car and rejoin the race so that, once the debris was cleared and the safety car was withdrawn, he could drive to the finishing line without interruption while all of his rivals would need to refuel. As the race progressed to the fourteenth lap, Alonso, having refuelled, was among the stragglers. At the agreed moment, Piquet pushed hard on his throttle and, sensing the car was beyond his control, pushed down even harder and crashed sideways into a concrete wall, risking a wheel coming off and hitting him on the head. The car bounced off the wall, across the track and into the wall on the other side. Not suspicious of any wrongdoing, television viewers across the globe, including Ecclestone in his office, watched as Piquet miraculously emerged unscathed. Once the race restarted, the line-up quickly changed. Every car stopped for fuel except Alonso's which sped into the lead to win Renault's first victory of the season. Ecclestone congratulated Briatore and flew back to London while the teams packed to fly to Japan. Briatore and Alonso featured in the media as returning heroes. Asked why he had decided to refuel so early in the race, Alonso replied, 'I did what I was told' and no, he did not ask why. According to Piquet, Briatore had executed a potentially lethal conspiracy to achieve success for Alonso.

Back in Europe Ecclestone flew to a meeting of FIA's world congress in Paris where, to Mosley's delight, he openly apologised for his disloyalty to the president. He also began discussing a special deal with Montezemolo to frustrate the breakaway. 'It's no point taking your line, Luca,' he told Montezemolo, 'because in the end you'll be the loser.' To strengthen his case he mentioned that Honda was planning to abandon Formula One. 'You can't rely on the manufacturers,' he added. To demonstrate his potency he scorned a delegation sent by the Quebec government to sanction the following year's Montreal race. Ecclestone wanted a guaranteed $175 million over five years. Without a commercial sponsor, the Quebec government tried to persuade Ecclestone to modify his terms. 'The demands of Formula One exceeded the taxpayers' ability to pay,' Ecclestone was told by the delegation worried by the subsidy. 'I'm owed over $30 million,' Ecclestone replied. 'I want that and a five-year contract. Without that, there'll be no Grand Prix in Montreal next year.' Then he flew to Japan. Helped by collisions and penalty points awarded against his rivals, Alonso also won that race. Ecclestone congratulated Briatore.

In the customary whirlwind, Ecclestone stopped briefly in London before flying on to Brazil. Six months earlier Slavica had bought a new house in Chelsea. 'Why have you done that?' he asked. 'I don't like this house,' she replied, referring to their home in Chelsea Square. 'Too many stairs. Up and down. When you get old, it will be too many.' Ecclestone was bewildered. As he packed to leave, his wife shouted, 'Maybe when you get back, I won't be here.' He had heard the same threat so many times that he ignored it. For the sake of their daughters, he told himself, divorce was unimaginable, but in reality his fate was dictated by Slavica. Her influence over his life was too powerful to exorcise.

The last race of the 2008 season in São Paulo proved to be thrilling. At the final corner Lewis Hamilton overtook a Toyota to win fifth place, securing the world championship by a single point over Felipe Massa, Ferrari's Brazilian driver. Ecclestone congratulated Ron Dennis.

During his stay Ecclestone had met many old friends including Nelson Piquet Senior. Beyond their banter, he was unaware that his former driver had privately pulled aside Charlie Whiting, FIA's race director, with whom he had worked for seven years at Brabham. 'Flavio's a shit,' Piquet said, explaining the intrigue behind his son's crash in Singapore. Whiting, a reserved man, cautioned Piquet: 'If you do something now it will be bad for Nelson Junior. He'll be forced out of Formula One.' Although Whiting had been sworn to secrecy, he repeated Piquet's allegations soon after to Mosley. Mosley gave it some thought but decided to do nothing. Under contract to Briatore, Piquet Junior would not testify and the data from the car was inconclusive. Nothing could be done until there was more evidence.

Unusually, Mosley did not tell Ecclestone. Local newspapers were reporting Ecclestone's surprise about hearing from reporters that Slavica had moved into a flat owned by a boyfriend of Petra and that she was filing for divorce. 'She moved out,' replied Ecclestone searching for an excuse, 'because they are doing building work next door and it is impossible to live in the house. She can't stand the noise. I don't know if she wants a divorce or not.' Over the next hours on the telephone from Brazil, he tried hard to persuade his wife to return to their home. 'I thought we would stay together for the good of the girls,' he told Katja Heim, a friend. 'I would never have left her. I would have died in that position. I've never walked out on anything.' He recalled Slavica's demand in Monaco that he retire. 'She was right,' he said mournfully. His later telephone calls were unanswered. Ecclestone felt humiliated, not least by an agency issuing a statement about Slavica's intentions on her behalf. 'Really?' responded Ecclestone, 'I didn't know she had a PR company.'

Flavio Briatore cared for Ecclestone. He sat and listened to the endless recriminations that are normal in those circumstances. Slavica, recalled the unusually vulnerable seventy-eight-year-old, was a good sportswoman, especially in tennis and skiing. 'I'm not a sportsman and she wants a new life at fifty before it's too late.' Gradually he accepted that she could no longer live with a workaholic. 'She wants to travel and I don't,' he said. She had bought a new Gulfstream for about $70 million and planned to fly with some friends to visit the Dalai Lama in India. The spiritual leader, assuming that Ecclestone himself was among the visitors, would be surprised. In London her husband's pain soon passed. He became reconciled to his new life. Intentionally he had avoided the paralysis of extensive self-analysis. 'If I did,' he admitted, 'I would be upset. I'm so busy I can ignore it.' 'How are you getting on?' he was asked by John Coomb. 'Very well, thanks. Now, when I wake up in the morning and it's raining, I don't get blamed.'

The reason he was no longer blamed was Slavica's refusal to answer his telephone calls. Urged by their daughters to attempt a reconciliation, especially so they could enjoy Christmas together, Ecclestone drove to Battersea Park at the time he knew Slavica would be walking with the dogs. Arriving just as she was leaving, he parked his car to block her exit and force a discussion. Eventually she agreed to celebrate a family Christmas. As they all parted in good spirits on Boxing Day, Ecclestone believed that the marriage could be saved. Instead, a few days later and much to his surprise, he received a lawyer's letter that Slavica was filing for divorce. Naturally the outstanding issue was the fate of about $3 billion in the family trusts. The demands received by Helen Ward, Ecclestone's solicitor, were disconcerting. 'This isn't Slavica's voice,' said Ecclestone, suspecting a partisan lawyer's influence on his estranged wife. Nevertheless, he wanted to avoid arguments. 'Tell her, I'll agree to anything she thinks is fair,' instructed Ecclestone. 'That leaves me with enough at my age,' he said, ruing that the man who was once hailed as Britain's highest earner had probably become the victim of the biggest divorce settlement in British history.

Having failed to save his marriage, he was doubly determined to protect his business. During their time together, Briatore had been frustrated that Ecclestone would not cooperate with FOTA. 'Bernie earns too much money,' he told Mosley, echoing Montezemolo's own recent comment: 'Bernie, you are rich, so we can take care of Formula One now.'

The confirmation that Honda was pulling out of Formula One was offset by Mercedes's declaration about the benefits of Formula One. Ecclestone called Montezemolo. 'The last thing you want, Luca,' Ecclestone told Ferrari's chief, 'is for everyone to go communist. You should look after yourself.' Montezemolo agreed but for a price. During December Montezemolo extracted an additional $80 million a year from Ecclestone to abruptly split from FOTA. Like a film star's billing for a big movie, Ferrari's star status required extra rewards. 'We bought Ferrari,' Ecclestone chortled. 'We bought Ferrari's loyalty. Our deal with Ferrari was that we bought them so they would not go to others.' Briatore and the other team principals were surprised by Montezemolo's self-interest. Having bought the betrayal,

Ecclestone could not resist some revenge for his humiliation at Maranello in July. 'It's a shame,' Ecclestone told *The Times*, 'that he [Montezemolo] is not in touch with the people that seem to run the company, as opposed to what he does: work as a press officer.' Ecclestone believed it was business as usual. Others were unprepared to allow familiar deals to conceal bitter divisions.

Over the previous thirty years Formula One had been plagued by many battles but few were so personalised as the one between Jackie Stewart and Ecclestone. At the end of 2008, reviewing the year's debacles, Stewart boldly accused Ecclestone of 'having such power that he can suffocate almost any performer who would dare to suggest there must be change'; while Mosley's refusal to resign after the sex scandal, Stewart insisted, was 'intolerable'. A line had been crossed, said Stewart, demanding the departure of the authoritarian 'Siamese twins'. Ecclestone ignored Stewart, whom he regarded as a moaner. Mosley also refused to retreat. He marched towards gunfire, enjoying the chance to slay Montezemolo, Briatore and Howett. The chances of reconciliation were diminishing.

The report that the growing banking crisis had allowed CVC to repurchase its debt on the secondary market at 90 per cent of the value, adding to its profits, reignited the argument about the sport's ownership.

Injudiciously, a CVC employee had revealed that they were earning about $500 million net profits every year from their investment and, by astutely registering the company offshore, it was all tax-free. Once again, Ecclestone was facing a coup, but he was handicapped. CVC had not only diluted his own authority but CVC's huge profits was an additional incitement for the teams to remove Mosley. Ecclestone understood the risk but was uncertain about his own vulnerability.

12

Götterdämmerung

On 18 March 2009, the eve of the 2009 Grand Prix season, Flavio Briatore, Ron Dennis and John Howett arrived at Princes Gate to urge Ecclestone to sign the 2007 Concorde agreement and end their warfare. If he continued to refuse, they warned, none of the teams would apply to race for the entire 2010 season and would race in a breakaway series. All three believed in their own reasonableness. None could imagine that in Ecclestone's eyes their mere presence in his office to deliver an ultimatum confirmed their vulnerability. Ecclestone looked at Howett – 'Toyota's MoT man' – with scorn. Toyota had poured $2 billion into Formula One and still failed to win a single race. 'I've had proper people threaten me,' he thought, 'and there's no way I would get on my knees to him and his pistol and let him pull the trigger.'

Howett's evident admiration for Briatore's professionalism also grated. 'We need protection from Mosley,' Briatore told Ecclestone, describing events the previous day in Paris. Mosley had threatened the teams that he would unilaterally impose severe cuts and technical changes unless each team agreed to limit its annual expenditure immediately to $42 million. The teams offered to reduce their costs gradually to $150 million but no less. 'Max is impossible,' said Briatore. 'He's like all lawyers. He grasps the problems but doesn't solve them. Instead, he makes everything more complicated.' Unless Mosley was quashed, said Briatore, the breakaway would happen.

'Flavio', thought Ecclestone, 'is presenting this as very personal against Max.' Picking up his telephone, Ecclestone ordered, 'Cancel the freight plane, there's no race.' The teams would need to fly to Australia for the first race in eleven days and Ecclestone was playing hardball. Ecclestone's visitors were jolted, although in hindsight Howett doubted that anyone was on the line. By the end of the meeting, the flights were 'restored' and Ecclestone seemed sympathetic but he would still not sign the Concorde agreement. 'Don't worry, boy,' he said, touching Howett's hand. 'I'm on your side.' Howett was bewildered. He could not grasp whether Ecclestone's relationship with Mosley was merely one of convenience or if they were really joined at the hip, not least because they blamed each other for the continuing failure to sign the Concorde agreement to prevent the breakaway. Ecclestone's strength, Howett realised, was to back three horses simultaneously, so there was an upside even if the slowest horse won.

Donald Mackenzie experienced the fallout of the revolt from Richard Branson. The aspiring tycoon, who pledged to sponsor the new Brawn team, had summoned Mackenzie to his office. 'I'm going to back the breakaway,' Branson announced, anticipating a financial advantage. 'Good luck,' replied Mackenzie and walked out. Soon after, at the opening of the season in Melbourne, Branson provoked uproar. Jenson Button protested about Branson's conversation with his girlfriend and later the entrepreneur was accused of 'borrowing a baby' from a stranger as a humorous stunt in a restaurant. To the teams' disgust Mosley was encouraging Branson and other non-runners to enter Formula One to stymie their revolt.

Two months later, on 15 May, after flying around the world and racing three times in Asia, all the teams were summoned by Ecclestone to a meeting at the Heathrow Hilton. Ecclestone was apprehensive about Mosley's performance. Ten days earlier, his son had died in tragic circumstances and he was exhausted by the pain. But 'Brother Mosley', as he affectionately called his partner, refused to avoid a fight. 'I'm taking the gloves off,' Mosley told

Ecclestone, personalising his own power against the 'enemies'. No one, he decided, would be allowed to dictate to him. His first target was Briatore. 'You're trying to take over Formula One,' Mosley said, regretting that Ecclestone had made Briatore one of the sport's richest men only to be rewarded by opportunism. 'Don't be so rude,' Briatore responded. 'What you're doing is wrong,' said Mosley, glaring. The tension rose. Howett suggested that all the teams abandon the meeting and leave. Mosley was scathing. In his opinion the Toyota manager was a small-time shop steward winding Briatore up for confrontation. 'You don't understand the complexities of running Formula One,' he told Howett. His attack was interrupted by news from Paris. Montezemolo had started a legal suit against FIA in the French courts. 'We're not backing down,' insisted Mosley. Montezemolo's manoeuvre was defeated. Four days later the teams arrived in Monaco for the race on 24 May. 'I don't want any more meetings with Mosley,' said Howett. 'All we're doing is supporting the water and biscuit companies.' Briatore agreed. A summit of the teams was arranged on his yacht on Friday, 22 May 2009.

The anger against Mosley had intensified. Unexpectedly Ross Brawn's new team, built on the foundations of Honda's sell-off, had won every race. Ferrari's former designer had included a double diffuser at the rear of Jenson Button's car to increase the downforce. Unnoticed by his rivals Brawn had pioneered a reinterpretation of the rules. 'We thought that it was illegal,' protested Briatore, 'but with Mosley everything is in the air. He has too much power.' Ron Dennis shared the anger. Mosley's agenda to help the small teams beat the big spenders had favoured Brawn at McLaren's expense. Even Montezemolo arrived in Monaco to participate in the showdown. Despite his deal with Ecclestone, Montezemolo declared that FOTA were united in their rejection of Mosley's latest changes of the rules. Briatore took the lead. The teams, he said, could earn more money if they left Formula One. They agreed to confront Ecclestone and Mosley the following day, 22 May, at Monaco's automobile club.

Ecclestone was in an odd position. While he was living on Briatore's yacht, his host was urging him to revolt against Mosley. 'I am your friend,' said Briatore, 'I won't do anything against you. I want you to join us. Just help us get rid of Max.' Ecclestone had good reason to doubt that loyalty. Briatore, he heard, had earlier met Mackenzie at his home near St Tropez and urged the CVC partner to replace Ecclestone with himself as the chief executive. 'Trust me,' Ecclestone told Mackenzie. 'What's good for Flavio isn't good for you or the teams.' As a poacher turned gamekeeper, Ecclestone believed that Briatore was unable to sabotage his juggling act in his lifetime and thereafter he was not concerned.

'I've got Flavio under control,' he told Mackenzie. 'It's not a problem.' 'What are you going to do?' Mackenzie asked. 'Nothing. It's like a girl smacking Mike Tyson. It's pointless to retaliate.' He continued, 'Most things in life are timing.' In the game of poker with the teams, the stakes were high. 'Let them guess our position and see if they get on with it.' Briatore, he believed, would never execute his threat. On reflection he added, 'Everyone thinks I have a nice job. It's true. They just can't have it. If you're quick on the draw, there's always people who will try to beat you.'

The threat from Montezemolo was different. Ecclestone was unsure whether he was bluffing. Montezemolo had injected buckets of testosterone into the argument but, Ecclestone calculated, was heading towards a brick wall. The economics of the sport were outlandish, he knew, and would be destroyed by a split. FOTA lacked credibility. 'I work for CVC,' Ecclestone told Montezemolo, 'and if you do a breakaway, all the television money will disappear. No circuit or broadcaster will need to pay a penny to show the races.' One billion dollars' worth of entertainment would be offered for nothing. Montezemolo laughed that Ecclestone's infallibility was no longer taken for granted.

Over the previous sixty years, Ecclestone had developed a masterly enigmatic performance. While he replied to Montezemolo and Briatore that Formula One was more important than individual teams – and Briatore argued the opposite – he agreed that Mosley was to blame for the problems. Throwing Mosley's fate into play encouraged Briatore's ambitions. His team was performing miserably and he wanted a new career. Mosley's weakness, Briatore believed, undermined Ecclestone's authority and offered him the chance of inheriting the crown.

Even the oldest personal relationships were frayed that afternoon in Monaco's elegant automobile club. Howett was surly. Montezemolo appeared angry. Briatore was spiky. The two Italians' unity, Ecclestone believed, was a facade. 'It's easy', he thought, 'for Flavio to load a gun, wave it around and pull the trigger. He has a lot less to lose than Luca.' But Montezemolo, he thought, 'would never pull the trigger'. Mosley looked at Montezemolo and was tempted to stage a victory dance about Ferrari's failed court action in Paris and Montezemolo's unexpected resignation from Fiat's board of directors. He succumbed to the incitement. 'Your English is poor,' Mosley told Montezemolo loudly, 'and you're no longer the head of Fiat.' The vitriol terrified Mackenzie. His bankers were threatening to call in his loans and close his business unless the Concorde agreement was signed and annoyingly Mosley was seemingly untroubled by CVC's plight. 'If CVC disappears,' Mosley told him, 'it doesn't matter to me. Whether I speak to you or your bankers is all the same.' Mackenzie turned to Ecclestone for help. Under pressure, Ecclestone was compelled to consider that Ferrari was not bluffing but Mosley was less willing to compromise. On 26 May he wrote to Montezemolo seeking a meeting and agreed to raise the limit for a team's budget to $200 million. But at the same time, to prove his authority, he ordained that teams wanting to race in 2010 needed to apply in July rather than October, and on his terms. If the established teams refused to apply, he would fill the Formula One race with what Ecclestone called 'crippled teams' – preordained losers.

***

Three weeks later Briatore was too fired up to pause. The threat from the major teams that they would not apply to race in 2010 if Ecclestone refused to sign the Concorde agreement remained. On his way to the annual Silverstone race he invited all the team principals to meet on the evening of Thursday, 18 June 2009, at Renault's factory in Enstone, near the circuit, principally, he would say, because there was a helipad. The agenda, everyone knew, was a showdown against Ecclestone.

Ecclestone and Mackenzie had been working overtime to persuade doubters not to join Briatore. They focused on Ross Brawn, whose team produced the 2009 champion and who was renegotiating his new team's contracts. 'Your whole business will fold if there's a breakaway,' Mackenzie warned Brawn before he arrived at Princes Gate. At the end of their meeting, Brawn approved an agreement with Mackenzie to stay loyal to Ecclestone. Soon after, at Princes Gate, he verbally assured Ecclestone that he would not deal with Briatore and FOTA. They shook hands. Six hours later at 11.45 p.m. in Enstone, Brawn signed the breakaway statement. Martin Whitmarsh, McLaren's principal, immediately telephoned his staff. 'The breakaway has been agreed,' he whooped. 'We're going to form a new company.' There was, the McLaren team agreed, a spring in their steps. 'Formula One stinks right now,' said Dennis. He blamed Mosley for 'pouring dirt'. They could race without Mosley and FIA. The counterblast was equally ferocious. 'The teams are loony,' Mosley told BBC television, 'and the chief lunatic is Flavio Briatore who wants to be the next Bernie.' 'Brawn double-crossed me,' Ecclestone claimed.

John Howett was euphoric. Ecclestone, he noticed on Friday, was not as usual walking around Silverstone's Paddock. 'Bernie's shocked,' he said. 'He hasn't come out of his motorhome. He's no longer in control.' On Saturday morning Ecclestone flew by helicopter to London with Briatore to meet Mackenzie at the Connaught Hotel. 'It's a madhouse,' Mackenzie commented, furious that two old men had put $2.9 billion at risk. 'We need an agreement,' he ordered with calm politeness. Ecclestone nodded and soon after confessed to Todt, 'Flavio believes what he reads in the newspapers about his abilities.' 'But you're close to him,' commented Todt, surprised by Ecclestone's admission. 'It's best to hold your enemies close to you,' sighed Ecclestone. Journalists spotting Ecclestone in the Paddock on Sunday morning noticed he was shaken. 'I haven't given all the years of my life to build this up,' he told Nigel Roebuck of *Motor Sport*, 'to see it destroyed now.' By Sunday night, after Brawn's string of victories on the Silverstone track were halted by Red Bull (the team had finally fitted a double diffuser), Mackenzie insisted that CVC's investment depended on Mosley's resignation. 'You're deliberately trying to destroy the business,' Mackenzie raged at Mosley. 'The idea is to retain teams, not lose them.' 'No, no, no,' replied Mosley holding his head in his hands, upset that no one appreciated his good ideas. 'You've got to go,' Ecclestone told Mosley on Wednesday 24 June. 'If these people keep telling me to go, I won't,' replied Mosley. But neither Mackenzie nor Montezemolo would tolerate delay. 'The teams will only sign the new Concorde agreement', Montezemolo told Mackenzie, 'after Max resigns.' Unsentimental about Mosley's historic contribution to Formula One, both would demand his departure when FIA's World Council met in Paris on the following Sunday. Ron Dennis cheered gleefully from the sidelines.

Ecclestone arrived in Paris on Saturday night determined to end Mosley's career. Amid emotional shouting, Ecclestone threatened, 'If you don't go, FIA will be blown up and be gone.' Mosley prevaricated. 'Mackenzie will sue you and FIA if you don't go,' Ecclestone added. Mosley's departure no longer satisfied Montezemolo. 'Max must go and also Bernie must go,' Montezemolo told Mackenzie before arriving in Paris on Sunday morning. Mackenzie appeared as a bystander while the stakes escalated for Ecclestone who, with Montezemolo, confronted Mosley on Sunday evening. Montezemolo, Mosley thought, was angered by '*piacheve*' – Mosley's failure to repay the Italian for his personal support in New York against Ecclestone; while Ecclestone himself, he decided, was irredeemably disloyal. Despite their forty-year relationship, Ecclestone was, he told himself, 'an impulsive, quicksilver, strange person whom I still don't understand'. His deadpan eyes were disconcerting. But ultimately the bulldozing by the two men had become irresistible. Reluctantly, at the end of the World Council meeting, Mosley invited the two men to his office. More arguments followed until he agreed to a dignified departure. He then revealed his heir.

Four years earlier, after Jean Todt had at the last moment withdrawn as Mosley's successor, the two secretly agreed that Mosley would stand for another term and Todt would take over in 2009. Now Todt's relationship with Montezemolo was fracturing and he was ready to move to Paris. 'The teams won't stand for Todt,' Ecclestone told Mosley, fearful of a Frenchman's bureaucratic tendencies and, worse, FIA's considerable power would be wielded by someone beyond his influence. 'The teams don't have votes,' replied Mosley pointedly. Ecclestone, he knew, hated change and, to retain his influence, still favoured Michel Boeri, the Grand Prix chief from Monaco. Montezemolo, Ecclestone told Mosley, was also opposed to Todt. On hearing the news, Todt was surprised because Montezemolo, after working with him for sixteen years, had pledged his support. 'One day he says, "You're my best friend," ' complained Todt, who had recently been offered a senior job at Formula One in London by Ecclestone, 'and the next he speaks against me. I don't trust him any more.' Montezemolo told Ecclestone that Boeri was unacceptable. Ecclestone gave up, uneasy that a forty-year partnership was over. 'I support Jean,' he said after his opposition proved to be forlorn. Montezemolo flew to Paris to extract Mosley's resignation formally and seal the succession. 'Do you know that I'm Jewish?' Todt asked Mosley. 'Of course,' replied Mosley, removing any suspicion of being anti-Semitic. Mackenzie was relieved. Peace, he believed on the Sunday evening, had finally broken out.

Knowing that Mosley would be replaced by Todt, his former employee, and that Ecclestone's position was weakened, Montezemolo walked out of FIA's offices into the Place de la Concorde and headed towards the Italian television cameras. Until then Montezemolo had allowed Briatore to speak on his behalf but he could no longer restrain himself. 'I have toppled the dictator,' he announced. The mockery was instantly repeated to Mosley. Of course he was a dictator. How else could the sport be run? As he had told Ecclestone: 'People only listen to dictators.' But Montezemolo's gloating outraged the wounded vizier. For years he had supported Ferrari and critics would say that Schumacher owed two world championships to Mosley's prejudice. Yet Montezemolo had behaved with crude ingratitude. 'I'm not resigning,' Mosley told Ecclestone, 'I don't give a damn. If the buggers want to take me on, I'll happily fight. I'm going to stand for re-election and I'll win. I'll sink Flavio and Luca.' To retaliate, he summoned the same Italian television company and offered an immediate interview. 'Luca is just a *bella figura*,' he scorned, suggesting that Montezemolo was merely a pretty actor, 'and no one in Italy takes any notice of him.' Ecclestone contemplated whether his friend was losing touch with reality when, on Saturday 4 July, the pack of cards collapsed again.

Some weeks earlier, Rachel Sylvester, a skilled political journalist employed by *The Times*, had approached Ecclestone for an interview. There was no particular reason other than that Ecclestone seemed an interesting person to feature in the newspaper's regular Saturday interview. Since Ecclestone did not employ a media adviser, Sylvester left messages with his secretary until, in the midst of the crisis, Ecclestone finally agreed. An invitation to be interviewed by the Top People's newspaper, considering his good relations with Ed Gorman, the motor correspondent, seemed a safe site to reassert his undiminished control over Formula One. As usual, he did not consult anyone. Critics would say that having forsaken secrecy he wanted recognition for his success.

Sylvester arrived in Princes Gate with Alice Thomson, an equally adroit journalist. Attractive, intelligent and beguiling, neither woman had been to a Formula One race or was aware that the sport, in the midst of a self-destructive conflict, was again testing Ecclestone's skill to beat off yet another challenge after four changes of ownership. They were simply intrigued by the character of a seventy-eight-year-old billionaire controlling the world's second most profitable sport. By then Ecclestone had been interviewed on countless occasions. He remained a car dealer who lacked any formal education, who had never read a book and partly relied on the *Daily Express* and television documentaries for an interpretation of world events, but conscious that his mystique could appear abrasive, he intended to disarm his visitors with charm. Because both were young and attractive, he underestimated them.

Few entering Ecclestone's ground-floor office could fail to be impressed. Overlooking a large, well-arranged garden, the leather upholstery, colourful mementoes and framed photographs of himself with the Queen, Nelson Mandela, Pelé and Fangio were a testament to a showman's extraordinary sixty-year career. The helmet, he often explained to guests, was needed because 'I'm a fire-fighter.' On his own turf Ecclestone felt comfortable offering his opinions, especially about politics. Formula One's success, he told his guests, owed everything to his dictatorship. After criticising the invasion of Iraq and Afghanistan, he revealed his cynicism about Western governments. 'If you look at democracy it hasn't done a lot of good for many countries – including this one,' he said. Formula One's autocrat not surprisingly expressed his admiration for strong leaders like Margaret Thatcher who 'made decisions on the run and got things done' and his disapproval of 'Gordon and Tony [who] are trying to please everybody all the time'. Developing his theme, he expressed his dislike of referrals rather than fast decisions. Max Mosley, he suggested, was his ideal prime minister and would do 'a super job'. The eccentricity of that opinion was matched by his support for Jeffrey Archer, the novelist imprisoned for perjury whom he nominated to be London's mayor. So far, his opinions were colourful and seemed inclined to favour dictatorship over democracy. So, he was asked whether he could name 'a favourite historical dictator'? After some thought, Ecclestone replied, 'In a lot of ways, terrible to say this I suppose, but apart from the fact that Hitler got taken away and persuaded to do things that I have no idea whether he wanted to do or not, he was, in the way that he could command a lot of people, able to get things done.' He continued, 'In the end he got lost so he wasn't a very good dictator. Either he knew what was going on and insisted, or he just went along with it – either way he wasn't a dictator.' The two journalists, aware that Ecclestone had been controversial, departed pleased to have collected some good quotations. Ecclestone was unaware that he had dropped a noose around his own neck.

Ecclestone's drift into rambling thoughts about dictatorship and Hitler undoubtedly reflected his own values of management. His autocracy, skulduggery and exploitation of his opponents' dysfunctional characters had sustained Formula One. In developing his theme, however, he seemed unquestioningly favourable to a mass murderer. Worse, he supported the neo Nazi argument that Hitler was unaware of the crimes committed in his name. One explanation for his opinions was nervousness. Seeing that the two women were uninterested in Formula One, he used sensational humour to catch their attention. His better excuse for the historical distortion was ignorance. Reliant on Hollywood for his knowledge about the Third Reich, he imagined that the Führer's strong government rescued Germany from bankruptcy by rebuilding the German economy and restoring the German people's self-confidence in the same way as Thatcher. In Ecclestone's 'book', nothing bad happened until Luftwaffe bombers flew across his home in Dartford in September 1939. The reality of the Nazi regime was, his admirers would say, beyond his comprehension. He was apparently unaware that

Germany was tyrannised by state-sponsored murder after 1933 and that Hitler's concentration camps were built and filled with thousands of innocent citizens before the outbreak of the war. To Ecclestone's good fortune, no one would realise that among his prize exhibits of vintage cars in Biggin Hill was the gleaming Lancia Asturia open-topped stretch limousine in which Hitler and Mussolini had driven through Rome in 1938 to sign the 'Pact of Steel'. Propped up against the car were framed photographs of the event. Mussolini had given the car to Hitler as a present. The nuances about his education interested no one on Saturday morning. Ecclestone had unintentionally portrayed himself as an anti-Semitic admirer of Hitler.

Soon after daybreak, Ecclestone realised his error. Every radio and television news programme repeated his lurid thoughts. Martin Sorrell, a CVC director, spoke for the majority condemning Ecclestone's sentiments as 'disgusting', an opinion echoed by Mario Theussen, the head of BMW. Sorrell briefed the *Daily Mail* that Ecclestone would be fired before the next race, appropriately to be held at Nürburgring. Ecclestone was unfazed by Sorrell's hysteria. Collateral damage rarely bothered him. Over the weekend, he was called by other famous Jews, including Philip Green and Richard Desmond, offering to say publicly that he was not anti-Semitic. Desmond proposed that in return for Ecclestone contributing £250,000 to charity, he would put two pages of the *Daily Express* at his disposal. Ecclestone declined the offer. He regularly donated to charities, even to the arts, although he admitted, 'I hate the theatre.' His greatest comfort was a call from Peter Mandelson. 'I thought they wanted to talk about Formula One,' he told the Labour politician. 'You should have called me,' said Mandelson. 'I would have told you that they would stitch you up.' That was not Ecclestone's conclusion. The journalists' report, he knew, was accurate.

On Monday morning he telephoned Sylvester. 'I seem to have caused some trouble with my Jewish friends,' he said sheepishly. 'Why don't you write a comment piece for the paper?' Sylvester asked, suggesting that an explanatory article by himself could mitigate the damage. With the help of *The Times* staff, Ecclestone composed a contrite apology without fully withdrawing his sympathy for Hitler's dictatorial government and, despite the uproar, he flew to Germany for the Grand Prix.

Unknown to Formula One's managers, Ecclestone's plane passed over Cologne and landed in Rome, and he drove with Donald Mackenzie to the villa of Marco Piccinini's mother. Escorted by elderly retainers through anterooms, the two were taken into the dining room where Luca Montezemolo was waiting. 'I've brought this for you,' said Ecclestone, proffering a package. Montezemolo cast the unopened gift aside and over the next two hours ignored Ecclestone's presence. Talking directly to Mackenzie, he said, 'Max must go, and so must Bernie.' 'We at CVC will decide that,' Mackenzie replied. After that desultory meal – interrupted by Montezemolo telephoning Mosley with demands for his immediate departure – Ecclestone and Mackenzie flew to Cologne. Flavio Briatore was waiting at a seedy motel. In a purple-painted basement conference room, Mackenzie and Sacha Woodward-Hill listened to Briatore and John Howett scream obscenities at Ecclestone, insisting, 'You don't matter any more.'

The scenario in the Paddock at Nürburgring was no more promising. Two old men had attached Nazi-loving to Formula One's reputation. Neither was in the slightest apologetic. In his motorhome, Ecclestone and Zimmerman repeatedly greeted each other '*Sieg Heil*' and, when Niki Lauda came in for a drink, Zimmerman put on the video of Lauda's crash on the same circuit in 1976. 'You stupid Austrian,' shouted Zimmerman, 'Why didn't you get out?' In Monaco Mosley thought, 'This is all annoying. It will remind people to mention my *News of the World* story.' In his conversations with Ecclestone, he barely mentioned the storm. His only concern was his own survival and settling accounts.

***

Soon after the German race, Mosley met Nelson Piquet Senior at the Rampoldi restaurant in Monaco, a favourite haunt. Amid tears, the former world champion retold the story of his son's misfortunes with Briatore. He blamed Briatore for withholding the necessary support for his son, who had come thirteenth at Nürburgring, practically his best result throughout the season. Their discussion inevitably drifted back to the deliberate crash in Singapore. 'We can't do anything unless Junior makes a statement,' said Mosley. 'He's around the corner,' said Piquet. 'I can bring him in now.' 'No,' insisted Mosley, 'he should give a statement to a lawyer.' Then Mosley added, 'And don't tell Bernie because he'll tell Flavio.' 'I already have,' replied Piquet.

Two months earlier, in Monaco, Piquet had told his old employer about the conspiracy. Ecclestone looked surprised: 'I was aghast that anyone wanted to risk killing Piquet,' said Ecclestone, 'and then I didn't believe it. There was no evidence and I thought it all a bit stupid.' His advice to Piquet was blunt: 'If you think that's true, you should tell Max'.

Fixing races between teams was not unusual, Ecclestone knew. In his last race in 1973, Jackie Stewart, the reigning world champion, had been asked by Ken Tyrrell not to win – it would have been his hundredth victory – but to drop back and allow François Cevert, his team mate, to pass just before the chequered flag. 'I'll think about it,' replied Stewart. He would have obliged but the issue disappeared after Cevert was killed on the track. Piquet's allegation, Ecclestone knew, was different but nothing more was said until Piquet Junior came twelfth in the Hungarian race on 26 July. To his father's horror, after watching the race Briatore fired his son. The father walked directly into Ecclestone's motorhome. 'First Flavio gave Nelson poor cars and now he's kicked him out,' he exclaimed. 'I'm going to fuck this guy.' 'Don't threaten anyone,' Ecclestone replied, 'If you want to do it, just do it.' Upset about Briatore's leadership of the breakaway, Ecclestone had lost sympathy for his friend. 'I helped him all the time,' he thought, 'and now look, he's fucking me.'

Ever since the unpleasant confrontation in the Cologne motel, Mackenzie told Ecclestone, Briatore had been calling about the succession.

Five days later, after three years of procrastination about the Concorde agreement, Ecclestone and Mosley surrendered to the teams and Mackenzie. Throughout July Mosley had negotiated the new terms and, on 1 August 2009, the revised 2007 agreement, 253 pages long, was signed by Ecclestone and Mosley. It would expire in 2012. Briatore welcomed a partial victory that FIA's powers were restricted and a team's annual expenditure was only notionally capped at $200 million. Renault and the other teams could now receive the delayed payments from CVC and, with Mosley gone, there was an opportunity to renegotiate Ecclestone's status. Briatore's satisfaction ignored Mosley's anger and Ecclestone's inability to offer his customary protection to FIA's justice.

Flavio Briatore was in Max Mosley's sights. Nelson Piquet Junior had given a statement to a lawyer and, at Mosley's request, to a former British police officer employed by Quest, the private investigators. In both Piquet had explicitly included Briatore in the Singapore conspiracy. Considering recent dramas, Mosley was particularly interested in the crisis, probably the last of his career. Unusually, Ecclestone had shifted towards neutrality, putting the most charitable gloss on the conspiracy. 'If Flavio didn't know about the plan, he should have,' he said. Enjoying Briatore's discomfort, Mosley agreed to have lunch with his target at the Rampoldi. The Italian emphatically denied Piquet's allegations. The idea, he scoffed, that he would conspire with Piquet and then fire him, was ludicrous and, he added, Piquet had crashed repeatedly during the season. Mosley nodded. 'Well, these summer events are not personal but business,' he said.

Throughout August Mosley secretly prepared for a formal hearing to be held at the Spa Grand Prix at the end of the month. Quest's investigations were supervised by a team of London lawyers. On 30 August, without notice, just after

Ferrari won its only race during the season, Mosley summoned
Renault's senior staff for questioning by a London lawyer. To
Mosley's disappointment, Quest's investigators had still found
no independent evidence confirming Piquet's allegations of
Briatore's involvement in the conspiracy. Solidly the Renault
witnesses questioned by FIA's lawyer all accused Piquet of
seeking revenge for his dismissal until Pat Symonds, Renault's
director of engineering who, according to Piquet, was a
co-conspirator, admitted being in the room during a discussion
between Piquet and Briatore. When asked directly about the
conspiracy, Symonds replied, 'I won't answer that question.'
Mosley was delighted. 'If he'd lied,' said Mosley, 'there would
have been no case. But the silence is self-incrimination.'

At the end of the day Globo TV, Brazil's main channel, broke
the embargo about the conspiracy. Across the world Formula
One was damned as corrupt. The sport, commentators repeated,
had sunk into a cesspit, run by unscrupulous multimillionaires.
When Mosley finally retired in October and Ecclestone
eventually departed, wrote Richard Williams in the *Guardian*,
they 'will leave behind a sport stripped of its integrity, its old
values replaced by a superficial prosperity that can no longer
conceal a putrescent core'. Briatore, portrayed as a symbol of
Formula One's permanent deception, was attacked by Piquet
as manipulative and uncaring: 'I was simply being used by him,
then discarded and left to ridicule . . . My situation at Renault
turned into a nightmare.' Briatore initiated libel proceedings
against both Piquets for their 'blackmail and outrageous lies'.

On Ecclestone's recommendation, Ali Malek QC, a commercial
silk, was hired by Renault to conduct an internal inquiry. Mosley
heard on 13 September, the day of the Monza race, that Malek
had found 'Witness X', Alan Permayne, Renault's chief engineer,
who confirmed that Briatore knew about the conspiracy.
Renault, Malek reported, would plead guilty. Picking up the
gossip in Monza, Jackie Stewart admitted, 'There is something
fundamentally rotten and wrong at the heart of Formula One.'

The sport was corrupt, he added, when even someone as decent as Pat Symonds could be ensnared.

Mosley arranged a formal FIA trial for 21 September in Paris. All Renault's employees except Briatore were given immunity. 'That's wrong,' protested Briatore. 'The prosecution is settling scores after the event,' agreed Ecclestone. Optimistically, Briatore expected a solution miraculously to solve his predicament but the continuing outrage was too great for Briatore to resist. On 16 September, he resigned from Renault, blamed by the corporation as 'morally responsible' for organising the crash. Briatore denied the allegation. As his reputation was shredded and his commercial interests were punished by banks calling in their loans, Briatore asked Ecclestone for advice. 'Follow your religion faithfully,' said Ecclestone, 'and confess. Say, "I didn't engineer it but as team chief I must take the responsibility." Then Max can be lenient.' Briatore was not attracted to the idea of contrition. 'I'm fixing everything in the World Council,' Ecclestone assured Briatore, but his attempts failed. To Mosley's satisfaction, the puppet-master was firmly sidelined. This was Mosley's last show and no one could interfere.

In approaching the trial, Mosley was realistic about cheating. Everyone in Formula One, he knew, attempted to bamboozle their competitors. 'In the old days,' Ecclestone reminded him, 'everyone ran cars underweight and cheated.' The challenge, Ecclestone knew, was to get away with it and on this occasion Briatore had failed the test. Mosley cast that argument aside. The evidence, he believed, was overwhelming. But to his disappointment, Briatore refused to attend a court where Mosley was both prosecutor and judge. Undaunted, in his absence Mosley sentenced Briatore to a life-time ban from Formula One. 'I did give a harsh sentence,' he admitted, 'because I feared leaving the building and walking into eight microphones and would be greeted with fury if I hadn't thrown the book at him.' Mosley's belief that he had fulfilled his duty was not shared by Briatore.

'Mosley is clever, very dangerous, very vindictive and mean,' said Briatore. 'He smiles in the front and stabs in the back. He likes power to inflict punishment rather than to spread benefits.'

Ecclestone was shocked. A lifetime ban, he announced, was 'too harsh and unnecessary'. If only Briatore had confessed and apologised, he lamented, he would have escaped the worst. 'Formula One needs colourful characters and Flav is one of those.' He urged an appeal. Ecclestone's lament was criticised by Martin Sorrell. 'We had "Hitler did good" and now we have "cheating is acceptable". Where will it end?' Ecclestone was defiant towards Sorrell: 'He is not in any position to get rid of me in any shape or form . . . He's supporting, I think, his religion against me making a little bit of a stupid statement some time ago, which just wasn't a stupid statement, really it was misunderstood.' They would make up over dinner at Mark's Club. 'Be a good boy in the future,' Sorrell told Ecclestone.

Ecclestone's support for Briatore's appeal to the French courts, claiming that he had been denied fundamental justice by Mosley's 'vindictive pursuit' of 'personal revenge', was shared by Montezemolo. Mosley's confidence that Briatore would lose was mistaken. On 5 January 2010 Briatore would defeat FIA and, under pressure from Ecclestone and Montezemolo, Todt agreed to settle rather than appeal. In return for Briatore 'recognising' his individual responsibility for the deliberate crash, Todt reduced the ban to three years.

Ecclestone's association with Briatore, especially his endorsement of the maverick as 'a real friend who I can rely on' bewildered many. Ecclestone was unapologetic. 'People say I shouldn't be associated with Flavio. I couldn't care. I know what I know. If people say that I shouldn't be associated with people who cheat, I wouldn't be able to speak to anyone. Everyone cheats, and he shouldn't have got caught, and he should have confessed.' His morality shocked the City financiers. Towards the end of the season, Mackenzie feared that his trust in Ecclestone had been misplaced. After 'Spygate', 'The Crash',

Nazi sympathies and compassion for Briatore, some sponsors and corporate chiefs were edging towards abandoning the sport. Formula One's publicity was only valuable for winners and there were too many losers. In Tokyo the board of Toyota, disturbed by the scandals, humiliated by constant defeat and insulted by Ecclestone's reluctance to display some deference, were poised to follow Honda, Ford and BMW and abandon Formula One. Even though Formula One gave manufacturers the cheapest advertisements, marketing a car which over eight years and 139 races had never even come third was difficult. Howett's fierce agitation for a breakaway rebounded and, to his undisguised shock, his headquarters unexpectedly announced its departure from Formula One.

Ecclestone expressed disdain. Toyota, he believed, had brought nothing but trouble to the sport and scuttled away when they lost. But the departure by the world's biggest motor manufacturer appalled Montezemolo and Mackenzie. There would, they feared, be insufficient quality competitors on the grid. The danger increased when Renault decided to withdraw after being condemned as guilty for cheating. Ecclestone instantly approached Bernard Rey, Briatore's replacement, to show how Renault could profitably remain in the sport by cooperating with Geni, a Luxemburg finance company, as the majority investor. To his satisfaction, Renault remained in Formula One.

By the beginning of August, even Ecclestone felt battered by the crisis. Unusually he decided to enjoy sailing on his yacht off the Croatian coast. Among his guests were David Merlini, the escape artist, and Tamas Rohonyi, an old friend and organiser of the Brazilian Grand Prix. Rohonyi arrived with some friends on their way to the Hungarian Grand Prix, including Fabiana Flosi, a thirty-three-year-old Brazilian lawyer who had worked for Formula One in São Paulo for the previous fifteen years. Attractive, intelligent, modest and diplomatic, the divorcee and Ecclestone had worked together during those years. Unexpectedly, as the yacht slipped between the islands in the Adriatic, a relationship developed. She was the peaceful company he had previously lacked. In that relaxing atmosphere, Ecclestone could reflect about the end of an era. Briatore and Howett were gone. Williams was struggling. Ron Dennis had been promoted after an ugly spat involving Lewis Hamilton and replaced as team principal by Martin Whitmarsh. Mosley's retirement had been celebrated at a farewell party by journalists presenting the president with a whip bought in Piccadilly. 'Woman D is off having a baby at the moment,' Mosley said laughing, 'but women A, B and C will love this.' Mercedes, tired by McLaren's scandals, announced their intention to sell the 40 per cent stake and resurrect the 'Silver Arrows', their own team which had been withdrawn in 1955 after their car crashed into a crowd at Le Mans, killing ninety-six spectators. Mercedes had also bought a stake in Brawn, confirming Mosley's argument that private teams were superior to the manufacturers. Mutual attrition had decimated the grid.

Looking back over that tumultuous year, Ecclestone reflected that so much had changed and only one factor remained constant – he himself. By trusting no one completely – even his closest allies – the master juggler had survived repeated attempted coups. Many who remained in the Paddock were his foes, yet the mood within that exclusive area was unusually calm for the remainder of the season. In mid-October, Ecclestone headed for São Paulo. The race in Brazil was always fun, Tamas Rohonyi was always a good host and Fabiana Flosi added to the excitement. Outside the Interlagos stadium, long queues of excited fans had waited all night to buy seats to see the spectacle. The passion was irrepressible. In a dramatic race, Jenson Button won the 2009 world championship in a Brawn. Ecclestone pushed his way through crowds to congratulate Ross Brawn personally. 'What a fantastic race,' he bubbled. 'What a fantastic season!'

13

Godfather

One year later, the mood was hectic. 'Come on Flav,' urged Bernie Ecclestone. 'I'm going.' Standing at the entrance of Karl-Heinz Zimmerman's motorhome at Monza on 12 September 2010, Ecclestone was shouting at Flavio Briatore over the roar of the twenty-two cars moving into position for the start of the year's fourteenth race around the 'temple of speed'. Briatore was hesitating. According to FIA's ruling, he was banned from professional involvement in Formula One, yet Ecclestone had not only flown the discredited businessman from Milan to Monza by helicopter but had encouraged him to walk around the Paddock. Stares and sporadic cheers from excited red-shirted tifosi – the fans – had greeted the Italian. Like a returning pop star, Briatore enjoyed the attention, the demand for handshakes and the photographers' frenzy. Now Ecclestone wanted Briatore to leave the sanctuary of the sterile Paddock and parade among Formula One's stars on the grid. The television images of Briatore's glad-handing would be seen across the globe. Notoriety, in Ecclestone's calculations, guaranteed gossip in the newspapers.

'It's Bernie's game with the rest of the world,' said Lauda watching television with Zimmerman. 'Bernie knows Flavio is out of Formula One. He's using him for his own purpose.' To show that he was in charge, Ecclestone enjoyed chastening Jean Todt whose indecisive grandeur infuriated him. 'He put the president's hat on and his personality changed,' carped Ecclestone, bereft without Max Mosley. To puncture Todt's self-importance, Ecclestone had even delayed the FIA stewards hoisting their flag as required by the regulations. On the eve of his eightieth birthday, he was parading Briatore to confirm himself as the undisputed king of the biggest show on earth.

In the hot sunshine, with Briatore in tow, Ecclestone and Fabiana Flosi pushed through the crowds on to the grid. Over the previous weeks, their relationship had deepened. Marriage and even children were now a possibility. Greeting Formula One's celebrities and posing for photographs with locals who bore striking resemblances to the Sopranos and their friends, the two headed towards Sebastian Vettel's car. 'No mistakes,' said Ecclestone, fearful that the recently anointed 'Crash Kid' would repeat the petulant folly which eliminated his car two weeks earlier at Spa. 'No stupid risks,' he repeated to a favourite whose chance to win the championship had been reduced. Immobilised by a helmet with the visor down, 'Little Schumi' blinked in obedience. Ecclestone spoke to no other driver; even Michael Schumacher was ignored, although they had spoken at length in Ecclestone's motorhome. The forty-one-year-old's comeback and talk of a resurrected dream team with Ross Brawn had been politely mocked. 'Schumi will get his own car next season,' said Ecclestone, certain that the super-fit former world champion would be a serious challenger in 2011.

Not far away, Briatore was cajoling a succession of Italian government ministers, members of Silvio Berlusconi's party. 'It's like he's been let out of prison,' smiled Ecclestone. 'I want him to be photographed with as many ministers as possible.' Although the seizure of Briatore's yacht after the Monaco race was shrugged off by Briatore as a 'bureaucratic error', his battered reputation had suffered further. 'I feel sorry for him,' said Ecclestone. He liked helping underdogs. During his summer holiday with Briatore in Sardinia, he had bailed out his partner's forlorn investment in QPR. Lending a few million pounds was painless but he dismissed the prospect of satisfying Briatore's aching desire to return to Formula One. 'Won't happen,' he snapped.

A siren warned that the race would start in two minutes. Hundreds of technicians, officials and sponsors hurried to clear the track. Fernando Alonso, the favourite chosen to restore glory to Ferrari, focused on the first bend. To be certain of victory, the Spaniard would need to win the challenge not to back off at the curve. To watch that decisive moment, Ecclestone's fast walk back to the motorhome turned into a 100-yard sprint. 'I bet Jumbo wins,' he told Briatore, using their nickname for Lewis Hamilton, as they settled in front of the television. 'Fernando will win,' countered Briatore. 'It will be decided by rubber at the first corner,' said Niki Lauda. Seconds later, on the critical turn, Jenson Button took the lead and Alonso followed. One minute later, on the fourth corner, Hamilton's wheel clipped Felipe Massa's Ferrari. The McLaren's steering cracked. 'You know you can't make mistakes,' Hamilton had admitted just before the race. 'It's the toughest contest I've had.' One former world champion was out, but three others remained in the tightest battle for years against the grit of Mark Webber's crusade to take the title instead of retirement.

After the storms and scandals of 2009, no one had predicted that 2010 would be the most thrilling competition for years. Feuds rather than fuel were propelling teams stunned by the performance of their rivals. Amid venomous duels between rival drivers in the same teams, the competition was electrified by tyre blowouts, engine malfunctions, brake failures and crashes, in warfare dependent as much upon technology and driving rain as strategy and human psychology. Unexpected innovation with the suspension, the distribution of weight and levels of downforce had rattled the eggheads employed to invent marginal advantages.

At McLaren a twenty-five-year-old aerodynamicist with a first-class degree from Cambridge and a PhD had caused mayhem during the season by inventing the F-duct. Operated manually by the driver's elbow as he turned corners at 200 miles an hour, the air was directed by the duct on to the car's rear wing to increase the downforce and the grip. On the straight, the duct was shifted to reduce the drag. Around Monza's circuit, the innovation increased speeds by four miles an hour and shaved half a second off the total time. Constant tweaking to shave milliseconds made the difference between victory and defeat. 'There's been some cheating with engines here,' revealed Briatore. 'Always happens,' replied Ecclestone, expressionless.

During his stay in Monza, Ecclestone had not disguised his certainty that the previous year Briatore had presented himself as his successor to Donald Mackenzie. The self-effacing 'owner' of the sport who had arrived in Milan on his new jet was still bemused by Briatore's ambitions. Although surprised to meet Briatore at Monza, Mackenzie trusted Ecclestone's judgement. Earlier that day, a snatched conversation between Ecclestone and Pasquale Lattuneddu, his Sardinian fixer, had confirmed him as the sport's Godfather.

Monza's police chief had called, whispered Lattuneddu, to report that he was about to serve a criminal writ on Tony Fernandes, the Malaysian owner of Lotus. The demand for $10 million had been issued by Vijay Mallya, the owner of Kingfisher, for the alleged theft of technical secrets. 'The police want to know', said Lattuneddu, 'whether they should arrive in force, in uniform, and handcuff Fernandes, and parade him through the Paddock?' Arrests for failure to settle arguments were a regular feature of Formula One. After a brief pause, Ecclestone replied, 'No, tell them to do it quietly.' He hoped that the lacklustre Lotus team would remain in Formula One. Later Fernandes would thank Ecclestone for preventing the embarrassment.

Ecclestone showed less sympathy for the Virgin team. Branson had not been seen for some months. 'He says he's a billionaire but he's put no money in,' said Ecclestone in the clipped tone that signified his displeasure. 'His cars hold up the race,' he added, suggesting that Virgin's departure at the end of the season would not be regretted. With the exception of Ferrari, McLaren and Red Bull, most of the teams bordered on insolvency. Without RBS's money Williams would struggle in 2011 but without Williams,

Ecclestone knew, Formula One's traditions would be doomed. 'I'll help you find a new sponsor,' Ecclestone assured Frank Williams. Finance seemed to be the sole topic of conversation. In succession, Luca Montezemolo and Norbert Haug of Mercedes harangued Ecclestone and Mackenzie for more money. 'If I give you more, all you'll do is spend it,' countered Ecclestone. Montezemolo's threat to bring Ecclestone and CVC down when the Concorde agreement expired at the end of 2012 was rebutted by Ecclestone's challenge: 'What odds are you offering? You know there won't be a breakaway. The teams won't buy it.' Montezemolo physically embraced Ecclestone but pretended to be wary. Ecclestone showed confidence. The big threatening beasts of 2009 had disappeared.

Two teams were expected to drop out of Formula One, yet Ecclestone was focused on expansion. Since landing at Monza, a stream of delegations had crossed the grass carpet to enter his motorhome. Eight arrived from Bulgaria, two men from Rome and six men representing Sochi in Russia all pressed their claims for a Formula One race. Ecclestone no longer needed to persuade politicians of their interest to finance the races and pay handsomely for the privilege. The Bulgarians were told they lacked the money; the Romans were assured of Ecclestone's support for a race around Benito Mussolini's New Colosseum district; while the Russians were equally reassured of a fixture if they paid the required millions. 'They've sent a message that they'll place the deposit after they get Putin's personal agreement,' Ecclestone was told by Sacha Woodward-Hill. 'They don't envisage a problem.' Exactly five weeks later, Ecclestone would fly at a day's notice to Sochi to sign a seven-year agreement at $40 million per event starting in 2014. The signing ceremony would be witnessed by President Putin after a fifteen-minute private conversation with Ecclestone. 'He's learning to speak good English,' said Ecclestone. One month later Putin invited photographers to record him testing a Formula One car in St Petersburg.

Despite the recession, Formula One's income kept rising. Sacha Woodward-Hill was collecting letters of credit from all the circuits for the following year. The Indian promoter of the Formula One race to be held near New Delhi also called at Zimmerman's motorhome to discuss the subcontinent's debut in 2011. The money had also been banked for a new race in Austin, Texas, in 2012. European fans would suffer to satisfy Ecclestone's global ambitions. 'Two or three circuits will hit the dust,' admitted Ecclestone, anticipating protests from Spain, Hungary, Belgium or Germany. 'But I won't throw out the dirty water until I've got the clean water,' he said confident that besides football, only Formula One would attract global sponsors for all its fixtures.

That confidence was bolstered by the constant stream of visitors from different backgrounds and nationalities including Eric Schmid, the chairman of Google, Emilio Botin, the founder and chairman of the Santander bank, and Vittorio Colao, the chief executive of Vodafone. The less famous brought gifts of wine, chocolates, books and a $25,000 Hublot watch designed for Formula One fans. In between those meetings, darting from his motorhome into Zimmerman's hospitality tent, Ecclestone greeted Niki Lauda, Jackie Stewart, the Crown Prince of Bahrain and Eric Clapton, the musician, talking at a table. The musician was a personal friend, while the crown prince was travelling after the race to a partridge shoot in Wiltshire. 'Tomorrow evening, after the shoot, I'm flying on to Palo Alto to visit Google,' the prince told Clapton. At a neighbouring table, Fabio Capello, the manager of England's football team, was explaining his unease about Wayne Rooney, the Manchester United striker. Outside, fans and the famous were waiting for the chance to pose for a photograph with Ecclestone. 'They keep squeezing me as if I'm gay,' he complained.

The race was proving to be a nail-biting thriller between Button and Alonso. 'Everything depends on the tyres,' predicted Lauda. 'Ferrari needs less rubber than McLaren, so the winner depends on who changes tyres first.' Even after watching thousands of races, Ecclestone was unusually gripped. Split seconds on the track and in the pits would decide the outcome. His excitement reassured his friends and even his erstwhile enemies that Formula One would prosper thanks to the machinations of the undisputed king of wheels and deals. 'Formula One is like a big stage for a pop concert,' the dream-broker liked to say for the public's consumption. 'Over the years, teams come and go like stars come and go. Elvis died. Things still went on. When I go the same will happen. Formula One will continue.'

His refusal to arrange a smooth transition annoyed many of Formula One's fraternity. Resented as the leader who thrived by cultivating ambiguity, he understood the randomness of life but refused to safeguard his legacy. The anti-hero's dictatorship, arbitrating between the foul and the fragrant, had defeated every attempted coup. His invincible self-image deterred, he hoped, any future revolt. His own fate was more secure than ever. The 100-year 'lease' bought from FIA would start in 2011. 'I bet I won't be here when it finishes,' he laughed. He was also certain that he would not be usurped by CVC. Three years earlier Mackenzie had broached the sensitive issue. 'I want to plan your retirement when you get to eighty,' the financier had said. 'I've got bad news for you,' replied Ecclestone. 'I'm eighty-one.' Running Formula One, Mackenzie knew, was an entrepreneurial rather than managerial task and no one could rival his deal-making. 'If CVC put someone in with me,' Ecclestone told Mackenzie, 'he would be either no good or would run away. And if he's that good I don't want him around. I have no intention of leaving. I love being involved in motor racing. I care now more than before.' Mackenzie abandoned the subject. Formula One, he knew, was a fragile structure which risked falling apart after Ecclestone's departure. But if for some Ecclestone appeared indispensable, the cemeteries, he could reassure himself, are full of indispensable people. Breaking private equity's tested formula, he abandoned the conventional timetable to sell the business within ten years. Rather than being the architect of a rebirth, he stepped back to enjoy a flinty maverick pour increasing profits into his account.

As a safety measure, however, Mackenzie had identified a successor who would wait until Ecclestone chose to leave. One person would be disappointed. Despite his ambition to inherit the crown, Ron Dennis was not on Mackenzie's shortlist. 'If one fish suddenly weakens, the rest have to decide whether they eat it up or hold back,' was a favourite expression on the grid. Dennis's ambitions were not sated but he knew that Ecclestone, in his lifetime, would never surrender.

Ecclestone was not a stranger to mortality but even he had been affected by the recent death from cancer of Tony Morris, his lifelong friend. He had sat by the bookie's hospital bed until the end. The companionship of Fabiana Flosi restored his vigour. Holding hands, forty-five minutes before the race ended, they bid farewell to their guests. Outside dozens of excited fans, too poor to buy tickets for the race, cheered as Ecclestone and Briatore walked to the helicopter. 'If we crash, Ruggiero,' Ecclestone had told the manager of the brand new Augusta-Westland, 'don't send the bill.' On his mobile, Ecclestone heard that Alonso had grabbed the lead after the McLaren entered the pits first. Button's team had taken 4.2 seconds to change the wheels while a lap later, Ferrari's mechanics had performed miracles in 3.4 seconds after Alonso had shaved more milliseconds in the fastest lap. Fortunes had changed in the blink of an eye.

By the time the helicopter landed at Linate airport for Ecclestone to transfer to his Falcon jet, Alonso was striding towards the podium to enjoy the adulation of 100,000 excited fans who had poured on to the track. Only seven weeks earlier, fans in Hockenheim had booed him after Massa had been ordered to allow Alonso to pass and win. 'Cheating' and 'theft' cursed Eddie Jordan, and Alonso had been asked whether his victory in Germany ranked with his victory in Singapore. Those boos and hisses were replaced by frenzy at Monza. After a poor season, Ferrari was back in the fight.

In the rankings, Mark Webber of Red Bull was still first, Hamilton was second and Alonso was third. With five more races, the unpredictability made 2010 a thrilling season. On the flight home with Briatore and Eric Clapton, Ecclestone looked pleased. In a maudlin moment the previous night he had confessed, 'I'm worried to shit it will all go down after me.' But in his jet above the Alps, he clearly anticipated another twenty years, at least.

Abu Dhabi, Sunday 14 November 2010

Bernie Ecclestone and Fabiana Flosi drove into the Paddock of the Yas Marina circuit just before noon. As usual his Mercedes was the only car admitted into the inner sanctum. Walking through the excited crowds towards his headquarters, Ecclestone shared the bookmakers' assumption that Fernando Alonso would win the world championship and told everyone seeking his opinion, 'Hamilton to win but not the championship.' Mark Webber's fate had been preordained by securing just fifth position on the grid. The wild card was Sebastian Vettel who had won pole position in the previous day's qualifying session by a fraction of a second. Even so, the odds were too heavily stacked against the twenty-three-year-old German for Ecclestone to speculate about his chances. Even the inveterate gambler refused to challenge the common wisdom despite Vettel's victory the previous Sunday in São Paulo, Brazil.

Unusually Ecclestone had stayed to watch the end of the race in São Paulo. Fabiana's family and friends were guests in his motorhome and he agreed to await the outcome of Vettel's challenge. During the helicopter ride to the airport, he congratulated his young protégé. 'All very exciting,' was the limit of his sentiments. There was no hint of anticipating a repeated success seven days later. During the overnight, non-stop flight back across the Atlantic on his jet, he reflected about the permutations of the finale of nineteen races in eighteen countries. There were four contenders and the cars would certainly be improved. Thankfully, speculation about the outcome would generate global media coverage. Abu Dhabi's ruler, Crown Prince Sheikh Mohammed bin Zayed al Nahyan, would be well pleased to have paid a premium to stage the last race of the season. Once again, Formula One had proved itself as the unique event to focus the world's attention on the most inhospitable locations, not least on Abu Dhabi's sandy wasteland which was being transformed for $40 billion into a tourist attraction.

At noon on Sunday in Abu Dhabi Ecclestone enjoyed his first argument. 'He always takes me to the difficult meetings,' sighed Donald Mackenzie, following Ecclestone into the heat. Jean Todt had complained about Ecclestone's refusal to provide a private office for the FIA president. The name plate outside Todt's office stated 'FIA president & FOM president'. To Ecclestone's glee, Todt protested, 'I don't want to share an office with you.' 'Right, I give you my half,' said Ecclestone. Todt was not pacified. Ecclestone, he knew, was playing power games. 'I told Bernie that he'd never get on with Todt,' said Niki Lauda as he watched Ecclestone walk back towards his headquarters. 'They're both physically small men.'

Waiting for Ecclestone in his headquarters was King Juan Carlos of Spain. Also present was the chairman of the board of Bahrain's Formula One corporation. Mr Zayed al Zayani was standing beside a huge wooden box. After greeting King Carlos and urging him to sit down for lunch, Ecclestone walked towards the robed Arab. 'This is in gratitude for everything you have done for our kingdom,' said the sheikh. Unpacking a four-foot-long curved sword, Ecclestone was told in a soft tone by the sheikh, 'You might want to use this gift to settle issues with the FIA.' Waving the gleaming metal above his head, Ecclestone replied, 'This is better than chocolates.' 'We don't make chocolates in Bahrain,' said the sheikh in a deadpan voice. Ecclestone's own present for chosen guests was a silver ruler.

At the nearby lunch table, Placido Domingo, the opera star, was being seated near King Carlos. The tenor had just arrived from San Francisco to watch Ferrari win the championship. He planned to fly back at 2 a.m. the following morning. 'We'll go and see Luca and Alonso,' said Ecclestone.

The two walked past the Williams headquarters. Frank Williams was outside, in the shade. Inside, the atmosphere was sombre. Without any success on the track and having lost their major sponsors, his team needed reinvigoration. Ecclestone waved. The next house was McLaren's. Ron Dennis was entertaining his Arab investors to a cold salad. To everyone's surprise, McLaren cars were positioned second and third on the grid for the last race. 'Everything will be decided in the first lap,' predicted Dennis. 'They'll be an accident and that will decide the championship.' In his dreams, Dennis hoped that Webber and Alonso would collide and Vettel's engine would blow up again, allowing Hamilton to glide towards the chequered flag. McLaren's mistake, he knew, had been to rely on the F-duct and not copy Adrian Newey's new floor wings, which increased the downforce. McLaren's success at the beginning of the season had been lost to the faster Red Bulls. Dennis was not despondent: 'A hundred million people could be watching today. That's amazing.' Ecclestone did not visit Dennis.

He had earlier called at the neighbouring headquarters of Red Bull, intentionally surprising Dietrich Mateschitz. The tall Austrian had glowed after Ecclestone emerged through the boisterous crowd and approached the small table that the reticent businessman was sharing with his wife. 'I want to thank you for all you've done for Formula One,' said Ecclestone pulling up a stool. 'It's magic.' Mateschitz had personally spent at least $700 million over six years in the hope of beating the major manufacturers. His financial reward had been vast, and envied by Richard Branson who passed by outside like a ghost, not approached by any of the hundred milling journalists. Ecclestone had long ago derided the adventurer as worthless to Formula One.

With the tenor at his side, he finally reached the laughing

crowds outside Ferrari's headquarters. All eyes and cheers were directed at the tenor. 'You're right to come and join the celebration,' said Italy's principal Formula One journalist. Domingo smiled: 'It's a great day.'

'Is Luca here?' Ecclestone asked once inside the building. 'He's busy,' was the reply. 'Tell him to come down. There's a surprise.' Minutes later, Montezemolo descended to be thrilled by his unexpected visitor. 'It's exciting,' confessed Montezemolo, glowing about Ferrari's rising fortunes during the last months. 'I couldn't miss it,' said Domingo. Alonso walked past and thanked the maestro for his good wishes. No one doubted that the crown was within his grasp. Beyond their hearing, a guest mentioned that Max Mosley had written in that morning's *Times* newspaper an article condemning Alonso's victory in Hockenheim in July as 'illegal' and predicted that his victory in Abu Dhabi would damn the new champion as 'a 'thief'. The Spaniard, accustomed to controversy, had ignored the accusations. He expected to win from his position third on the grid and that his victory would automatically suffocate the argument.

Leaving the party, Ecclestone and Domingo hurried back to Ecclestone's headquarters. Mercedes had been ignored. Dieter Zetsche, the chief executive of Mercedes, had arrived for the race but he could only survey the disappointment after his corporation's massive investment. Their hopes were now pinned on 2011, and a new car designed for Schumacher.

King Carlos was waiting. At 4.30 p.m. the Spanish monarch expected the Crown Prince of Abu Dhabi to arrive. Even the ruler's son could not drive into the Paddock. 'We don't want a Vettel victory this year,' Mackenzie was saying, explaining the commercial disadvantage. 'And we don't want Alonso.' The CVC director's financial calculations were too sophisticated for his audience. 'He's here,' announced Ecclestone. King Carlos and his nine bodyguards walked into the heat. The monarchs kissed and were led by Ecclestone towards the grid. 'It starts in twenty-five minutes,' he said.

The crowds in the stands stood and shouted, mostly for 'Bernie'. As the monarchs stood beside Alonso, Carlos could not resist clasping an arm around his countryman. From the stadium, a group of Spaniards started shouting 'ETA, ETA,' in support of the Basque terrorists. 'Say hello to Vettel,' shouted Ecclestone above the noise. The two monarchs clasped the gloved hand and headed towards their reserved seats in the stadium to watch the race begin.

Returning to his building, Ecclestone told Lauda, 'Hamilton to win and Alonso the championship.' The Austrian agreed. 'Right, Karl-Heinz, are we finishing our game?' he said pointing at the backgammon board. 'They're off,' said Lauda. As he ate a steak, the Austrian maintained a running commentary. Schumacher's early crash brought Ecclestone back to the television. No one anticipated how the decisions by the teams – especially Alonso's – to change tyres while the stewards cleared the track would destroy their predictions. 'Troubles are coming,' said Lauda as the race approached the halfway point and Alonso was struggling to advance from twelfth position, with Vettel leading. Even Lauda, the great Austrian, could not imagine the result. Standing behind him, Herman Tilke, the circuit's designer, confidently insisted that Alonso would find no difficulty in overtaking. At that moment Ecclestone was seated nearby as a silent prop alongside Dmitry Kozak, Russia's deputy prime minister, who was answering questions for a Russian television crew. Ecclestone assumed the politician was heralding the imminent arrival of Formula One in Russia. Even a decisive race did not interrupt business.

'We're off,' Ecclestone announced as the Russians departed. 'We'll see the end at the airport.' During the twenty-minute dash to the private airfield, Ecclestone anticipated Alonso storming through to take the lead. The news that the Spaniard was still seventh, stuck behind Vitaly Petrov's stubborn Renault, was heard in silence. Tilke was wrong. Overtaking had proved impossible. Ecclestone watched Vettel's victory in silence. The unpredicted, unprecedented end to a unique season left him speechless. 'He's crying,' said Mackenzie as he watched the youngest champion uttering 'unbelievable' by radio from his car. 'It will be good for business in Germany.' Slowly a smile crept across Ecclestone's previously expressionless face. 'I told him not to make any mistakes,' he said.

Even before the new champion was lifted from his car, Ecclestone's Falcon jet was roaring down the runway and banking towards Iran for the flight to London. Fabiana offered Ecclestone and his friends a tray of sandwiches. For those left behind at the Yas Marina circuit Ecclestone anticipated there would be scenes of chaos and congratulation. In Ferrari's headquarters, there would be despondency and recrimination. Next door, Red Bull's team would be partying until daybreak and beyond. After some reflection, Ecclestone decided to call Vettel using his satellite telephone. Inevitably the reply from Vettel's mobile was a recording inviting a message. The ringmaster uttered just one word, 'Bernie', pushed the red button and stuffed the telephone into his pocket.

Notes

I first met Bernie Ecclestone in late 2009. At the end of the meal, he suggested that he would cooperate in writing this book. I said I would think about his offer but that if I accepted he would not be able to dictate the content, read it before publication or have any rights of approval. However, I would agree to check facts and opinions with him. Subsequently I sent a letter to him confirming those terms as the basis of our relationship.

After February 2010 I met Ecclestone regularly in London and flew with him to several Grand Prix races. During those trips, we had endless discussions. My work method was to elicit facts from him and others, and put to him his critics' point of view, and challenge him about the discrepancies.

One essential contribution by Ecclestone was to call many involved in his personal and professional life and ask them to speak to me. Hence my access has been unique. Many of the people, including Max Mosley, Ron Dennis and others, I have met many times. They all asked Ecclestone, 'What should I say?' He replied, 'The truth. Don't worry about me.'

Therefore most of the quotations by Ecclestone (BE here) were expressed by him to me. Similarly, the thoughts of Max Mosley and others were recorded during interviews with me. To avoid lengthy notes, the reader can assume that unless otherwise attributed below, the speaker quoted in the text is the source of the quoted matter.

1 MONACO

6 'I couldn't care'   BE
7 'You don't want to believe people'   BE
9 'I'm not going to lose to Todt'   BE

2 GAMBLING

15 'Short people have to fight a lot'   BE
19 'That Ecclestone' John Surtees; 'I had a decent sense'   BE
21 'Keep up with me'   John Young
22 'I don't like others'   BE
24 'Going into racing'   Terry Lovell, *Bernie Ecclestone: King of Sport*, 2008, p. 20; 'The race continued'   Ted MacAuley, *Grand Prix Men*, 1998, p. 204
26 'I realised that I didn't want to risk'   *Sunday Telegraph*, 10 July 1983
27 'I suppose if you've only got'   Lovell, *Bernie Ecclestone*, p. 42
28 'He was irritated'   Ann Jones; 'I couldn't live with Ecclestone'   Lovell, *Bernie Ecclestone*, p. 21; 'It's the price of freedom'   BE; 'It was a major property'   Lovell, *Bernie Ecclestone*, p. 42
29 'Buying and selling'   BE
30 'Competing against thirty entries'   Lovell, *Bernie Ecclestone*, p. 25
31 'a knack of knocking back'   John Young; 'All my cars'   BE
33 'I don't like the customers'   Peter Warr; Telephone engineers were frequently summoned   Ann Jones
34 'I didn't terrorise my father'   BE; Spotting a bunch of flowers   Ann Jones; 'We had very little trouble'   BE
35 'Have you got a good second-hand MG?'   Peter Rix
36 As Rowe's agent   Lovell, *Bernie Ecclestone*, p. 26
37 'Most successful businessmen'   BE
38 'If you're the richest man'   Johnny Humphries
42 'I'm like a mouse'   Tuana Tan

3 EMBRYO

45 The secret adjustments were not enough   Herbie Blash
49 'I've seen things no man should ever see'   Jackie Stewart
52 'Because you've been bloody awkward'   Lovell, *Bernie Ecclestone*, pp. 36–7; Mr Justice Goff described Ecclestone's 'machinery'   *Economist* 15 July 2000
53 Ecclestone was displeased   BE and Lovell, *Bernie Ecclestone*, p. 39; 'there were 23,000 miles on the clock'   John Young and BE; 'Someone's going to bump Bernie off one day' and 'a new Jaguar'   John Coomb
55 'Nobody told him to do anything'   BE and Lovell, *Bernie Ecclestone*, p. 32; 'I get rid of people who offer opinions'   BE; 'Everyone is dispensable'   BE
56 'You can't do without me'   BE; he intended a 'major assault'   Lovell, *Bernie Ecclestone*, pp. 44–5

57 Gordon Murray watched him kick the headlamp   Herbie Blash
58 'Shut up or piss off'   Lovell, *Bernie Ecclestone*, p. 51
61 'an immediate natural alliance'   Max Mosley
62 'Bernie can handle the lies'   Max Mosley
63 'At least it hasn't cost you much to run'   Max Mosley
64 'There wasn't a strategy'   BE
66 Ecclestone collected the television money   Herbie Blash
67 he dived into the waste-paper basket   Max Mosley
68 Williams had stopped at his bank   Peter Warr; 'Bernie's Boys'   Herbie Blash
70 'Just pouring money into your sinking ship' Lovell, *Bernie Ecclestone*, p. 45; 'It was nothing to do with me'   BE; 'Seeley upset other people at Brabham'   BE
72 'I gave up worrying'   Max Mosley

4 SQUEEZE

75 'Bernie asked me' and Thirty-seven years later   Patrick Duffeler; In 2004 Ecclestone was challenged   Lovell, *Bernie Ecclestone*, p.77; Philip Morris considered Duffeler to be 'a fantasist'   BE
77 'The cars weren't clean'   Herbie Blash
80 'It doesn't look like fuel to me'   Niki Lauda and BE
83 'Bernie, why did you do that?'   Patrick Duffeler
85 'I know that in the past' *Daily Mail* 25 November 1976
86 'I have taken nothing'   ibid.; 'I could take you to the cemetery'   BE
87 The combination   *Sunday Business* 18 February 2001
88 He emerged   Patrick Duffeler
91 'if you are going to run a brothel,   Max Mosley
92 'I prefer close, silent wrestling'   BE; 'grind me down mentally'   Niki Lauda, *To hell and back*, 1986 p. 62; 'I was happy that my departure'   ibid., p. 60
93 He twists and turns   ibid., p. 64
95 'The challenge'   ibid., p. 71
96 To continue staging   Lovell, *Bernie Ecclestone*, p. 93
97 Partly in revenge   Niki Lauda
99 'disastrous and expensive'   *Daily Mail* 21 March 1978
101 'We can't count'   Herbie Blash; 'You're just little men'   *Sunday Times* 14 December 1980
103 'circling each other'   Alistair Caldwell
104 Without a word,   Alistair Caldwell; 'He's a sad, little, unfulfilled twerp' Alastair Caldwell; 'He did whatever had to be done'   BE
105 'Why would I want'   *Sunday Telegraph Magazine* 10 July 1983

5 HARD MAN

110 'He's got all the cards'   Max Mosley
113 'These people'   *Sunday Times* 14 December 1980

114 'If someone wants to cross me'   BE
116 Balestre approved   BE
117 Dennis was criticised   John Hogan and BE; 'It's the Big One'   Tuana
Tan
119 'the spruce, spry look'   *Sunday Telegraph Magazine* 10 July 1983
120 the grim atmosphere   *The Times* 18 January 1982
121 'We have got to get our act together'   *Sunday Telegraph Magazine*
10 July 1983; like a Mafia Don   Niki Lauda; 'If you're not in my
car'   Nelson Piquet
122 Piquet had mentioned the same fear   Max Mosley
123 'When a driver dies'   *Sunday Telegraph* 18 July 1983
124 'Get out of here'   Monty Shadow
125 'a mysterious figure'   *The Times* 18 January 1982; *The Times* wrongly
asserted   ibid. and *Sunday Telegraph* 18 July 1983
127 'Everyone knows'   *Motor Sport*, January 1998
128 three-year deal with the European Broadcasting Union: this was
extended in 1985 for another five years.

6 COUP

133 'She says that if I do not live with her'   Tuana Tan and BE
134 'I did some stupid things'   *ES Magazine*, November 2008; 'I wasn't
very happy'   BE
135 Ecclestone denied   *Daily Express* 13 May 1987
136 Volatile and occasionally tearful   Ron Shaw; 'Shit shirts,
darling'   John Bloom; 'Are they having an affair?'   Ann Jones
137 'See you later'   BE
138 'It's a shambles'   *Sunday Telegraph* 10 June 1983; In Piquet's
opinion   Nelson Piquet
139 'You get paid so little by Bernie'   *Motor Sport,* January 1998
140 'a grumpy man'   Niki Lauda, *To hell and back*, 1986 p. 182;
'In retrospect'   Lovell, *Bernie Ecclestone*, p. 160; 'I was pissed
off'   Gordon Murray
141 'I've never done anything bad'   BE and *Daily Telegraph* 4 July 1998
141 As they landed   Max Mosley
144 'The trouble with people'   *Financial Times* 8 April 1989
146 'I never sue'   *The Times* 12 August 1995
146 'I suppose I'm a bit like a headmaster'   *Financial Times* 8 April 1989
and *The Times* 5 February 1988
147 'I carry out my business'   *The Times* 5 February 1988; 'I am forty-
seven'   *Independent* 9 July 1988
148 'I would have taken'   BE; To prove his argument   *Autosport* 1 August
1985; 'We're too sophisticated'   *Sunday Times* 4 March 1990
151 'Bernie took one look'   Max Mosley
152 'Anyone who says we tried to kill it off'   Lovell, *Bernie Ecclestone*,
p. 254; 'You mustn't blame it all on Bernie Ecclestone'   *Autosport* 17
August 1988; 'I used Paddy'   BE

153 McNally's approach to Balestre   BE
154 Ecclestone's lament was a smoke screen   BE and *Financial Times* 16
     November 1998
155 'Ron's become arrogant'   Private source; 'In my opinion'
     RaceFax:ftoo112
156 FIA, having forsaken   *Panorama* and *Financial Times* 16 November
     1998; 'an amazing windfall' and 'more revenue'   Private source
157 occasionally Ecclestone speculated   BE; 'Bernie is in it for
     money'   Max Mosley; His guarantee to protect all the
     perks   *Autosport* 3 October 1991; 'Balestre had become a bit of a
     handful'   BE
159 The glow lasted one season   *Evening Standard* 9 July 1993
160 he had a reputation   Max Mosley
161 'Drivers are overpaid' and Facts about Ecclestone's background   *Mail
     on Sunday* 20 September 1992
162 Within seconds, Ecclestone had dashed across   John Surtees; 'I said I
     was going to supply them'   *Guardian* 10 December 2004
163 'I persuaded Flavio Briatore'   BE
164 'Noise and lifestyle'   *Evening Standard* 13 April 1994; 'a form of
     natural culling'   *Daily Express* and *The Times* 5 October 1993
165 'I would prefer'   *Observer* 10 October 1993
167 'like crucifying Jesus Christ'   *Sunday Business* 30 April 1997; 'What
     they are saying is'   *The Times* 2 May 1997
170 'The re-fuelling accident'   *Autosport* 4 August 1994; 'I never ask
     people questions'   BE; 'I arranged it'   *The Times* 12 August 1995
171 'You don't chose your parents'   Flavio Briatore
172 'We're looking for changes'   BE, Max Mosley and Flavio Briatore;
     'damaging ego'   Timothy Collins, *The Pirhana Club: Power and
     Influence in Formula One*, 2001, p. 194); 'There are no miracles in
     motor racing'   ibid., p. 196
173 'Schumacher is a ruthless, brutal driver'   BE
175 'You'll never get me to discuss'   *Sunday Times* 16 July 1995; 'The
     teams know'   *The Times* 12 August 1995
175 'I remember when'   *The Times* 12 August 1995
176 'I tell them up front'   BE
177 'Why do you allow her to do this?' Tuana Tan
178 'My mother's funeral'   Ann Jones; 'I'm staying with Slavica'   Tuana
     Tan; 'If somebody is dead'   Lovell, *Bernie Ecclestone*, p. 6

7 BILLIONAIRE

180 'The pain I feel'   Collins, *The Pirhana Club*, p. 194; 'I have
     higher standards'   ibid., pp. 185, 192; 'Dennis has an inferiority
     complex'   BE; 'Bernie doesn't love me'   Ron Dennis
181 'Bernie could have said'   Max Mosley
182 Mosley did not agree and 'Bernie, you're not a liar'   Max Mosley
183 Mosley left Ecclestone to complete a separate deal with the teams.

Before the 1995 fifteen-year agreement, FIA had the Concorde agreement with the teams governing their entry to race in Formula One and Ecclestone had the FOCA agreement with the teams; but Ecclestone did not have an agreement with FIA. The new fifteen year deal gave Ecclestone the right to exploit FIA's control over the world championship races and excluded FIA from any television income; Mosley did not fear accusations of corruption   Max Mosley

184 'You've done a double'   Ron Dennis; 'I don't think this is fair'   Frank Williams; The teams, he knew   BE; 'There's no Queensberry rules here'   Ron Dennis

185 'Bernie carries a grudge'   Ron Dennis; Grateful for Ecclestone's previous help   Eddie Jordan; 'Eddie Jordan is as honest as he can afford to be' and 'There's no need to wind Eddie up'   BE

186 'I was not putting up a fight'   *Daily Mail* 8 July 1996; 'I'm not intending to die'   *The Times* 10 July 1996

187 'You cross me'   *Sunday Telegraph* 24 June 2001

188 'I don't cultivate it'   Lovell, *Bernie Ecclestone*, p. 374

189 More recently   *Sunday Times* 15 October 2000

190 'They would prefer to have'   *The Times* 10 July 1996; 'I did the deal with Bernie' and 'Bernie, this is the last time'   Luca Montezemolo

191 'I feel betrayed by Luca'   Ron Dennis; "You idiot"   *Mail on Sunday* 8 September 1996

192 'If they can't speak English'   *Guardian* 4 August 2000

194 In February 1996   Sacha Woodward-Hill; 'I don't want a bun fight'   *The Times* 16 November 1997

195 'Bernie doesn't like'   Brian Shepherd; 'You need someone to fly'   *Observer* 5 May 2002; 'This isn't what I want'   Eddie Jordan

196 'The float was his idea'   BE

197 'If you can get Bernie to give'   Max Mosley

198 'I believe that it would be difficult'   RaceFax:ft00291

199 'I want to help Max look good'   BE

200 'We just want a transition period'   David Ward

201 'I felt Bernie was being greedy'   Ron Dennis

202 'The more they talk'   *Sunday Times* 16 March 1997; Ron Dennis and Frank Williams threatened   *Daily Mail* 25 March 1997

203 'The client from hell'   *The European* 10 July 1997

204 The Lex column   *Financial Times* 22 May 1997; 'I don't want to stand up'   BE; 'It's the peanut under the cup trick'   Ron Dennis

205 'you've stolen Formula One'   Eddie Jordan; 'The teams can go to hell'   Lovell, *Bernie Ecclestone*, p. 294; 'Ron was not disloyal'   BE; 'If the teams owned it'   *Financial Times* 3 October 1997

206 Rushing from one meeting   *Evening Standard* 23 July 1997; he would receive £2 billion   *Guardian* 9 June 1997

207 Levy thought that Ward was employed   Lord Michael Levy, *A Question of Honour*, 2008, p. 136

209 'I'm sure Mercedes is financing this'   Max Mosley; 'something none of us could swallow'   Collins, *The Piranha Club*, p. 304; 'Ron has left it

too late'   BE; 'I feel we should make one final effort'   *Sunday Times* 5 October 1997

8 TOBACCO

210 'He'll see us on 16 October'   BE
212 'How's it going?'   Max Mosley
214 'You should have said nothing'   Max Mosley; 'I said to those clowns'   *Sunday Times* 19 March 2000
215 Blair had already asked Derry Irvine   Andrew Rawnsley, *Servants of the People*, 2000, p. 95; the letter was 'catastrophic'   BE; 'Labour are like boy scouts'   David Ward; David Hill began prevaricating   Rawnsley, *Servants of the People*, p. 96
216 according to Tory officials   *Sunday Mirror* 18 January 1998; depicted as a villain   Lovell, *Bernie Ecclestone*, p. 357
217 Labour, he moaned   *Sunday Times* 5 April 1998
218 expressed their 'disappointment'   Collins, *The Piranha Club*, p. 253; 'it's no use banning Schumacher'   Max Mosley
219 Off-message, Jack Straw   *Evening Standard* 13 November 1997; 'I've been hung out to dry'   BE
220 'I'm pissed off'   *The Times* 16 November 1997; In an interview with *The Times*   *The Times* 20 September 2000; 'Being nice to people'   Collins, *The Piranha Club*, p. 148–9
221 'I don't believe that Bernie' and 'You know he'll do anything'   Ron Dennis; 'I never worry'   BE
222 'Blair played a crooked hand' and 'If you appear'   BE; 'Blair is hateful'   *Sunday Times* 19 March 2000
224 'will never be the same again'   *Guardian* 3 August 1998
225 a Panamanian corporation   This was Larmoran Participation Inc
226 In 1998 Ecclestone's companies   In 1998 Ecclestone's principal corporation was FOM Ltd; 'the entrepreneurial side'   *Guardian*   28 August 1999
227 he considered Mosley effeminate and 'You should relax'   Ron Dennis; Dennis required psychiatric help   Max Mosley
228 'Bernie promised us a share in the cake'   Luca Montezemolo; 'the ill-informed and misleading background noise'   *Sunday Times* 22 November 1998; 'just a few minor issues to resolve'   *Financial Times* 29 September 1998; 'There's been too much noise'   *Evening Standard* 26 November 1998 and *Daily Telegraph* 21 November 1998
229 'It seems to be difficult for them'   *Sunday Telegraph* 7 November 1999
230 Mosley had just released viewing figures   Racefax: ns00996; 'She was the one kicking arse'   *Sunday Business* 12 September 1999; Saunders reduced the loan to $1.4 billion   The $1.4 billion was loaned to Bambino, the owner of SLEC. FOM transferred the fifteen-year rights to Formula One Administration (FOA), so FOM became a subsidiary of FOA
231 'I'll only stop working'   *Financial Times* 4 July 1999

232 van Miert's apology *The Times* 27 July 1999; 'He does whatever he can get away with' BE; At those prices, Formula One was worth $2.6 billion Morgan Grenfell PE bought 12.5 per cent of SLEC Holdings, the holding company of Formula One, through a specially created company called Speed Investment Ltd; 'all rich, flaky and wanted to get into the deal Scott Lanphere

234 'Lanphere's an idiot' BE; 'They've messed up a bit' *Sunday Business* 20 February 2000

235 'Money doesn't drive me' BE

236 'Think about this for two minutes' BE; Powers and Lanphere who together still owned 50 per cent of Formula One Legally Formula One was owned by SLEC. Formula One Administration was owned by SLEC and in turned owned by Bambino, the Ecclestone family trust; 'Their fifty per cent is like 5 per cent' BE

237 Excitedly, Haffa accepted Ecclestone's offer Bambino sold a put option to the Formula One shares to 'Speed', EM.TV's vehicle for buying Formula One which was exercised in February 2001

238 'I don't ask questions' BE

239 'Bernie's deals are his deals' Jackie Stewart; Stewart . . . made some ungenerous comments *Guardian* 15 July 2003

240 'We don't want your money' John Coomb; 'The people running Silverstone' *Evening Standard* 16 July 2003

241 'let's play games with someone' BE

242 'He fitted us up' Private source

243 'I could not take him seriously' Luca Montezemolo

245 Ecclestone paid Peter BE

247 'We thought a 100-year deal' Frank Williams.

248 'Unfortunately he finds all this' Racefax: ftdt003

249 Worst was Mr Justice Longmore's criticism *Economist* 15 July 2000; 'Nearly all of Formual One's affairs' *The Times* 21 September 2000

250 'I have a position' BE

251 'All they do' BE; 'I would not underestimate' Lovell, *Bernie Ecclestone*, p. 216

252 'Bernie seems to have been trying' Racefax: ns08777

9 REVOLT

254 'Slavica can be a pain' *Sunday Mirror* 18 January 1998, *Mail on Sunday* 23 April 2000 and *Daily Telegraph* 12 July 2001

255 'My girls are always with me' *Guardian* 8 July 2000; 'One day if I go back' *Sunday Times* 19 January 2000; permanently angry Pasquale Lattundeau

256 'He's been tucked up' Ron Shaw; with a black eye Katja Heim; 'Slav thought I was being serious' BE; With Ecclestone's help *Sunday Mirror* 29 March 1998; *Bild*, the German tabloid newspaper BE and Katja Heim; 'He was like a loony' *Mail on Sunday* 23 April 2000; As therapy *Daily Telegraph* 12 July 2001

257 Keterman sold the story   *Mail on Sunday* 25 August 2002 and   BE
258 'Europe is going to become a third-world economy'   Racefax: ns14945
259 'It's a great shame'   Racefax: ns02633
260 The German media tycoon   Technically, EM.TV bought the 25 per cent with a guarantee from Kirch
263 'Those muppets'   Eddie Jordan; the opportunity to buy Kirch's 75 per cent share in Formula One   i.e. SLEC shares
264 'I fly by the seat of my pants'   *Daily Telegraph* 1 October 2004; 'Part of my life's work'   *Observer* 5 May 2002; 'That's a stupid way'   Gerhard Gribkowsky
265 Gribkowsky engineered Fischer's departure   He would be fired from his next job in 2007, as chief executive of the WestLB, after the discovery of financial irregularities causing $334m losses; 'Bernie attaches strings to the shares'   Martin Brundle; 'they can't do a thing without Bambino's permission'   BE. Ecclestone had fixed that FOH had seven directors and he appointed himself and three others, including Luc Argand and his wife Emmanuele Argand-Rey. Under the shareholder agreement made between Bambino and EM.TV (whose position was stepped into by Kirch and then the banks), when their respective stakes were at 50 per cent each of Bambino and Speed Investments (for the latter read EM.TV/Kirch/the banks) could appoint four directors to the FOH board. When Speed (EM.TV/Kirch) exercised its option to take a further 25 per cent holding, Speed became entitled to appoint six directors and Bambino two. Under a further agreement between SLEC and WestLB, WestLB could appoint somebody (Robin Saunders) to the FOH Board, to count towards Speed's allocation of Board seats. Bernie Ecclestone and Stephen Mullens were both on the FOH board but were appointed before the shareholder agreement was made and Bambino claimed that it had never appointed either of them to be its chosen directors, so after the banks got involved, Bambino appointed Luc Argand and Emmanuele Argand-Rey to be its first two directors (so Ecclestone, Mullens and the two Argands were all on the board and, with Robin Saunders friendly, that made five).
266 'He's helpful and very bright'   BE. FOM is owned by SLEC, which is 75 per cent owned by Speed Investments Ltd (owned by the banks) and 25 per cent by Bambino. Although the banks have a majority ownership of SLEC, they have no voting control over FOM. FOM is in turn owned by FOH and then FOA. Ecclestone secretly appoints two more directors to the board of FOH which denies the banks any influence over Formula One.
267 'Mullens is a arsehole'   Gerhard Gribkowsky and BE
268 'What happened on the podium'   *Daily Mail* 24 May 2002
269 'I don't think reckless risk'   *Guardian* profile 4 November 2002
270 Within minutes   John Howett
272 'It's quite incredible'   *Guardian* 4 November 2002
273 'We will not compromise'   *Guardian* 8 April 2003; 'huge amounts of money'   Luca Montezemolo

274 'They want to get control'   BE and *Sunday Times* 4 May 2003
275 'Writs will fall'   *Sunday Telegraph* 6 April 2003
276 'Ferrari are good at their job'   BE; Ecclestone deployed his trusted ritual   *The Times* 3 March 2003
277 'Bernie always does a special deal'   Max Mosley; 'I do have parents'   *Observer* 12 December 2004 and *Sunday Telegraph* 9 March 2003
279 'The GPWC'   *The Times* 4 May 2004
282 'I just do not understand'   Racefax: ns11491; 'Boy was I wrong'   *Financial Times* 16 June 2002; 'the biggest mistake I ever made'   Forbes.com 17.9.07 and Lovell, *Bernie Ecclestone*, p. 221
283 Stewart 'went berserk'   Ron Dennis
284 Ecclestone capitulated   *Daily Mail* 10 October 2004; He sued Jackie Stewart   BE
285 Without provocation   Gerhard Gribkowski; 'For outsiders looking in'   BE
287 'I knew that Ferrari would see sense'   BE
288 Certain that Dennis's rebellion   *The Times* 21 January 2005; 'The teams are saying'   Racefax 14 March 2005; 'Max has this Machiavellian streak'   Ron Dennis
290 'It'll cost €100,000' and he had slipped a copy of a letter   Gerhard Gribkowsky and BE; 'This is unhelpful'   BE; 'We now have the power'   *Independent* 26 March 2005; 'I don't care who's on the board'   BE

10 CHEATING

292 'It's about the lifestyle'   *Formula One Business Magazine*, p. 1028; Good drivers from his team   *Mail on Sunday* 20 September 2009
293 'How can you be such buddies'   Eddie Jordan; 'In this game'   BE
294 'The Concorde agreement'   Adam Parr and Ron Dennis
296 'We didn't have a good car'   Jean Todt
297 'I suspected' said Mosley   *Guardian* 27 June 2005; 'Ecclestone and the teams'   Max Mosley; 'Max had a strong argument'   BE; 'Bernie knows that I'm not good at backing down'   Max Mosley; Mosley was accused of 'posturing'   *Daily Mail* 9 July 2005
298 'we wouldn't have had all this nonsense'   *Evening Standard* 10 August 2005; 'Before we had more or less a dictatorship'   *Daily Mail* 8 July 2005; 'Unless I run it the way I want'   BE
302 His stake would be sold to CVC   The purchase of the shares was executed through Delta Topco, a Jersey-based company which is 70 per cent owned by CVC with other shares belonging to J. P. Morgan, Lehman Brothers, the Ecclestone family trust Bambino and Bernie Ecclestone. CVC investors received their profits through the CVC European Equity Partners IV Fund; Six weeks later, on 25 November 2005   CVC bought 100 per cent of SLEC shares for $2.9 billion through Delta 3 and Bambino bought back 10 per cent of the newly

formed Formula One Group. Lehman brothers bought an 8 per cent stake. Finalised 28 March 2006.

305 Pointing his shotgun   Peter Warr and Ron Dennis
306 'Max doesn't like peace'   BE; Regardless of any agreement   Ron Dennis and Racefax: ns11077
307 'Bernie, what's wrong?'   Niki Lauda
308 'Are you having sex?'   Ron Dennis and BE; 'All he wants is money'   Tamas Rohonyi
309 Montezemolo had even asked   Gerhard Grobkowsky
313 Alonso wanted to leave McLaren   Racefax: ns19723
314 no one was convinced   Transcript, FIA hearing p. 20 and   Max Mosley
315 'Max doesn't like Ron taking the piss'   BE; "Until now'   Max Mosley; 'Under Mosley', 'colouring the evidence' and 'Max has always been jealous'   Ron Dennis
316 'Max is enjoying my trauma'   Ron Dennis; 'He turned up'   BE
317 'Dennis has lost all credibility'   Jean Todt; 'a menu for punishments'   BE
318 'Stewart never stops talking'   Max Mosley
319 'I don't care what happens to Ron'   BE

11 SCANDAL

324 'It's not on the tape'   Ed Gorman
326 'You fucking amateur'   Adam Parr
328 he could be trusted   BE
331 'It's nothing to do with me at all'   The Times 24 June 2008; 'The FIA has a clear, clear'   The Times 12 July 2008
332 'I don't want to have a war with Max   John Howett
333 'There are a lot of balls in the air'   BE
336 'Bernie is simpatico'   Luca Montezemolo; 'He attacks you in public'   Max Mosley
337 The breakaway is good for Flavio'   BE
338 'Poor little bugger'   John Coomb; 'Bernie, I'm off'   Niki Lauda
339 'I've given him my life'   Monty Shadow and BE
342 'She was right' and 'I'm so busy'   BE
343 'I'll agree to anything'   BE
344 'It's a shame'   The Times 20 December 2008; 'intolerable'   The Times 6 January 2009

12 GÖTTERDÄMMERUNG

345 'I've had proper people' and 'Flavio is presenting'   BE
348 'Just help us get rid of Max' and 'Everyone thinks I have a nice job'   BE
350 'pouring dirt'   Ron Dennis
351 'Its best to hold'   Jean Todt

352 'an impulsive, quicksilver, strange person'   Max Mosley; 'I don't trust him any more'   Jean Todt

358 'I was aghast' and 'I helped him'   BE

359 'If Flavio didn't know'   BE

360 'If he'd lied'   Max Mosley; 'I was simply being used'   *The Times* 22 September 2009; 'blackmail and outrageous lies'   *Guardian* 12 September 2009; 'There is something'   *Guardian* 18 September 2009

361 'Follow your religion' and 'In the old days'   BE; 'I did give a harsh sentence'   Max Mosley; 'Mosley is clever'   Flavio Briatore

362 'too harsh and unnecessary'   *Daily Mail* 26 September 2009; 'He is not in any position'   *The Times* 28 September 2009; 'People say'   BE; Todt reduced the ban   The FIA's statement recorded about Briatore and Symonds: 'Each of them recognising his share of responsibility for the deliberate crash involving the driver Nelson Piquet Junior at the 2008 Grand Prix of Singapore, as "Team Principal" of Renault Formula One where Mr Flavio Briatore is concerned, they have expressed their regrets and presented their apologies to the FIA.'

13 MONZA

367 'You know you can't make mistakes'   *Sunday Times* 29 August 2010

Index